The Gaga Years

The Gaga Years

The Rise and Fall of the Money Game, 1981–1991

EDITED BY
Brett Duval Fromson

A Citadel Press Book
Published by Carol Publishing Group

To

Carmel Snow Wilson

AND

James Wilson Fromson

Acknowledgments of permission to reprint previously published material appear on page 372.

A Citadel Press Book
Published by Carol Publishing Group
Citadel Press is a registered trademark of Carol Communications, Inc.
Editorial Offices: 600 Madison Avenue, New York, N.Y. 10022
Sales & Distribution Offices: 120 Enterprise Avenue, Secaucus, N.J. 07094
In Canada: Canadian Manda Group, P.O. Box 920, Station U, Toronto, Ontario M8Z 5P9
Queries regarding rights and permissions should be addressed to Carol Publishing Group, 600 Madison Avenue, New York, N.Y. 10022

Carol Publishing Group books are available at special discounts for bulk purchases, for sales promotions, fund raising, or educational purposes. Special editions can be created to specifications. For details contact: Special Sales Department, Carol Publishing Group, 120 Enterprise Avenue, Secaucus, N.J. 07094

Design by Arthur Hamparian

Manufactured in the United States of America
10 9 8 7 6 5 4 3 2 1

Library of Congress Cataloging-in-Publication Data

The Gaga years : the rise and fall of the money game, 1981-1991 /
    edited by Brett Duval Fromson.
        p.   cm.
    "A Citadel Press book."
    ISBN 0-8065-1329-2
    1. United States—Economic conditions—1981- 2. United States—
    Social conditions—1980- 3. Wall Street. 4. Stockbrokers—United States.
    5. Inside trading in securities—United States.
    I. Fromson, Brett Duval, 1955-
    HC106.8G3 1992
    332.64'273—dc20   92-26769
                                                      CIP

Contents

ACT 2

THE PARTY GETS WILD
(1986–1989)

ACT 3

A WICKED HANGOVER
(1990–1991)

My clever publisher, Steve Schragis, came up with the idea for this book. My industrious literary agent, Michael Carlisle, proposed that I execute Steve's idea. My estimable editor, Bruce Shostak, nursed the project from beginning to end. A host of excellent journalists wrote the stories that appear here. And Joe Nocera came up with the title.

To one and all, thank you.

Introduction

THE EIGHTIES was the party to end all parties, an orgiastic financial blowout the likes of which we shall not see again in our lifetime, if we are lucky.

It was the Money Decade. The desire for money sup· planted the lust for a good roll in the hay as the national obsession. Otherwise intelligent people actually said things like, "Greed is good." It was that kind of decade.

Nowhere was the itch for money more scratchable or the financial screwing more frequent than on Wall Street.

I like to think of Wall Street as a red-light district; the investment banking houses as bordellos; Mike Milken and John Gutfreund as madams; CEOs and institutional investors as the Johns; and the SEC as the sleepy cop on the beat. We in the press were the piano players.

If you don't understand what happened at the party and how things got totally out of control, you will never understand why the economy is having so much trouble getting out of bed in the nineties. This book intends to show you what happened as chronicled by some of the better journalists writing for some of the best publications.

The money game was one of the big stories of the decade and attracted a host of excellent journalists. Many of the writers represented in this book are familiar to any reader of the financial press: Bryan Burrough, Tony Bianco, Laurie Cohen, Steve Coll, Susan Faludi, Jim Grant, John Helyar, Daniel Hertzberg, James Kaplan, Michael Lewis, Carol Loomis, Joe Nocera, Ron Rosenbaum, Allan Sloan, Jim Stewart, Michael Thomas, and David Vise. Among them they have won almost all of journalism's major awards from the Pulitzer Prize on down.

The book is arranged chronologically to give you a sense of how things got gaga. After all, it took time for complete financial mania to rule the day.

I have divided the book into three parts, three acts if you will. Given the dramatic nature of Wall Street in recent years, it did not seem a stretch to think of the story as a morality play.

In Act 1, "Let the Party Begin," the scene is set; the lead players introduced; and the action started. The stars of Act 1 are Ronald and Nancy Reagan, Mike Milken, and Dennis Levine.

Act 2, "The Party Gets Wild," tells two stories. First, the widening insider scandal: the busting of Ivan Boesky, the naming of SEC chairman John Shad as chairman of the criminal brokerage Drexel Burnham Lambert. But this act also covers the frenzy of the bull market and the LBO boom that could not be stopped, not even by the crash of October 1987.

Act 3, "A Wicked Hangover," is about the pain resulting from the debt-financed, speculative binge of the eighties: the death of Drexel; the nailing of Mike Milken, the downfall of Salomon Brothers and John Gutfreund; and most tragically, the rich getting richer and the poor being left further behind.

I have tried to pick the most memorable pieces of the decade, the ones that not only show what happened, but also capture the mood of the times. That is why I have included breaking news stories about momentous events like 1981's first Reagan inauguration, 1986's busting of Ivan Boesky by federal agents, 1988's takeover of RJR/Nabisco by LBO maestro Henry Kravis, and 1991's Salomon Brothers scandal.

But most of the stories in this book go far beyond the breaking news. These are stories that in their own ways made history because they told it so much better than anyone else has: Michael Thomas's story of the first obscenely profitable LBO that set investment bankers salivating, Susan Faludi's report on the human cost of the LBO of Safeway, Carol Loomis's saga of the rise and fall of Robert Campeau, David Vise and Steve Coll's look at SEC chairman John Shad, Joe Nocera's piece on the eighties mania for investing, and others.

I have also included stories that reflect the feel of the decade. Some of these—like Steve Coll's "A Wall Street Trader's Bad Day," about the October 1987 crash—are brilliant. Others—like Julie Connelly's love note to trophy wives—are not. But breathless pieces about the rich make amusing reading in retrospect and are important reminders that in some sense we all bought in the pretense of the decade that greed is good.

ACT 1

Let the Party Begin (1981–1986)

Freed Americans Land in West Germany; Reagan Sworn in as the Fortieth President; Action Vowed on Economy

Haynes Johnson

January 21, 1981, the *Washington Post*

Ronald Reagan set the decade's shoot-the-moon tone in his first inauguration speech. And Washington Post *political writer Haynes Johnson wrote the most comprehensive news story about that moment. He saw the psychological connection between Reagan's sunny message of economic prosperity and the liberation of the hostages in Iran. The clear implication of Reagan's speech was that as the hostages were liberated from the ayatollah, so, too, Americans would be liberated from the affliction of Jimmy Carter and the Democrats.*

RONALD REAGAN, his first moments in office accompanied by a happy ending for the nation, assumed the powers of the president of the United States yesterday amid emotional circumstances unmatched in America's forty eight previous inaugurations.

Only minutes before he took the oath of office as the fortieth president, dramatic news bulletins, which turned out to be minutes premature, were flashed from Iran bringing the word the nation had been waiting for fourteen frustrating months—the hostages were free.

3

Reagan's message to the country—delivered in confident tones before a vast throng gathered below the Capitol's West Front and millions more watching on television—was in keeping with his campaign promise. He pledged immediate action to deal with what he called "an economic affliction of great proportions" confronting the United States and promised to "curb the size and influence of the federal establishment and to demand recognition of the distinction between the powers granted to the federal government and those reserved to the states or to the people."

President Reagan's theme was optimism, a rejection of a belief that the nation's problems are beyond solution. He spoke of the time of heroes not being over, quoted Churchill on triumphing over adversity, and told his fellow citizens, "We are too great a nation to limit ourselves to small dreams." And: "Can we solve the problems confronting us? The answer is an unequivocal and emphatic yes."

After his address, obviously in an ebullient mood, the new president brought up the release of the hostages before congressional leaders who hosted a Capitol luncheon in his honor. The planes carrying the prisoners to freedom had cleared Iranian airspace just thirty minutes before, Reagan announced, raising a glass of California wine. "So we can all drink to this one," he said, "to all of us together."

It was a theme for a day that held far more than the usual elements of national celebration. Those two events, the coming to power of a president who promises to reverse the force and size the federal government accumulated over two generations and the freeing of the hostages, provided a unique framework for Reagan's inauguration.

But there were other elements that distinguished this inauguration. Ronald Wilson Reagan, who will be seventy on February 6, becomes the oldest person to take office. Only Dwight D. Eisenhower, who had celebrated his seventieth birthday two months before leaving office, was older in the presidency.

Reagan, while not the first president to come out of the West (Herbert Hoover and Richard Nixon also had California backgrounds), brings to power a new era of conservatism, backed by the increasing political strength of the western states. Reagan's first act as president was an earnest gesture in support of his assertion that he intends immediate action to fulfill his conservative promises. He ordered an instant federal hiring freeze, and said he would permit only rare exceptions to it necessary "to maintain vital services."

Despite the usual euphoria of the event, the political scraps and squabbles resumed quickly, even before the new president went to work for the first time in the Oval Office. In the Senate, two of Reagan's conservative supporters, Sen. Jesse Helms and Sen. John P. East, Republicans from North Carolina, voted against Casper Weinberger's confirmation as secretary of defense and promised to oppose Reagan's nominee for deputy defense secretary as well. Helms explained on the Senate floor that, in his view, Weinberger is "not at this moment prepared to make the clean break with the very policies of the past which have managed our military and international decline."

As in every ceremony for a new administration, there were vivid reminders of the other side of the political process that culminates in an inauguration—the cruelty of defeat and the fickleness of a capital city that glories in winners and quickly forgets losers.

Throughout the day, Jimmy Carter, the thirty-ninth president of the United States, seemed a fading, almost forgotten figure. Indeed, the outgoing president, defeated after one term in office, suffered one last frustration as the time ran out that would have permitted him personally to greet the hostages on his last day as president. His farewell words were delivered in husky tones after his arrival home in Plains, Georgia. While his wife, Rosalynn, stood beside him with tears in her eyes, Carter spoke at length on the agony of the hostage ordeal, a speech he had wanted to give in his closing days in Washington.

Their daughter, Amy, who had pranced her way down Pennsylvania Avenue exactly four years before at her parents' side, showed more poignantly the emotional impact of defeat. She was a study in sorrow, choked with tears and remorse, as she waited to board the plane for Georgia.

Reagan, as Carter had four years before, went out of his way to speak gracious words about his erstwhile political rival. Turning toward the outgoing president, Reagan said he wanted Americans to know how much Carter had done to carry on the tradition of an orderly transfer of power.

"By your gracious cooperation in the transition process you have shown a watching world that we are a united people pledged to maintaining a political system which guarantees individual liberty to a greater degree than any other," the president said to the ex-president. "Thank you and your people for all your help in maintaining the continuity which is the hallmark of our Republic."

Reagan, in another friendly gesture, also appointed Carter as his emissary to greet the hostages in Germany.

In any other inaugural, the shift of presidential power and the corresponding intense focus on the new leader provides its own drama. But yesterday, to an unprecedented degree, both the incoming and outgoing presidents were almost secondary to the extraordinary drama of the hostages. Both became pawns in a game of power and frustration played out to the last second and before a watching world by the leaders of Iran.

Neither Carter nor Reagan could escape the developments that kept them both, as well as their country, hanging in suspense up to the very moment that another historic shift of American power occurred.

Their day began with new hopes that the hostage ordeal, finally, would be over. Even as the crowds were taking their places along the inaugural route and across the Capitol grounds, the last elements of the story were wrung out, piece by piece, but with uncertainty remaining to the end. Those closing moments had all the elements of a fictional thriller—or a Reagan melodrama from his Hollywood years—and they drew the attention of the nation.

While the two men were having tea in the White House, in another of those traditional rituals that serve to make the bitterness of campaigns, word came that buses bearing the hostages were approaching the Tehran airport.

When they entered the presidential limousine, carrying the seal of the President of the United States, the news was that the hostages were about to board waiting planes.

When their motorcade was proceeding slowly down Pennsylvania Avenue, the historic "Avenue of the Presidents" that has been the scene of moments of national joy and sorrow, of inaugural parades heralding new political leaders and funeral corteges mourning those that have passed, news reports said the planes were preparing to depart.

When Reagan was only four minutes away from the beginning of the formal presidential ceremonies, at 11:36 A.M., a news service bulletin was flashed saying simply: "Hostages freed."

In fact, neither Carter nor Reagan knew for sure what had happened. Carter told Reagan, just before the formal ceremonies began, that the planes were on the runway in Tehran, ready to go. But Reagan didn't get the official word until after he had finished his address and walked back inside the Capitol Building.

The actual departure from Iran took place five minutes after the new president concluded his address.

Reagan's inaugural will be remembered for those events, but it also made history in other respects. For the first time, the inaugural stage was situated on the West Front of the Capitol. All others had occurred on the east steps looking out over the Capitol Plaza grounds and the Supreme Court and Library of Congress buildings beyond.

The change was notable. From the promenade of the West Front, the inaugural party had a sweeping view of the capital and its most celebrated memorials in the distance, obscured by a slight haze on an otherwise perfect, almost balmy day; beyond was the Potomac River and the land stretching out to the west. Below them were the broad avenues and the central mall of Pierre L'Enfant's original plan for Washington.

Reagan took note of the special location toward the end of his speech.

"This is the first time in our history that this ceremony has been held on the West Front of the Capitol building," he said, from a lectern shielded by bulletproof glass and bearing the presidential seal. "Standing here, we face a magnificent vista, opening up on this city's special beauty and history. At the end of this open mall are those shrines to the giants on whose shoulders we stand."

He referred to the Washington Monument, the Jefferson and Lincoln Memorials, and the hills of Arlington Cemetery, using them as symbols to evoke a message that was designed to rekindle a sense of national heroism and sacrifice.

The Capitol itself never looked finer. The new president delivered his address beneath huge American flags and red-white-and-blue bunting hung from the building.

By eleven o'clock the grounds had filled, and the crowds awaited the ceremony by standing, chatting, and listening to patriotic music—"Yankee Doodle" and "The Battle Hymn of the Republic"—played by the Marine Band, resplendent in their bright red uniforms, directly below the presidential platform. At 11:15, as news circulated among the crowd that Pars, the Iranian news agency, was reporting the "imminent departure" of the hostages eight thousand miles away, the lights of the presidential motorcade could be seen coming down the Avenue to Capitol Hill.

The strains of "Hail to the Chief" at 11:22 signaled the arrival of Jimmy Carter on the inaugural platform. It was the last time that presidential salute would be sounded for him; some of those watching recalled how Carter had ordered it not to be played in an effort to minimize the ceremonial trappings of the office. Now, four years and a lot of history later, "Hail to the Chief" was back in vogue among the formal striped pants and mink coat attire of his successor's inaugural.

Mark Hatfield, a Republican senator from Oregon and chairman of this year's Joint Congressional Committee on Inaugural Ceremonies, stepped to the lectern. The formal ceremonies had begun.

Hatfield spoke of "a day when a tide of new hope is running through the land." Then he asked the crowd to join hands in the singing of "America," rendered by Michael Ryan of the Marine Band.

Reagan's pastor, the Rev. Donn Moonaw, delivered an invocation in which he offered thanks for the freeing of the hostages. It was the only mention of the imprisoned Americans during the ceremony.

Supreme Court Justice Potter Stewart administered the vice-presidential oath of office to George Bush, who repeated the words in clear tones and then waved to the crowd, his wife, Barbara, at his side.

After the playing of another hymn, "Faith of Our Fathers,"

the moment for the presidential transfer of power had arrived. It was 11:55 A.M. when Reagan and Chief Justice Warren Burger moved forward to the platform under slightly overcast skies and unseasonably warm sunshine.

"Governor, are you ready to take the constitutional oath?" Burger asked Reagan. "I am," Reagan replied.

His left hand on the *Bible*, his voice firm, Ronald Reagan repeated the simple thirty-five-word oath that made him the fortieth president of the United States and the possessor of the nation's problems. He waved to the crowd, both in front of and behind him, and stood with a look of bemused pleasure while the band struck up "Hail to the Chief" for the first time in his presidency, and the muffled reports of a twenty-one-gun salute echoed off the Capitol walls.

Then he turned toward the crowd, and the nation beyond, and delivered his twenty-minute inaugural address. As he finished, the new president delivered an impromptu benediction of his own.

"God bless you and thank you," President Reagan said.

With his wife, Nancy, at his side, he acknowledged the applause of the crowd, and moved back from the lectern while the National Anthem was sung by Juanita Booker and his minister gave a brief benediction.

The ceremony was over, and the president led the way back into the Capitol. There he learned that the other side of the day, the one that always will now be associated with his inauguration, had been successfully completed, too.

The hostages were coming home just as his presidency was beginning. For that moment, at least, it seemed possible to believe his appeal for a national renewal had more than rhetorical meaning.

Reagan Regalia: Nancy's $25,000 Inaugural Wardrobe

Nina Hyde

January 19, 1981, the *Washington Post*

Nina Hyde's piece on Nancy Reagan's $25,000 inaugural wardrobe—complete with a $1,650 alligator handbag—sent a message to wealthy matrons from coast to coast that sartorial excess was in. I love her comparison of what the Reagans spent with "what the wife of the president of France might spend." (Of course, it later came out in the press that Nancy had simply used her position as First Lady to "borrow" the clothes from top designers, who in turn were taking advantage of her name to promote their clothes.)

NANCY REAGAN has come to town with a wardrobe of clothes and accessories worth at least $25,000 to wear for the inaugural period. That tally comes from estimates given by designers and stores familiar with Mrs. Reagan's purchases and it includes the hand-beaded inaugural ball gown and coat designed by James Galanos and a Maximilian mink coat, a Christmas gift from her husband. The Maximilian replaces the black mink she has owned for twenty-five years, which designer Adolfo has recycled into a lining for her raincoat.

The tally of private purchases and gifts does not include the spangled dress she wore last night to the Kennedy Center, her outfits for today's events other than the gala, her jewelry and some of the shoes and underwear, or the cost of her hairdresser. It does include a $1,650 American alligator handbag by Judith Leiber.

Nancy Reagan has many designer clothes, which she

10

wears over and over again, and the wardrobe for the inaugural no doubt will be used the same way. Below is a shopping list for her inaugural attire with approximate prices.

A top-quality, full-length mink coat by Maximilian, the exclusive New York furrier whose mink coats usually start at $8,000 and generally go up to $12,000 for the best. Anna Maximilian Potok, who fitted Nancy Reagan, would not reveal the exact price of the coat. She did say that the midcalf length was suitable to be worn over daytime clothes as well as full-length gowns. "I'm sure Mrs. Reagan will wear it for different kinds of occasions," said Potok.

A hand-beaded inaugural night ball gown by James Galanos, America's most inventive designer, took several women four weeks to embroider. His gowns are mostly sold from sketches and swatches picked from a sample book and then made to order by hand in his Los Angeles workroom. A gold embroidered gown on the rack at Neiman-Marcus last year had a price tag of $10,000. Last fall, a plain gown and jacket costume with embroidery just on the jacket could be ordered from his sketches for $5,000. Galanos "donated his services" for the inaugural dress, as he did the dresses she wore to the two California inaugural balls. And like the others, which were contributed to the Los Angeles County Museum, this one will join other First Lady gowns in the Smithsonian's Museum of American History.

Nancy Reagan will be wearing a matching Adolfo dress and coat on inauguration day. She has long worn Adolfo suits, which start at $800. His dresses start at $600; his coats rarely are priced under $900.

Bill Blass evening gowns start at $1,200. When they have fur trim—and Mrs. Reagan's dress for the gala at the Capital Centre has a fox-trimmed shrug—the price zooms up to more than $2,500. (Barbara Bush also is planning to wear a Bill Blass hammered satin gown for the inaugural ball.)

David Evins makes a lot of special-order shoes based on his basic design but adapted to the color and fabric choice of the client. Lady Bird Johnson wore his shoes, Jackie Onassis still does and so do a lot of movie stars and models. The shoes are made in Florence, and start at about $125, depending on the fabric. Special-order shoes cost a minimum of $200, "and it is a very common thing," says Evins. The shoes that go with the inaugural ball gown have the same embroidery motif on the front and a totally beaded heel.

Judith Leiber was so afraid the white satin handbag she made for Mrs. Reagan might be soiled from sewing machine oil that she made two. Both are shirred white satin with silk straps; one has a rock crystal scarab surrounded by rhinestones ($400), and the other is the same shape with different beading ($350). Leiber and Reagan together decided that a Louisiana alligator handbag in a classic square shape would be most suitable for daytime use. (The Louisiana alligator is no longer on the endangered species list.) Neiman-Marcus has two of these bags in stock for $1,700 each.

The amount of money the Reagans personally spent on the inaugural wardrobe, tallied from the minimum or maximum viewpoint, is high for a personal wardrobe. But it is not out of line with what the wife of the president of France might spend. "In fact, one should think of it like a coronation," said a Washington woman who buys top designer clothes.

"Spending a lot of money [on clothes] has to have some proportion to what your resources are," says Philip Miller, president of Neiman-Marcus. "I wouldn't say it would be a good investment for a young couple starting out and getting their home settled to go out and spend $1,000 on a dress for a ball. For someone who is established and has an upper-level income, I think the pleasure of fine clothes, both in terms of how they feel when you wear them, how you look and how they are perceived, is a real benefit."

Says Betsy Bloomingdale, a close friend of Nancy Reagan's, who has guided her on many of her clothing purchases, "You don't buy clothes like these. You collect them."

The Great Ghastly Post-Inaugural Lear-Lock

Stephanie Mansfield

January 22, 1981, the *Washington Post*

Stephanie Mansfield coined the term "Lear-lock" in her delightful satire on the rich and famous trapped in their private jets on the tarmac at Washington's National Airport the day after the Reagan inauguration. Her piece captures the brassy style of the eighties that was set by Ronnie and Nancy and aped by the monied and the powerful across the country. I especially love the quote from the stunning blonde in the red fox coat, who snapped, "Most of these men have to get back to work." Right.

FROM DAWN TO DUSK the inaugural veterans came, wearing minks and lynx, cashmere and cowboy boots, clutching copies of *Town & Country*, bearing Louis Vuitton and Gucci garment bags, the heady aroma of Bal à Versailles mixed with jet fuel.

They leaped out of limo after limo, descending upon the tiny general aviation terminal at Washington's National Airport to make their inaugural exit. Some were owners of private planes, others just passengers. In all, there were more than 230 private jets trying to take off yesterday.

By noon, it was Lear-lock.

"It's wild," said Butler Aviation general manager Admiral James Morin. "They all want to leave at the same time. Some damn corporation pilot is raising hell because he can't get fueled up. He's said he's hauling a couple of senators and he wants to leave."

13

The mass exodus of the private jets owners (more than twice the normal number for any given day) not only set their own departures back two hours, it also caused up to one-hour delays for commercial passengers at National Airport's main terminal.

"My God," said Morin, racing around in a brown leather bomber jacket, "everybody wants to leave. Some guys are prima donnas. They want special attention. Well, nobody gets priority around here."

Not even Bob Hope, whose trip back to Palm Springs yesterday aboard the Spanos Construction Co.'s Lockhead Jet Star was delayed about one hour.

"This is crazy," said Hope, surveying the scene in a tweed hat and pink plaid pants. On arrival several days ago, Hope had walked into the terminal, spied a picture of former president Gerald Ford on the wall and claimed it as a souvenir.

"I didn't steal it," he said. "They told me I could take it. I'm planning to paste it on my golf bag. Every time Ford makes a bad shot, I'm gonna swing the bag around to show him."

Every few minutes, the intercom crackled:

Mr. Mellon's party, please call the desk . . .

Eli Lilly Group, your pilot is waiting . . .

Passengers with Ford Motor Company, please report to . . .

Hoffman LaRoche party, please check the desk.

The message board overflowed with memos, among them a scribbled note: "Sen. John Warner, please call your Taylor."

Fortified by forty gallons of free coffee and twenty dozen doughnuts, the tony travelers (destinations Miami, Chicago, Detroit, Dallas, Fort Worth, Greenwich, Salt Lake City) squished down into plastic chairs, chatted about the inaugural ("That ball last night was absolutely ghastly!"), and did what most people in their tax bracket try hard to avoid: They waited. And waited.

"I thought this was the reason I bought my own plane," huffed one beefy businessman.

"Most of these men have to get back to work," snapped a stunning blonde in a red fox coat.

There was Wayne Newton's red, white, and blue turboprop (with the words "Boomtown, Reno, Nev." on the tail).

Henry Ford II's Grumman G-2, Occidental Petroleum's mammoth 727, Mel Tillis's "Stutter One" and a flotilla of Fortune 500 Sabreliners, Jet Stars, Lears and Cessnas owned by Atlantic Richfield, Bethlehem Steel, Tenneco, Goodyear, Whirlpool, John Deere, General Motors, Gannett Newspapers, U.S. Tobacco Co., Time-Life, Inc. and a gaggle of lesser-known corporations.

Outside on the tarmac, the luxury skyliners sat snout to tail, winged victories temporarily clipped. Inside, the pilots sat in the lounge, waiting for takeoff times and placating their passengers.

"LADIES AND GENTLEMEN, PLEASE DON'T PICK ON YOUR PILOTS," Jim Morin announced testily over the intercom.

"About ten percent will bitch no matter what," said Morin. "Some are nice, but some are inconsiderate as hell."

"I've never seen such a mess," said Jim Sturgis, corporate pilot for Tenneco's Lockheed Jet Star.

The pilots, distinguishable by their navy blue raincoats, said they can earn up to $40,000 a year flying board chairmen and executives across America. Some are former Air Force pilots who shunned commercial airlines for private work to log more flying time.

"Basically, I'm a chauffeur," said Eddie Lawsche, who co-pilots a Sabreliner 60 owned by the Fort Worth-based Western Co.

He flies thirty-five to fifty hours each month and earns $25,000 a year.

"We're kind of like the king's carriage driver," said another pilot who wished to remain anonymous. He earns $40,000 a year flying for a Chicago-based corporation, flies about fifty times a month, stays in the best hotels, eats in the best restaurants and is on call twenty-four hours a day.

The life, he said, has its ups and downs.

"You can't belong to a bowling league," he said before gathering up his party.

Back at the Butler Aviation desk, there was Sen. Lowell Weicker (R-Conn.) elbowing into the crowd with a group of friends. "I'm not going, I'm dropping off," he said.

There was former senator George Murphy in a blue beret,

admiring a Texas oilman's blinking red and blue elephant pin. Murphy was waiting to board a friend's Cessna Citation for a flight to West Palm Beach. Did he mind the wait? "I don't mind anything anymore," the seventy-eight-year-old Murphy replied.

There was former Democratic Committee chairman Robert Strauss on his way to a board meeting in Michigan, shaking hands with fellow Texans in ten-gallon hats.

There was a procession of Yves St. Laurent luggage preceded by Robert Tish, Loews' Hotel magnate. Behind him, a bellhop carried two wicker baskets draped in gingham napkins, goodies for the flight.

"The money walking through here," sighed Val Settle, a Marriott employee selling $17 sandwich trays to the airborne. "You can just smell it. They're amazingly nice, though," Settle confided. "If they bump into you, they say excuse me."

Piled in the corners was enough designer luggage to start a discount outlet.

"I just can't take my eyes off it," said Evelyn DiBona, wife of the president of American Petroleum Institute. "It all has to be signature luggage."

Admiral Jim Morin was racing around his office. "Where are my damn glasses?" he screamed at no one in particular.

Morin and his crew have been deluged with over seven hundred private aircraft landing and taking off from the general aviation terminal since last Saturday. He managed to borrow a "taxiway" from the main terminal to accommodate the private planes parked there for the inaugural. (The parking fee is approximately $15 a night.)

He also has clients (Paul Mellon, International Brotherhood of Teamsters, Southern Railway Corp.) who pay from $350 to $2,000 a month for hangar space.

"They have private planes for the convenience," said Morin. "And they don't have to be pestered by people in lobbies."

Also, he pointed out, you can write it off as a business expense.

Meanwhile, back at the terminal, the limos were backed up almost as far as the Lears. "You won't see this again," said FAA policeman Jim Chaffin. "At least not until four years from now."

Windfall

Michael M. Thomas

August 8, 1983, *New York*

I recall reading Michael Thomas's outraged attack on the leveraged buyout of Gibson Greeting Cards by former Treasury Secretary William Simon when it appeared in New York *magazine. I was dumbfounded that you could buy a company by borrowing against the assets of the company. Thomas deserves credit for seeing that the seductive profits and fees offered Wall Street insiders by the LBO game would change the face of American business, and not necessarily for the better.*

IN JANUARY 1982, a group headed by William E. Simon—energy czar under Nixon, treasury secretary under Ford, and evangel of free enterprise—bought the Gibson greeting-card company from RCA for $80 million. Simon and his partners put up only $1 million of their own money—the rest was borrowed against the assets of Gibson, which, among other cards, publishes a line featuring Garfield the fat cat. Eighteen months later, Simon took Gibson public in an offering underwritten by Lehman Brothers Kuhn Loeb that valued Gibson at $290 million. Simon's share of the windfall was enormous—his personal cash investment of just $330,000 turned into nearly $66 million in cash and stock—and it was all perfectly legal. "We were just darn lucky," he says.

Ronald Reagan said recently that he liked to think that America was still a country where a man could get rich. His particular sense of history notwithstanding, the president probably had in mind the sweat and toil of Horatio Alger's heroes, the inventiveness and vision of Ford and Edison. The

17

saga of the Gibson deal is a tale of enrichment as compelling as any of the "boys' lives" that young Americans were once given to ponder and emulate. The values and accomplishments making up the rungs of this ladder of success are hardly traditional in character, yet a study of them speaks volumes about the way in which wealth can be created today.

On its face, the Gibson offering prospectus isn't an imposing document. Cover and all, the booklet runs to sixty pages of closely printed figures and related footnotes. The title is hardly seductive:

3,500,000 Shares
Gibson Greetings, Inc.
Common Stock

Yet, this seemingly innocuous prospectus, one of hundreds hatched in this fertile bull market, is a textbook of "executive suite" financial culture. It provides insights into an elitist network of insider deal-making that most outside Wall Street don't grasp, possibly including those who invested in the Gibson offering without digging beneath the surface. It illustrates to perfection the "paper entrepreneurialism" so passionately denounced by Robert Reich and others, a business culture dominated and defined by people for whom business has no reality beyond the numbers.

The Gibson story also raises the issue of the proper use of the nation's financial resources, including not only the cash and credit provided by the marketplace but also tax breaks and other incentives handed out by Washington in the well-meant, but mistaken, belief that they would stimulate the creation of new, more productive business assets and more jobs. Such tax subsidies have been most opportunistically seized to facilitate the frenzied trading of secondhand assets and businesses, which has little to do with the mainstream industrial objectives to which the president and his men continually proclaim their dedication. In 1983, this trend has been epitomized by leveraged buyouts—the purchase of a company using its own assets as collateral for the necessary loans. Their growing allure, says *Business Week*, "can be explained in three words: Gibson Greeting Cards."

Between the time William Simon, fifty-five, bought Gibson and the time it went public, the company's internal structure, business, and, most important, management, did not change materially. (Simon never even became an executive of the company.) Its outlook was enhanced, says William M. Kearns Jr., a Gibson director and a managing director of Lehman Brothers Kuhn Loeb, by the bankruptcy of two minor competitors and the malaise of its two substantially larger competitors, Hallmark and American Greetings. (As it happens, American Greetings is growing at over 25 percent annually.) Only Gibson's paper framework and the composition of its capitalization were fundamentally changed. Because the purchase of Gibson was financed by borrowing against the company's assets, its net worth was substantially replaced by debt: It now owes $59 million, including financial leases, versus $22 million a year earlier. Thanks, however, to ingenious paper shuffling, the continuation of Gibson's nice earnings trend, and, most of all, the appearance (not to be minimized) of a roaring bull market, Simon made a profit of 20,000 percent in a year and a half.

The sheer magnitude of Simon's windfall and the relatively short time it took to cash in would be newsworthy in themselves, as finance columnist Dan Dorfman was the first to point out. The alchemies of capitalism have seldom achieved so extraordinary a transmutation of values. It might be helpful to note that Gibson's 400 percent increase in valuation over the period prior to the public offering was equal to that of Coleco, the best-performing stock on the New York Stock Exchange, over roughly the same period. Coleco is an innovative marketer of video games and home computers, two areas with which investors have been infatuated. Since 1982, Coleco's sales and profits have increased nearly 500 percent. Over a comparable period, Gibson's sales and profits also increased handsomely, but by about 50 percent.

Unlike Coleco, Gibson did not obtain its increase in value from a rolling ground swell in investor enthusiasm urged on by perceptive security analysts who discerned the future unfolding in a series of remarkable product and marketing breakthroughs. Lehman Brothers Kuhn Loeb, the managing underwriters of the offering (and also RCA's longtime investment bankers, who advised that company on the sale of Gibson to the Simon group), simply decided that $27.50 per share, the amount the public paid, was what the market would bear.

Gibson Greeting Cards is a small (8 percent of the market), 133-year-old maker of greeting cards, or, as the prospectus calls them, "social expression products." In 1964, Gibson was acquired by C.I.T., the big consumer-finance company that merged with RCA in 1980. In late 1981, RCA decided to dispose of Gibson. In January 1982, it sold the card firm to a group organized by Simon, which included Gibson's top management, who presumably had access to the sort of financial information relied on by lenders when appraising credit-worthiness. The total consideration received by RCA was roughly $80 million: $22 million to repay an intracompany loan from C.I.T. to Gibson, and $58 million for RCA's equity in Gibson, which was valued on RCA's books at $87 million.

The Simon group raised the purchase price, plus another $8 million (largely for closing costs), from various financial institutions, among them General Electric Credit Corporation (G.E.C.C.), a multi-billion-dollar financing subsidiary of General Electric. As its contribution to a financing package totaling $88 million, the Simon group put up $1 million in cash, purchasing roughly seven million shares at 14 cents a share. Gibson has operated under the Simon aegis since January 1982, during which time its revenues and profits have continued in an upward trajectory already well established when the company was part of RCA.

On May 19, 1983, the syndicate headed by Lehman Brothers Kuhn Loeb offered 3.5 million shares of Gibson to the public at $27.50 a share. Half of these shares were sold for members of the Simon group, who netted (after underwriting commissions) $25.75 a share for stock that they had purchased for 14 cents.

Except for the sheer scale and speed of the profit realized by the insiders, this is not an uncommon business tale. A bunch of smart guys made an admirable deal for themselves and took advantage of an investment climate in which almost anything goes. That's what bull markets are for. And Simon himself seems to subscribe to the theory of Kismet in the Gibson deal. Asked about various aspects of the operation, he keeps saying, "We were just darn lucky." Perhaps, but when one examines the behavior of the principal figures in the Gibson saga, it all seems curiouser and curiouser.

Take RCA, a company that for twenty years has seemed to be very uncertain of its grand design. The company has long been an investment banker's dream: It has needed large amounts of fresh capital to keep going, and it has seldom turned a deaf ear to an acquisition proposal. Investment bankers collect handsome fees when companies are bought and sold; sometimes, when they latch on to an RCA, they can enjoy a double dip, as in the case of RCA's frozen-food business, Banquet Foods, bought through Lehman Brothers Kuhn Loeb and later sold through the same firm. Over the last fifteen years, RCA has consistently done better for its investment bankers than for its stockholders. RCA keeps an investment banker on its board: Peter G. Peterson, a commerce secretary under Richard Nixon. Peterson is the chairman and co-chief executive of Lehman Brothers.

Beginning in 1980, RCA launched the systematic divestiture of a number of companies, which, to quote RCA's 1982 annual report, were "outside the areas of electronics, communications, and entertainment . . . or which offered less-than-satisfactory promise of attractive return on the required investment." Although some might argue that greeting cards are a quintessential form of communication, Gibson must have fallen into the former category. Financially, Gibson could more than hold its own with the other members of the RCA family, which still includes C.I.T. and Hertz. In 1981, the year during which its sale to the Simon group was being negotiated, Gibson earned approximately 15 percent on RCA's equity investment; by comparison, in the same year, RCA earned about 4 percent on its own equity.

Moreover, Gibson appeared to be on a roll. A new management was installed in 1978. In 1979, Gibson netted $4.3 million, the next year $6.9 million, and $11.6 million in 1981. Gibson's 1981 profit represented over 20 percent of RCA's *total* reported net income. In 1982, under the same management but now flying the William E. Simon flag, Gibson Greeting Cards earned $14 million, continuing the trend of the preceding three years. In terms of the interests of RCA stockholders, it might have been preferable to have had Gibson divest itself of RCA.

Of the purchase price, RCA received $58 million for its equity in Gibson. Since RCA had valued Gibson on its books at $87 million, it sustained a loss of $29 million on the sale of a going business, the earnings of which were increasing at an annual rate of over 30 percent. Ingeniously, RCA treated the tax reduction resulting from selling Gibson at a loss as an item of operating profit, and included it as income for 1982—a good example of tax laws' facilitating essentially unproductive transactions, not to mention the use of accepted accounting prestidigitation to turn broken eggs into omelets.

RCA has defended the Gibson sale, in an official statement, on the grounds that the company had been widely shopped but that only two offers had developed; that it needed the cash, that the price was good, relative to 1980 earnings; that factors impossible to predict, such as the explosion of the 1982–83 bull market, "enabled [Simon] to cash in on the gamble [he] took." The first seems inarguable. As to RCA's need for cash, if Simon's group raised $87 million on Gibson's assets, why couldn't RCA itself have done substantially the same? As will be seen, the Simon group realized $35 million through a sale and leaseback of Gibson's operating properties; this is a type of transaction for which Lehman Brothers Kuhn Loeb has been actively advertising its expertise to its corporate clients for some years. The argument with respect to 1980's earnings sounds plausible, given that RCA shook hands with Simon on the deal in June 1981; it didn't sign a contract until December of that year, however, by which time Gibson's excellent, 68 percent year-to-year increase in profits over 1980 must have been evident to someone at RCA. Deals are often killed or renegotiated on the basis of drastically improving or deteriorating results.

Finally, as I've mentioned, the "risk" of the Simon group was limited to 1.2 percent of all the financing involved. RCA's explanations scarcely stand up under the question "How come you couldn't do what Simon could?" One strong possibility is that RCA had conceptually locked itself into a divestment program that assumed a relentless momentum of its own. A spokesman for RCA implies that this is the case, suggesting that the Gibson deal took place during a period of transition: Chairman and C.E.O. Thornton Bradshaw arrived at RCA at a point of financial crisis, which meant that not all decisions, especially those that promised to provide some cash, could be reviewed as carefully as they might be today.

There is some confusion about the exact nature of Lehman Brothers Kuhn Loeb's advice to RCA, for which the firm was paid $200,000. The investment bankers claim that they were paid for finding a buyer, an assertion denied both by a spokesman for RCA and by Simon himself. In this writer's experience, investment bankers are hired to "bless" a deal, to pronounce it fair and reasonable for the client who pays the fee. For this kind of advice to an old client, the fee of $200,000 mentioned in the prospectus seems to be about right. In any case, financial consolation would come later for Lehman Brothers Kuhn Loeb: For putting together the underwriting group in the May 1983 offering, and for seeing the offering to market, the firm would realize gross underwriting fees and commissions exceeding $1.8 million.

In retrospect, RCA cannot fairly be accused of having left $232 million "on the table." No one could then have foreseen the bull market that got going in August 1982. Certainly, at the time Gibson changed hands it would have been impossible to give away the sort of new issues for which investors would beg in 1983. It does seem, however, that RCA was unduly generous in parting with a growing, consumer-oriented, low-ticket business at substantially below its book value. It is difficult to accept financial desperation as a rationale; the impact of the Gibson sale on RCA's earnings statement and balance sheet and cash flow, to judge from the latter's 1982 annual report, was nominal. There are any number of ways RCA might have protected itself, especially given Gibson's continuing earnings momentum. RCA sticks to its contention that under the circumstances it made a good deal.

The role of Lehman Brothers Kuhn Loeb seems less excusable, if only as a matter of taste. The firm did not prevent one of its oldest, most valued clients from taking 5.3 times earnings for a business it would later value for public consumption at twenty times earnings. The subsequent performance of

Gibson—the stock is selling today at around $23—suggests that the offering was overpriced, especially when, as Lehman Brothers Kuhn Loeb admits, approximately two-thirds of the offering found its way to "retail" (i.e., individual) accounts. It is almost a matter of form to price retail-oriented offerings so as to be certain of at least a small increase in the value of the shares in the months after the offering. Simon denies pushing Lehman Brothers on price; he says, "We adhered to what Lehman Brothers Kuhn Loeb recommended. Any leaning was minimal." One can only wonder at the 133-year-old firm's willingness to price a piece of new business at a level that could only—admittedly in hindsight—reflect poorly on the argument of one of its clients.

Lehman Brothers Kuhn Loeb rejects any findings of inconsistency. The sale by RCA and the offering by the Simon group are perceived by chairman Peterson as entirely unconnected, having been handled by different executives of the firm. Peterson, who is leaving Lehman Brothers this year, chooses to remain above the controversy. He describes himself as "totally uninvolved in the process" regarding the Gibson transaction. He disclaims any detailed knowledge of the services Lehman Brothers Kuhn Loeb rendered RCA on the Gibson sale, and says he had nothing to do with the Gibson offering.

The pattern of institutional eccentricity with respect to Gibson, Simon, et al., is most wondrously strange in the case of General Electric Credit Corporation. To appreciate this, however, requires an understanding of the financing package assembled to buy Gibson.

As I've said, the Simon group raised significantly more than the $80 million needed to pay RCA. In one way or another, a total of $87 million was raised on the strength of Gibson's assets; according to the prospectus, close to $7 million of that would be paid out in "closing and related costs," which is legalese for finder's fees, accounting charges, and lawyers' billings. Almost 10 percent of the total value of the transaction thus went to middlemen.

Of the money borrowed for Gibson itself, $13 million was a relatively conventional secured loan from an affiliate of Barclays Bank. The next $31 million was funded in a somewhat more complex manner. A new company, Gibson Realty, Inc., was organized by Raymond Chambers, Simon's partner. Simultaneously with the RCA closing, Gibson Realty bought Gibson Greetings' land and buildings with a promissory note for $31 million. Gibson Realty then sold these properties immediately to a pair of unidentified public real-estate funds for $35 million cash. Already, it had made $4 million. It now lent $31 million *back* to Gibson Greetings—of which Simon was in the process of becoming the owner—so Gibson could forward the money to RCA as part of the acquisition package. In addition, Gibson Realty charged Gibson Greetings 12 percent annual interest on its loan, while Greetings (now with substantial public ownership) is getting only 11 percent on the $31 million promissory note from Gibson Realty. And, needing a roof under which to operate, Gibson Greetings leased its former properties back from the real-estate funds that now owned them.

This raises the question of the $4 million difference between the $35 million received by Gibson Realty for properties that it had purchased from Gibson Greetings for $31 million only minutes earlier. On this, the prospectus is roundabout. On page 2, it is stated that among the benefits accruing to Simon (and his partner) are "net proceeds . . . from the purchase and resale of certain real property of Gibson in 1982 of $250,000 and other benefits." The reader is counseled to turn to page 4 for amplification, but there finds no direct word of such proceeds or benefits. The section does indicate that over $4 million, or almost all the difference between Gibson Realty's cost and what it sold the properties for, was paid out in "fees and expenses to unrelated parties." By doing sums with the information furnished in the prospectus, it *does* appear that Simon and Chambers ended up with $250,000 to compensate them for the trouble of forming a shell corporation to make all this excitement possible. Oh, yes, Chambers also picks up (via Gibson Realty) another $290,000 a year, representing the difference between the 11 percent rate on Gibson Realty's note to Greetings and the 12 percent rate on Greetings' note to Gibson Realty. The prospectus explains that this "reflects business arrangements between related parties."

In any event, between Barclays and the real estate deals

(after expenses), the Simon group had accumulated $44 million to pay RCA. It now obtained $39 million from General Electric Credit Corporation, a financial giant that is one of the largest and most profitable units in the General Electric family.

G.E.C.C. negotiated stiff terms for its participation as a lender. It took a lien on everything connected with Gibson except Bill Simon's famous grin. It pegged the interest rate at 6.45 percent over its own cost of money. And to ensure that it participated in what the business schools call "the best-case scenario," it got an option permitting it to buy roughly a quarter of the company (2.3 million common shares) at the same price as the Simon group—14 cents a share. Finally, it wrote into the loan a provision that if a dividend was paid on Gibson's common stock G.E.C.C. would be entitled to extra interest on its loan.

By February of this year, when *Forbes* discussed the Gibson transaction, it was clear that a public offering of Gibson stock was intended and that G.E.C.C. stood to make a fortune on its stock option. At that point, the price under discussion appears to have been around $12 a share, although this is an inference based on *Forbes*'s conversation with William Kearns, of Lehman Brothers Kuhn Loeb. In March, Gibson paid its stockholders, still consisting solely of the Simon group, a special dividend of $2.8 million; this triggered G.E.C.C.'s right to receive extra interest of $1.88 million.

G.E.C.C. was thus by mid-March in the position of putting all or a piece of its 14-cent stock in the forthcoming public offering, at $12 a share, although two months later the stock would actually be offered at $27.50. It was also entitled to the special interest. It had, by any measure, negotiated a wonderful deal.

And yet, G.E.C.C. elected not to receive the extra interest it was due. It further chose not to exercise its option, but instead to sell it in early April for $13 a share, or about half of what it could have got a few weeks later. Half of the option shares were bought by Gibson itself, and half by the Simon group. This was consummated in early April 1983 and is addressed in the prospectus in a strange aside: "The Company believes that such price reflects, in part, GECC's desire to realize the value of its entire equity interest in the Company at this time."

It can be argued that $30 million in the hand is worth $59 million (2.3 million shares times $27.50 less underwriting expenses and fees) in the bush, but the argument loses force when hand and bush are separated by a matter of a few weeks. G.E.C.C. says that market uncertainties prompted it to accept a price that would seem low only weeks later. Doubtless G.E.C.C. was pelted with the hoary investment-banking argument that the addition of its stock to the offering would kill the deal by making it top-heavy. Whatever the answer, G.E.C.C. elected to forgo roughly $30 million in profit on its option plus $1.88 million in cash interest to which it was clearly entitled, and that is simply inexplicable.

Further, G.E.C.C. hardly "realized" on its investment. "Realized" makes it sound as if G.E.C.C. had been paid cash on the barrel for its option. Actually, G.E.C.C. took back $30 million in notes, $15 million (payable over ten years) from Gibson itself, and $15 million (payable *after* ten years) from the Simon group. Thus, not only did G.E.C.C. hand Simon and friends a windfall of over $15 million (since they were able to double in the public offering what they had paid G.E.C.C. two weeks later), it also let them pay for it down the line, and on better terms than Gibson, the company they were about to sell to the public, got.

G.E.C.C. offered a variety of justifications when I asked why it had passed up over $30 million in realizable profit. At first, a number of tax and technical motivations were offered by a spokesman. Simon also says that G.E.C.C. had "tax reasons"; he adds that the company wanted to cash in its entire investment and asked him for an offer. A clear possibility is that the closer G.E.C.C. looked at this deal—the special March dividend being the last straw—the more the idea of continuing in a putative partnership with the Simon group became unappealing. Preferring to remain only as lenders, G.E.C.C. took what it could get and departed the stage. G.E.C.C. will not comment on this hypothesis.

Classical mythology instructs that he who is favored by the gods should go for broke, which is surely what the Simon group, and especially Simon himself, has done. So far, the group has taken out $45 million from sales of stock for which it paid $250,000. Adjusting for the buyback and exercise of the G.E.C.C. option, it retains shares worth $154 million, against which it owes $15 million with ten years to pay.

This seems hardly to have sufficed for Simon himself. Not content with millions from sales of stock plus a share of the special dividend, which came to around $900,000, he has shown he really knows how to "cut a fat hog," as they say in Texas. Private companies of which he owns 50 percent have to date collected a $580,000 finder's fee and a first-year consulting fee of $440,000 (on a contract that has nine years to run, at $390,000 per year); he has even sliced off a piece of roughly $80,000 in insurance fees channeled through Simon-controlled insurance brokerages. Might this not appear greedy in view of the fact that he has earned millions? Simon replies that taking these fees is simply good business practice, and he hasn't been criticized for having done so.

Thus, in the brief period since he and his group bought Gibson, Simon has personally taken out, *in cash*, something over $15 million. He retains stock worth $51 million, against which he owes a little over $5 million, secured only by his stock itself. His twenty-plus percent stake in Gibson has proved in a year and a half to be worth more than he and his group paid RCA for the entire company.

This brings us to the question of what purchasers of the public offering got for their $27.50 a share. By buying into a company that had a load of cheap stock in the hands of insiders, they got Gibson stock now having an underlying (or book) value per share of $5 and change. From the opening bell, they have had a market loss; the stock has sold at as low as $23 and to this writing has not sold at its offering price. Investors in the offering have also indirectly underwritten Bill Simon's future peace of mind. In a most unusual arrangement, Gibson has agreed to foot 60 percent of any tax bill that may be presented to the Simon group in the event that its cheap stock should be interpreted as "compensation" by the I.R.S.

There won't be any substantial dividends for a while, either. The special dividend the insiders paid themselves in

March left Gibson with a total leeway of $933,000 with which to pay dividends, or less than a dime a share. Simon is categorical that there was no intention to pay dividends for some time after the sale to the public. This presumably represented a policy shift following the March payment to the insiders. In any case, much of Gibson's future cash flow will have to service the debt created when Simon acquired the company. It is to be hoped that existing facilities and resources can support the kind of growth indicated by a public-offering price representing around twenty times the prior year's earnings. As a basis for comparison, I.B.M. sells at sixteen times last year's earnings, and American Greetings, four times larger than Gibson, sells at fourteen times last year's earnings.

In the Gibson prospectus, nothing technically went undisclosed; an army of lawyers saw to that. Yet, nothing was made clear, certainly not to the layman considering taking up a few shares in this offering.

From the character of the prospectus to the tax laws that underwrite the cash flow, the Gibson transaction exemplifies the distortion of well-intentioned governmental policies. It is questionable, in fact, whether Simon could have pulled this off without Uncle Sam's arm draped lovingly across his shoulders.

There is an irony in all this. On leaving Washington, Simon wrote two best-sellers—*A Time for Truth* and *A Time for Action*—preaching Pleistocene self-reliance, free-marketry, and, above all, freedom from government. But if anyone owes his fortune to Washington, it is William E. Simon. Like Gerald Ford and Henry Kissinger, he began simply by putting up his Washington credentials for sale or rent as a consultant and adviser. In the simplistic canons of Republican economics, he became a prince of philosophers. *Fortune* would write, with admiration and a straight face, "Simon fully exploited the enhanced status that a businessman can acquire from a few years of Washington prominence." This prominence set Simon on a path to wealth available only to men with access to large amounts of credit and privileged information. His post-Washington career is a miracle wrought as if by an invisible hand, a hand belonging to Uncle Sam. It's hardly what we might expect from a man who has preached, also to his considerable profit, a gospel that says if we're going to make anything of ourselves we have to cut loose from Washington.

Simon has first-class media relations, and the financial press has been eloquent in making him out to be a shirt-sleeves entrepreneur. With all due respect, however, if his Gibson maneuverings are anything other than paper shuffling, then this writer is Marie of Romania.

That still doesn't answer the question of why RCA and G.E.C.C., two great corporations, and Lehman Brothers Kuhn Loeb, a highly respected conduit to the public market, have made their resources and purses available to him in such a surprising fashion. That the investing public went for the Gibson offering is *not* surprising; in markets like these, new issues are sold, not bought, and prospectuses are mailed to the customer along with the confirmations that inform him how much he owes for what he has been told to buy. Certain deals, like other types of processes, acquire a momentum of their own, inexorable and powerful, strong and seductive enough to sweep all but the most steadfast and commonsensical along with them. The stock-market drought of the last decade pretty much ensured that when the time came there would be in place a backlog of greed more than sufficient to overcome the declining store of clear thinking.

Happily, it's not a problem for the progenitor himself. As Simon explained to *Fortune,* "I keep wondering why more people are not doing what we're doing." He made this statement, *Fortune* reports, "with an air of genuine bafflement." This seems a mite disingenuous coming from a man who has arguably outnegotiated two of the nation's larger companies and made himself an important fortune in less than two years.

In any event, like Garfield, Simon has earned the right to purr.

Junk Debunked

James Grant

September 24, 1984, *Grant's Interest
Rate Observer*

Jim Grant, editor of Grant's Interest Rate Observer,
*is the wittiest financial journalist I know. He is
also one of the most perceptive. His "Junk
Debunked" was written in 1984, but remains the
most authoritative critique of Michael Milken's
thesis that junk bonds were a lot less risky than
people thought. It may have taken awhile for Grant
to be proven correct, but the unfortunates who
invested in such Milken-financed disasters as
Executive Life, the now-bankrupt insurance
company, could have profited from this line in
Grant's piece: "The truth is that markets are bigger
than market makers, and that nearly every
investment enthusiasm has an unhappy ending."*

Payment of interest on a bond is fixed, and if not paid when
due, failure is precipitated. Most corporation directors, no
matter how successful the enterprise may be, hesitate to
burden it with fixed charges, even if the future gives promise
of earnings that exceed the charges many times over. And
even in those instances when there seems no reasonable
doubt but that the new money obtained from the sale of
bonds will be invested so as to earn immediately, through
new or improved equipment, more than sufficient to pay the
charges, there is no assurance that this increased earning
capacity will continue through the life of the bonds.

—Arthur S. Dewing, *The Financial Policy
of Corporations*, Volume IV, 1920

IN THE BOND MARKET, this is a day of high hopes and low interest-coverage ratios. It is a day of the near extinction of the triple-A corporate credit and the rise to investment respectability of the sub-Baa credit. It is a time that has nurtured the junk-bond movement and has taken to heart the junk-bond investment philosophy. As recently as a decade ago, only three "high-yield" corporate bond funds existed; their combined assets were $400 million. At last count, there were thirty two such funds with assets running to $6 billion. In the mid-1970s, it was a rare speculative-grade new issue that was admitted to the public debt market; nowadays it's a rare triple-A issue that sees the light of day. (In fact, according to Salomon Brothers, no triple-A debt security has been sold this year, while the average monthly volume of Ba-or-lower merchandise is running just below the record pace set last year.) Merrill Lynch, describing the growth of the "high-yield" market, notes that there now are junk-minded insurance companies (it counts a dozen or so with a "major" commitment to speculative bonds), junk investment advisers and junk savings and loan associations. Not coincidentally, Drexel Burnham Lambert, the principal force in the junk market, is the fastest growing investment banking house in Wall Street.

To junk proponents, of course, all this is as it should be. Better to own the low-rated debt of an up-and-coming business, they say, than the investment grade debt of the next International Harvester. They invoke Michael Milken, dean of junk at Drexel Burnham, who says: "Risk is a function of knowledge." In general, they say that the rating agencies are backward looking while markets exist to discount the future ("I'm much more interested in the future"—Milken). In credit analysis, they emphasize the significance of prospective growth in earnings and downplay the importance of historical balance-sheet ratios. They observe that the rate of default on corporate debt is vanishingly low, and they say that diversification will reduce such risk as may exist in one given portfolio. They recite the excellent junk investment record. "The total return to investors in high-yield securities has been very impressive," writes the corporate-bond research unit at Merrill. "An investment of $100 in high-yield securities made in 1935 would have grown to $4,056 at the end of

1983, while a $100 investment in high-grade securities would have grown to $713 in the same time period. Using more recent data, a $100 investment in high-yield securities in 1965 would have grown to $446.73 by the end of 1983, while a $100 investment in high-grade securities would have grown to $271.25."

So apparently airtight is the case for junk, so much of it has been sold and so great is the institutional appetite for it that one is obliged to doff one's hat to the junk pioneers. Standing there hatless, however, one also must scratch one's head and ask if this Wall Street concept will go the way of all fads. The question must concern everyone, in and out of the bond market. For one thing, the junk phenomenon reflects the chronic weakness in insurance company operating results; as underwriters lose money in price wars, or through wind-damage and asbestos settlements, they are increasingly obliged to reach for yield in their investment portfolios. More basically, the rise of speculative bonds is a symptom of the piling up of debt and of the long-running deterioration of corporate finances. In that sense, the gentrification of junk amounts to the making of virtue out of unpleasant necessity.

Grant's is anti-junk. While conceding the extraordinary record of high-yield bonds, we would observe, to start with, that the present-day world is very long on debt and very short on equity. It is long on debt that may well be repudiated. According to an old investment adage, one should own the thing in short supply and shun the thing in surplus. What an illiquid world needs is cash; what it owns (or owes) in superabundance is debt. In the circumstances, the type of income-producing security to own is probably the one that affords the greatest margin of safety—that is, the one that offers the highest ratio of cash flow to interest expense. By definition and as the accompanying table illustrates, junk bonds of any description are claims on companies without much financial leeway. (Moody's defines Ba, the highest junk grade, this way: "Bonds which are rated Ba are judged to have speculative elements; their future cannot be considered as well assured. Often the protection of interest and principal payments may be very moderate and thereby not well safeguarded during both good and bad times over the future. Uncertainty of position characterizes bonds of this class.") Needless to say, the averages conceal both good and bad, and as far as the BB and B rating categories are concerned, the numbers vary enormously within each class. For instance, in 1982, while the bottom of the pile of the BB sample reported a ratio of cash flow to long-term debt of 15 percent, the best of the class reported a ratio of 36 percent. However, as a general rule, the headroom in speculative issues is short.

We have two more anti-junk declarations. The first (of which more in a moment) is that the holdings of certain speculative bonds are concentrated in a handful of financial institutions, and that that fact tends to rob the safety-through-diversification argument of some of its force. The second is that the junk idea has been carried too far. The signs (to us) are clear that a faddish consensus has formed around the person of Mike Milken and around the firm of Drexel Burnham. There is, we think, an unspoken faith that Drexel *is* the market and that it won't let anything happen to it. ("We get up at 4:00 A.M.," a Drexel bond salesman told the *Los Angeles Times* earlier this year, "and we don't go out to lunch, we don't take personal phone calls, we don't tell jokes, don't talk about the ball game. No one in America works as hard as we do.") The truth is that markets are bigger than market makers, and that nearly every investment enthusiasm has an unhappy ending.

Junk bonds have recently underperformed. Since the rally began in June, low-rated debt has trailed not only the Treasury market but even an average of nuclear-fired electric utility bonds. (The numbers are striking. On May 31, the Merrill Lynch low-grade index yielded 194 basis points more than the Merrill high-grade index did; on August 31, the difference was 298 basis points.) Paul H. Ross, director of corporate-bond research at Salomon Brothers, puts down the laggardliness to the specific woes of airline and oil-drilling issuers. He says that, as a matter of trading history, junk has tended to bring up the rear of bond-market rallies—it lagged governments by five months in 1982. Barring a recession, he adds, spreads between junk and Treasuries should close; however, if there is a slump in the offing, credit-quality concerns will heighten, and junk will suffer.

For ourselves, our hunch is that this time things will be different, that, in some basic way, junk has had its day.

Taking in Each Other's Laundry

Allan Sloan and Howard Rudnitsky

November 19, 1984, *Forbes*

"Taking in Each Other's Laundry" was a breakthrough article. Long before the world had ever heard of Michael Milken, Forbes *magazine's Allan Sloan and Howard Rudnitsky pierced the veil of the Drexel Burnham Lambert money machine. Their story is the financial equivalent of a Madison Square Garden program complete with the names and positions of key players in the Drexel network—Milken, Spiegel, Carr, Steinberg, Lindner, Belzberg, and Posner.*

AH, THE WONDER OF IT! Five years ago the investment banking firm of Drexel Burnham Lambert was distinctly minor league, an also-ran in the race for survival in a fast-changing Wall Street. Today Drexel is one of Wall Street's all-stars. While many Street firms are retrenching and pinching pennies, Drexel is expanding. It is up to 6,200 employees, from 3,000 in 1979. Drexel, which is privately held, doesn't disclose profits, but *Forbes* estimates the firm earned at least $150 million last year, up from a mere $6 million in 1979.

The secret? Being in precisely the right place at the right time with the right product. Some call them junk bonds. Drexel would prefer they be called by the more dignified name "high-yield." But by whatever name, these securities—not rated investment grade by either Moody's or Standard & Poor's—have become hugely popular. That's in good part because Drexel, recognizing an opportunity, has both stimulated the demand and provided the supply.

Trading in high-yield, low-rated securities was something that most brokerage firms were embarrassed about in the 1970s, when a young Wharton M.B.A. named Michael Milken (*Forbes*, December 5, 1983), scarcely into his thirties, started dabbling in them. No other reputable firm was interested. Classy it was not.

Milken saw opportunity: a gaping market imperfection. What was wrong with lower-quality bonds? What was so hot about quality bonds? In today's era of high debt, declining equity ratios and wrenching economic changes, many once-proud securities issuers have been reduced to junk status: Consumers Power, International Harvester and Bethlehem Steel, to name a few. In an age of discontinuity, the boundaries have fuzzed between quality and junk.

Milken, of course, was hardly the first to recognize the merits of junk bonds. Years ago, academic studies had concluded that over long periods of time, even after deducting defaults, low-quality bonds tended to yield better results than quality bonds. The extra margin of interest was crucial.

Milken began his crusade for low-quality bonds in the Philadelphia office of Drexel Firestone, which later became part of Drexel Burnham. He was giving investment advice part time during his days at the Wharton School of Business, becoming a full-time broker after graduation. Milken later became famous at Drexel headquarters in downtown Manhattan because he commuted there by bus from his home in suburban Philadelphia. He took the bus rather than the train, which was quicker and more comfortable. Why so? He wanted to avoid running into any acquaintances on the train. Not that he was antisocial. Milken simply wanted to make sure no one would interrupt his reading of prospectuses. Thus did he make himself the guru of junk bonds.

Milken, still only thirty-eight, now runs a 135-person department in the heart of Beverly Hills, ensconced in posh offices in a five-story building that he and his associates own. Among his associates is his brother Lowell, thirty-six.

Mike Milken no longer rides buses in obscurity. He is in such demand that he can schedule appointments at 5 A.M. and people will actually show up. Milken seems to live only to do business. He talks about adding dormitories in his building so that his subordinates can put in longer hours, and he may not be kidding.

Milken took home an estimated $15 million last year as his share of Drexel Burnham's profits. Few of the other executives complained. Milken's activities contributed about half of the firm's profits, according to brokerage industry observers.

Thanks in good part to Milken and Drexel, low-rated issuers such as Circus Circus Enterprises, Coastal Corp. and Charter Medical can now raise hundreds of millions of dollars by issuing junk paper through Drexel. This single firm runs a good half of the trading in the junk securities market.

What's interesting, however, is not where Drexel is today—that's an oft-told tale—but how it continues to dominate the high-yield market, whose profitability and growing size are luring an increasing number of competitors. By now, Drexel's dominance and profit margins should have been significantly eroded by competition, but they haven't been.

An important factor in Drexel's continuing dominance is the close ties that it has forged with a number of major clients, among them some of the most controversial figures in North American finance. Who are these clients? They constitute almost a Who's Who of American wheeler-dealers. There is Saul Steinberg, head of privately held Reliance Group Holdings and a member of The Forbes Four Hundred list of the richest people in the U.S.; Carl Lindner of American Financial Corp., who is also a Four Hundred member; Victor Posner, head of a conglomeration of heavy-industrial companies, a Four Hundred member, too; Fred Carr, chairman of First Executive Corp., one of the fastest-growing insurance companies in America; the Belzberg family, the most famous corporate carnivores in Canada, who have moved some of their operations to the U.S.; and Thomas Spiegel, president of Columbia Savings & Loan Association of Beverly Hills, which has grown from $370 million to $4.4 billion in assets in the past three years and has put about $1.1 billion to work in the junk securities market.

A second tier of Drexel customers includes Stephen Wynn of Golden Nugget; Ivan Boesky, the arbitrager; and the irrepressible Meshulam Riklis of Rapid-America, which is 60 percent owned by him and 40 percent owned by Lindner. Riklis's West Coast office is in the same building that houses Drexel's junk trading operation. Because Mike Milken and his associates own the building, that makes Riklis not only a client but also a tenant.

For these well-loaded Drexel clients, Milken and his associates have provided both a source of money and a place to put it. It's a case of mutual convenience: I'll finance you by buying stocks and bonds that you issue, because I think they're a good investment. You buy my securities, because you think my issues are a good investment. Some of the capital I raise becomes capital for you, and some of the capital you raise becomes capital for me. Because we all believe our paper is good and Drexel helps make liquid, stable markets in it, our paper really is good. A self-fulfilling prophecy.

Generating business like that is the reason Milken is among the highest paid Americans and why Drexel Burnham is one of The Street's most profitable firms.

Mike Milken's pitch, which falls on increasingly receptive ears, is that buying a diversified portfolio of junk securities is less risky than investing in so-called safe securities. He points out that many investors buying and holding high-rated paper have been slaughtered two ways. Persistently high interest rates have destroyed their capital, and many once-sound issuers have become more than a little shaky. It wasn't long go that International Harvester and Consumers Power Co. were top-drawer credits. Now, their main concern is survival. Investors buying and holding paper of a company like IH are down 40 cents on the dollar.

By contrast, the so-called junk bonds have an extra measure of protection, partly because the 200 or so basis points in extra yield provide a margin of safety that "quality" bonds lack. And fertile minds at Drexel have come up with many kickers that add value to junk bonds. For example, there are the Hovnanian Enterprises bonds that pay 16⅞ percent interest plus a share of the firm's profits; bonds backed by commodities; notes with "springing" warrants that take effect only if someone tries to take over the issuer. Drexel has even registered an offering of puttable common stock for Arley Merchandising.

Fred Carr may be Milken's best customer. In the late 1960s Carr was known as a gunslinger who bought small, hot issues for his Enterprise Fund, rode the market up and then got out before the bubble burst. He denies all blame for Enterprise's fall. First Executive has had a remarkable record since Carr took over ten years ago. A continued good showing would restore his reputation.

Then there is savings and loan magnate Tom Spiegel, who is little known outside the securities industry. Spiegel, whose family controls Columbia S&L, joined the junk securities party about two years ago. He did so after the persuasive Milken convinced him there were millions to be made in using S&Ls' new, expanded powers to invest aggressively in junk securities. Why lock your money away in thirty-year mortgages at 12 percent when you could buy junk bonds and earn 16 percent? Columbia has money to invest because it has floated some $2 billion of long-term, fixed-rate retail certificates of deposit through stockbrokers and has $600 million of long-term, fixed-rate borrowings from the Federal Home Loan Bank of San Francisco.

Today, therefore, Spiegel is a big source of commissions for Drexel Burnham. Like Spiegel, other key junk clients buy paper through Drexel and also use the firm's services to raise capital, although some of the customers occasionally use other underwriters as well.

Mike Milken not only helps raise money and create investments for his good customers, but he also makes markets in their securities. With his big, well-heeled customer base, Milken can provide the market with liquidity and stability—qualities junk bond markets once lacked.

Milken has earned his customers' loyalty because, when an issue goes sour, he tries to fix things by doing additional financings or helping to restructure the company. Unlike some investment houses, which have been known to dump junk issues onto the market and run, leaving the issues' holders to their own devices, Milken and Drexel provide service after the sale.

Not that Milken doesn't produce some losers. Take the $400 million of convertible bonds Drexel floated for MCI Communications last year. These bonds recently traded at 65 percent of face value, giving investors a $140 million paper loss. Nucorp Energy, a Drexel issuer, has gone into Chapter 11, and another issuer, MGF Oil, said recently it will file soon.

The biggest fiasco in Drexel's junk underwriting history was a $25 million issue of Flight Transportation bonds and warrants in 1982. Drexel's diligence was less than due. Shortly after the deal closed, the SEC cited Flight for fraud and the firm's bank accounts were frozen before most of the $25 million was disbursed. Various Flight creditors, plus Drexel, claim the money.

Rather than rescind the deal, as many of its customers wanted, Drexel told them they will get back most of their investment by the end of this year. Without interest, of course. The Flight issue was widely placed, rather than concentrated in a few hands, and Drexel's handling of it provides an interesting contrast to the way it rescued an unfortunate issue of Integrated Resources preferred.

Milken is such a persuasive man that he can sometimes say outrageous things and yet sound convincing. He likes to argue that debt-laden companies are often safer than unleveraged ones. The reason is that if a highly leveraged company can swap all its debt for stock, it will save enough on debt service to turn cash flow positive. But if a company has no debt and gets into trouble, it has no debt-service costs to eliminate through an equity swap. That's something like saying a drunk is better off than a teetotaler because a drunk can sober up and a teetotaler can't.

However, his customers seem to overlook some of this excess enthusiasm and to forgive bombs like MGF and Nucorp. So far, Milken's winners far exceed his losers, and his services remain immensely valuable to the wheeler-dealers he serves.

At first Milken served them by simply making markets in existing low-quality issues. The relationship between Milken and his clients began to move into the truly big time in 1976, when Drexel Senior Executive Vice President Frederick Joseph brilliantly conceived the notion of floating original-issue junk. Until then, junk securities were fallen angels (once highly rated securities whose issuers had been downgraded) or securities issued as currency in takeovers or in stock buybacks. The thought of selling original-issue junk to Drexel customers who were already trading junk paper was a breakthrough the world was ready for.

Fittingly, the first two junk issues Drexel underwrote raised capital for junk-securities mutual funds, which invested most of the proceeds of their Drexel underwritings in paper that Drexel made markets in. That broke the ice. The supply of junk bonds could now be expanded to meet a growing demand.

Now the market is booming. In one week last month, Drexel announced a $1.3 billion deal for Metromedia, $1.2 billion for Occidental Petroleum, $325 million for Saul Steinberg and $100 million for a leveraged buyout done by Kohlberg, Kravis, Roberts & Co., a new client. Drexel has become the nation's largest underwriter of stock and debt issues for industrial companies. Drexel's ability to place original-issue junk gave clients rated below investment grade a reliable distribution channel for raising capital. Now clients could finance each other by buying new-issue paper. One hand was washing the other.

In some ways original-issue junk was real pioneering. Drexel opened the public securities markets for issuers such as Golden Nugget, which had a sound business plan but lacked the history to get favorable ratings from the credit agencies. Agencies emphasize issuers' past performance, which doesn't help a firm with a glittering future but a difficult past. Junk analysts use an approach more suitable for today's changing world. They try to project cash flow, to see if the borrower can pay the debt, rather than extrapolating from history as the rating agencies do.

Understandably, companies such as Golden Nugget are eternally in Drexel's debt. "They made me," says a grateful Steve Wynn, Nugget's chairman. Wynn, whose firm has raised more than $400 million through Drexel since 1978, is a believer. The company has about $250 million invested in high-yield paper, he says, about half of it bought through Drexel. And, he adds, he holds some junk paper in his personal portfolio.

The relationship between Drexel and its more aggressive clients reached full flower a year ago, when the firm designed a new strategy: the junk takeover. This was another product the world embraced eagerly. Most hostile takeovers are funded by bank loans, which people such as Saul Steinberg and T. Boone Pickens have found difficult to raise on terms they consider reasonable. But in Pickens's assault on Gulf Oil and Steinberg's greenmail of Walt Disney, some Drexel clients bought target company shares, others committed money, and Drexel was poised to raise hundreds of millions by issuing junk securities quickly. It's like a big self-help group, along the lines of your local fuel-oil-buying co-op, except that billions of dollars are involved. Until rival investment bankers find a way to derail junk takeovers, Drexel-backed raids will be exceptionally difficult to stop. Watch out, world.

The major Drexel clients don't act as a formal group. They don't meet with Milken over $4 glasses of orange juice in the Polo Lounge so they can rig markets together. It's a community of interest, not a cabal. Its ties are thus stronger than any formal agreement could forge.

Clients do gather en masse at Drexel's annual high-yield bond conference, a Los Angeles financial extravaganza that has attracted guests as diverse as Frank Sinatra (access to whom was provided by Steve Wynn of Golden Nugget) and James Walker Michaels, editor of *Forbes*. Otherwise, however, there aren't any meetings in smoke-filled rooms.

Are there common threads among special Drexel customers? Only that all are aggressive, are outsiders to the conventional financial community, have a trading mentality and can make quick multimillion-dollar investments without going through a corporate bureaucracy. A conventional observer would say they tend to be buccaneers much more interested in money than in running businesses. An admirer would call them financial entrepreneurs, redeployers of capital.

To understand what makes Drexel's bond world work, we examined scores of transactions, concentrating on those in which key Drexel customers bought one another's paper at original issue, thus providing the issuer with an infusion of capital.

Over and over, we found key Drexel customers buying one another's securities in the secondary market, too, as well as chipping in to buy issues that it was particularly crucial for Drexel to place.

For instance, if Drexel had not helped Columbia Savings

raise $115 million of capital this year (an insignificant number compared with the S&L's $4.4 billion of total assets), Columbia would not have been able to grow as rapidly as it wanted to. Under S&L rules, $1 of equity or subordinated debt can support more than $30 of deposits. Thus, Columbia's $115 million could in theory support more than $3 billion of new deposits, which Columbia could raise by having brokers sell retail CDs. Some of that money, in turn, could be channeled into Drexel's paper.

A similar multiplier exists for the money Drexel has helped raise for the Belzbergs' savings and loan. There is also a multiplier, albeit a much smaller one, at work in the cases of Lindner, Steinberg and Carr, who run insurance companies that have raised money through Drexel. The more capital an insurer has, the more business it can write, the more premiums it can take in, the more money it has available to invest.

Which brings us to a key requirement: To be a major player in the Drexel high-yield bond game you should control one or more pools of capital—capital not necessarily your own. The pool may be an insurance company. Or it may be a savings and loan. In any case, you can tap it to provide a market for Drexel offerings.

Having a group of loyal customers who can buy big pieces of an issue quickly can be crucial. Take this example: In early 1984, as part of a package defending its client, Gearhart Industries, against a hostile takeover by Smith International, Drexel placed a $98.7 million issue of Gearhart notes and warrants. It was an unusual issue, containing "springing warrants," triggered only in the case of someone buying a big piece of Gearhart.

Is such a warrant legal? How do you value it? Most investors would hesitate to invest pending definitive answers to these questions. But Gearhart couldn't wait. Drexel's big customers, though, could step up to the plate. Of the $98.7 million, Executive Life and a 50 percent-owned subsidiary bought $52 million, Columbia Savings bought $20 million and a Belzberg company bought $9.7 million. Just three customers bought more than 80% of the issue.

Or take the $75 million of 14¼ percent fifteen-year notes Drexel placed in August 1983 for Circus Circus Enterprises, a casino client with the potential to develop into a customer like Golden Nugget. Of the $75 million issue, Executive Life bought $27.5 million, Columbia Savings bought $27 million and a Belzberg company bought $10 million.

Drexel and Milken are in the middle of long-running, mutually beneficial deals among Carr, Steinberg, Posner and Lindner. In June 1980, when First Executive was in search of capital, Carr privately placed a $3.5 million issue of convertible bonds. The biggest buyer was a Posner insurance company, Chesapeake, which took $1.3 million of them. In this case, it was a business acquaintance of Carr's, not Milken, who brought Posner into the deal.

Later in 1980 Drexel made a $10 million placement of preferred for First Executive. The buyers: Steinberg's Reliance, $6 million; a Lindner insurance company, $3 million; DWG, a Posner company, $1 million. This money was important not only to First Executive, but also, for personal financial reasons, to Mike Milken and some of his Drexel associates.

Incestuous? That's one way of putting it.

Drexel and its clients contend that his type of analysis focuses on only a few deals out of many hundreds.

That's true. But these deals are disproportionately important to the sellers of the securities.

Drexel clients Posner and Steinberg simultaneously held large equity positions in First Executive, both later selling out at a profit. Posner got his stock by converting his $1.3 million bonds; Reliance bought shares in the market. Reliance says it bought and sold First Executive stock on investment value, and Posner's position had nothing to do with it. Posner, who got a six-to-one return, says that he, too, was looking for a good investment and could not have cared less about Steinberg's activities.

There's no reason to doubt what these men say, but it sure was convenient. Fred Carr is now helping finance Posner and Lindner through private placements arranged by Drexel. For example, in 1982 Carr ($21 million) and Lindner ($4 million) bought an entire Posner issue. In June 1984 Carr bought $39 million ($53.4 million face value) of Posner paper to help finance Posner's buyout of Royal Crown.

Says Posner: "I don't know who buys my paper, and I don't care. All I know is that we get a good rate [from Drexel]. If we didn't get a good rate, we wouldn't deal with them."

First Executive has invested in a number of American Financial private placements. "I buy it because it's a good rate, we view the paper as safe, and we can make money on it, not because Mike Milken is selling it," Carr says.

Be that as it may, First Executive was a major buyer in the February 1984 offering of $200 million of 14¼ percent notes and $148 million ($506 million face value) of zeros issued by Rapid-American, the Meshulam Riklis-Carl Lindner joint venture. Columbia Savings bought chunks of these Rapid-American issues, too.

To round out the picture, the Belzbergs now hold 6.8 percent of First Executive common stock, which was bought in the market rather than directly from First Executive. When First City Properties, a Belzberg company, sold $50 million of notes and warrants in January, First Executive and a 50 percent-owned subsidiary bought $20 million (of the notes) and 800,000 warrants, a potential 7.5 percent stake in First City.

You take in my washing and I'll take in yours, and we'll all end up richer. Columbia Savings bought $22.1 million of a $75 million First Executive issue of convertible preferred in July 1983. In early 1984 First Executive bought 275,000 shares of a one-million-share Columbia stock offering.

Then there's Saul Steinberg. In 1981 Drexel brokered a deal in which Steinberg bought a 20.5 percent share of Zenith National Insurance Corp., a worker's compensation firm. Among the sellers of Zenith National shares were Eugene Klein, Steve Lawrence and Eydie Gorme.

Later, Zenith did a $50 million notes-and-warrants offering through Drexel. The buyers included Reliance ($10 million), First Executive ($16 million) and Charter Corp.'s insurance companies ($5 million). Within a few weeks Zenith had bought enough preferred shares of Integrated Resources, which raises money through Drexel, to file a 13d and has bought other Drexel paper.

Thus does Drexel-raised money frequently flow back and forth among Drexel clients. Thus does Drexel maintain its firm hold on the high-yield bond market. There is nothing illegal about this. It is simply a case of one hand washing the other—to the mutual profit of customers and broker.

Steinberg, of course, used Drexel and his fellow clients to finance his attack on Disney—an attack from which he walked away with $59 million in greenmail profits.

Will some of these Drexel customers pull together for further corporate raids? It's pure speculation that they might, but not outrageous speculation. Drexel raised $600 million for Oscar Wyatt this August, six months after his Coastal Corp. made a pass at Houston Natural Gas. Drexel Burnham raised more than $250 million for Boone Pickens's predatory Mesa Petroleum and lined up hundreds of millions of dollars to help Mesa go after Gulf Oil. Arbitrager Ivan Boesky and the Belzbergs have benefited from Drexel's money-raising services.

The mind spins. With that kind of money could Mobil Oil be a target? Isn't Mobil too big? Maybe, but the Bass brothers took on giant Texaco and walked away with $280 million in greenmail.

Drexel doesn't operate in a vacuum. Now that the junk bond market has been made respectable and billions of dollars have flowed in, the very market imperfection that Milken capitalized on has been at least partly closed. Junk bonds are probably less of a relative bargain than they used to be. Foreigners and bank trust departments are investing in junk now, so are pension funds, and Drexel talks of selling junk unit trusts to individual investors. Will these changes affect the risk-reward ratio of buying low-quality bonds? Most likely. But Drexel and Mike Milken are running what almost amounts to a private capital market and, barring a real financial crash, are likely to go on reaping the rewards for a long time.

Playing With Fire

Anthony Bianco

September 16, 1985, *BusinessWeek*

---

*In "Playing With Fire," Anthony Bianco reveals how
the financial markets in the 1980s were becoming
little more than betting parlors for short-term
speculators. To my knowledge, he was the first
journalist to notice that the U.S. was evolving into
a "casino society." In the nervous nineties, this
line from his story seems chillingly prescient: "A
strong case can be made for the theory that the
spread of financial gamesmanship is diverting
resources from truly productive enterprise." He
made the case. Unfortunately, too few people
listened or cared.*

IN SPARE MOMENTS on the floor of the New York Stock Exchange in the early 1900s, Bernard Baruch would bet a
fellow member whether the next trade to cross the tape would
be up or down. If he were still alive, the famed speculator
could simply stroll over to the stock-index futures trading pit
just off the NYSE floor and, by putting down $6,000, place a
$95,000 wager on the direction of the entire stock market.

Ah, progress. Spurred by deregulation, the financial investors have been working overtime. They've churned out a vast
array of new instruments and created whole new markets. It's
now possible for the average citizen or company to take a
financial position almost instantaneously on just about anything, anywhere. What was an oppressively restrictive financial system only fifteen years ago has been recast in recent
years in a pluralistic, almost-anything-goes mold.

This financial revolution has improved the immediate lot
of almost everyone with money, from the small saver earning

the going market rate of interest to the giant pension fund able to hedge its risks in the futures market. But by stoking a pervasive desire to beat the game, innovation and deregulation have tilted the axis of the financial system away from investment toward speculation. The U.S. has evolved into what Lord Keynes might have called a "casino society"—a nation obsessively devoted to high-stakes financial maneuvering as a shortcut to wealth.

On the NYSE, 108 million shares change hands daily, up from 49 million five years ago. In the government securities market, trading volume is averaging $76 billion a day, quadrupling 1980s level. Yet this growth seems tame compared with the action in financial futures and options trading pits. For example, daily volume in Treasury-bond and T-bill futures tripled to $26 billion in 1984 alone.

"You can argue all you want that this is motivated by the free market, but the fact is that we don't need these high transaction volumes to produce the current level of gross national product," says Albert M. Wojnilower, chief economist of First Boston Corporation, a top Wall Street investment bank. In 1984 First Boston alone handled trades worth $4.1 trillion—which is a bit more than the GNP. "People simply must enjoy all this maneuvering," muses Wojnilower.

But what price fun? A strong case can be made for the theory that the spread of financial gamesmanship is diverting resources from truly productive enterprise. "We've become expert in trading all kinds of financial assets and companies . . . but all the while, productivity lags," noted Paul A. Volcker, chairman of the Federal Reserve, in a speech at Harvard University last year.

Indeed, the casino society's coming of age coincides with marked deceleration of the U.S. economy. From 1979 to the present, the GNP, adjusted for inflation, grew at an annual rate of only 2.1 percent. That compares with 3.1 percent during the seventies and 4.2 percent during the sixties. The annual rate of gain in productivity has slipped to 1.3 percent since 1979, down from 1.5 percent during the previous 10 years and 2.9 percent in the decade before that.

Moreover, the U.S. financial system, which fuels the economy's wealth-producing machinery, has become perilously fragile. The number of manufacturers filing for bankruptcy has risen dramatically. Banks and thrifts are failing by the dozen, and runs by depositors have become a frequent reminder of the crash of 1929.

The great crash was preceded by rampant stock-market speculation—much of it with borrowed money—that drove share prices to fanciful heights. When the market collapsed, it took down the rest of the financial system. Today the tables are turned. Stocks are not grossly overpriced, and margin borrowing is modest. But the speculative use of debt and other forms of leverage is pandemic in the rest of the financial world. "The markets," says NYSE chairman John J. Phelan, "are leveraged to the teeth."

Washington, of course, is setting the standard of profligacy, running a $180 billion annual budget deficit. Federal debt doubled during the seventies and hit $1 trillion in 1981, the Reagan administration's first year in office. This year, it is expected to top $2 trillion.

Meanwhile, borrowing surges all across the economy. Total debt of households, corporations, and governments jumped by a postwar record of 14 percent to $7.1 trillion, in 1984. That's considerably faster than the economy is growing. Credit-market debt now stands at an ominous 1.95 times the GNP, compared with 1.68 a decade ago.

There is also a sharply expanding, hidden debt that doesn't show up in the figures. For example, the official tally doesn't consider the immense leverage inherent in financial futures and options. Buying a stock-index future, for instance, requires a down payment of only 6 percent. By using one security bought on margin as collateral for other purchases, leverage mounts up.

A Mountain of IOUs

Much of this mountain of IOUs rests on a comparatively tiny base—the capital of banks, thrifts, brokerages, and other middlemen. The base has grown, but at nowhere near the pace that financial obligations have proliferated. This means that the financial sector's ability to cushion shocks is diminishing at a time when the increasingly venturesome ways of financial institutions and their customers trigger such shocks with greater frequency.

In cleaning up the wreckage left by the crash of 1929, the New Dealers tried to prevent a recurrence of the speculative insanity of the twenties by chaining the financial system to interest-rate ceilings. Congress set a series of limits on the rates banks could pay depositors. The "Regulation Q" ceilings, as they were called, weren't an issue until interest rates started surging in the sixties. Spurred by rising inflation, rates climbed to a higher plateau in the seventies and, worse, started seesawing wildly.

These swings periodically opened huge gaps between the government ceiling and interest rates in the money markets. Depositors shifted huge sums from their bank accounts into Treasury bills, money-market funds, and other instruments with freely fluctuating rates. Consequently, banks couldn't meet the demand for loans, which resulted in "credit crunches" that wreaked havoc with the whole economy. By 1980 Congress decided to phase out all deposit ceilings that had not already been dismantled during the crises of the seventies.

Like the deposit, the loan was gradually restructured. The thirty-year, fixed-rate mortgage all but disappeared in the early eighties, replaced by shorter-term home loans with variable rates. The corporate loan, too, was overhauled to allow the interest rate to float with the market.

All this remodeling work on the ground floor of the financial system put into circulation a vast pool of formerly inert funds. To divert some of this cash into their own vaults, financial institutions had to keep escalating their promises to the consumer. Bankers, brokers, and insurers discovered modern marketing and began churning out a dazzling array of financial packaged goods to stimulate and satisfy demand. Financial consumers, underserved for decades, suddenly found themselves beckoned and cajoled from all sides. The cumulative effect was to compel belief in a kind of magical world where everyone came out ahead.

Surging inflation gave rise to the casino society, and now, ironically, the taming of inflation is extending the gamblers' domain. Investors and corporate America alike have become addicted to the easy, double-digit returns of the inflation-hyped seventies and early eighties. Rather than endure withdrawal pains as inflation declined, these investors and companies have gone adventuring.

High-Risk Gambling

Most of the casino society plays the game by chasing after outsized rewards—which inevitably come with higher risks attached. Money is moving from the floodlit center ring of the stock-and-bond markets to their shadowy periphery. Witness the explosion of the over-the-counter market in equities, which features many small, unseasoned companies. OTC volume is running at 80 million shares a day, up from only 26 million in 1980.

The stampede into "junk" bonds—the fixed-income equivalent of the OTC stock—has been equally dramatic. Once virtually excluded from the public markets, companies with credit ratings below investment grade have issued $30 billion worth of bonds in the last five years. These junk bonds typically bear interest rates anywhere from 3 to 5 percentage points above those for blue-chip issues.

Investment promoters have also turned out to be remarkably adept at repitching real estate, previously sold as the ultimate inflation hedge, as a steadily appreciating asset blessed by tax breaks galore. Despite the Reagan administration's reduction of income tax rates, investing to avoid taxes has assumed fetishlike proportions among the wealthy. Sales of publicly traded real estate trusts and partnerships amounted to $6.7 billion in the twelve-month period that ended in June 1985. That compares with a mere $1.6 billion in 1981.

But big money's speculative play of choice at the moment is the corporate takeover. The $140 billion in mergers, acquisitions, and leveraged buyouts announced in 1984 exceeds the previous record of $54 billion, and the pace has not slackened. Says Kenneth H. Miller, who runs Merrill Lynch Capital Markets' merger department, "You can sell almost anything you can call a business."

The current merger wave started in the mid-1970s, as the

gap between companies' stock-market value and their underlying asset value yawned invitingly wide. But in sharp contrast to the epidemic of stock-for-stock acquisitions by which the conglomerate was created in the sixties, the economics of the latest acquisition binge hinge on the prolific use of debt.

By borrowing heavily to buy control, an acquirer can use the target company's own assets to finance the deal. Once in charge, the new owner can sell pieces of the company to pay off acquisition loans. When the original gap between the stock-market value and the split-up value of the acquired company is large—and the acquirer's equity investment negligible—the returns on investment are breathtaking. Some companies, taken private in the bear market of 1980–81 and resold to the public in 1983, returned $10 for every $1 of equity invested.

Numbers like that have institutional investors slavering to put up equity financing for takeover deals. When Kohlberg Kravis Roberts & Company, the premier practitioner of the leveraged buyout, put together a $1 billion buyout in 1983, it predicted it could take five years to invest it all. Actually, the money was gone by July 1985, and the company set about raising $2 billion as an encore.

More important, bank lenders stand ready to provide copious quantities of debt financing for any deal that makes even a shred of sense on paper, regardless of the identity of the buyer. Every era has had marauders probing the defenses of an outraged business establishment. What's particularly galling to the corporate powers-that-be this time is the extent to which they are being betrayed from within. T. Boone Pickens Jr.'s largest backer in his 1984 run at Gulf Oil Corporation was Citicorp, the nation's largest bank holding company.

Although takeover speculation has sharply driven up share prices in such trendy areas as broadcasting, the overall market still sells at about 80 percent discount to what it would cost to replace company assets. And increasingly, targets of unwanted buyout bids are fighting debt with debt.

The surge in debt-financed acquisitions and share repurchases is distorting corporate America's balance sheet. In 1984 some $78 billion in equity vanished, and companies added a staggering $169 billion in new debt. That's the widest such yearly gap ever, according to the investment-banking firm Salomon Brothers.

Increasing reliance on debt made sense during the high-inflation days of the seventies. Because government ceilings in effect prevented interest rates from rising above the inflation rate, the real cost of borrowing was zero or, at times, negative. But with inflation now at 4 percent and short-term interest rates at 7 percent, the economics of borrowing have boomeranged. "To be a debtor in today's world is very dangerous," says Allen Sinai, chief economist for Shearson Lehman Brothers. "Heavy borrowers are betting, whether intentionally or not, that inflation will bail them out down the road."

If the casino society has a birthday, it's April 26, 1973, when the listed stock options began trading on the brand-new Chicago Board Options Exchange. Rescued from the obscurity of over-the-counter trading, stock-option volume soared to new heights. As the first major new security derived from another security, the listed option was a harbinger of the brave new world of "derivative" instruments now rapidly unfolding.

A share of stock is itself a financial abstraction representing fractional ownership of a corporation, whose assets usually include such things as factories, equipment, and inventories. An option is the right to buy or sell stock at a set price. The option's allure is leverage: it trades at a fraction of the price of the underlying stock.

Twice-removed from the tangible realities of productive enterprise, the option exists only to be traded. It is a "wasting asset," worthless upon expiration. The listed option was followed by a flood of other derivative instruments, which recently included a futures contract based on the consumer price index and several OTC stock-index futures. As they proliferate, more and more of what transpires on the trading floors of Wall and La Salle streets has no direct connection to the factory floors of Main Street.

Investment Shields

The exchanges promote financial futures and options as devices to shield investment portfolios from market fluctuations. But their inherent leverage makes them tempting proxies for stocks and bonds as well. It takes 50 percent down to buy stock on margin but only 6 percent to buy a stock-index future. Someone who sold short one S&P 500 future at the opening bell on August 7, 1985, made $1,925, or 32 percent, on a $6,000 investment by day's end. Yet the index dropped by only 2 percent.

The advent of the listed option also marked the debut of the computer as a weapon in the markets—one that altered the character of the markets by putting the trader in charge. The Street didn't automate even simple clerical tasks until the early seventies. But trading in options without instantaneous stock-price data was a death wish.

As the major stock-market players were drawn into listed options, they realized that high-speed technology could be used to advantage as all markets became volatile. The wiring of Wall Street began in earnest. Today, from Wall Street to Los Angeles, traders by the thousands sit before computer terminals, orchestrating the movements of vast sums to the rhythms of the numbers flashing on their screens. Ceaselessly maneuvering for short-term advantage, the trader is king in the casino society.

The trader's rise coincided with a shift in the Street's revenues and hence its priorities. Brokerage firms now generate more revenues in trading for their own accounts than they do in commissions, once their main source of income. Naturally, the Street's attention is shifting from servicing customers to positioning itself so that it can fully profit from market swings.

Over the last decade, for example, brokers have deployed huge chunks of capital in risk arbitrage—the art of trading in the stocks of companies facing buyout proposals. With astonishing frequency, a stock's price will soar just before a buyout bid is announced. This suggests that trading on information has become institutionalized.

Each new financial instrument is mathematically related to existing instruments. Until these complex relationships are broadly understood, the prices of related instruments will tend to become misaligned. By simultaneously buying one instrument and selling short the other, a trader can turn a price discrepancy into large profit.

Ironically, the use of hedging techniques to beat the game

is becoming so prevalent that it is unsettling the stock market. At the moment, relationship traders are earning 9 percent to 10 percent by playing the S&P's 500 index future against one hundred individual stocks that closely track it. When traders unwind their positions en masse by selling the one hundred stocks, it can pull down the whole market—as happened on August 6, 1985, when the Dow Jones industrial average dropped 21.73 points.

High-Profit High Rollers

The arrival of the casino society has brought something of the rapacious flavor of the robber-baron era back to the markets. Not since Baruch's day has the high roller been so evident. A disproportionate share of the spoils is going to those who are willing and able to grab enormous leverage and chances to throw the dice. The megadeal—the bold, decisive stroke that makes fortunes overnight—is becoming the standard against which achievement in the business world is measured.

The debate over the economic effects of what is nothing less than the reinvention of the U.S. financial system over the past fifteen years will be resolved only in retrospect, if ever. Takeover artists, for example, may in fact be "maximizing shareholder values," as they claim to be. They may also be spurring a much-needed restructuring of corporate America by terrorizing inept and arrogant managements. But if so, it's by accident. Like all the other games the casino society plays, the object of the takeover game is to get rich today, come what may.

Depository institutions are free to take greater investment risks but still have access to low-cost federal funds and to the imprimatur of deposit insurance. If a financial institution is big enough and its blunders sufficiently catastrophic, Uncle Sam apparently now stands ready to bail out everybody concerned. In a system in which the government both encourages risk-taking and provides unconditional shelter from the consequences, excess and hypocrisy can be expected to flourish.

"We spend our days issuing debt and retiring equity—both in record volume—and then we spend our evenings raising each other's eyebrows with gossip about signs of stress in the financial system," lamented Volcker in his Harvard address.

"We rail at government inefficiency and intrusion in our markets, while we call upon the same government to protect our interest, our industry, and our financial institutions."

In the end, speculation simply has too large a constituency to be tamed by any force other than self-restraint. Only when fear overcomes greed will the casino society rein itself in. The question nagging all concerned is how big a jolt is needed to alter the seductive calculus of speculation.

Drexel Official Accused by SEC of Inside Trades

Scott McMurray and Daniel Hertzberg

May 13, 1986, the *Wall Street Journal*

In retrospect, the decade's most important event on Wall Street occurred the day the Feds busted investment banker Dennis Levine for insider trading. But no one, not even the enforcement arm of the Securities & Exchange Commission (SEC) realized that nabbing Levine signaled the beginning of the end of the "smart money" on Wall Street who were using inside information to cheat other investors and undermine the financial markets.

THE SECURITIES AND EXCHANGE COMMISSION charged Dennis Levine, a Drexel Burnham Lambert Inc. managing director, with making $12.6 million by illegally trading in stocks and options on nonpublic information. The SEC said it was the largest insider trading case ever.

Mr. Levine, thirty-three years old, a senior member of Drexel's mergers and acquisitions department, illegally traded in the securities of fifty-four companies between June 1980 and last December, the SEC alleged in a suit filed in federal court here. In all fifty-four cases, Mr. Levine traded while possessing "material nonpublic information" about actual or proposed tender offers, mergers, leveraged buyouts and other business combinations, the SEC charged.

Mr. Levine's wife, reached at their Park Avenue apartment, said he wouldn't be available for comment. "I don't think he'll be saying much before he talks to his lawyers," she said.

The commission charged that Mr. Levine did the illegal trading over a five-and-a-half-year period during which he worked for a total of four major Wall Street firms, none of which were named in the suit. According to the SEC, Mr. Levine joined Drexel in February 1985 from Shearson Lehman Brothers Inc. In November 1981, he joined a Shearson Lehman predecessor, Lehman Brothers Kuhn Loeb Inc., after having worked at Smith Barney, Harris Upham & Co. since June 1978.

Frederick Joseph, Drexel's chief executive officer, said in an interview that the charges against Mr. Levine were "shocking and sad." He said Drexel was "cooperating fully" with the SEC in its continuing investigation of Mr. Levine, and that the firm hadn't been aware of Mr. Levine's allegedly illegal trading.

In a prepared statement, the firm said that "the SEC allegation, if true, would be a most serious breach of Drexel Burnham Lambert's standards. In fact, this is the first such allegation made against a (Drexel) employee in our fifty-one-year history."

David Hershberg, senior executive vice president and general counsel of Shearson Lehman Brothers, said, "We are just in the process of reviewing the complaint and we are evaluating it. We have been cooperating with the SEC in the course of its investigation and expect to continue."

A Smith Barney spokesman declined to comment.

Investment bankers said the charges against Mr. Levine are potentially damaging to Drexel's reputation because the firm has been in the forefront of the merger and acquisition boom of the 1980s.

The Levine case indicates that the SEC is stepping up its policing of takeover-related trading, an area that many people on Wall Street privately assert is riddled with insider trading. The case follows an SEC insider trading action last week against First Boston Corp., a major investment banking firm. First Boston, without admitting or denying the charges against it, consented to findings that it traded in the stock and options of Cigna Corp. earlier this year based on nonpublic information about a pending $1.2 billion Cigna charge against earnings. First Boston agreed to give up profits of $132,138 and pay a record $264,276 fine.

A source close to the SEC said that the agency also expects to file soon another major insider trading case.

"Nearly every firm on the Street has been hit" by insider trading scandals, said one investment banker. "But they were all junior people." The Drexel case involves "a top partner in mergers and acquisitions."

Named as a defendant in addition to Mr. Levine was Bernhard Meier, described in the complaint as a Swiss resident who acted as a broker for Mr. Levine's trades. The SEC said that from mid-1982 to late 1985 Mr. Meier was a portfolio manager at a "foreign financial institution located in the Bahamas." Mr. Meier copied some of Mr. Levine's trades and made $152,000, the SEC said.

Mr. Meier couldn't be reached for comment.

Although the SEC didn't name the institution, an international banking directory, the Hambro Euromoney Directory for 1986, lists a Bernhard Meier as an assistant vice president at Nassau-based Bank Leu International Ltd., a subsidiary of the Swiss bank Bank Leu. Reached by telephone in Nassau, Graham Jones, an assistant vice president, said he was aware that Mr. Meier was being named in an SEC complaint.

Mr. Jones said that Mr. Meier left Bank Leu last December. "He returned to Zurich. Since then I haven't heard from him," Mr. Jones said.

Also listed as defendants are two Panamanian companies allegedly controlled by Mr. Levine—International Gold Inc. and Diamond Holdings S.A. The SEC said that Mr. Levine funneled his trades to Mr. Meier through accounts opened in the name of those companies. Mr. Levine also had a similar account under the code name of Mr. Diamond, the SEC charged.

The complaint alleged that Mr. Levine placed his orders with Mr. Meier via collect calls over pay telephones, apparently to avoid having his orders traced to him. Mr. Meier in turn entered Mr. Levine's and his own orders via unidentified brokerage firms in New York, the SEC said.

SEC court documents list six stocks in which Mr. Levine

allegedly traded while working as an investment banker on transactions involving the companies. They are Sierra Research Corp., Maryland Cup Corp., Esquire Inc., Cone Mills Corp., American Natural Resources Co., and Crown Zellerbach Corp.

The SEC added that Mr. Levine also illegally traded in the stocks of thirteen companies in which his employers were involved as investment bankers, but where he personally wasn't involved. They are: Alexander & Alexander Services Inc., Bendix Corp., Carter Hawley Hale Stores Inc., Criton Corp., Crocker National Bank Corp., Four Phase Systems Inc., Itek Corp., Continental Group Inc., Jewel Cos., Nabisco Brands Inc., A.C. Nielsen Co., G.D. Searle & Co., and Sperry Corp.

Mr. Levine traded in thirty-five other stocks using nonpublic information gleaned from stock market sources, the SEC charged.

The SEC asked for a preliminary injunction against further securities law violations by the defendants and is seeking to have their assets frozen. A hearing on the preliminary injunction is set for May 22.

The agency is also asking for a permanent injunction plus treble penalties for alleged profits earned after August 10, 1984, the effective date of the Insider Trading Sanctions Act of 1984. Based on about $7.6 million of such alleged profits by Mr. Levine and about $96,000 by Mr. Meier, treble damages would amount to about $22.8 million and $288,000, respectively.

The complaint claims that Mr. Levine opened his accounts by depositing about $170,000 at the Bahamian bank in 1980 and currently has about $10.3 million there "derived from illegal trading profits."

The SEC also charged that the defendants tried to cover up the alleged scheme beginning in mid-1985, after they learned of the SEC investigation. And last Friday, with the SEC preparing to charge Mr. Levine, he allegedly tried to transfer $10 million from the Bahamian bank to an unidentified bank in the Cayman Islands, the suit charged. But the Bahamian bank hasn't yet complied with his request, the SEC said.

The agency said Mr. Levine and Mr. Meier tried to hide

their tracks by "presenting a false explanation of the trading activity under investigation, (and) withholding and altering documents." The SEC said that the defendants also destroyed documents and created new ones to conceal their activities.

An SEC official declined to comment on whether the agency would refer the case to the Justice Department for possible criminal action.

In Washington, Gary Lynch, the SEC's enforcement director, said, "This is the largest insider trading case we've ever brought, not only in terms of profits but also the number of securities involved and the length of time over which the violations occurred."

Noting that the defendants were accused of trading through a financial institution in the Bahamas, SEC attorney Michael Mann said, "It really proves we can really get them anywhere."

Mr. Levine is widely known and well-liked in the closely knit fraternity of Wall Street lawyers and investment bankers who dominate the takeover business. One investment banker called him "likable, cherubic." He and others said they were stunned by the SEC charges against Mr. Levine.

To many on Wall Street, the youthful Mr. Levine personified the legendary, get-rich-quick world of dealmakers, where the best and brightest earn million-dollar-plus salaries and bonuses while still in their thirties. Mr. Levine earned about $1 million in salary and bonuses last year at Drexel, investment bankers said.

Mr. Levine was wooed away from Shearson Lehman Brothers to Drexel, where he was given the title of managing director and guaranteed minimum compensation of $1 million a year, industry sources said. Mr. Levine was chief strategist for Drexel as it assisted Pantry Pride Inc.'s $1.83 billion hostile takeover of Revlon Inc. last year. The SEC action made no mention of any illegal trading in that transaction.

Mr. Levine enjoyed his new wealth. Colleagues say he recently bought a red Ferrari Testa Rossa auto for $105,000.

Wall Street sources said Mr. Levine holds a bachelor's degree and master's of business administration from Baruch College in New York. Before joining Smith Barney, he worked at Citibank in 1977 and 1978.

ACT 2

The Party Gets Wild (1986–1989)

Widening Scandal on Wall Street

*James B. Stewart
and Daniel Hertzberg*

November 17, 1986, the *Wall Street Journal*

When federal agents captured Ivan Boesky, they got their hands on one of the great rats in Wall Street history. And thank god he had the morals of a rodent. Otherwise how would the government have trapped those other voles and weasels. The Wall Street Journal's Jim Stewart and Daniel Hertzberg were wired into the federal government investigation like nobody else. Other reporters said that this duo was simply the fortunate recipients of leaks by government lawyers. Perhaps so, but we would all have liked to be in their shoes.

Iₙ Iᵥₐₙ F. Bₒₑₛₖy, government enforcement agents have captured the ultimate font of information about the inner workings of Wall Street. Market professionals now fear that what began as the Dennis B. Levine insider-trading case last May will soon shake Wall Street's very foundations.

"This ranks among the scandals of the century," says Daniel J. Good, a managing director and takeover specialist at Shearson Lehman Brothers Inc. "Boesky was at the top of the spiral. His relationships go very high with very important people."

Mr. Boesky, America's richest and best-known arbitrager, agreed on Friday to pay $100 million to settle Securities and Exchange Commission charges of insider trading. In addition, he agreed to plead guilty to one felony count that carries a

65

prison term of one to five years. Under the settlement, he will be barred from the securities industry for life.

The announcement by SEC Chairman John Shad and Manhattan U.S. Attorney Rudolph Giuliani, made after the stock market closed Friday, brings to an abrupt end one of the most dazzling careers on Wall Street. The payment, consisting of a $50 million fine and the return of $50 million in illegal profits, is said to strip the forty-nine-year-old Mr. Boesky of most of his fortune and is the largest penalty in the history of the SEC.

Like Mr. Levine before him, Mr. Boesky (pronounced BOEskee) is cooperating fully with the government's investigation of insider trading. Lawyers familiar with the investigation confirm that, in return for agreeing to plead guilty to only one felony count—a lenient plea bargain given the extent of Mr. Boesky's crime—Mr. Boesky has implicated other major figures on Wall Street, including professionals at some of the country's top securities firms.

The lawyers add that government investigators are closely examining Mr. Boesky's relationships with officials of Drexel Burnham Lambert Inc., the securities firm that arranged $660 million in financing for Mr. Boesky's most recent limited partnership offering and that owns a stake in Northview Corp., Mr. Boesky's hotel company.

According to the lawyers, beginning Friday at 4:30 P.M., the SEC issued subpoenas seeking information about trading in a dozen securities and the role in those transactions of, among others, Drexel; Michael Milken, the head of high-yield, "junk bond" financing at Drexel; Carl Icahn, one of the country's best-known corporate raiders; Victor Posner, another well-known corporate raider; and Boyd Jefferies, the chairman of Jefferies & Co., a Los Angeles-based brokerage firm that often assembles blocks of takeover stocks from arbitragers.

The fact that the SEC is seeking information about these and other individuals and their relationships with Mr. Boesky doesn't mean that they are guilty of any wrongdoing or that any civil or criminal charges will be filed against them. Mr. Icahn declined comment on the subpoenas. Mr. Posner didn't respond to a message left with an employee who said he would contact Mr. Posner. The others couldn't be reached for comment over the weekend.

An official close to the investigation estimated that twelve individuals could eventually be charged with securities-law violations as a result of Mr. Boesky's testimony. Others indicated that certain Wall Street firms may become targets as well.

The government's investigation now seems to have come full circle: Drexel is the firm where Mr. Levine was working at the time of his arrest. Moreover, Drexel, because of its ability to finance practically any transaction by issuing high-yield, high-risk junk bonds, has fueled the merger boom that has been the source of much of Mr. Boesky's fortune.

Government prosecutors and Gary Lynch, the SEC's enforcement chief, declined comment on all aspects of their continuing investigation, including any examination of Mr. Boesky's ties to Drexel. A spokeswoman for Drexel, reached at home over the weekend, declined to comment but promised to seek comment from Drexel's top officials. No comment was forthcoming. Frederick H. Joseph, Drexel's chief executive, couldn't be reached. A top Drexel executive, reached at home, declined comment and asked not to be identified.

Drexel is hardly the only firm with cause for concern. Mr. Boesky is believed to have traded information with many of Wall Street's best-known figures. There is a pervasive fear among market professionals that a government and public backlash will result, leading to lasting changes in the marketplace. For example, Felix G. Rohatyn, a general partner of Lazard Freres & Co., predicts that there will be "congressional investigations spurred on by a Democratic Congress. It wouldn't be surprising," he says, "to see new legislation or regulation."

The SEC's complaint against Mr. Boesky suggests that despite his reputation for having lots of Wall Street sources, it was Mr. Levine who recruited Mr. Boesky into an insider-trading scheme in February 1985, the same month that Mr. Levine moved from Shearson Lehman to Drexel. (Mr. Levine and his lawyers, who have consistently declined comment on the case, couldn't be reached for comment on the SEC's latest allegations.)

The complaint suggests that Mr. Levine baited his hook by passing on some tips, gratis, to Mr. Boesky. Among the deals about which Mr. Levine had inside information at the time were merger negotiations between ITT and Sperry, Coastal's bid for American Natural Resources, and a leveraged buyout of McGraw Edison.

The contacts between Mr. Levine and Mr. Boesky soon turned into a torrent. A Wall Street executive and a lawyer say that Mr. Levine's telephone records, obtained by the SEC, show hundreds of calls to Mr. Boesky, sometimes as many as twenty a day.

Had the relationship stopped there, lawyers say, the government might have had difficulty proving an insider-trading case against Mr. Boesky. The SEC acknowledges that, at least at the outset, Mr. Levine didn't tell Mr. Boesky the sources for his information. Mr. Boesky himself, as an arbitrager, didn't breach any fiduciary relationships with insiders. He might have argued that he didn't know he was receiving inside information that Mr. Levine had stolen from his employer or had obtained from others who had stolen the information. Moreover, stock trades by Mr. Boesky, who routinely speculated in the stocks of rumored and real takeover targets, wouldn't necessarily have corroborated claims by Mr. Levine of trading on inside information.

But according to the SEC's complaint, Mr. Boesky was evidently so impressed by the quality of Mr. Levine's information that he entered into an explicit profit-sharing agreement with Mr. Levine. He promised to pay 5 percent of the profits from information that triggered a purchase of securities and 1 percent of the profits earned on stock positions influenced by information obtained from Mr. Levine. In reaching this agreement, lawyers say, Mr. Levine made explicit what was already obvious: Mr. Boesky was getting inside information.

The two pledged themselves to secrecy, and Mr. Boesky, using his vast capital and Mr. Levine's information, embarked on a highly profitable stock-buying spree. For example, the SEC alleges that Mr. Boesky made $9.2 million in profits from just three stocks—Nabisco, Houston Natural Gas and FMC—involved in takeovers or restructurings. He also profited from trading Boise Cascade, General Foods, Union Carbide and others. In all, the SEC says, Mr. Boesky made more than $50 million in unlawful profits. Mr. Boesky's illicit earnings dwarf the unlawful profits earned by others accused of insider trading.

Beginning around September 1985, lawyers familiar with the case say, Mr. Levine knew that he was under investigation by the SEC. He curtailed his own insider trading somewhat, but he apparently thought that his arrangement with Mr. Boesky would continue to reap substantial profits without attracting the attention of the SEC. He accelerated the flow of information and began to press Mr. Boesky for some of the proceeds of the profit-sharing arrangement. Mr. Boesky stalled, quibbling about just how much Mr. Levine was owed. Finally, in April, the two agreed that Mr. Levine would receive $2.4 million as his share of the profits.

But unknown to Mr. Boesky, Mr. Levine had already breached the secrecy pledge. An inveterate name dropper, Mr. Levine had told at least one of his co-conspirators, Robert M. Wilkis, a former investment banker at Lazard Frères & Co., some details of his arrangement with Mr. Boesky.

For Mr. Boesky, an enormously successful career turned nightmarish on May 12, the day of Mr. Levine's arrest.

Rumors that Mr. Boesky was also involved started almost immediately. Mr. Levine was well-known for his contacts among arbitragers, and Mr. Boesky was by far the best known of them. Former prosecutors reasoned at the time that the government was unlikely to strike a plea agreement with Mr. Levine—apparently the ringleader of the largest insider-trading conspiracy in history—unless he had delivered a bigger name to investigators. And sources familiar with the investigation had confirmed to this newspaper that a major arbitrager was a target of the investigation.

But Mr. Boesky was also the least likely of suspects by virtue of his wealth and success. To many on Wall Street, it was inconceivable that a man of Mr. Boesky's stature, with a fortune beyond the reckoning of most, would place his fate in the hands of a Dennis Levine by entering into an illegal insider-trading pact. Despite occasional flurries of rumors, as the summer wore on without any government action, the suspicions about Mr. Boesky faded.

As the rumors subsided, Mr. Boesky's own assessment of his chances of avoiding prosecution and conviction progressively worsened, say lawyers familiar with the case. He assumed that his name had been divulged by Mr. Levine. But he had never actually paid the $2.4 million (Mr. Levine's arrest came before delivery of the funds, leading some to question whether Mr. Boesky would ever have honored the commitment). As a result, the case might have turned on Mr. Levine's word against Mr. Boesky's, a case his lawyers thought Mr. Boesky could win.

However, the government's case proved to be far stronger. Investigators painstakingly compiled telephone and trading records, and they were too consistent with Mr. Levine's disclosures to be coincidental. Moreover, the government had a corroborating witness in Mr. Wilkis, who is cooperating with the government and hasn't yet pleaded guilty to any charges. Mr. Wilkis's testimony, though hearsay, would be admissible in any trial against Mr. Boesky.

Harvey Pitt, Mr. Boesky's principal counsel and a partner in Fried, Frank, Harris, Shriver & Jacobson, long Mr. Boesky's principal law firm, says settling with the SEC and agreeing to plead guilty was the only feasible option. "Both Mr. Boesky and I are pretty tenacious," Mr. Pitt says, "but you have to assess the situation in a cold and realistic way." He adds that if Mr. Boesky ever considered flight and the life of a fugitive, he isn't aware of it. Mr. Pitt says that widespread reports that Mr. Boesky had a net worth of $200 million are wrong and that Mr. Boesky will keep "very, very little" of his wealth.

After Mr. Levine's arrest, Mr. Boesky's arbitrage activity declined significantly, though he continued to manage the limited partnership and his other businesses. A previously reported *Wall Street Journal* analysis of SEC filings required of investors acquiring 5 percent or more of a company shows that Mr. Boesky's filings fell sharply in the months following Mr. Levine's arrest.

In August, Mr. Boesky told fellow directors of Beverly Hills Hotel Corp. that he was the subject of an SEC investigation. That is believed to have been his first acknowledgment to outsiders that the government was closing in. Though no one will discuss details of his plea negotiations, he is understood to have approached the government, through his lawyers, a short time later about resolving the case.

Even his closest friends, investors in his limited partnership, and employees say that they knew nothing until just before or after the SEC's press conference Friday afternoon. One friend says Mr. Boesky called him Friday, just before 5 P.M. "He said he had some bad news," the friend says, "and I thought maybe he was going to tell me he was getting a divorce. I was stunned, but he sounded more embarrassed than anything else."

A friend who spent Thursday evening with Mr. Boesky says he seemed relaxed and gave only one clue to Friday's momentous announcement: "He asked me where I'd be Friday afternoon."

Mr. Boesky met with staff members at Ivan F. Boesky Co. at about 3:30 Friday afternoon to break the news. It was received in stunned silence, and the staff was given strict instructions not to discuss it with anyone until it appeared on the Dow Jones News Service ticker.

A statement Mr. Boesky had read to employees was released a short while later to news organizations. The government "justifiably holds me and not my business associates or business entities responsible for my actions. I deeply regret my past mistakes, and know that I alone must bear the consequences of those actions," Mr. Boesky said in the statement. "My life will be forever changed, but I hope that something positive will ultimately come out of this situation. I know that in the wake of today's events, many will call for reform. If my mistakes launch a process of reexamination of the rules and practices of our financial marketplace, then perhaps some good will result."

This weekend, though, many of Mr. Boesky's colleagues were assessing the short-term threat to themselves of Mr. Boesky's fall rather than any possible long-term benefits.

While lawyers working on the case would give few clues about where the case might go next, one noted that Mr. Boesky's plea agreement largely insulates him from prosecution for other crimes, assuming that he cooperates fully and makes a truthful and complete confession. That suggests that the kind of explicit insider-trading agreement Mr. Boesky had with Mr. Levine was the exception rather than the rule.

Other lawyers familiar with the case say that Mr. Boesky is implicating high-level Wall Street professionals who used what they knew to be inside information to reap profits by means other than trading in stocks. For example, charges of mail or wire fraud could be filed against investment bankers who traded inside information with Mr. Boesky and used the information to attract takeover-defense clients, or financiers who tipped Mr. Boesky to upcoming takeover bids so that a large block of stock would move into sympathetic hands, thereby enhancing chances for a takeover that would be lucrative for the financiers. The SEC subpoenas issued Friday, lawyers say, are consistent with this approach.

Charles Carberry, the assistant U.S. attorney prosecuting the Levine case, declined to comment on the specifics of the case or where the Boesky investigation might lead. But he emphasized that while the courts have sometimes wavered on what constitutes insider trading, they have repeatedly affirmed convictions of mail or wire fraud when people profited indirectly from what they knew to be inside information.

In this area, the line between legitimate and criminal conduct may be somewhat blurry. "Everybody talked to Boesky," says a top merger professional. The result is "a lot of sleepless nights for a lot of people," says Joseph Flom, a leading takeover lawyer at Skadden, Arps, Slate, Meagher & Flom. That unease is expected to intensify as the government investigation of insider-trading reaches what one top Wall Street executive calls the "golden triangle": the relationship between corporate raiders, arbitragers and the purveyors of junk bonds, most notably Drexel.

Beyond the eventual impact on individuals and their firms, most think that the penalties against Mr. Boesky will ultimately have a positive effect on the markets by countering public skepticism about their integrity. "I don't think the public distinguishes between arbs, Drexel's takeovers" or anything else, says Mr. Flom. "It's all one big mess as far as they are concerned. By and large, the typical attitude is that these Wall Street types are screwing up America."

Chronology of the Dennis Levine Case

May 12, 1986 — SEC charges Dennis Levine of Drexel Burnham Lambert with making $12.6 million since mid-1980 from insider trading. SEC also names defendant Bernhard Meier, Mr. Levine's broker at Bank Leu International in Nassau.

May 13, 1986 — Mr. Levine is arrested and charged with obstructing justice for attempting to destroy records. He is released on a $5 million bond.

June 5, 1986 — Mr. Levine pleads guilty to four felony charges and agrees to cooperate with the government in its investigation. Settling civil insider-trading charges, he agrees to pay $11.6 million.

July 1, 1986 — SEC charges Robert Wilkis and Ira Sokolow, former investment bankers at Lazard Freres and Shearson Lehman Brothers, with exchanging confidential information with Mr. Levine. They settle with SEC. Mr. Wilkis allegedly made about $3 million from insider trading. Mr. Sokolow agreed to give up $120,000 in profits.

July 3, 1986 — David Brown, investment banker at Goldman Sachs, resigns amid SEC investigation.

July 14, 1986 — Ilan Reich, takeover lawyer at Wachtell, Lipton, Rosen & Katz, resigns amid government investigation.

Aug. 19, 1986 — Litton Industries Inc. sues Shearson Lehman and Mr. Levine, charging that Mr. Levine's insider trading made Litton pay more than necessary to take over Itek Corp. Suit seeks $30 million in damages.

Sept. 4, 1986 — Mr. Sokolow and Mr. Brown plead guilty to criminal charges of passing stolen information to Mr. Levine.

Oct. 3, 1986 — Mr. Reich is indicted by federal grand jury in the Levine case.

Oct. 9, 1986 — Mr. Reich pleads guilty to two criminal counts for his role in the Levine case.

Nov. 6, 1986 — Mr. Sokolow is sentenced to a year and a day in prison for his role in the Levine case.

Nov. 14, 1986 — Ivan Boesky agrees to pay $100 million penalty for trading on insider information supplied by Mr. Levine from Feb. 1985 to Feb. 1986; agrees to plead guilty to unspecified criminal charges.

The Wall Street Career of Martin Siegel Was a Dream Gone Wrong

James B. Stewart and Daniel Hertzberg

February 17, 1987, the *Wall Street Journal*

This is the story for which Jim Stewart and Daniel Hertzberg of the Wall Street Journal *won a Pulitzer Prize. It is the quintessential inside story of how a weak man is corrupted by his desire for money.*

Last November 14, thirty-eight-year-old Martin A. Siegel, one of Wall Street's leading investment bankers, was spending the afternoon in the Park Avenue offices of Martin Lipton, an eminent takeover lawyer and a man Mr. Siegel had come to regard almost as a father.

Suddenly a federal marshal burst in upon the two men, thrusting a subpoena into Mr. Siegel's hand. When Mr. Siegel read the subject matter of the investigation—Ivan F. Boesky—and the accompanying list of his own takeover deals at Kidder, Peabody & Co. in the 1980s, he knew his career was over. He began sobbing, as a horrified Mr. Lipton rushed to comfort him.

The public end to Mr. Siegel's career, once one of the most spectacular success stories on Wall Street, came last Friday. He resigned his year-old position as co-head of mergers and acquisitions at Drexel Burnham Lambert Inc. and pleaded guilty in federal court to two felony counts for his role in the Boesky scandal. Coming just a day after the stunning arrests of three top Wall Street professionals, Mr. Siegel's pleas still managed to shock Wall Street. More than anyone else so far

75

implicated in the scandal, Mr. Siegel personified the American dream.

He also embodied the new breed of investment banker who has ridden the takeover boom of the '80s to the top. Inside information was inextricably linked to his own rise, and he is cooperating fully in the government's continuing investigation. His testimony has already implicated the three men arrested last week, and he has described the pressure for profits from high-level Kidder Peabody officials that allegedly led to the misuse of inside information by the firm's arbitrage department.

In sum, Mr. Siegel's testimony is a vivid chronicle of how systemic the abuse of inside information has become on Wall Street.

This is the story of Mr. Siegel's rise and abrupt fall. It has been pieced together from scores of interviews with people who know Mr. Siegel and with people who are familiar with at least portions of Mr. Siegel's recent statement to the government as well as those of others who have testified in the government's continuing investigation.

(Mr. Siegel couldn't be reached to comment on this account. The government wouldn't identify his whereabouts, citing his continuing cooperation and importance as a potential witness. His lawyer, Jed S. Rakoff, declined comment.)

In the eyes of many Wall Street observers, the takeover boom came of age on August 26, 1982, when Bendix Corp. launched a $1.5 billion hostile bid for Martin Marietta Corp., the opening salvo in what became the now-legendary four-way battle involving Bendix, Martin Marietta, United Technologies Corp. and Allied Corp. And thrust into the center of the action, in his role as Martin Marietta's chief strategist, was a young, hitherto little-known merger specialist at Kidder Peabody named Martin Siegel.

By the time of the Bendix bid, Mr. Siegel had known Ivan F. Boesky for years. Kidder Peabody, where Mr. Siegel was the key mergers and acquisitions strategist, didn't have an arbitrage department so Mr. Siegel couldn't use his own firm for the information about stock positions and company valuations that is crucial to takeover strategy and is the arbitragers' stock-in-trade. He had come to rely on Mr. Boesky, whose persistent phone calls had led to a close relationship. Indeed, they spoke on the phone for five years before they met in person in 1980.

Mr. Siegel had become awed by the vast wealth he saw Mr. Boesky amassing. Two years before the Bendix bid, Mr. Siegel had been invited to dinner at Mr. Boesky's sprawling estate in suburban Westchester County; the Boesky house dwarfed the house that Mr. Siegel was planning to build on Long Island Sound. On two other occasions, Mr. Boesky had come out to the Siegel home to play tennis, a game Mr. Siegel loved and played well. Mr. Boesky arrived in his pink Rolls-Royce.

Mr. Siegel's awe at Mr. Boesky's possessions was all the more pronounced because he came from a modest family background that had been marked by financial struggle. When he was twenty years old, his father, then in his forties, had filed for bankruptcy, an event that left an indelible impression on the son. Indeed, friends say that Mr. Siegel was haunted by the fear that someday, like his father, he would fail just as he reached the prime of life.

For the same reason, he saved money compulsively. For years, he had lived as a bachelor on his relatively modest $50,000 annual salary at Kidder Peabody, saving all of his much larger bonuses. But in 1981 he married his second wife, another investment banker at Kidder Peabody, and they had their first child the next year. They built a large home in Greens Farms, one of the most exclusive enclaves on the Connecticut coast. They had a New York apartment as well and hired a nurse for the child. Mr. Siegel's salary wasn't enough to cover these burgeoning expenses; he was depleting his carefully saved capital.

Several days before the Bendix bid, Mr. Siegel, then thirty-three, trim, dark-haired and strikingly handsome, pushed through the double doors of the grill room at New York's Harvard Club. Mr. Siegel spotted Mr. Boesky and the two settled down for what would become a fateful conversation.

Mr. Siegel aired some of his personal financial concerns to Mr. Boesky. He must have known that to do so in front of an arbitrager was like placing red meat before a lion. "I'll make some investments for you," Mr. Boesky volunteered, and one thing led to another. By the end of that conversation, the two had forged an agreement: In return for information furnished by Mr. Siegel, Mr. Boesky would pay him an unspecified percentage of Mr. Boesky's own profits from trading on the information.

At the beginning, Mr. Siegel didn't expect to be leaking inside information; he thought he would simply be using his expertise as an investment banker to identify companies he deemed likely takeover targets. Indeed, Mr. Boesky had agreed that to trade on inside information just before a deal was publicly announced, or during the course of a deal, was too risky. The goal was to get Mr. Boesky into a takeover stock so early that the purchases couldn't possibly attract the interest of the Securities and Exchange Commission or other market watchers.

Bendix/Martin Marietta, however, provided an opportunity too good to resist. Martin Marietta, Mr. Siegel's client, had responded to the Bendix bid with the most audacious of tactics: the "PacMan" defense, named after the video game, in which the target tries to devour its suitor with a counterbid. Martin Marietta offered to pay $1.5 billion for Bendix.

In some ways, the tactic showed Mr. Siegel at his best. Although it wasn't the first time it had been employed, "it was wildly creative to do it on this scale," recalls one participant. Says another colleague, "You see the creative impulse in the literary and artistic worlds, only rarely in law or business. Marty had it."

But the PacMan defense, to be effective, needed some market momentum to get Bendix into play, pushing up its stock price so it would realize the market was taking the Martin Marietta attack seriously. So just before Martin Marietta's bid was unveiled, Mr. Siegel called Mr. Boesky and leaked the top secret plan, fully aware that he had just crossed the line of illegality. It was the last time he ever used the telephone to convey inside information to Mr. Boesky; shortly after, his feelings of guilt manifested themselves in a paranoid belief that his phone was tapped.

Using Mr. Siegel's information, Mr. Boesky bought Bendix stock, eventually realizing a profit of about $120,000. The PacMan defense succeeded. Bendix lost its independence and was acquired by Allied, and Martin Marietta survived, though at a cost so high that the PacMan defense has never again been attempted on such a scale. The battle was a coup for Mr. Siegel, thrusting him into the limelight just as the nation's takeover boom erupted. And it put Kidder Peabody, considered an established but sleepy firm in decline, at the forefront of merger-defense work.

Mr. Siegel parlayed that fame into a thriving defense-oriented merger practice, modeled in part on the successful takeover law firms. Mr. Siegel tirelessly traveled around the country, persuading chief executives of major corporations to pay Kidder Peabody a retainer to defend them should they become the target of a hostile corporate raid. Over time, he succeeded in scores of instances. "Marty was the most persuasive, most charming investment banker I'd ever met," recalls one chief executive who joined the Kidder Peabody fold. "He had a terrific bedside manner with [chief executive officers] and boards."

But his success wasn't immediately reflected in a significantly higher salary. Over the years he complained about Kidder Peabody's stinginess, its refusal to recognize his contributions to the firm and its penchant for doling out money to unproductive senior partners. In December 1982, a few months after the Bendix/Martin Marietta battle began, he turned to Mr. Boesky and asked the arbitrager for a cash payment of $125,000.

Mr. Boesky readily agreed even though the sum exceeded his profits from Mr. Siegel's information about Bendix. To avoid detection, Mr. Boesky placed the cash in a suitcase and gave it to a courier who met Mr. Siegel in a public place. Mr. Siegel gave the courier an agreed-upon password, and he handed over the suitcase. Mr. Siegel kept the cash hoard, dipping into it throughout the year to pay employees, such as his child's nurse, and for spending money. He thought of the money as a "consulting fee."

With the exchange of money, Mr. Siegel's relationship with Mr. Boesky settled into a pattern. When Mr. Boesky wanted information, or when Mr. Siegel had information he wanted to leak, the two got in touch by telephone. The signal was "Let's have coffee," and they then met in person to exchange the information, first in an alley behind 55 Water

Street, the financial-district building where Mr. Boesky worked, and later, after Mr. Boesky moved into the former Fifth Avenue offices of fugitive commodities trader Marc Rich, at a nearby midtown coffee shop.

In early 1983, Mr. Siegel leaked inside information about a bid by Diamond Shamrock Corp. for Natomas Inc. and a bid for Pargas Inc., later acquired by Freeport-McMoRan Inc. In September he told Mr. Boesky that Gordon Getty, one of Mr. Siegel's clients, was dissatisfied with the management of Getty Oil Co. and that a sale of the company was likely; it was eventually acquired by Texaco Inc. In 1984, he told Mr. Boesky about a bid for Midlands Energy Co. and used inside information about Carnation Co. to predict it would be sold. Nestlé S.A. eventually acquired Carnation, and Mr. Boesky earned a profit of more than $28.3 million on that deal alone.

The insider trading in these instances was extremely clever. In at least three cases, Natomas, Getty and Carnation, Mr. Siegel used inside information to make an educated prediction that a major corporate transaction would ensue. Mr. Boesky was thus able to take enormous stock positions ahead of any final decision to make a bid. Even if detected by the authorities, such trading didn't look like it could possibly be insider trading. And in every instance, it could be argued that Mr. Siegel's leaks actually worked to his clients' benefit by driving up the stock price at which they were eventually acquired, and to Kidder Peabody's benefit by boosting its fees that were based on the sale price.

At the end of both 1983 and 1984, Mr. Boesky and Mr. Siegel met to tally up Mr. Siegel's fee. Mr. Boesky began by saying, "What did you do for me this year?" and Mr. Siegel responded with an analysis of his leaks. The two end-of-year cash payments totaled $575,000.

Mr. Siegel, however, was becoming increasingly anxious about the scheme; and during the summer of 1984, he received a tremendous jolt from an article in *Fortune* magazine. Buried in the text of an otherwise-flattering profile of Mr. Boesky was one sentence: "Boesky's competitors whisper darkly about his omniscient timing, and rumors abound that he looks for deals involving Kidder Peabody and First Boston."

Panicked, Mr. Siegel hastily sought a meeting with Mr.

Boesky. But the arbitrager was unfazed, noting that the magazine had nothing specific and suggesting that he could set up a
foreign bank account for Mr. Siegel if he was really worried.
Mr. Siegel demurred, appalled by the image of himself as a
fugitive. He vowed to stop passing inside information, even
though he couldn't bring himself to tell Mr. Boesky, and he
accepted the 1984 payment.

The Carnation deal, details of which Mr. Siegel leaked
from April through June 1984, was the last about which Mr.
Siegel passed information to Mr. Boesky. Indeed, the pattern
of Mr. Siegel's leaks is almost as conspicuous for the deals in
which he didn't leak inside information as for those in which
he did. For example, one of Mr. Boesky's greatest windfalls
came when he correctly anticipated that Lenox Inc. would
give in to a hostile bid from Brown-Forman Distillers Corp. in
1983. Mr. Siegel represented Lenox, but he wasn't the source
of any leak. Mr. Boesky apparently had inside information
even before Mr. Siegel knew it.

Similarly, Mr. Siegel defended Richardson-Vicks Inc. in a
hostile bid by Unilever in 1985, but he didn't pass information
to Mr. Boesky. Rather, Mr. Boesky passed valuable information about the transaction to Mr. Siegel indicating the presence of another source. The Richardson-Vicks transaction has
been named in government subpoenas related to the Boesky
investigation.

In these and other transactions, Mr. Siegel learned the
value of inside information in the day-to-day workings of
mergers and acquisitions. He continued to listen to Mr.
Boesky, even after he stopped giving him inside information.
At the end of 1985, when the two met for their annual session,
Mr. Boesky told Mr. Siegel that he wanted a written list of the
deals Mr. Siegel had helped him on, indicating that he was
disappointed in the arrangement. "Don't you love me anymore?" Mr. Boesky asked.

By then, Mr. Siegel had allegedly forged a far more valuable
relationship, one in which he was able to tap into one of Wall
Street's greatest repositories of inside information: Goldman,
Sachs & Co.

At Kidder Peabody, Mr. Siegel had developed into the
model investment banker, idolized by many he worked with.

The firm began having its annual summer party for interns at Mr. Siegel's home in Connecticut, the message being, as one participant recalls, "that if you come to Kidder and work hard, you're going to be like Marty—a beautiful home, beautiful wife, beautiful kids. It was like a stage set for *The Great Gatsby*."

Mr. Siegel commuted from the house to lower Manhattan by helicopter. At home, he pursued his two hobbies, tennis and sailing on adjacent Long Island Sound. Colleagues say Mr. Siegel was never swept up into the fast-paced whirl of Manhattan society. "He disdained the charity-ball set," says one friend. "He was not a social climber. He didn't globe-trot. His main interest was his children." (In addition to a daughter, the Siegels had twins, a boy and a girl, who were born in 1985.)

Despite his growing success, Mr. Siegel was coming under mounting pressure from within Kidder Peabody. Many of its areas were not doing well, and many partners feared for the firm's future. In March 1984, Ralph DeNunzio, the firm's chief executive, told Mr. Siegel that in addition to his merger and acquisitions work, Mr. Siegel had to help create an arbitrage department. The firm allotted $30 million to that effort.

The directive seemed to undermine the "Chinese Wall" that is supposed to limit the exchange of information between arbitrage departments and mergers and acquisition departments at investment-banking firms. Evidently in recognition of the inherent conflicts in having the firm's top mergers and acquisitions specialist directly involved in trading on takeover rumors, Mr. DeNunzio also indicated that Mr. Siegel's involvement in arbitrage not be disclosed publicly; it never was. Indeed, when the government identified Mr. Siegel as the Kidder Peabody arbitrager it had previously identified only as "CS-1," it came as a shock even to some Kidder Peabody employees who had no idea that Mr. Siegel was involved in arbitrage.

Repeated efforts to reach Mr. DeNunzio, both at home and in the office, over the holiday weekend were unsuccessful. A Kidder Peabody spokesman denies the account of Mr. DeNunzio's involvement. The spokesman says Mr. DeNunzio's role in arbitrage at Kidder Peabody "is the same as any chief executive officer who supervises departments of a firm." Any inference that Mr. DeNunzio was aware of, or condoned, any misuse of inside information or other wrongdoing "is false and absurd," the spokesman adds.

Despite pressures from the firm's officials to generate large profits, Kidder Peabody didn't have the resources to succeed at arbitrage. Assigned to officially head the new unit was Richard Wigton, generally regarded as a loyal but plodding trader; assigned to work with him was Timothy L. Tabor, a young and headstrong former accountant. (Messrs. Wigton and Tabor were among the three arrested by the government last week.) Mr. Siegel despaired that the unit could generate legitimate profits and complained at the time that his own role in arbitrage was untenable.

Apparently, the result was the alleged arrangement with Robert Freeman, the head of arbitrage at Goldman Sachs, who, when he was arrested by the government last week, was charged with entering into an agreement with Mr. Siegel to swap inside information. It was information that gave Mr. Siegel a tremendous edge in his own merger and acquisitions work. Mr. Freeman, too, became a highly valued strategist on Goldman Sachs merger deals.

The arrangement turned Kidder Peabody's arbitrage unit, virtually overnight, into one of the firm's principal profit centers. In an extraordinary first-year performance that aroused amazement within the firm, the arbitrage unit accounted for more than 25 percent of Kidder Peabody's pre-tax profits the first year it existed. Although that percentage declined slightly in subsequent years, the unit generated "millions of dollars in illegal profits to Kidder," the government charged last week. Confidential profit figures from Kidder Peabody obtained by this newspaper show that arbitrage profits in 1985 were $6.9 million out of total profits of $47 million, or 15 percent, the firm's third-highest profit center. In 1984, arbitrage profits were also about $6.9 million out of a total profit of $39 million.

The alleged arrangement with Mr. Freeman seemed foolproof. The idea was that Kidder Peabody would trade on information from Goldman deals and that Goldman Sachs would trade on information from Kidder deals, so there were no obvious leaks within the firms. (The government, however, hasn't said whether there was any trading by Goldman Sachs on information Mr. Freeman allegedly received from Mr. Siegel. It did allege that Mr. Freeman traded in his own account, which, if true, breached the alleged understanding with Mr. Siegel.)

Moreover, arbitrage departments took positions in so many stocks rumored to be takeover targets that a few striking successes wouldn't appear unusual. There were no messy exchanges of cash, no unsavory-looking couriers. Goldman Sachs said last week that its own internal investigation suggests no wrongdoing on the part of either Mr. Freeman or the firm.

During 1985, as the alleged Goldman Sachs/Kidder Peabody scheme flourished, Mr. Siegel's communications with Mr. Boesky diminished. They didn't meet until the end-of-year session, and it didn't result in any more money changing hands. Mr. Boesky kept pressing hard for more information from Mr. Siegel, but Mr. Siegel resisted.

Then, in January 1986, Mr. Siegel decided to move to Drexel as co-head of its merger and acquisitions department, in part because the pressure so sustaining the Kidder Peabody arbitrage operation while building the firm's mergers and acquisitions practice had become nearly unbearable. Mr. Siegel arranged to meet again with Mr. Boesky, fearful that Mr. Boesky would be furious that he had made the decision without consulting Mr. Boesky. Mr. Boesky was furious, though apparently for reasons unrelated to Mr. Siegel's concerns. Dennis B. Levine, then an investment banker at Drexel, was already leaking inside information to Mr. Boesky at Kidder Peabody. (Last year, Mr. Levine pleaded guilty to four felony counts and is scheduled to be sentenced tomorrow.)

Even at that meeting, Mr. Siegel couldn't bring himself to tell Mr. Boesky that the relationship was over. Mr. Siegel's paranoia about the scheme had continued unchecked, and he increasingly viewed Mr. Boesky's swarthy, muscular couriers as potential hit men. Behind his usual cheerful, outgoing facade, Mr. Siegel lived in a state of fear.

But at Drexel, Mr. Siegel put insider trading behind him. He severed his ties with Mr. Freeman. He had come to Drexel to wed his defense expertise to Drexel's legendary financing capabilities, and the result was hugely successful. Mr. Siegel represented blue-chip clients like Lear-Siegler Inc., Holiday Corp. and Goodyear Tire & Rubber Co.—the kind of client Drexel desperately wanted to attract. Ironically, Goldman Sachs was furious when Goodyear, a longstanding Goldman Sachs client, insisted that both Drexel and Goldman Sachs represent it in its defense against a hostile bid by Sir James Goldsmith.

Last summer, Mr. Boesky tried several times to get in touch with Mr. Siegel. In August, almost exactly four years after their fateful Harvard Club meeting, Mr. Boesky called to say, "I must meet with you" to discuss their "arrangement." Mr. Siegel resisted, then suggested a public place—the Harvard Club. Mr. Boesky said it had to be private; Mr. Siegel declined. Mr. Boesky was presumably wired at the time, but the government never obtained convincing recorded evidence of Mr. Siegel's guilt.

On November 14, the question of the government's evidence became moot. After news of Mr. Boesky's settlement with the government and after he sobbed in Mr. Lipton's office, Mr. Siegel determined almost immediately to plead guilty. He returned to Drexel's offices that evening, where, without going into details, he offered to take a leave of absence. Frederick H. Joseph, Drexel's chief executive, wouldn't hear of it, saying the firm would back him.

But Mr. Siegel's career was effectively over. Though he kept coming into the office, he ceased active participation in pending transactions. The Connecticut home he loved was hastily sold. He moved his family away from New York. He quickly agreed to the government's offer of a guilty plea to two felony counts; negotiations with the SEC over the financial terms of his settlement took longer. Under his agreement, he is paying $9 million to settle the charges. When he resigned from Drexel, he also forfeited approximately $11 million—$7 million in compensation due him and about $4 million in Drexel stock.

On Friday morning Mr. Siegel, flanked by his lawyers, Mr. Rakoff and Audrey Strauss, appeared in Manhattan federal court. He was dressed like an investment banker in an expensive dark gray suit, blue shirt and red tie. Occasionally wiping tears from his eyes, Mr. Siegel pleaded guilty to a single count of conspiracy to violate securities laws, as well as to one count of tax evasion for failing to declare the Boesky payoffs on his tax return.

Later, U.S. Attorney Rudolph Giuliani and Gary Lynch, the SEC director of enforcement, held a crowded press conference to celebrate Mr. Siegel's guilty plea. Said Mr. Guiliani, "His cooperation is very valuable, and Mr. Boesky's cooperation is very valuable. The value of this will be apparent as time goes on."

Mr. Siegel's negotiations with the U.S. Attorney's office didn't include any explicit promises to name others in the scandal, but he is cooperating fully in the government's continuing investigation. He is familiar with the inner workings of Kidder Peabody and has implicated Messrs. Wigton and Tabor. He is expected to provide testimony about the involvement of other Kidder Peabody executives in the firm's arbitrage activities as the government considers possible criminal charges against the firm.

To a lesser extent, Mr. Siegel is knowledgeable about the inner workings of Drexel, a firm also under investigation for reasons unrelated to Mr. Siegel's activities. As for Goldman Sachs, it is known that Mr. Siegel is not the government's principal witness against Mr. Freeman, but his testimony could be valuable corroboration if the government's case against Mr. Freeman goes to trial.

In addition, Mr. Siegel is intimately familiar with many important takeover deals, including the role inside information may have played in them. For government investigators, Mr. Siegel's guilt plea is thus the biggest coup since the capture of Mr. Boesky.

For his part, Mr. Siegel faces a maximum of ten years in jail and a $260,000 fine on the two charges. He also settled, without admitting or denying guilt, SEC charges that he tipped Mr. Boesky about six takeover stocks. Mr. Siegel was permanently barred from working in the securities industry. In a statement read afterwards by Mr. Rakoff, Mr. Siegel said, "I hope that, by accepting responsibility for my mistakes, I have begun to make up for the anguish I have caused my family, friends and colleagues."

In the end, it was Mr. Siegel, seemingly blessed with nearly every attribute for success, who was his own worst enemy. By embracing the use of inside information for personal gain, to advance his career, and to benefit his firm, Mr. Siegel sealed his fate. Mr. Siegel's fears that his career, like that of his father's, would end in financial ruin, proved self-fulfilling.

The Wrong Dream

Ron Rosenbaum

April 1987, *Manhattan,inc.*

Ron Rosenbaum's "The Wrong Dream" is the perfect follow-up to "The Wall Street Career of Martin Siegel Was a Dream Gone Wrong." Offended that the American dream "has become so debased that it can be applied to a life single-mindedly devoted to the accumulation of excess material wealth and empty symbols of status through the pursuit of a useless and parasitic 'profession,' " Rosenbaum let loose with this comic rant against those of the yellow tie and red suspenders.

THERE IT WAS on the front page of the *Wall Street Journal*—perhaps the most revealing and wrongheaded summary of the insider-trading scandal: the headline applied to the otherwise well-reported Martin Siegel story, the headline that called Siegel's pathetic saga "A Dream Gone Wrong." Martin Siegel, we are then informed, "personified the American dream."

It's astonishing—and sad—that the notion of the American dream has become so debased that it can be applied to a life single-mindedly devoted to the accumulation of excess material wealth and empty symbols of status through the pursuit of a useless and parasitic "profession"—even disregarding the crude suitcase-full-of-cash criminality this "dreamer" brought to investment banking.

In fact the story of Martin Siegel and the whole yuppie-investment-banking culture of which he was an avatar is not the story of a dream gone wrong. It's the story of the wrong dream.

Still, one must have a little sympathy for all those led astray by the false yupoid dream. This is a time of rude awakening for these deluded clones. The twin pillars of eighties yuppie culture—the Reagan administration and the investment banking business—have suddenly been unmasked and revealed to be little more than sordid criminal conspiracies, with all the once-proud big-time operators of both now reduced to ratting on each other to save the condos for the families they'll abandon when they go off to jail.

Maybe I'm giving yuppies too much credit, but I have a feeling that there are going to be a lot of them so ashamed and revolted by the behavior of their culture heroes that they're going to want to dissociate themselves from the whole disgraced and discredited culture—*but fast*. They're going to want to eradicate all traces of their yuppie past, obliterate the style and mannerisms that link them with the repulsive behavior of their fallen idols. But they're not going to know how. They're going to need a crash course in transforming their identities.

And so, as a public service, I'd like to present a modest proposal for a new kind of institution to service the needs of those seeking to escape the stigma of yupoid life-style: Yuppie Re-Education Camp.

Although the name suggests the gulag-like re-education camps of Oriental communist dictatorships, we're not talking about forcible detention here. This will be a strictly voluntary program designed for as-yet-unindicted investment bankers (both of them), although it may come to be a popular institution with those already-convicted inside traders seeking to convince their sentencing judges that they've seen through the fraudulence of the life-style that led them to the dock.

But the chief beneficiaries of Yuppie Re-Education Camp will be all those would-bes and wanna-bes, the people whose idea of a culture hero was Martin Siegel and who now want to purge themselves of the taint of their former life-style.

Yuppie Re-Education Camp, as I envision it, will not require the use of actual brainwashing techniques, although the strenuous "self-criticism sessions" *will* suggest to some the way the Red Guards humiliated big shots during the Chinese Cultural Revolution by forcing them to denounce themselves as "pig-dogs." But basically we're talking about something more American here, something more eighties, something on the order of Betty Ford clinics for greedheads, detox centers for money-junkies, self-help clinics for sleazeballs.

You laugh, you don't think I'm being serious, but you'll see: there's going to be a real demand for this service. Already the rats are beginning to scurry off the sinking ship: There's a recent report that suggests that while last year the pinnacle of dreams for top law-school graduates was to work on deals at First Boston or Drexel, the tide of sentiment among the consummate opportunists of this year's graduating class has shifted. Now the SEC reports an increase in applicants who profess the desire to go to work for enforcement director Gary Lynch, pursuing the deal-making criminals of last year's graduating class and their mentors. Although this sudden infusion of idealism must be regarded with some suspicion (farsighted preemptive plea bargaining for future crimes?), nonetheless, even if it's hypocrisy, it's an indication that it's become something of a social embarrassment to admit to wanting to be an investment banker.

Clearly, in the months and years to come, the shame of having been a yuppie, an investment banker, a condo-flipping sleazeball, is going to grow. The problem for those seeking to sneak off the sinking vessel of this venal life-style is how to shed all the telltale signs that they once were yuppies. Not just the clothes and the food but the whole moronic "go-for-it" mentality. It's not going to be easy getting people who have known nothing but the lust for possessions and status symbols to discover new ways of approaching life, disguising the habits of a decade.

That's where Yuppie Re-Education Camp comes in. Herewith a preliminary outline of some elements of the core curriculum:

How to Hold Your Pants Up Without Red Suspenders

You know, of course, the old joke:

Q. Why do firemen wear red suspenders?

A. To hold their pants up.

The mystery of why investment bankers wear red suspenders is a far more profound and troubling one. After all, the first person in the eighties who made a conspicuous spectacle of his red suspenders was the fatuous discount-drugstore tycoon and failed gubernatorial candidate Lew Lehrman. It couldn't be Lew, could it, that investment bankers were imitating? No, that's unfair—even to investment bankers. In fact the ridiculous red-suspender trend probably had its origin in the slavish Anglophilia of the upscale end of the investment banking fraternity, a transparently fraudulent attempt to create the impression one's forebears had worked "in the City" for centuries with the ancestors of Montagu Norman.

Or it might just be that the very silliness of the red-suspender look was what fueled its popularity. It may have been a way of saying, "I'm so successful and powerful and arrogant that I can dress like an idiotic tyke and you'll still have to keep a straight face if you want a crack at the capital markets."

But whatever the origin of this stylistic tic, the party's over for red suspenders unless you're Bozo the Clown. Throw them out, fellas. Wearing red suspenders these days is like wearing a sartorial scarlet letter that says: I BELONG TO A SHAMEFUL PROFESSION, I AM PROBABLY A CROOK.

How will you hold your pants up? Well, you investment bankers heading for federal correctional institutions won't have to face that problem for a few years, since I hear many of our better prisons have adopted these kinda neat one-piece jumpsuits that don't present the belt-versus-braces dilemma.

But for all you yuppie types at Re-Education Camp who will have to learn how to hold your pants up all over again, we're recommending a switch to something aggressively tacky and unstylish: Sansabelt double-knit polyester slacks with the miracle no-belt "continental style" Flexo-waistband. Not only will you not need a belt (these pants practically glue themselves to your legs), you'll have taken the symbolic step of distancing yourselves—in a violent way—from enslavement to the disgraceful conformity of your past.

What to Wear Around Your Neck Instead of a Gold Tie

Those of you who pass the initial Re-Education Camp style seminar ("How to accessorize your wardrobe so your cuff links won't clash with your handcuffs") will graduate to the tie-selection seminar. We will probe the origins of the Wall Street version of yellow fever: the craze for yellow and yellow-gold ties that caught on in 1984 and has yet to exhaust itself. A yellow tie remains the definitive "Say it loud/I'm yuppie and proud" neckwear.

We will analyze why you all slavishly followed this trend as if you'd been hypnotized en masse into tie-color conformity. Was the yellow tie a symbolic "yellow streak" that reflected the cowardliness of your career choices and your security-obsessed, herd-following life-style? Did it symbolize your enslavement to the power of gold, like a slave manacle around the neck? Or did it just seem to go well with red suspenders?

In any case, a full week at Re-Education Camp will be devoted to the problems of buying clothes that will harmonize with other tie colors, followed by an intensive seminar in alternate neck ornaments—string ties, love beads, puka-shell necklaces—that represent bold stylistic breaks with the yupoid past.

Learning the Difference Between Making Money and Making Love

This isn't as elementary as it seems if you listen to the rhetoric of fast-track types of late. For instance, here's a quote in the *Times* from an unnamed "prominent investment banker" apropos of the big-fee, anything-goes climate of aggressive M & A investment banking in the eighties that led to the insider-trading scandal: "It was like free sex."

Now, setting aside for a moment the question of what "free sex" actually means (does it mean he ordinarily pays for sex?), there seems to be a profound confusion of realms here. It's one that recalls the conflation of economic and sexual imagery in Victorian pornography. In *The Other Victorians*, Columbia professor Steven Marcus points out that the overheated prose of nineteenth-century porn often appropriated metaphors from the economic realm to describe moments of sexual ecstasy. The most common phrase for having an orgasm in this literature, he points out, was "to spend."

It's become a commonplace by now that, in the yuppie hierarchy of urges, the lust for money has replaced the lust for pleasures of the flesh; that the avatars of eighties go-for-it culture tend to seek orgasm *by* spending.

In Yuppie Re-Education Camp we will go back to the basics and carefully try to spell out the difference between having orgasms and spending money, a distinction that can make a crucial practical difference in how you treat the sales-clerk at Bloomingdale's.

Learning to Distinguish Between the Peace Symbol and the Mercedes Hood Ornament

In the precipitate rush to disguise their identities and avoid being associated with yuppie culture, some panicky individuals are going to go overboard and make mistakes that will give them away. Recently there was an item in the news about a Midwest college that was holding some sort of "sixties" festival and the students decorated their banners with what was intended to be the peace symbol. In fact what they'd inscribed turned out to be something closer to the Mercedes-Benz hood ornament. There *is* a difference, so for those of you at Yuppie Re-Education Camp who seek to cover up your old stylistic preferences with sixties symbols and icons, we will offer a refresher course on such crucial distinctions as:

The difference between Eldridge Cleaver and Beaver Cleaver

The difference between Huey Newton and Helmut Newton

The difference between Rasta and Pasta

The Difference Between Crack Dealing and Investment Banking, As Professions

Recently, in the course of spending time with detectives investigating a crack murder, I learned a fascinating fact that suggests an eerie point of confluence between the crack-dealing and the yuppie life-styles. It seems that one telltale sign of the presence of a crack-refining lab in a neighborhood is the presence of large quantities of empty jugs of spring water in trash cans and dumpsters. The classier crack-dealing operations turn up their noses at using city tap water in the process of refining cocaine into crack, because the presence of iron and other impurities in tap water can give the final product an unappetizing brownish hue. And so crack dealers—like yuppies—have become huge consumers of bottled water.

When you think about it, there are other instructive similarities between crack dealers and Perrier-drinking Martin Siegel clones. Both life-styles involve destructive addictions to substances: one to cocaine, the other to money. Both involve choosing these substances over any human values or ideals. Both usually lead to the purchase of flashy possessions and, as the addiction grows, to the commission of illegal acts to maintain that life-style. Come to think of it, there's not much of a philosophical difference between crack dealers and investment bankers at all. Except that these days most decent people would rather admit they're crack dealers than investment bankers.

Perfect Family

James Kaplan

June 1987, *Manhattan,inc.*

---

*"Hype Gone Haywire in the Eighties," this
hilarious story by James Kaplan, pokes fun at the
eighties mania for self-promotion and publicity.
Having received a press release from a family
named Evans that began, "Here's a family that
belongs on the cover of* Manhattan,inc.*," Kaplan
decides to find out who in the hell these people are
and what they think they are doing. It's a hoot.*

THEY COME BY THE BUSHEL, the press releases; you quickly
become inured to their relentless yodeling hype. You discount, severely, and then you dismiss; or, if an eyebrow rises,
you learn to translate, as you would translate a page from
Pravda, combing the positivist rhetoric for the stray bit of
truth or interest.

At first glance this release looked like any other. Then you
saw the opening sentence. "Here's a family that belongs on
the cover of *Manhattan,inc.*," it said.

An eyebrow rose.

[The release continued:] Father Tom (Thomas W. Evans) is a
partner in the New York law firm of Mudge Rose Guthrie
Alexander & Ferdon; according to *The Making of the President*, it was Evans and two other colleagues who persuaded an
attorney named Nixon to head for the House [*sic*]. . . . His
book about preschool education, *The School in the Home*,
was published by Harper & Row in 1973.

Mother Lois Logan Evans is an investment banker, chairman of the Federal Home Loan Bank of New York, and former

assistant U.S. chief of protocol. . . . She is also president of Acquisition Specialists Inc., a New York-based consulting firm that represents clients in discussions of mergers and financing and that has venture capital interests.

Tom and Lois Evans are the parents of three children. . . . It is with their eldest daughter, Heather, and her fiance, artist Matthew Baumgardner, that the couple should be featured. Until recently, Heather, twenty-seven, was vice president and head of an exclusive selling assignment team at Bear, Stearns & Co. Before that, she founded Heather Evans Incorporated, a line of dresses for businesswomen.

Heather Evans, who has also been a fashion model represented by Ford Models, Inc., New York, and L'Agence Pauline, Paris, is a graduate of Harvard Business School and Harvard College. She served as publisher of the *Harvard Advocate*. She has received significant media attention following her cover story (November 1984) in *Working Woman*, "The Plight of the Corporate Nun," as well as a follow-up cover story (April 1985) in *Management Review*, "The Hedonist in the Grey Flannel Suit."

In the February 1985 edition of *Institutional Investor*, Heather Evans was featured as a risktaker. As the magazine's writer asked, "If Jim Palmer poses on television in his jockey shorts, is there any reason an ambitious young woman in investment banking shouldn't lend her endorsement to a line of intimate female apparel? . . . As Heather Evans, a twenty-six-year-old mergers and acquisitions associate at Bear Stearns noted in her recent bra-and-panty ad in the *New York Times Magazine*: 'There's always high risk on Wall Street. That's why being confident is important.' "

Fiance Matt Baumgardner is a young artist whose work has been on loan to the White House. . . . Heather and Matt will be married on December 20, 1986, in a Red Hook, Brooklyn, social club hung with Matt's art; they declined her parents' invitation to be married at the Century Association. That typifies the old/new, establishment/arts mix which makes the Evans family newsworthy. That they are also highly photogenic makes this profile even more worthwhile. After all, have you ever heard a story of a family which is a better mix of talented men, talented women, Park Avenue meets Wall Street meets Avenue A meets . . . .

Now, flackery is as old as the hills, and self-promoters are not exactly scarce in this town, but it is usually clear what is being pushed: a new product, a real estate empire, a career, a debut. What was being promoted here? What was being sold? A *family*? If so, to what end? Was this family somehow being touted as ideal? Did such a category even exist? Or was this merely publicity for its own sake? And who, precisely, was doing the selling?

Both eyebrows rose, higher and higher.

Thomas Evans came downstairs to the reception area himself. If this was some sort of ploy, it was a clever one—but it didn't seem to be a ploy. Evans, a partner in the law firm of Mudge Rose Guthrie Alexander & Ferdon, formerly Nixon Mudge Rose Guthrie & Alexander, was tall, handsome, well tailored—and almost apologetic. His handshake was neither aggressively hale nor overbearing: no hard sell was going on here. In fact, the vibe Evans emitted was scarcely the vibe one would have expected from the press release. This was no triumphant superlawyer, but a quiet one: a distinguished, reticent man.

"This initiative to you came from my daughter, as you may know," Thomas Evans said, once we had sat down in his office, a large, bright room on the thirty-sixth floor of 180 Maiden Lane. Beyond the picture windows, the East River stretched north into a gray mist. "Or," he said, "someone on her behalf, one of her friends, who thought this would be a— good idea."

Thomas Evans's tone distinctly implied that it wasn't.

As Evans began to talk across his big antique walnut desk, he loosened up a bit, and one could start to see how he had done all he had done, why he had evoked trust and generosity. His speaking voice was deep—the accent was subtly mid-Atlantic, with odd Southern tinges in the diphthongs, despite the fact that Evans grew up in Garden City on Long Island and went to school at Williams and Columbia. He was deliberative but not boring; charming but not slick; strong but not domineering; open but not spilly. Not very humorous—at least in journalistic company. But humor wasn't what you wanted in a topflight litigator. *A man,* I thought, *that Richard Nixon would trust.*

I asked how he had happened to write a book on preschool education.

"We had a country house with a lot of empty book-shelves," Evans said. "And we bought books by the yard. . . . A series of books that we bought were called *Berle's Self Culture* by Adolf A. Berle. I had had a professor at Columbia Law School named Adolf A. Berle Jr. His father had written these books in the early twentieth century, and a number of other books on a method of bringing up children. Now—the two Berle boys and the two daughters all went to Harvard and Radcliffe in their early teens and graduated before they were twenty. Adolf passed the entrance exams when he was twelve and a half; he got his undergraduate degree, a master's degree, and a law degree all by the time he was twenty-one. But the interesting thing about the Berles was that not only did they have great attainment in their academic lives but they went on to very productive lives."

Evans condensed Berle's writings into about a hundred pages, wrote a foreword talking about the Berle family, and then wrote an afterword, in which he described how he had used Berle's methods with his own family.

A bell rang in my mind. Could parents somehow raise scientifically ideal children?

"It wasn't elaborate or overladen," Evans said of his own program. "It was just worked into play, and worked into dinnertimes, and other such things."

What was it?

"When you're trying to clean house, or write something, or do whatever you're doing," Evans continued, "and a kid is asking why the sky is blue, or, you know, what something on television means, it's *very* demanding to get back and talk with the child. But that pays tremendous dividends, and Berle was one of the first people to see this.

"The important thing was to answer the questions, and to establish the dialogue, and let the child know that you were interested. . . . Berle would also say that if the child asked a question about tennis, that you might use that occasion to teach him about right angles."

There were also the trivia quizzes. But more on that presently.

It turned out, in further conversation, that Thomas Evans had been an adoptive child. He hadn't found this out until he was twenty-six. And although his upbringing was pleasant— wasn't it interesting to consider Evan's status as an only and adoptive child in light of his extreme care in raising his own children? I asked whether he had ever had any interest in finding his natural parents.

Evans went off the record.

When it came time for me to leave, I asked him for his opinions on an article about his family.

He laughed, a bit nervously, and went off the record again.

How long had he been at Mudge Rose Guthrie, et al.?

"I came here in 1965," he said. "When I graduated from law school, I went to Simpson Thacher. I was there for, I think, about four years, then went with a New York State Commission of Investigation, which is no longer around, and was there for about a year and a half. . . . In Brooklyn Heights one day, I had one of my kids at a playground and bumped into Leonard Garment, who was then the head of the litigation department at Nixon Mudge, and he invited me in to be interviewed and to fill a spot in the litigation department, which was bursting at the seams at the time because the firm had so much new business, was expanding rapidly.

"Of course, a lot of my life at that time was in working for Nixon, whose litigation I handled, with the exception of the case that he argued in the Supreme Court, which was Leonard Garment's case. And then [I] had occasion to work in his campaign, and then came back to the firm after the campaign, and have been with it continuously since."

There was a hint of displeasure at the former head of his firm—using only his last name—but something in Evans's demeanor asked one not to go into that. In fact, something in his demeanor seemed ill at ease with the fact of being interviewed at all. I was struck that he went off the record on important personal matters, yet this didn't make him look evasive; it only indicated a certain natural, even laudable, reticence.

A reticence that seemed—in light of the press release—dissonant. At the very least.

What was going on here?

Lois Evans met me in the board room of the Federal Home Loan Bank of New York, a windowless room on the 103rd floor of One World Trade Center. She was a strikingly pretty blond woman of a certain age, wearing an emerald green dress. Like her husband, Lois Evans radiated dignity, probity, accomplishment, and, above everything else, reticence.

Things were getting curiouser and curiouser.

"I think [this story] basically was my daughter's idea," Lois Evans told me.

She had a light, dry, intelligent voice, with a hint of the slight drawl of privilege. But as she talked, there was no hint of the vacuity that a prejudiced auditor might associate with such a drawl, such a blond-and-emerald-green gestalt. The look may have been *Town & Country*, but the talk was Eastern Power Corridor, advanced version. Here was no helpmeet for Thomas Evans, but a (fortuitously attractive) counterpart.

Lois Evans discussed the op-ed piece she recently wrote with Heather, on why no women have been involved in the insider-trading scandals. She then began to speak of the arc of her own career: how she quit work as a copywriter at Grey Advertising to have her first child, raised the children until the youngest was in school, then went back to work—as a member of the U.S. delegation to the UN under George Bush.

I remarked that the shift from house mom to UN delegate was not quite a usual one. How had that happened?

"Basically because we knew George Bush," Lois Evans said. "He liked the idea of having public members on the delegation. There are officially three public members on the delegation; I wasn't one of those, and I wasn't paid at that time, and the State Department people didn't like that. It was a real learning experience for me. I hadn't spoken before; it was just—I had been raising three children. . . . It was very nice that [Bush] gave me that opportunity, because it changed my life, really."

"How did you know Bush?"

"We had a mutual friend in Texas, the Cattos. Jessica Catto's [husband, Henry,] had been in college with my husband. And they are very close to the Bushes. And so that's how we met him."

So. Thomas Evans and Lois Evans knew Leonard Garment and Henry Catto and George Bush, and both had reaped the rewards. But while acquaintance sometime elevates the unworthy, Thomas Evans and Lois Evans hardly seemed to fit that category.

After Lois Evans's job at the UN, Gerald Ford had replaced Richard Nixon, "so I knew I wouldn't get another political appointment," she said. "So I thought that this would be—to get into business in something that would be somewhat creative, working on deals. And of course, a lot of our friends through my husband's work are investment bankers and businessmen who are looking for acquisitions and all, so I guess that's how I got into it. Again not with much knowledge. . . . But then I got on-the-job training."

Lois Evans started her own investment-banking firm, Acquisition Specialists, Inc. in 1975, working as an independent entity in partnership with several others.The firm has continued to this day. She has also combined that work with other jobs: a stint as assistant chief of protocol for the United States in New York (1981–82) and her present position as bank chairman.

Wildly distinguished, yes; but hypeable? It was getting more difficult by the minute to figure out how the Evans press release had happened. Grasping at straws, I thought back to the Berle book and asked Lois Evans if she had shared her husband's interest in pedagogy. Had her children had an unusual upbringing?

"Well, a lot of it was. Our children had, you know, a great curiosity, too," Lois Evans said. "[My husband might have seen it] as more of a parental initiative, but I'm not so sure it wasn't the child's initiative.

"I mean, my husband's basically a teacher—I think he'd like to have been a teacher. So if a question was asked at the table—we thought it was very important to eat with the children. He would always have breakfast with them. So he had that time with them. And then in the evening we'd eat with them, too."

"But that's pretty unusual."

"Well, I certainly didn't think it was. But I know when my children would have friends over that they were often very intimidated by our dinner-table conversations—"

"Was there a system at the dinner table? Did you and your husband purposefully set about playing certain types of games, or starting certain discussions, at the dinner or breakfast table?"

"Well, some of the games we played were a little structured, but a lot of it was spontaneous. . . . We'd play word games like, [one person would say] 'dog,' and the next person would say 'bark,' and then the person after that would say 'tree'—if they're doing it correctly— then from 'tree' they'd go into another word which would have some relationship to 'tree' but would be a different usage. . . . And they can do that when they're fairly young. And, you know, we'd have quizzes, too; [my husband] liked to give quizzes."

Quizzes?

"Oh, world-events kind of quizzes, mostly. Or something that they're studying in school. And they could ask questions. You know, they could do it, too."

"They'd give you quizzes, too?"

"That's usually when I got up and left the table."

What was CSB Holdings? Was it somehow behind the Evans press release?

I had decided to be blunt with Heather Evans. We were sitting under a *ficus benjamina* in the sublet loft on Great Jones Street that she shares with her husband, painter Matthew Baumgardner. Baroque harpsichord was playing on the stereo. The loft was spotless, airy, and, for a loft, reasonably elegant. We were drinking grapefruit juice and club soda. Baumgardner was due home momentarily.

"What was the genesis of the press release?" I asked her right off the bat.

"That's what I was going to tell you," Heather Evans said. She seemed a little nervous. She was an attractive if not precisely beautiful young woman, large-eyed, *gamine*, slim and long-legged, with short, streaked hair and pale, flawless skin. She was wearing a simple but stylish gray cotton dress, heels, pearls, and a large, expensive-looking flowered silk scarf over her shoulders. I emphasize these details because I somehow felt they had been emphasized for me.

"I had never planned to go into investment banking," Heather Evans said, sipping at her drink. "I left Bear Stearns in July to help a new Lazard Frères banking venture—it's actually a commercial-banking venture which has not yet gotten approval—to help them with their marketing. We had expected them to get going much faster than actually has happened. And so one of the things I had done was retain a public relations firm—for that banking venture.

"[The venture] was called CSB Holdings. And the person who I retained was somebody who I had known, although not well, before: Marian Salzman. In the course of this, she knew about my family. And—she sort of said, 'Well, your parents haven't gotten nearly as much press as they should have. Why don't we put together'—and she put together that press release. And she had this concept of, you know, just four interesting individuals in sort of this financial-world-downtown-art-world kind of mix. And I still am not sure how it comes out as a story. I think both of my parents have done really fascinating things, and they're not—I've even seen my mother interviewed, because my mother is a really dynamic person in a cocktail-party conversation or in a business situation. But I think she gets nervous when she talks with the press. But in any case, this is the genesis of it. It was more just because [Salzman] was getting paid a retainer by my firm, and she had nothing else to do. Because the *product* that Lazard is preparing is confidential, so there was nothing for us to market, and it was kind of on a lark." She laughed, uneasily.

"So neither of my parents knew what—I mean, I sent them copies of the letter, both of them have forgotten what was in it—"

Heather Evans laughed again.

But why *have* a story? "What do you think?" I asked her. "Are you still interested in doing a piece?"

"Yeah!" Evans said.

"One of the things I'm most interested in now," she continued, "is Matt's work, so I really love the idea of doing photographs of Matt's work. And as I say, I still think my parents both do a lot of interesting things and have never—it's funny. None of us have, except for Matt, who is very much an artist and, really, that is his, you know, it's his calling—I'd say that the three Evanses in the group are more—'dilettante' doesn't have a good connotation—"

She laughed nervously and started again. "I mean, we all do a lot of different things," she said. "And so we've never really—you know, I got a lot of publicity when I started the dress company. But—so in terms of—you know, I think they're very interesting people. But as for how the story will come out—that's your job!"

A big, gulping laugh.

The point of the story was Matt's work?

The point of the story was Heather's parents?

The point of the story was to repair past media neglect of the Evanses?

In fact, it seemed, more and more, that the point of the story was Heather Evans.

We were discussing Heather Evans's current role as technical adviser on Oliver Stone's new movie about Wall Street, talking about how her passion for correctness about Street details has occasionally collided with purely cinematic concerns—when the buzzer buzzed.

Heather Evans walked to the front of the loft to answer it, her heels echoing like hammer strokes on the lacquered floor. She spoke into the speaker. It was Matt. He had forgotten his keys.

Presently the doorbell rang and Evans let her husband in. He walked into the living area. He made an arresting sight. In fact, if you gathered a Somali tribesman, an Aleutian fisherman, and Matthew Baumgardner in a room, you'd have a tough time deciding which one was most opposite to Thomas Evans, partner in Mudge Rose Guthrie, et al.; Lois Evans, chairman of the Federal Home Loan Bank; and Heather Evans, former investment banker, fashion model, and dress designer.

And yet—this was perhaps the point. When we shook hands, it occurred to me that Matt Baumgardner had his own peculiar appropriateness: he was the *sauvage*. Tall and husky, with close-set dark eyes, a wide nose, a flattop haircut shaven on the sides—the face of a boxer—he was wearing untied high-tops, black jeans, and three shirts. The outermost was a beige chamois work shirt, untucked; next came a dusty-purple polo shirt with the collar flipped up; innermost was a V of olive T-shirt. The combination and the effect were perfect. This was . . . a Painter.

Baumgardner hulked down on the other side of the couch from his wife—and suddenly it hit me. There they were: a picture! Photo opportunity! Heather, cool and analytical in her shawl and pearls and heels, and Matt, nonverbal and picturesque in his Great Jones best. On opposite sides of the couch, like the left and right sides of the brain.

"It's funny when I remember my childhood," Heather Evans was saying, a bit later. "Because I was very—all three of us were pretty—not that we were very school-oriented, although we did well in school—but we were very intellectual. Which is not really typical of, like, an Upper East Side, Spence School upbringing, actually. Although, you know, I certainly grew up with lots of smart people whose parents were all well educated, but, you know, I also was just really lucky in terms of all my exposure. I mean, my childhood and Matt's are very different, just in terms of our exposure." She turned to her husband, as if for confirmation. "But I don't think that you were exposed to the same sort of conversation," she said to him. "Also, I went to Europe every summer from the time I was eight."

"I've never been to Europe," Baumgardner said, with a wry smile.

Heather Evans laughed.

"I'd rather take her around the United States on a Harley-Davidson," Baumgardner said. The line was perfectly delivered, in a kind of growl. His wife laughed, a little less comfortably.

"Were you aware of your parents' efforts to educate you?" I asked Heather Evans. "Did it sit easily with you? Did it make you feel different from other kids?"

"I think by and large it was something I didn't notice," she said. "Maybe my brother would have noticed it more, because he probably fought against it more. I did really well in school naturally, so I never felt as if my parents could care less how I did in school. And so I never felt pressure that way. We did have one thing which I really hated. We used to have these quizzes, at the table."

We surveyed Heather Evans's career to the present date. She has not let the grass grow under her feet. She worked as a fashion model from the end of her junior year of high school through college. She graduated from Harvard at twenty, in 1979, then went to work as an investment banker for Morgan Stanley for two years. She then entered Harvard Business School. In her second year of graduate school, she started her own company, designing and selling to speciality shops dresses for businesswomen. She would fly to Cambridge on Monday morning, go to classes on Monday and Tuesday, then fly back to New York to run her company. When the ethics (or lack of ethics) of the dress business frustrated her, she went back to investment banking, at Bear Stearns. When the self-seriousness and moral vacuity of investment banking alienated her, she left Bear Stearns. Today she advises Oliver Stone; she serves as chief financial officer for a TV-and-film production company; she sits on the board of a dance company; she promotes Matt's career. She has written a book proposal. The topic is a secret. She and Matt are living on her last bonus from Bear Stearns and his earnings from painting—mostly the former, she hints.

The bra-and-panty ad. "That was a pretty funny story," Heather Evans said, laughing. "I tend to not talk about that. Marian [Salzman] likes that story. This ad had a little photograph of me—my head—and it said something like, 'Mergers and acquisitions is a high-risk business, and I'm willing to take risks.' And then this lingerie—this woman in bra and underwear next to me—"

"So it was not you?" I said.

"No, it wasn't me. But the weird thing is, in the mock-up that I saw of it, the woman was black or something—it was clearly not me. In the one they used in the *Times*, the woman had pretty much the identical haircut to me. So it was slightly confusing. . . . This caused a *huge* scandal—first of all, people thinking it was me, and just thinking this was inappropriate on Wall Street."

It turned out that Heather Evans had a copy of the ad, and now we looked at it. There was a large picture of a model in bra and panties and a small head shot of Heather Evans. The model *did* resemble Evans. Markedly. It turned out Evans had done this ad for an acquaintance in the fashion industry. As a favor. And yet wasn't there a strange parallel—wasn't there possibly more than one parallel—between the deceptive but titillating) lingerie ad and the (deceptive but titillating) press release?

"I have to say," Heather Evans said of the lingerie, "the worst story about this stuff is that the stuff was terrible merchandise."

Heather Evans's parting handshake was *very* firm. Matthew Baumgardner took me downstairs on the old-fashioned freight elevator. We rode for a bit in silence, then he turned to me. "They're a wild family," he said. I looked at him for elaboration, but just then his nonverbal side prevailed. We shook hands in the doorway. "Good meeting you, man," he said.

As a favor (the lingerie ad). On a lark (the press release). The public relations person has nothing else to do. Here is Marian Salzman, over whose name the release was released:

"She [Heather Evans] had just switched from Bear Stearns to Lazard Frères—or to what she called CSB Holdings. They became a client of this firm, so we did a lot of their preliminary media plans. It was in that context that she had asked me if I could put together something to do some publicity for her and for her family, particularly for her husband, in that he's launching a career as a painter. And I think she was doing what she could to try to raise his profile, kind of piggybacking off the fact that *she* has had a pretty high profile—I don't know if she showed you that she'd done the Trendsetters bra ads. And she's done a lot of other things."

"What kind of things?" I asked.

"I would call them kind of promoter-personality type

things. I mean, kind of in line with the fact that this is the kind of book that she's trying to write right now. [The book] is about that type of approach to your career? She's been a real good self-promoter."

"What's the book going to be about?"

"I don't know if I should be telling you—but I think it's called *The Promoter Personality*. It's just basically about different ways to sort of achieve success and how to kind of call yourself to the attention of the people you work for.

"At any rate," she continued, "I obviously knew of the reputations of her mother and father, so it kind of made the idea of doing some promotion for her more appealing, just because they have such *unbelievable* reputations in the kind of the New York business elite. And particularly her father. I mean, Tom Evans is probably the nearest thing to *God* if you talk to most people on Wall Street, in terms of just being one of the kind of real ethical, ethical kind of—almost legendary. And so that's kind of how I agreed to do it: it was sort of more as a *favor* than it was part of the client assignment, where we were doing some very straightforward financial promotions for the firm she was involved with."

As a favor.

"Was tying the parents into the story your idea or Heather's idea?" I asked.

"I'm not really sure," Salzman said. "It's kind of one of those lunchtime ideas? For which no one should probably take credit and everybody probably does?"

"I see."

"I mean, it certainly makes them a very, very appealing New York story," Salzman said. "And if you've seen them, I mean, they're all so *ridiculously* photogenic."

Heather Evans called the Monday after I met her, from Ohio—she and her husband had gone to visit his sick grandmother. She wanted to be sure I understood that the point of the piece was *really* her parents, how much they had done and how little they had been recognized. She gave me a list of people I should ask about them. The list included Alfonse D'Amato, Nathan Quinones, and John Shad, the chairman of the SEC. That was fine, but I had another subject on my mind, one that had impressed me more by its absence than its presence.

"Would it be possible for me to talk to your brother?" I asked.

"Yeah," she said. "You know, the reason my brother hasn't really come up is that he's basically a pretty serious drug abuser."

"I see," I said.

Heather Evans then went on to tell me more about her brother and his problems and volunteered his phone number.

Something else had struck me as strange. In her article, "The Hedonist in the Grey Flannel Suit," Heather Evans had discussed the problems managers have in attracting increasingly high-paid and jaded young employees. She had talked about two-salary couples without children and had mentioned her husband—her husband Peter.

Had she been married before?

Heather Evans laughed, shakily, over the phone. "Yeah, I kind of ignore that," she said. "Yes, it's true. My parents aren't too happy about that."

"About the fact—?"

"I got married, and then I was married for three years, and then I got divorced and met Matt about six months after I got separated, and we got married very quickly after we met. . . .

"I think I mentioned," she said, "I do everything in fast motion. I think I've slowed down a little, which is good now, but . . . "

Heather Evans called from New York on Tuesday to correct her brother's phone number and to give me her sister's number in Rome. She also gave me the numbers of some people I could call at Bear Stearns, and a few other numbers, too.

Heather's brother's phone was disconnected. I called her sister in Rome. Mozart's *Requiem* was playing in the background. Paige Evans was in the middle of dinner and sounded a bit annoyed. "What's the purpose of this article?" she asked.

It was an awkward moment.

The conclusions I was beginning to draw about the article were conclusions I was hesitant to share with her. I told her about the press release. I mentioned I had had difficulty getting through to her brother.

Paige Evans told me to call back when I had some specific questions to ask.

Thomas Evans returned my call from a car on its way to Newark Airport. He sounded jovial. "I had one loose end that I wanted to tie up," I told him. "when we talked the other day, I asked for your opinion about the article on your family, and your answer was off the record. But I forgot to ask—did you ever see the press release?"

"No, I didn't," Evans said.

There was a pause.

"Was my answer about the article off the record?" he asked.

"Yes, it was."

"I was possibly a little negative [about the article]," Evans said. "I look forward to it."

Lois Evans called the next morning, very upset. "I think this article should stop," she said. Her daughter Paige had phoned her from Rome to say that a reporter had called with personal questions about the family, that the reporter had been trying to get in touch with her brother.

I told Mrs. Evans I had only been following the avenues that had been indicated to me and that Heather had given me the other children's phone numbers.

"She shouldn't be doing that," Lois Evans said. She said that, for obvious personal reasons, they were concerned that their son not be written about. "Maybe that would happen when you're a public figure," Mrs. Evans said. "But we're not public figures."

Had she ever seen the press release, I asked.

Mrs. Evans said she hadn't. "That was Heather's idea," she said. "She should tell the people who are in it."

Thomas Evans called me the next morning. He had the number of some people I could talk to about his wife, his daughters, and his son. He asked for my address. He wanted to send me his book.

Shortsellers in the Bull Market

Brett Duval Fromson

August 31, 1987, *Fortune*

In the midst of the bull market, writing about shortsellers—investors who make money when the stock market goes down—was considered a bit offbeat. Who knew that the market would crash seven weeks later? I didn't.

Y OU MIGHT THINK that the great American bull market of the past five years must have been tough on shortsellers. A shortseller, after all, makes money on a stock only when it goes down—and stocks have gone up by 230 percent on the Dow since the bull market began on August 13, 1982. But in fact, the professionals whose principal business is selling short have done quite well. Interviews with shortsellers, their brokers, and knowing observers indicate that the pros as a group have performed better than the Dow—which means much better than the average stock mutual fund. Some shortsellers have achieved *annual* returns on capital higher than 100 percent.

How have they done it? In shorting a stock, you want to do much the same thing as a long investor—buy low, sell high. But in shortselling you sell the stock before you buy it. You do that by borrowing shares from a broker whose customers own them in margin accounts. Eventually, you will have to cover, meaning purchase the same number of shares and thereby close out the transaction. You make a profit if you buy the securities for less than you earlier sold them for.

When an amateur ventures to short a stock, he usually expects to cover within a few weeks, or a few months at most.

Success or failure depends on timing. If the timing proves unfortunate and the stock price rises instead of falling, the amateur is likely to lose his nerve and cover at a loss.

The pros don't operate that way. They sometimes have to cover at a loss, of course, but they minimize the risks of timing by basing short-sale decisions on painstaking analysis of value—or lack of value. When they take a short position, they do so with enough confidence to hang on if the price goes up. Sooner or later, their analysis has told them, it will come down.

Professional shortsellers, or shorts as they're often called, speak of the importance of doing homework, and they do a lot of it. Says Mike Murphy, publisher of the *Overpriced Stock Service*, required reading for shortsellers: "We look for overvalued companies to short, which you can only do if you have a firm grounding in classic security analysis." From San Francisco, Murphy sends his newsletter, a tip sheet of short-sale prospects, to over a thousand subscribers at $495 a year. As evidence that most shorts are value players, Murphy points out that many hold positions a year, two years, and even three while waiting for the market to recognize the overvaluation.

Shorts dig like badgers in looking for dirt on companies. Some spend months doing research on a target company before deciding whether to take a position. If they need industry experts or private detectives to help, the shorts get them. They do whatever it takes "within the letter of the law," as one of them puts it. Consequently, their analysis is often superior to buy-side research done by investment firms.

A broker who counts some of the top West Coast shorts among his clients attests to the quality of the shortsellers' studies. He set up a phone conversation between his firm's medical technology analyst—"who is no dummy"—and a shortseller. The purpose was to discuss a particular company. Says the broker: "She explained the bull story for about fifteen minutes, and then he began asking questions. By the end of their conversation, *she* was asking *him* questions. He was well beyond her understanding of how vulnerable this business was and how tricky the accounting was."

The number of professional shortsellers in the U.S. is quite small—there may be fewer than fifty. They tend to share certain characteristics, notably tough-mindedness. They need it to discern corporate weaknesses that other investors do not see and that managers are trying to conceal. They also need it to hold on when the price of a shorted stock keeps going up. And they need it to delay covering when the price goes down, to wait until the stock hits bottom. Their minds seem exceptionally sharp, as if the work keeps them well honed.

Most of them guard their anonymity. Some who were interviewed for this story agreed to talk only on condition that their names would not be mentioned. Low visibility is a help in gathering intelligence. As one short puts it: "Some companies won't return a phone call or send quarterly reports if they know you are short their stock. It's as if you were calling up the CEO to ask if someone in his family has AIDS."

With certain exceptions, the pros can be divided into two categories: those who short large-capitalization companies and those who go after smaller companies. One of the best-known shortsellers in the large-company group is James Chanos, twenty-nine, who won renown for predicting the collapse of Baldwin-United, the financial services company that went bankrupt in September 1983, with Chanos holding a large short position in the stock. He now does business as a one-principal firm, Kynikos ("cynic" in Greek) Associates Ltd. He has two unlisted phones, at home and at his office.

Chanos was born and raised in Milwaukee, and though he graduated from Yale and now lives in New York, he thinks of himself as a Midwesterner. Every working day at lunchtime he takes the subway to Brooklyn to play basketball with employees of Brooklyn Union Gas Co. He feels that his Midwestern upbringing gave him a certain common sense that helps him spot overvalued stocks. He leans to companies that are carrying a lot of debt, and he quotes with approval a friend's dictum: "Asset values are contingent, but debt is forever." Baldwin-United, he says, exemplifies the kind of company he looks for—"stupendously leveraged, no operating earnings, and a stock price dependent on asset values that were not sustainable."

He likes to short companies that are followed by few analysts because he thinks they are probably not well understood. "As a rough-and-ready guide to the quality of cover-age," he says. "I look at total capitalization, including debt, and then divide by the number of analysts who cover the company."

Southland Financial, a Texas real estate development out-fit, was an example of a hot-stock company covered by few analysts. Because management advertised that the company was for sale and because then-renowned Ivan Boesky owned 10 percent, the stock spiked to $28.50 a share. The market capitalization—number of shares times price per share—bal-looned to $478 million despite Southland's 1986 loss of $41.9 million on revenues of $58.8 million. "It had all the things I like," says Chanos. The stock tanked to $5.75 a share when investors discovered that no one wanted to buy Southland at anywhere near its inflated valuation. Chanos, like most shorts, prefers not to say whether he has covered his entire position.

Chanos loses some, of course. The first quarter of 1987 was bad for him, and only a solid second quarter let him break even for the first half of the year. "I've been short the cable TV stocks, and that has been a fiasco," he says. "They've all doubled on me. People trade the cable systems at ever higher asset values per subscriber."

Another shortseller who prefers to short sizable compa-nies is Jim Rogers, forty-four. Rogers, originally from Ala-bama, has made many millions selling short. He lives in a sumptuous townhouse overlooking the Hudson River on Manhattan's Upper West Side. Partly retired from Wall Street, he teaches security analysis at Columbia University's busi-ness school.

While Rogers and Chanos do not work in concert, they meet once or twice a year for lunch to discuss investing ideas. Their first meeting, in 1983, came about because Rogers—who also went to Yale—was interested in hearing the younger man's short-sale ideas. It is a rite of passage for rookie short-sellers to meet stars and try to impress them with the quality of their stock analysis.

Rogers still sells short, and these days his main targets are big financial companies. "I'm short a raft of financial services companies because that is where I see excesses in the economy." Morgan Stanley is a favorite of his. "It's nothing personal, truly," he says. "Morgan Stanley is a great investment bank. Just overvalued in my opinion." If Drexel Burnham Lambert were publicly traded, Rogers adds, he would cover Morgan Stanley and all his other financial services short sales and go short on Drexel. He thinks that firm's heavy involvement in junk bonds will make it vulnerable in an economic downturn.

In contrast to Rogers and Chanos, some shortsellers concentrate on small, seamy companies where hype, fraud, or dubious accounting is often found. Connoisseurs of sleazy stocks are the three Feshbach brothers—fraternal twins Joe and Matt, thirty-four, and their older brother, Kurt, thirty-five. The Feshbachs go for what Joe calls "terminal" stocks that will drop even if the Dow goes to 3000. "We want to be sure we short lousy ones," he says. "Frauds and bankruptcy candidates and accounting fiascos."

The brothers work from messy offices in Menlo Park and Palo Alto, California. Since they began shorting in June 1982, when the Dow sat on its tuffet around 800, the Feshbachs have yet to endure a down year. Their fund was up 248 percent in 1984. In the worst year so far, 1985, it rose 44 percent. They made 62 percent last year, but the fund is up only 13 percent for the first half of 1987 because the brothers made a mistake and shorted a large block of Reebok International shares. After watching the price rise, they covered at a loss.

Reinvested profits and money from outside investors have pushed the total under Feshbach management to over $100 million. The fund is not open to new money just now. When it does reopen, the minimum investment in the partnership will be $2 million.

The Feshbachs must be the only big-time shortsellers who are also converts to Scientology, founded by science fiction writer L. Ron Hubbard. They keep copies of Hubbard's book *Dianetics: The Modern Science of Mental Health* at the office. Matt recently opened a second office in Florida to be closer to a teacher of Scientology, which purports to free people of psychological problems. What role Scientology plays in the brothers' investing is unclear. Perhaps it strengthens their confidence and discipline to short as aggressively as they do.

One of the Feshbachs' most profitable short sales in the past year was ZZZZ Best, a carpet-cleaning company that went bankrupt in July. They investigated the company after the chief financial officer was accused by customers of having stolen over $92,000 from them by charging flowers to their credit cards at a florist business he owned. To the Feshbachs' surprise, ZZZZ Best's twenty-one-year-old president did not fire the executive. Their suspicion grew when they saw ZZZZ Best's claim to have a $7-million contract to restore damaged carpets in Sacramento, California. A young analyst with the Feshbachs quickly discovered by talking to reputable carpet cleaners that no contract that size had ever been won anywhere in the U.S., let alone in Sacramento. "So we started to short the stock at $6," says Joe. "It ran all the way to $10 and we kept shorting." ZZZZ Best currently trades at 25 cents a share.

Other shortsellers admire the Feshbachs for their work on the Cannon Group, maker of such schlock films as *The Last American Virgin* and *Death Wish II*. Kurt heard about Cannon from a broker when he was living in Los Angeles in 1984. Wall Street was in love with the stock. The company was reporting impressive earnings. Says Kurt: "They claimed in their reports to shareholders that by preselling movies for cable and videocassettes and foreign rights they had already covered production costs." But since Cannon was making ever more expensive films and almost none were box-office hits, the Feshbachs could not figure out how the company was paying its overhead, interest, and other expenses.

Talking with former employees and the people who booked Cannon's films, Kurt discovered that management was understating costs, which dramatically boosted reported earnings. Rumors that the SEC was investigating Cannon's books began to surface in June 1986, and the stock peaked at $45.50 a share. It bombed to $2.63 and is now at $4.

Though professional shortsellers make good livings and some get rich, money is not their only motivation. They could also make money on the long side of the market, where their combination of diligent research, analysis, and fortitude would serve them well. Says a Texas shortseller: "My wife teases me, 'Why don't you just be happy and buy stocks?' " One reason is that shorts find winning on the short side more pleasurable than winning on the long side. James Grant, publisher of *Grant's Interest Rate Observer*, offers an explanation: "It might have been sweet owning Cannon Group when it went from $10 to $40, but it must have been triply sweet being short on the way to $3 a share because you saw the optimists in disarray when the company's preposterous claims and cockeyed accounting exploded in their faces."

New York psychiatrist Wilbert Sykes thinks he knows why shortsellers get such kicks from shorting. He suggests that they see themselves as outsiders and enjoy undermining the investing game. "Shortsellers," he says, "like an atmosphere that justifies their picked-on feeling. When the hostility and envy and jealousy cascade upon them, they see it as proof that they are getting the kind of attention they deserve." According to Sykes, shorts may actually enjoy the snide remarks, hate mail, and lawsuits heaped on them by corporate executives, shareholders, and investment bankers.

A shortseller demurs: "I don't want to be thought of as a destructive person. But not everybody understands what we do and likes us."

Some shortsellers admit to getting satisfaction from shorting companies they despise. Says a New Yorker: "Most of these really good shorts are run by charlatans, thieves, and dogs." Having shorted a tobacco company, he worries that his investment may stem more from hatred than from cold-blooded desire to earn a profit. "Those people are selling chewing tobacco to kids, telling them it's macho. I would be delighted to see those guys go under. I would cheer."

Another facet of shortseller psychology can be glimpsed in the following true story. On a grim down day on Wall Street, two veteran shorts were gleefully chatting on the telephone about what a wonderful day it had been. One said, "Bill, I don't understand it, but when a short goes my way it is really fabulous." The other replied, "Jonathan, don't you realize? It *is* fabulous. It's sexual. You're screwing somebody."

A sense that somebody gets "screwed" may help account

for the negative attitude many people have toward shortselling. They feel there is something disreputable about it. Quite a few Americans would agree with Robert Price, president of Price Communications Corp., a New York radio and television company. "I find no redeeming feature in shortselling, nor is it necessary or proper in a free-enterprise society," Price says. "It is just not sympathetic to the American philosophy, which is positive. Shortsellers are not a positive force. I wouldn't want my daughter to marry one." Price is no impartial observer, though: There is a big short interest in the stock of his company, and he does not like it.

Two Texas companies targeted by shortsellers have formed a posse to get them. Commonwealth Financial Group, a troubled Houston savings and loan, teamed up with Carrington Laboratories of Dallas, which claims to have an AIDS treatment using aloe vera, to attract attention to alleged illegal shortselling of their stocks. They say that shortsellers spread false and misleading information about companies to knock their stocks down. Commonwealth is using its public relations firm, Hill & Knowlton, to help put the message across.

The two companies also complain that shortsellers use the press to get publicity for negative stories on stocks they have a position in. Shortsellers retort that the press hears a lot more from companies and long investors than from shorts. Says Jim Rogers: "Go to Harry's Bar and see the gigantic amount of pumping that goes on for stocks people own. Lies being told. Exaggeration and hyperbole."

So far, SEC officials do not think much of the attacking companies' allegations. Says Richard Wessel, associate director for market regulation: "One company has come to us in person—officials and lawyers from Commonwealth, who claim they and other companies are being injured. I personally was not overwhelmed with their arguments. I have not yet been presented with proof that it really is a problem." Wessel's peer on the enforcement side of the SEC, associate director William McLucas, says he cannot remember an instance in which he took action against a shortseller for manipulation.

In defending themselves against target-company complaints, shorts can point to a 1986 study of shortselling by Irving Pollack, a former SEC commissioner. Pollack examined eleven cases and found no basis for company allegations that shortsellers misused the press.

Encountering hostility during a bull market, shorts sometimes wonder what a bear market will bring. Financially, they should do fine: The overvalued stocks they had sold short would top out sooner and fall faster. But some shortsellers, Jim Rogers among them, fear that negative feelings about shorting could turn venomous in a bad bear market, as battered investors see their assets and hopes shrivel.

Jim Grant thinks the stage is being set for a congressional inquisition, like the hearings on shortselling after the market drop in 1937. He says that if the 1930s were repeated, "shorts would be literally or figuratively hanged." Shortsellers may find some consolation in the thought that if these dire forebodings come true and they are hauled up before Congress, they will have made enough money on the short side to afford expensive lawyers.

Wall Street Traders' Ghastly Day

Steve Coll

October 19, 1987, the *Washington Post*

Steve Coll's story is the single best piece written about the October 1987 crash. He had the simple but brilliant idea to sit next to a stock trader and chronicle the guy's reaction to the debacle. This trader's nightmarish day captures the terror and despair that was rampant on Wall Street that day.

AT THE END, when the market capitulated into free fall, Mark Mehl, the thirty-five-year-old director of institutional stock trading at the large Wall Street firm Drexel Burnham Lambert Inc., lapsed into an eerie and private silence.

Chaos raged around him—hoarse voices shouted orders, shirt-sleeved traders juggled telephones, news flashed across the big electronic screens in Drexel's open stock trading room—but Mehl just sat there, staring at his computer screen. All day he had been trying to provide some leadership: standing and clapping at his traders like a football coach, barking encouragement into a microphone, and sometimes banging on a cookie tin to make himself heard above the din.

Now, just after 3 P.M., he sat sullenly behind his module of telephone banks, computer terminals and electronic tickers. His shoulders were slumped and his chin rested on his hand.

"The honest answer is, I've been a little humbled," Mehl said when asked what had come over him. "And when I get humbled, I stay quiet. We took our bet earlier today. We made a mistake."

At midday, Mehl had bet the market had bottomed out, and he was wrong.

"I was a superstar for four hours," Mehl reflected a little later. "Then I was a [expletive]." Mehl was hardly alone on Wall Street today. In the trading rooms of the financial district's great investment houses, on the floor of the New York Stock Exchange, and in the hundreds of small brokerages and investment firms nestled in Wall Street's towering skyscrapers, young traders and investors watched history being made at their expense.

They cracked jokes about it, they slapped each other on the back and talked about changing careers, they shouted wild, profane curses into the air—and sometimes, as happened to Mehl, they sat still and let it all sink in.

Just after 4 P.M., when the market had closed and the day's bottom had finally been measured, some of them poured into the streets, congregating at the historic corner of Broad and Wall, over which the powerful, columned investment house of legendary financier J. P. Morgan still looms some fifty-eight years after the 1929 market crash that shattered his grip on the nation's economy.

Cranes hoisted television cameras above the crowd that swarmed in front of the New York Stock Exchange to record this latest, and even more dramatic, market dive for posterity.

Just a few doors down from the stock exchange, on the ninth floor of 60 Broad Street, Mehl, Sam Hunter, the Drexel senior vice president who oversees all the firm's stock trading, and other executives of the firm drifted into evening meetings called to assess the day's devastation.

"I'm a little blown out," Mehl said when he emerged from one gathering. "My intellect—which is now totally useless after today—tells me that the [stock] markets may get a big lift tomorrow. But the markets can do what they want. They proved that today."

Just seven hours earlier, at 11 A.M., Mehl, Hunter, and the others had been certain that they had beaten the market—they thought they were winners. The Dow Jones industrial average was down about 250 points, a drop so steep it was almost unimaginable on Friday. Mehl, who directs stock trading for his firm as well as its clients, thought the worst was over. And he decided to make a multimillion-dollar bet. The bet would affect both his firm and its clients.

Over the next five hours, until the market closed, Mehl, Hunter, and the dozens of stock traders under their supervision rode an emotional and financial roller coaster that sapped their spirits as well as their wallets.

"We're having a ball here—we've finally got this thing turned around," Hunter shouted at 11:26 A.M., slamming his fist on the desk in front of him. The computer screen before him flashed the good news: After plummeting straight down from the beginning of trading, the Dow was finally on the rebound. And it was climbing fast.

Mehl, a lanky man wearing round wire-rimmed glasses, a pink shirt and a brown paisley tie, was nearly beside himself with enthusiasm.

"All you little weasels! I want your orders!" he shouted to the dozens of traders standing at partitioned, open desks in front of him.

With the Dow rising and the bond market improving, Mehl wanted to buy stock—and buy in big amounts. He was confident.

"You've seen the lows for a long, long time," he shouted into his microphone to his traders. "I want to be long [a buyer of stock] the limit! I want to be long the limit! We saw the bottom!"

His energy and enthusiasm were palpable. Grasping his telephone cord, he twirled the receiver as if it were a baton.

Mehl sat back down and looked at Hunter, his superior, a gray-haired, twenty-seven-year Wall Street veteran. Hunter patted Mehl on the back. "The arbs [speculators in takeover stocks] are being destroyed," Hunter remarked.

For a while, it looked like Mehl and Hunter had bet it exactly right. The Dow drove up steadily, until it was down 150 points, then 125, then down just over 100 points. The index was moving faster than it ever had before.

At fifteen minutes before noon, Mehl turned to one of his traders and said: "Did you cancel that vacation? We've got a lot of work to do this week. We're going to make a few million dollars."

"Only in America!" the trader yelled. "Go Twins! Let's do it!"

"This market's going to be tested again," Mehl said, turning to a visitor to explain his strategy. Still, Mehl said, while the Dow was already at a record low, and while he believed it would go lower again before the day was through, he was confident that he had seen the worst, and that now was the time to be a buyer of stock.

"Adversity creates opportunity," Mehl declared. "I think we've seen the lows for three or four months {to come}."

It didn't turn out that way.

Just after noon, the Dow began to slip again. From being down 108 points, it slipped to down 120. Ten minutes later, it was down 150. Mehl could feel that the ground was breaking, he said. This was the test he had anticipated.

At 12:35 P.M., the Dow was down 177 points.

"Let's put our money where our mouth is and find some stocks to buy," Mehl said.

He was still standing and shouting, rallying the troops, answering questions from his traders, pushing them on. He had flown in from business in Tokyo on Sunday, he said, and was working on just one hour's sleep. Jet lag, he said.

"I'm doing the best I can, boys," he shouted at his traders.

At 2:05 P.M., it was clear that the market was not going to pass this latest test. Volume was at 426 million shares— almost 100 million shares above Friday's record for an entire day. The Dow was down 287 points. Mehl was losing his bet.

"This is a day I'm going to remember the rest of my life," he said. Then: "We had a good two hours and then a bad one hour."

There was still hope in his voice. The market had two more hours to go. Perhaps it would come back.

Mehl huddled with Hunter and two other traders. "Unless the world's coming to an end six months from now and we just don't know it, this market's out of whack," Mehl told them. "If the world's coming to an end, I don't feel so bad."

It was 2:14 P.M. A minute later, Hunter stood up and shouted to the floor: "Don't let any of these buyers get out of the house!"

But after thirty minutes or so of firmness, the market began to fall again, and this time it fell hard. The Dow measure blinking on Mehl's computer screen changed virtually every second. Down 250. Then 300.

With more than an hour to go and the market spinning wildly down, the mood in the Drexel trading room began to change. Mehl fell into a private silence and stared at his computer. Hunter disappeared for a while. The traders grew more angry, more profane.

At 2:27 P.M., a message came over the large electronic Dow Jones news ticker at the far end of the room. It said President Reagan might make a statement about the market's plunge after the market closed.

The traders began to hoot and laugh. "It's Herbert Hoover all over again," Hunter declared loudly.

A trader approached Mehl and asked him, given the market's progress, whether it didn't now make sense to sell a particular stock short—that is, bet that its price would soon go down.

"Eight days ago that stock was at $82," Mehl snapped. "I don't feel like shorting it at $59."

At 2:40 P.M., Mehl's computer screen told him that declining stocks on the New York exchange outnumbered advancing ones by a forty-to-one margin.

"The government has to intervene," Mehl said with exasperation in his voice.

The free fall began just after 3 P.M. The Dow was down 350 points. Then 400. Then 450.

"I can't imagine it going any lower than that," Mehl said when the Dow was down 400. "I guess I should learn to imagine anything."

"There's not a [expletive] thing we can do," Hunter said.

The Gaga Years

Joseph Nocera

February 1988, *Esquire*

This book would probably be titled something incredibly dull like Wall Street in the 1980s *if not for Joe Nocera, who wrote "The Gaga Years" for* Esquire. *Herewith you will find a fabulous history of how the bull market seduced Americans and "brought money lust out of the closet." There is no better, no more entertaining story of the rise of personal investing in contemporary America. Nocera covers all the key players, from master investor Peter Lynch of Fidelity to master promoter Marshall Loeb of* Money *magazine. Thanks, Joe.*

JANUARY 28, 1987. DOW JONES opening average: 2163.39 It's ten in the morning, and the Dow has already risen eighteen points. Amazing. Like everyone else, I've become transfixed by the astonishing upward spiral of the Dow, up almost 250 points since New Year's Day, four and a half years into the greatest bull market in history. Usually, though, I try to wait at least until the evening news. Today I am standing in a posh storefront in Manhattan, at the corner of Fifty-first Street and Park Avenue, a vantage point from which it would take a supreme act of will not to keep track of the Dow's every tick. This is the New York City beachhead of Fidelity Investments, the giant Boston-based mutual-fund company that manages more money for more people than any other company in the world.

It's quite a spectacle here at Fifty-first and Park. Right now I'm staring up at an electronic board that resembles one of those overhead scoreboards you find in modern arenas. Only

125

instead of scores, it's spewing out the current value of Fidelity's Select funds—high-risk mutual funds that invest in only one industry. A light show for the 1980s. Amber numbers flicker across the screen, disappear, and then blip up again. Every hour the numbers are updated. At the bottom of the board flashes the most dazzling prop of all: the Dow itself. Which has just gone up another six points.

If money is the new sex—and isn't that what everyone is saying?—then this place is the whorehouse. The scent of the market is powerful here, intoxicating. All around me I can see the blandishments of money, the seduction of wealth, the lure of financial security. A recorded voice entices: "Choosing an investment should be as easy as watching TV." The aisles are lined with fund prospectuses. FIDELITY MAGELLAN, says a sign in front of one stack, ONE OF AMERICA'S MOST POPULAR FUNDS. MUNICIPAL BONDS, purrs another a few aisles over, THEY'RE NOT JUST FOR THE WEALTHY ANYMORE. I leaf through a few prospectuses. Is it my imagination, or is there a certain furtiveness to this act, like the way men thumb through *Penthouse* at an airport newsstand?

I see a woman outside, her face pressed hard against the window. She is a meter maid, young and black, and to judge from her expression, this place might just as well be Tiffany's. "She comes by every day," whispers a Fidelity saleswoman. "She really wants to make an investment, you can tell." Just then the woman steps haltingly through the revolving door. Once inside, she looks gaga at all she sees. This strikes me as the only appropriate response in the face of such irresistible come-ons. If the bull-market late 1960s were the Go-Go Years, then surely these are the Gaga Years.

I wander over to a bank of computers to punch up a few stock quotes but become distracted by a couple standing next to me. Complete strangers, they are deeply engrossed in conversation. The man looks like Robin Williams, only 20 years older; the woman is that classic type, the little old lady who dabbles in the market. In any other setting, it would be impossible to guess that these two are part of the Gaga Years. Yet this is what I hear them say:

She: "My mistake was selling my Carter-Wallace. You know, because of the AIDS thing. Sold it over a year ago."

He: "I hear Pan Am is supposed to be sold."

She: "A Philip Morris man said to me, 'You won't go wrong investing in Philip Morris.' " She sighs. "But I didn't."

He nods in sympathy. "Philip Morris is the finest of the tobacco companies."

They dawdle for most of the afternoon, talking, comparing investment notes, calling up stock quotes. Finally they walk out together. They are friends now. They met at Fidelity. They have the market in common. So did we all.

It seems so long ago, doesn't it—those days of gaga, when the market looked as if it would never stop rising? Black Monday, it is safe to say, will mark the end of the Gaga Years. And what images will remain? After the Go-Go Years of the 1960s, the names that stuck were Gerry Tsai and Bernie Cornfeld. This time the symbols will undoubtedly include Drexel Burnham and Boone Pickens and Ivan Boesky. And Fidelity. Just as Drexel will stand for the rise of the junk bond and Boesky for the wages of greed, so will Fidelity conjure up the return of the equity mutual fund.

At its peak, Fidelity had $85 billion in assets, which made it a larger investor of people's money than even Merrill Lynch. It had the most funds—more than one hundred—and in Magellan, it had the largest fund, which was run by the most famous portfolio manager, Peter Lynch. Fidelity became such an icon of the Gaga Years that on Black Monday reporters scrambled not to the stock exchange to get reactions but to Fidelity.

I spent much of last year hanging around Fidelity, seeing in this exercise both a means of coming to terms with the Gaga Years and a way of getting at the modern history of money in which Fidelity has played such a crucial role. I was at Fidelity when the Dow made some of its great gains. I was there when the crash came, too. Fidelity was always moderately enthusiastic about my endeavor, allowing me considerable access— though never so enthusiastic as to give me free run of the place. This, I was told, was the way things were, the way Mr. Johnson wanted it. Edward Johnson III, a reserved and somewhat eccentric Boston Brahmin, had run Fidelity since 1972 and was universally credited with being the genius behind the company's rise. As I began my quest, I wanted to learn more about him, too. Not least, I wanted to know how he saw the Gaga Years coming and got there first.

The History of Money: A Preamble

Gerry Tsai began his career at Fidelity—he not only got his start there but also became famous there: the first portfolio manager to get the press of a rock star. It was a different world then, a world in which the middle class still squirreled away its money in banks and small mutual-fund companies such as Fidelity were easily dwarfed by a superstar fund manager. Fidelity was also run by a different Mr. Johnson—Edward Johnson II.

Johnson was a Boston Brahmin in a profession dominated by Boston Brahmins. But though he was one of them by virtue of class and bearing, he had nothing but scorn for the way they approached money management. He believed that mutual funds should be managed by one person using his own instincts to trade stocks. And of course he was right. By the early 1960s, Johnson had created an entirely new species, the fund manager, and had charged it with one simple (and radical) mission: to beat the market by as much as possible.

Because Johnson believed that money management was too important to be left to Brahmin money managers, he wasn't afraid to hire Gerry Tsai, a young, untested immigrant from Shanghai, as a stock analyst in the early 1950s. When Tsai began running a fund in 1957, he became the embodiment of Johnson's theories. No one had ever run a fund the way he did. He bought all the glamour stocks of the day: the conglomerates with their bloated price-equity ratios. The turnover in his portfolio was dizzying: 120 percent in 1965 alone. The same year Capital Fund gained an unheard-of 50 percent. Tsai's performance made him famous, and his fame brought him customers; by the mid-1960s, he was managing well over $1 billion.

And then he was gone. Legend has it that the departure was precipitated by a meeting with Mr. Johnson in which the younger man asked about succession, and the older man replied that he expected his son to take over when he retired. Edward Johnson III, known as Ned, was running another Fidelity fund and outperforming the master as often as not.

Tsai moved to New York City to start a new fund, called the Manhattan Fund, hoping to raise $25 million. But so many people wanted to bottle the Tsai magic that when his new fund began life, in February 1966, it had an incredible $247 million. And of course that's when Tsai's touch deserted him. In 1968 the bottom fell out of the Manhattan Fund, and Tsai's fall from grace became the parable for the Go-Go Years. Shortly thereafter the bottom dropped out of the Dow itself, and everyone got a similar comeuppance. But Tsai went first and loudest, and for that he will be forever remembered.

Fidelity itself was hardly immune to the market downturn. Mutual funds can never gain while the broader market is losing; the best a portfolio manager can do is lose less than the market. But during the Go-Go Years, funds had been spectacularly hyped; now, as profits turned to losses, people felt burned, and they began doing exactly what you'd expect: redeeming their mutual-fund shares with a vengeance and putting their money back into the bank, where (they now thought) it should probably have been all along.

The result was that when Johnson II finally handed the baton to Johnson III in 1972, Fidelity was in trouble. Some of the younger Johnson's first acts as boss included firing people he had worked with for years. That wasn't enough. He needed something else, something more dramatic. And then he saw it. A man named Bruce Bent, operating out of a tiny office in New York City, had invented a strange new fund. It was called the money-market fund, and its creation marked the start of the modern history of money.

March 5, 1987. Dow Jones Average: 2276.43

"The idea came to me in the summer of 1969," Bruce Bent is saying. It is late on a brisk afternoon in March, and the market has closed for the day. (Up twenty points today! More than three hundred on the year!) We're sitting in Bent's corner office on the thirty-fifth floor of a slightly seedy Manhattan office building. He is a trim, handsome man, fifty years old now, with a face like Jack Kemp's—a face enhanced by the first few creases of age. Yet there is a certain prophet-without-honor quality about him. The carpet is faded. The furniture is old—not antique old but 1950s old. Bent's company, called the Reserve Fund, handles only money-market funds, which puts it at one remove from the bull market. While I was waiting in the lobby, I took a look at Bent's prospectus. His funds have only $2.7 billion in assets—peanuts compared to even a small mutual-fund company. If this bothers him, he hides it well.

"It was the summer of 1969," he begins again, smiling as he recalls the time he changed the world. "My partner and I had started our own investment firm. We didn't have any capital, and I was stuck on one question: How could you get money to come to you? Well, the answer was plain as day. *You had to pay higher interest rates than anyone else!*"

In those days, bank savings accounts were limited to 5¼ percent because of something called Regulation Q, a government-imposed ceiling on the interest a depositor could earn. Banks loved Regulation Q because it meant they took in money at an artificially low rate and then turned around and loaned the same money at whatever the market would bear. Bent wanted to find a way around Regulation Q, which he did by inventing the money-market fund. A money-market fund uses "deposits" from investors to make extremely short-term loans to corporations or the government. Like a bank, a money fund could charge market interest rates for those loans. But since it wasn't a bank (no Regulation Q!), it could also grant those same rates to its investors. The fund itself would make money by charging a management fee.

"In February 1970," Bent says, returning to his story, "we filed with the Securities and Exchange Commission. The guy said, 'I think we're going to have a problem with this thing.' For the next year and a half we went back and forth on it. The SEC people just didn't get it. Finally, in November 1971, they let us go ahead. I'm sure they only let us do it because they thought it was going to die."

Can you guess what comes next? Our prophet is rebuffed at every turn. Meanwhile, Bent is trying to support a wife and two children on zero income. "On bad days, I ate franks," he recalls. "On good days, I ate in the Penney's cafeteria. I took out a home-improvement loan and used it to buy food. I starting having trouble handling things, to tell you the truth. My wife, thank God, she understood I had this vision."

On January 7, 1973—more than a year after the SEC approval—Bent got a big break. A *New York Times* reporter wrote a short article about the fund. "The next day we got a hundred phone calls," says Bent. "By the end of the year we had $100 million in assets. People I knew on Wall Street would send their mothers to me. Little old ladies would say to me, 'My son told me you have a good thing.' Then they'd say, 'I'm nervous and I don't want to lose my money.' "

And, as we all know by now, they didn't. Money-market funds turned out to be great investments for little old ladies, because unless the fund manager was stupid beyond belief, the principal was never at risk. Only the interest fluctuated. However, since most of us didn't have sons working on Wall Street, it took a long time to figure that out.

It did not, however, take the mutual-fund industry long to see what the money funds were: salvation itself. Here was the means to win back some of those dwindling assets.

"And then," says Bent, finishing his story, "Ned Johnson figured out how to let people write checks against a money-market fund. That really added value."

The History of Money: The Early Years

Do you remember 1974? Do you remember any of your friends' investing in money-market funds? I do. I remember exactly one couple. I thought they were out of their minds. So did all their other friends.

Actually, the mutual-fund industry thought Ned Johnson was pretty crazy back then too, what with this check-writing nuttiness. Check writing violated the principle that was closest to the industry's heart: make it simple to get into a fund but hard to get out of one. But somehow Johnson saw what no one else did. The money fund wasn't just a temporary stopgap: rather, it marked the beginning of a new era, an era in which people would have options for their hard-earned money. To get them to hand their money to Fidelity, Johnson realized that he would have to treat the buyers of Fidelity "products" the same way McDonald's treated the buyers of hamburgers. Like *customers*. This was his revelation.

Johnson's check-writing feature was the second great invention in the modern history of money. The addition of checks gave the impression that money-market funds were like banks—they felt safe. People who invested in them could still think of themselves as savers. In effect, Johnson had begun to blur the distinction between investor and saver.

Fidelity's money-market fund opened for business on June 12, 1974, and was an immediate hit. It was called the Fidelity Daily Income Trust, or FIDIT. Its logo was a frog (*fidit, ribit*—get it?), and Johnson began scattering frog images about his office. This only reinforced his image as an eccentric, an image that was then approaching legendary proportions.

Certainly what he was doing to Fidelity seemed eccentric, even to the people on the inside. *Especially* to the people on the inside. Here was this company still starved for cash, and the boss was spending millions upon millions of dollars. And on what? Well, there were all the fancy new computers Fidelity suddenly had. Now, no one was saying that Fidelity didn't need computers. But the computers Johnson bought were so full of bells and whistles that they seemed all out of proportion to Fidelity's needs.

And the telephones! Fidelity employed six reps who worked in an awful windowless room answering calls at random. The six had been hired after Fidelity started running its ads and quickly discovered—and my, wasn't *this* interesting—that people would phone in with questions. Overnight, Fidelity had as sophisticated a system as an airline.

Johnson made Fidelity completely self-sufficient, with its own systems company and its own service company and, eventually, its own taxi company. By 1978, Fidelity had gone from being a company that could monitor phone calls weekly to one that could monitor them hourly. But *why?*

Do you remember 1978? You should; that was the year you started to think about your money again. Not that you had much choice; inflation was approaching double digits and interest rates were already there. Both were gnawing away at your standard of living. By then, though, the money revolution had come. As you looked around, you suddenly realized that there were ways to outsmart inflation. If you owned a house, you felt great. Houses were great inflation-beaters You hired an accountant for the first time, and he told you to borrow as much as you could against your Mastercharge, on which the interest was fixed by law, and put that money in a money-market account earning a few percentage points more. And you did it. And it was a real kick: you were making money on the spread. And then there was the night you woke up with a start and realized what an absolute idiot you'd been to keep your savings in the bank, where Regulation Q and inflation were robbing you. This was a truly terrible moment. You felt a little panicky, and you vowed that the very next day you would switch to a money-market account, the way all your friends were doing.

Do you remember the moment? That was the moment Ned Johnson had been planning for.

May 14, 1987. Dow Jones Average: 2329.68

"Fidelity Investments. This is Wendell Weaver. How may I help you?"

Weaver, who is twenty-three years old, who is wearing a pair of oversized glasses that make him look like an exaggerated character out of a Jeff MacNelly sketchbook, who exudes a naive wholesomeness that would do Jimmy Stewart proud, is sitting in a tiny cubicle on the eighth floor of a banal Dallas high-rise answering the phones. He is joined, on this hot Texas night, by twenty-seven other phone reps manning similar stations in a long, open room. He sits erect, his gangly frame on red alert as he awaits the next call. They come with some frequency.

"Let's see," he says into the receiver, glancing over at a sheet filled with the day's closing prices. "Magellan, up .15. Puritan, down 1. Overseas Fund, down .59 to 40.88. Looks like there was some profit-taking in the Japanese market." Next call: "Yes, sir. The Ginnie Mae Fund has been taking some substantial losses. Why? Well, when interest rates go up, bond prices go down." Next call: "The price of the yen? Just a minute." He pulls out his copy of the *Wall Street Journal* and rattles off the price of the yen. The calls stop coming for a minute, and he glances at his watch. It's a little after midnight. Welcome to the graveyard shift at Fidelity.

It's May. The Dow is still going up, though it's had a few little tumbles lately—those triple witching hours are murder. No one seems too worried, though. Certainly there is no sense of worry here on the eighth floor. Off in the distance I can see downtown Dallas, giving off the illusion of quiet that big cities often emit at night. Things are quiet in here, too, despite the low buzz of telephone talk.

If the portfolio managers in Boston are the beating heart of Fidelity, then this phone operation in Dallas is the belly of the beast. When Johnson put those six people in that little room, the phone became the company's weapon of choice. People who want to switch from one fund to another can do so by picking up the phone. They can call to make stock trades through Fidelity's discount brokerage. They can call just for the hell of it, twenty-four hours a day, seven days a week.

And Lord knows they do. In a way, the Fidelity phone centers—there are similar setups in Boston and Salt Lake City—are the belly of the Gaga Years, too. Especially at night. Why, I wonder, are people calling Fidelity instead of going to bed? In February 1986, when Fidelity began answering the phone all night, it didn't even bother doing market research. It just knew.

Neither Weaver nor anyone else in Dallas can recall the phones' ever shutting down completely, except on the day the space shuttle blew up. Then, as the shock wore off, the lines were suddenly jammed, the callers all asking the same warped question: *"What's it going to mean for the market?"*

Here in the middle of the bull market, one can see how firmly the gaga mentality has taken hold. Weaver detects a certain frantic tone from callers lately, as people who know nothing about the market try to climb aboard, worried that the train is leaving the station. "I spend a lot of time explaining what a dividend is," is how he puts it.

By the time Weaver came on duty at 11 P.M., the day's market headline was obvious. So jaded has everyone become by big gains that the Dow's rise on this day, a "mere" seven points, is a snore. Instead, most callers want to talk about the *Japanese* market, which has dropped 172 points, a fact of passionate concern to the many shareholders of a fund called Fidelity Overseas. Overseas was the number-one fund in the country in 1986, which was due in no small part to its Japanese holding. As a result of that record, it now has some one hundred-thousand shareholders, most of whom seem to be on the other end of the phone tonight.

At one in the morning an anxious shareholder calls to say that he has $36,000 in Overseas and what should he do? Weaver gives him a by-now-practiced speech. "It's not nearly as bad as two weeks ago," he says. "There's some profit-taking. And they're trying to stabilize the dollar. You're still looking at a 34 percent gain since the beginning of the year." Then a note of caution: "There is some instability in the foreign markets. You need to be aware of that."

It seems a little strange to me that this twenty-three-year-old kid is discussing the market with doctors and lawyers making ten times the $20,000 or so he makes. Or maybe it's not so strange. The doctors and lawyers can't see Weaver; they can only hear him. They hear his reassuring voice offering, in some weird way, comfort. "People want me to say it's okay," admits Weaver. But do you know what the whole thing reminds me of? It reminds me of the phone-sex business, in which women in curlers iron their husbands' shirts while talking dirty to some desperate soul in a hotel room.

One-thirty: a sudden upsurge in calls as Salt Lake City closes down, leaving only Dallas open. Weaver takes one from Fresno. New Mexico calls. At 3 A.M. Alabama calls, wanting to talk about the downturn in the Japanese market. After Alabama hangs up, Weaver tells me that he could hear the man eating breakfast. "I talk to people with toast in their mouth every day," he says.

The History of Money: The Middle Years

Early in 1980 there occurred one of those small, seemingly ho-hum events that later turn out to be fraught with significance. The event was the announcement by Time Inc. that Marshall Loeb had been named managing editor of *Money* magazine; its importance, in terms of the Gaga Years, was that by some happy accident, Time Inc. had managed to put precisely the right man in the right spot at the right moment.

Loeb, a nattily dressed man who resembles nothing so much as a leprechaun, was (and is) on the fast track at Time, while *Money* was the company's most snakebit publication, having done nothing but lose millions in its eight-year existence. Loeb's mandate, plainly, was to turn things around, which he did in classic golden-boy fashion, doubling the cir-

culation within two years. He did it by openly and shamelessly selling money as the new sex.

1980: time for another trip in the way-back machine. Interest rates had come down just a bit, but oddly, no one
seemed to be happy about it. Why was this? It's because,
thanks to the money-market fund, we'd become a nation of
interest-rate junkies. 1980 was also the year the banks tried to
put the clamps on the money funds, having finally realized
that Regulation Q was slowly killing their business. But the
banks never had a chance. The secret was out. Only suckers
put their money in savings accounts.

As interest rates declined, the fund pushers showed us
their other wares. We were interested now. We were curious.
As we looked for ways to keep making double-digit gains, we
saw . . .

"Choices!" Marshall Loeb practically leaps off his couch
in the Time-Life Building where he now edits *Fortune*. "Just
think of all the choices you had by then!" he exclaims. "You
had bond funds. You had tax-free bond funds. You had money-
market funds. You had *tax-free* money funds."

Eventually, you also had the bull market. When the market took off in August 1982, it became the new fix. Money
streamed into stocks and into their surrogate, the mutual
fund. This influx dwarfed anything that had come before
because so many more people were thinking about money
now. Here was the moment that the transformation from
saver to investor was complete.

Loeb believes that money became, in his words, "the most
discussed topic among consenting adults," as two-income
couples began talking about their money over dinner; it was
only a matter of time before those private conversations became cocktail-party talk. My own belief is that Loeb had a
microphone in the saltshaker, so sure was his feel for those
conversations. *"Money* magazine did good journalism," Loeb
insists defensively. But who was buying it for the journalism?
People were buying it for the fantasy—for the sex.

No one was more gaga during the Gaga Years than Loeb.
His trademark was the magazine's cover, on which he regularly put a wholesome young couple next to a headline that
read HOW TO TURN $50,000 INTO $250,000 IN JUST FIVE YEARS

What was this conceit if not the equivalent of *Playboy*'s centerfold? That you had as much chance of getting rich by following the example of the *Money* centerfold as you did of sleeping with a Playmate scarcely seemed to matter. People bought the magazine, took it home, and drooled.

Inevitably Loeb's magazine began intersecting regularly with Johnson's company. The first and most revealing incident came in April 1983, when *Money* chose a wholesome young Fidelity fund manager named Michael Kassen for its cover. The headline read HOW TO MAKE MONEY IN MUTUAL FUNDS. Underneath that: THEY'RE THE SUREST, SAFEST WAY TO INVEST IN A SURGING MARKET. And finally, the clincher: KASSEN, 30, RUNS A TECHNOLOGY FUND THAT HAS JUMPED 131 PERCENT SINCE AUGUST. A hundred and thirty-one percent!

Kassen's appearance in *Money* marked a kind of coming out for Fidelity. Ever since Tsai had left, portfolio managers had been forbidden to talk to the press, the lone exception being made for Peter Lynch, who was allowed guest appearances on Louis Rukeyser's show, *Wall Street Week*. That Johnson would now allow Kassen to speak freely to a *Money* reporter about his stock choices spoke volumes about how the world had changed. Fund companies needed every little edge now. In this new world, Johnson's decision to open Fidelity to the press was a given.

What was not a given was *Money*'s choice of Kassen to represent the "safety" and "sureness" of the mutual fund. Despite his undeniable talent for picking stocks, he was, in fact, probably the worst choice imaginable. His fund was anything *but* safe. It was called Fidelity Select Technology, and it did not invest broadly in the market like most funds but only in one segment: high technology. This caveat, however, never made its way into the *Money* article.

Kassen wound up feeling a little embarrassed by the publicity, but for Fidelity the experience exceeded its fondest hopes. When the article hit the newsstands in April, Kassen's fund was already an established hit, with a little more than $200 million. By July, it was closing in on $650 million. And then—poof!—the joyride was over. In August, technology stocks crashed, and so did Kassen's fund. He was working furiously now, trying to keep his head above water. And by any objective measure, he succeeded brilliantly. "Technology stocks were down 20 percent," he recalls, "and I was only down 10 percent."

Unfortunately, this was not much consolation to the people who had first learned of his walk-on-water mutual fund from *Money*. As Select Technology fell back during the second half of 1983, a lot of people discovered something about mutual funds that they hadn't quite comprehended before. The funds were not necessarily "sure." To be an investor, rather than a saver, meant accepting risks; and funds like Kassen's, geared to make the quick gain, also involved the most risk. But the lesson had not been learned from *Money* magazine. It had been learned with cold, hard cash.

July 28, 1987. Dow Jones Average: 2493.94

"Quite a paper this morning," says Peter Lynch, shaking his head in mock wonder. It is eight o'clock, and he is leaning back in the chair of his small corner office, leafing through the *Wall Street Journal*. Lynch, who is rumored to make $3 million a year managing Fidelity's Magellan Fund, is wearing a light blue seersucker suit, slightly worn and in desperate need of dry cleaning.

"Did you see what Boone did today?" Lynch asks. Pickens has announced plans to buy a $15 million stake in the giant airplane manufacturer Boeing. "I've got 20,000 shares of Boeing," Lynch says—a position worth a little more than a million dollars, pocket change for the $11 billion Magellan fund. Like most portfolio managers, he tends to refer to himself when he means his fund. "Someone forgot to tell that whole sector there's a bull market going on," he says with a shrug.

As Lynch makes his way through the paper, he finds a story that affects his life on almost every page. He groans over a report that American Express intends to buy back some of its shares. "Look at this." He shows me a printout that lists the previous day's performance of Magellan's 1,700 stocks. At the top of the sheet, written in pen and underlined for emphasis, are the words BUY AMEX. "I wrote it on the way in this morning. If only they had waited a month.

"Yup," says Lynch, shaking his head again. "It's quite a paper today."

Lynch may be the most famous portfolio manager of the Gaga Years, but he's not famous the way Gerry Tsai was twenty years ago. There is nothing flamboyant about him, nothing exotic, nothing larger than life. He is forty-three years old, tall and thin, his hair completely white, with classic Irish features. The only thing that sets him apart is this: for ten years now he has been the best mutual-fund manager alive.

Of all the smart moves Johnson made in the 1970s, the smartest may have been giving Magellan to Lynch. When he did so, back in 1977, Magellan was a nice little $22 million fund, and Lynch was head of research. Ten years and $11 billion later, Lynch could lay claim to one of the most fabulous statistics of the Gaga Years: if you had put $10,000 into Magellan when he took it over, you'd have made $175,000.

The result of Lynch's performance is that Magellan was a symbol of the Gaga Years even before they were over: a few years ago, it was an answer on the game show *Jeopardy*. It is the greatest marketing tool Fidelity has ever had, a powerful magnet pulling people into the company, making it the single biggest mutual fund in America. "Around Fidelity," says one former marketing aide, "Peter Lynch is God."

Well, maybe not *God*. But as the man who manages the franchise fund, his influence on the other portfolio managers is enormous. His lack of flash is part of the ethos of the equity shop. The suspender quotient is low here. Nor is there any flamboyance in the way Lynch and his colleagues buy and sell stocks. On this day in late July, fifteen companies will visit Fidelity; Lynch will see as many as he can. Frank Lorenzo touted Texas Air at breakfast. The officers of a small company in which Magellan holds a large position are scheduled for lunch. An oil analyst is coming by. When you have 1,700 stocks in your portfolio, your job can be defined rather simply: you have to know everything about everything.

At ten o'clock Lynch goes to his first meeting. "I bought a lot of your stock," he begins in a surprisingly soft voice. "Thanks for making me some money." Although there are a dozen people in the room, Lynch asks almost all the questions. As everyone settles into a chair, the CEO says, "We've had a good quarter, which we're reporting in three days. As you are valued shareholders, we'll trust you—" Lynch cuts him off. "We don't want to know that stuff," he says. Just tell us about the company."

Lynch dashes out of the meeting and heads back to his office. Suddenly everything seems to be happening at once. The phone rings—it's a company he's been trying to reach. The oil analyst has just arrived. A young Fidelity hand pops in to announce some second-quarter results. In the midst of this chaos, Lynch looks at me and says, "You know, the last two and a half years have been the worst in the last twenty." What's he talking about? The last two years have been great. Sensing my disbelief, he adds, "Eighty percent of the pros have lost in this market."

Well, sure. But to me, all that proves is the difference between the way Lynch thinks about money and the way the rest of us do. His goal is to beat the Standard & Poor's 500, while ours is to make more money than we could make in a bank or a money-market fund. Because of its enormous size, Magellan can no longer beat the market the way it once could; Lynch himself advises people looking for big gains to try another fund. But they don't. Magellan is where people want their money in the Gaga Years. And when they look up later and see he's made them 20 percent, they are very happy. Who cares if he hasn't beaten the Standard & Poor's 500?

In fact, most of the time he has. "I'm a little behind right now," he says. So far this year the Standard & Poor's 500 is up 33.8 percent. So I take it back. Maybe the guy *is* God.

Late in the afternoon Lynch turns his attention to me again. In the past few months, the mutual-fund backlash has been gaining ground. Magellan has been criticized for charging a high management fee. The industry has been criticized for peddling funds without explaining the risks, as happened during the excesses of the 1960s. But the worst cut of all came in May from the novelist Michael M. Thomas, who predicted a crash of the bull market triggered by the mutual funds. "When mutual-fund shareholders hit the panic button and start clamoring for redemptions of their shares," he wrote in *The Nation*, "the funds have no legal recourse but to come up with the money, and that could trigger a selling panic."

Has Lynch heard the criticism? "My mother used to say,

'Never play the market, because you'll lose it all,' " he tells me now, with more passion than I've heard from him all day. "But people don't have any choice anymore. They've been pushed into the market. I'm happy to beat the market by 4 or 5 percent. Last year I was up 23.7 percent or whatever the hell I was up last year. That's after the management fee, after the commissions—after everything." His voice is rising. *"This is a very efficient method for the public,"* he says with finality. He gives me a steely look that says, "This is not a point you want to argue with." Not today anyway.

August 13, 1987. Dow Jones Average: 2669.32

The whole thing is starting to get a little weird. The Dow was down today, eleven points, but it's been going up so far and so fast—up forty-four yesterday, up forty-three the day before, a new record every day—that there is a lot of talk that we're due for a correction. Or worse. Surely it can't go on forever.

Right now, though, I've got more important things on my mind. I'm sitting in Ned Johnson's office. Johnson, I've been told, does not give many interviews, and there was some question as to whether I'd be granted one. But at long last the moment has arrived.

Johnson's office is full of perfect Brahmin touches—tasteful paintings, discreet antiques—and also, I notice, the odd frog here and there; he likes to keep a few reminders of the old days. I spot a Quotron machine by his desk. Although Johnson hasn't managed a portfolio in years, I've heard he still loves the market. A few years ago, when Gerry Tsai joined American Can Company, Johnson called the person who manages his holdings and said, "I worked next to Tsai for five years. Buy twenty-thousand shares of American Can."

At fifty-seven, his hairline is long gone, but over the years his face has gotten thinner and longer, more dignified. There is still that sense about him that though his body may be here, his mind is a million miles away.

After some preliminary chitchat, I start the interview. "Mr. Johnson," I begin, "how did you come up with the idea of adding the check to the money-market fund?"

He instantly seems uncomfortable. "Oh, I don't know," he

replies with a sigh. "Ideas bubble up and down, and the ones that keep coming back up usually have the most merit." That's it. That's the whole answer.

Oh boy, I'm thinking. He's not going to make it easy. One more try. "Sir, what compelled you to do what you did in the 1970s? What did you see that no one else saw?"

This time he gives a helpless shrug. "I just assumed the equity market would come back. It always has before."

Do you know how I'm feeling here? I'm feeling like Dorothy in *The Wizard of Oz*, and I've just pulled back the curtain. This is the insight that changed the world? That the equity market was going to come back?

We talk for an hour, but the interview never really gets off the ground. Finally I thank him for his time and flip my notebook shut. And then a funny thing happens. Johnson becomes comfortable again. The act of closing the notebook has somehow freed him to talk. I can see it now: the wisps of sentences, the flash of ideas. I'm not saying I see genius, not in a ten-minute conversation, or even that I have any better understanding of where this very private man learned to see the future. But I am willing to concede now that he is capable of such a feat.

Just before I leave, I pop one last question. I ask him how long he thinks the bull market will last. But immediately Johnson reverts to his Dalai Lama–like pose. "How do you ever know when you've reached the top?" he replies. "Each crash is a little different from the one before it." He stares off into space. "They're all a little different," he repeats.

The History of Money: The Late Years

How do you know when you've reached the top? It's mid-August now, and the question is being asked with increasing frequency. I saw Loeb on television the other night pooh-poohing the bears. Then I saw Elaine Garzarelli of Shearson Lehman Brothers on CNN, making it sound as if collapse is imminent. It's hard to know what to think anymore.

And what is Fidelity saying about the market—Fidelity with its hundred delicious options for making money? Fidelity isn't saying anything. Fidelity believes that its job is simply to provide the choices. "There are huge attitudinal changes in this country," Rodger Lawson told me in August. Lawson heads Fidelity's giant marketing operation, and he was outlining Fidelity's official world view. "People want control," he said. "They want to make their own decisions."

But I'm not so sure. I think back to my night with Wendell Weaver, listening to callers practically plead for help. And I recall, too, an investing seminar I attended in Cambridge. The most memorable speaker was Dick Fabian, described by the master of ceremonies as "the father of mutual-fund switching." Flailing his arms like an evangelist, Fabian had proclaimed that everybody should be able to attain "20 percent-annualized - compounded - growth - with - no - down - side - risk-as-measured-over-a-five-year-period." He kept repeating these words like a mantra, until they hypnotized.

When Fabian left the podium, he was blocked by a mass of people who quickly surrounded him. To watch these people crowd around Fabian, to see the longing in their eyes, to listen to the desperate quality of their questions, was to realize that they did not feel freed by the new financial marketplace. They felt paralyzed by it. They were drowning in an ocean of choice, and they wanted Fabian to throw them the life preserver. They wanted him to tell them what to do. This, I think, is what people most crave as the Dow approaches 2700. But it is the one thing Fidelity won't provide.

On the fifth anniversary of the bull market, a balmy day in August in which the market had opened four-forty points up, I sat in on a meeting of Fidelity portfolio managers. More than sixteen people jammed into a small conference room, all members of the "income growth" group, which consists of more conservative funds than pure growth funds such as Magellan.

Leading the meeting was Bruce Johnstone, who manages both this group and his own huge fund, Equity-Income, which had returned 600 percent in ten years and bulged with $4.5 billion worth of conservative money. Short, balding, quick to laugh, Johnstone so overflows with guileless enthusiasm that he can get away with saying things like "I can't believe I've been so lucky to work with a genius like Ned. It's been great!"

The meeting was a freewheeling discussion of the market: where it had been, where it was going. Someone mentioned that the *Boston Herald*, the local Murdoch paper, had begun carrying a stock-market game. I'd noticed that, too. What could it mean, I wondered, when the lure of the Gaga Years had become so pervasive that Rupert Murdoch could use it as a circulation booster? Maybe it meant the end was near.

Certainly most of the people in this room felt that way. "You simply cannot justify this market on the fundamentals," I heard Francis Cabour say vehemently. Cabour is a legendarily conservative portfolio manager who is always predicting doom. But today everyone agreed, Johnstone included. "Four or five months ago, we thought we were in the ninth inning," he said. "Now it looks like we're in extra innings." Everyone laughed, but it was a nervous laughter—the kind that means the joke has hit home. I looked around the room at this handful of fund managers, all furiously working the bull market for every last dime, and the thing I noticed most was the complete lack of euphoria, that giddy sense of jumping in headfirst that had characterized the Go-Go Years, or the Roaring Twenties, for that matter. And it suddenly occurred to me that these portfolio managers were feeling what I was feeling—what everyone was feeling. In the last few months, as the Dow made some of its most majestic gains, there was none of the joy that usually accompanies such gains. We watched the Dow in awe, not understanding, and not really believing, either. We were just gaga.

In five years the Dow has risen two thousand points, and everybody is supposed to have had such a great time. And it has been fun. It's been exciting. So why isn't anyone smiling? I think it's because although we've become investors, in our heart of hearts, we wish we were still savers. We wish we didn't have to worry about whether to stay in or get out. We wish we didn't have to learn about the effect of interest rates on bonds or the difference between a growth and an income fund. We wish the world were simple again.

October 20, 1987. Dow Jones Average: 1738.74

Is this how it ends? Not with a whimper but with a bang—a huge, amazing bang? Yesterday was Black Monday: the Dow

Jones lost 508 points, 22 percent of its value, on a staggering 604 million shares. The worst day ever. A year's worth of gains wiped out. Those tremors I felt in that meeting with Johnstone have suddenly turned into an earthquake.

And here I am right back where I started, at a Fidelity investment center, in Boston this time. I am transfixed by the Dow again, just as I was that January day in New York City. Now as then, I am staring at that magical Select scoreboard, which in Boston is placed in the window so people can see it as they walk by. Except no one is walking by. They can't walk by. They stop, and they stare, their mouths hanging open. They—we—look like zombies, unmoving and uncomprehending.

It is a strange and frightening scene. The crowd has grown so large that it has spilled onto the street. Truck drivers honk their horns angrily. I hear someone say, "It just dropped another two points in two minutes. It's all over now." I see a tourist taking a picture of the Select board—something to show his grandchildren in fifty years? I hear someone else say, "I thought it would recover today. Wishful thinking." It seems a fitting end to the Gaga Years, if indeed this is the end. What could be more gaga than the greatest crash in history?

Fidelity, of course, was hit hard by Black Monday. By the end of the week, its $85 billion in assets will shrink to $76.7 billion, and the company will consider it a victory just to keep that much in the family—much of it now in money-market funds. Although no one will give out redemption figures, it is clear that shareholders were bailing out like crazy and that mutual funds played at least some role in creating Black Monday, just as Michael Thomas had predicted. On Wednesday, the *Boston Globe* will describe Magellan as a $7.7 billion fund. [Editor's note: In March 1988 Fidelity laid off about eight hundred employees, affirming that a period of rapid growth in the mutual-fund business has passed.]

The market opened two hundred points up this Tuesday morning, but by the time I get to the investment center, around eleven-thirty, most of the gain is gone. As it drops the crowd keeps growing, making the street impenetrable to traffic. Who has time to worry about traffic? Every time the Dow makes another downward blip, there are groans.

At twelve-thirty with the market down 20 points, the police arrive. They want Fidelity to shut off the Select board so that people will get out of the street. Fidelity complies—and everyone moves twenty feet to stare at the block trade tape in the other window. Fidelity shuts that off, too. No one moves. People are now staring at two blank screens. A man on a bicycle rides up and asks, in a foreign accent, "How's the New York?" Down twenty, I tell him. "I hear up fifty," he says.

I go inside and walk down a flight of stairs to the Quotron machines. There must be twenty people crowded around them. The hard core in this group first got here early yesterday. They look dazed and tired as they stare at the Dow. It reminds me of a poker game at four-thirty in the morning—you're sick of playing, and the games all seem stale, and you want to quit. But you can't. You're too deep into it. When I go back upstairs a half-hour later, the Dow is up ninety points.

I wander back downstairs. "Where's the Dow?" I ask. "Up ten," someone says. "It was just up ninety," I say.

"That was ten minutes ago," comes the reply. "Where have you been?" Everyone laughs, myself included. But it's all too crazy. I can't take it anymore. About two o'clock, with the Dow creeping up again, I leave Fidelity and retrieve my car from the parking garage. For most of the drive home, I resist the impulse to find out how the market is doing. But then four o'clock arrives, and the market closes, and the impulse is too strong to resist. "For those of you who haven't heard," the announcer says, "the stock market closed up a record 102 points." Good God, 102 points! Now what do I do?

The Slow Death of E. F. Hutton

Brett Duval Fromson

February 29, 1988, *Fortune*

"The Slow Death of E. F. Hutton" is a yarn. Hutton had been a great brokerage. It was murdered by the stupidity, selfishness, and greed of its top executives.

EVEN AT SIXTY-THREE, ROBERT FOMON can't sit down. For five hours he paces his living room, trying to explain the demise of E. F. Hutton, the brokerage house he ran for sixteen years. A haze of cigarette smoke covers the English antiques and sporting paintings that decorate his Fifth Avenue apartment. "Did I let the firm down?" he asks. "Did I let the employees down? No, I don't think so." To hear Fomon talk, there are no good explanations for Hutton's collapse and subsequent sale to Shearson Lehman Brothers, no large lessons to be learned.

Fomon just doesn't know a good story when he hears one. The Hutton saga is a managerial morality tale that has everything but a hero: an actress, a baseball commissioner, several villains, pretty girls, not to mention mismanagement, selfishness, arrogance, and greed. Call it "The Fall of the House of Hutton."

Was Hutton's collapse inevitable? Had the eighty-four-year-old franchise outlived its usefulness? As a laid-off former Hutton employee—one of five thousand—asks: "Did we have to be laid naked at the feet of Shearson?" The answer to each question is "No." Hutton's problem, says a former management director, is that it "made every mistake in the book, and no one was ever punished."

147

The blunders ranged from the ridiculously extravagant (investing $100 million in a glitzy new headquarters when the firm was losing money) to the downright illegal (check kiting). But the seminal error was allowing Robert Fomon to wield absolute power for so long. He hired and promoted whomever he wanted, including close friends. He personally reviewed the salaries and bonuses of more than one thousand employees. Like a feudal lord, he banished organization, budgets, and planning from his domain. "His whole life was holding court, making all the large and small decisions," says a former Hutton managing director and Fomon confidant. "When Friday night at six o'clock rolled around, a tear would come down his cheek because he was wondering what the hell he was going to do till Monday. Outside of work, he was the loneliest man who ever lived."

As Hutton grew, however, it became far too complex to be run so autocratically. After a broken leg and two small strokes between 1983 and 1985, Fomon, says a former Hutton officer, "lost control of the firm and no one ever regained it."

Hutton's senior officers contributed to the chaos because so many lacked managerial skills. In the firm's entrepreneurial culture, executives usually came up through the ranks of brokers or dealmakers; they did not regard managing as macho. Bad decisions by the officers tended to be ratified by the board of directors. Until 1986, eighteen of the twenty-three members, on average, were insiders. The outside directors included actress Dina Merrill, E. F. Hutton's daughter, and Edward Cazier Jr., one of Fomon's personal lawyers, whose firm, Hahn Cazier & Smaltz, received large fees from Hutton.

The firm's vaunted but poorly organized retail brokerage, which produced about 75 percent of Hutton's revenues, had problems too. Executives focused so much on increasing revenues that they lost sight of costs. Hutton did not know which brokers made money and which ones did not. Retail brokers retained large clients whose orders could have been executed more cheaply by lower-commissioned institutional brokers. Two executives cite an example of run-amok management: Hutton was expensing party girls from escort services as temporary clerical and secretarial help. From 1981 on, profits slipped steadily at the retail brokerage. Still, Hutton's legendary perquisites continued. Though the firm lost $90 million in 1986, according to a former top executive, it spent $30 million to send its best-producing brokers and their wives on all-expense-paid trips.

Between 1980 and 1982, Hutton was not just squandering its own money; it was also using funds from a $4 million check-kiting scheme. Hutton managers intentionally over-drew the firm's checking accounts for a day or two to earn additional interest income. The firm pleaded guilty to two thousand counts of mail and wire fraud in 1985 and never recovered from the scandal. Not even Robert Rittereiser, a top-notch manager brought in as president from Merrill Lynch, could save Hutton.

Fortune has learned that Fomon's loyalty to longtime associates snared in the check-kiting scheme led him to try to protect them from criminal charges. He pleaded the company guilty, in part to avoid indictments of certain top officers. And Fomon himself says that while he answered all the questions put to him by federal prosecutors, he did not tell the grand jury everything he knew. Several former top Hutton employees also maintain that Fomon tried, unsuccessfully, to alter the criticisms of executives named in the report of former Attorney General Griffin Bell, who was appointed by Hutton to help restore its reputation.

The check-kiting fiasco was, in many ways, a logical out-growth of bad old habits. Staid, sleepy Hutton had revenues of $85 million and employed just 1,275 account executives in 1970, when Hutton Chairman Alec Jack chose his protégé, Robert Fomon, the head of corporate finance on the West Coast, to become chief executive of the private partnership. Two years later Fomon took the firm public. Between 1972 and 1982, Hutton's share of the brokerage trade expanded from 2.9 percent to 7.6 percent as it opened over two hundred new offices.

Because revenues were growing much faster than costs, Hutton soon began making nouveau riche returns. In the 1970s, profits grew 22 percent a year, compounded annually, and net worth increased 21 percent a year. By 1980 almost four thousand account executives worked for Hutton, and the brokerage had revenues of $1.1 billion—more than any firm but Merrill Lynch. "We used to look down our noses at the Paine Webbers, the Dean Witters, and the Shearsons as they went through their traumas in the 1970s," says a former executive, referring to the mediocre management and slow growth that was common on Wall Street. "We were sure that nothing like that could happen to us."

While Fomon concentrated on corporate strategy and investment banking, his chief aide, George Ball, built up the retail brokerage. Ball put together an elite corps of salesmen who generated more commissions per account than any competing firm. Says a former Hutton broker: "Ball was like a big brother to us, a leader, a Napoleon. He kept us together, created an esprit de corps." In retrospect, it appears that Ball tried too hard to keep his troops happy. "George gave them whatever they wanted," says a former Hutton manager who worked closely with the brokers. "Up-front money, interest-free loans. In one region he had about forty such deals with brokers." Ball disputes this, but declines to elaborate.

In 1975 the Securities and Exchange Commission deregulated brokerage commissions. As competition from discount brokers increased, Hutton's revenue growth slowed. Costs, however, continued to rise. Former company officers say that by the mid-1980s, many of the top brokers were losing money because their take was so high. At the time, Hutton paid salesmen 40 percent of the commission, vs. an industry average of 30 percent. Every few years the company tried to reduce its brokerage costs. But the retail brokers had such influence within the firm that they could successfully beat back any cost-cutting assaults, sometimes by threatening to quit.

Hutton's investment bankers did not add much to profits either. "We were never any good," recalls one of the senior bankers. Under Fomon's direction, they sallied forth in a feckless attempt to do battle with the likes of Goldman Sachs and Morgan Stanley. "Investment banking was the plaything of a few officers," says a former close associate of Fomon. "There was no strategy. They had a *Gunfight at the O.K. Corral* style: Shoot a lot of deals and see which ones work." One debt instrument cooked up by Hutton's bankers in

1982—a floating-rate, tax-free corporate note—ended up costing the firm $55 million in 1986. Hutton had sold the notes with the understanding that holders could redeem them at par. When the creditworthiness of some of the securities deteriorated, Hutton felt obliged to reimburse clients.

Despite disappointing earnings from investment banking operations, Fomon and his entourage continued to spend pots of money. One top banker charged $900,000 in travel and entertainment expenses in 1986, according to Hutton records. "That's a hell of a lot even for an investment banker," says an officer at another Wall Street firm. Two corporate jets sat on the tarmac in New York, fueled and ready to fly off to Hutton apartments in Paris, London, and San Francisco.

Twice married and admittedly fond of women he calls "pretty young girls," bachelor Fomon lived more like Adnan Khashoggi than Paul Volcker. "He liked nothing better than being in a jet at thirty thousand feet with talented young women," says a former top Hutton official. Back in New York, he bedded a number of Hutton employees and put girlfriends on the payroll, according to those closest to him. "He considered it the spoils of war," says a Fomon confidant. Another officer says, "One of the roles I played was to keep him out of trouble. And I would say that I was consistently unsuccessful."

Fomon's most memorable public gaffe occurred in August 1986, when he agreed to a profile in *M*, a men's fashion magazine. One photo shows Fomon sitting at a Long Island party with his arms around two good-looking young blondes. "I'm old enough to be grandfather to some of the girls I take out," he told the interviewer. "They're decorative, nice to look at, they have keen senses of humor." Some people at Hutton did not find the article funny. "It was embarrassing for the firm," recalls an executive. At a board meeting, Dina Merrill criticized Fomon for bad public relations. Says Fomon: "I don't understand why people got upset. I can't help it if I appear in the papers with young girls."

The pandemic disorganization and mismanagement at Hutton became acute in 1982, when George Ball left to be chief executive of Prudential-Bache Securities. He had no obvious successor. Fomon temporarily took on the job of running the retail brokerage, but it proved too much for him. So he asked Scott Pierce, Vice President Bush's brother-in-law and an affable municipal bond manager, to replace Ball. Many people at Hutton were flabbergasted that Pierce had been chosen, since he had never worked with the retail brokerage. "I wasn't the best man for the job," says Pierce, who nevertheless agreed to take it.

Whether from overwork after Ball's departure or from heavy smoking and drinking, Fomon broke his leg and had two strokes in the mid-1980s. "He had more serious health problems than anyone has written about," says one of his confidants. He fractured his right leg in three places in 1983— getting undressed for bed, he says—and was out of the office for a month. Because the bones never set properly, he has been in considerable pain ever since. Then in September 1984 he had the first small stroke. Says a friend and former officer: "He wasn't the same again."

Eight months later Hutton stunned Wall Street by pleading guilty to check kiting. "The guilty plea was the worst decision I ever made," Fomon now says. "We should have fought it in court. I never understood what the aftermath would be. I thought it would soon be ancient history." Around Hutton the crime quickly became known as the F (for federal) matter.

Fomon says Hutton's outside law firm, Cahill Gordon & Reindel, persuaded him and the board to admit guilt during a forty-five-minute meeting. The attorneys pointed out that the Department of Justice was planning to indict several senior Hutton officials—but not Fomon—on criminal charges. They advised pleading guilty to avoid a long legal battle that would smear Hutton's name. But the guilty plea had precisely the same effect. Says Fomon: "I should have let the Justice Department indict whomever it wanted."

Back in 1985, however, he was feeling more charitable to those caught up in the scheme. Even Fomon's critics concede that he is a loyal friend. "Bob just couldn't stand seeing his buddies dragged through the mud," says a close associate. Former Hutton executives describe a meeting between Fomon and two senior officers a few days before Griffin Bell issued his final report. Fomon, say these executives, wanted to kill the Bell report. "We said, 'No way, Bob. You can't do that,' " recalls one of the officers. If Fomon could not scrap the inquiry, he could try to water it down. Several former Hutton executives say that he asked Bell to soften his criticisms of specific officers. Bell admits that Fomon lobbied him about one officer but says he did not give in. Fomon denies that he interfered with Bell's report.

The brokers were furious that Fomon had hired Bell in the first place. Says one: "The guilty plea was humiliating enough, but then these dummies went and hired a guy to come in, tell us what we already knew, and republicize it to the world." In July 1985, shortly before the Bell report was released, fifty top Hutton managers and brokers flew to New York. At a rebellious meeting in a midtown hotel, they complained to Fomon and Robert Witt, second-in-command of the brokerage, about management ineptitude. Fomon was unfazed. He introduced the hostile audience to Bob Rittereiser, a plain-spoken man he had just hired from Merrill Lynch. Fomon described Rittereiser, then forty-seven, as the firm's bright new hope and savior.

At Merrill Lynch, where he had spent most of his working life, Rittereiser was one of several candidates in line to replace Chief Executive William Schreyer. But he jumped at the Hutton offer because it seemed to give him a surer shot at the top. Ritt, as he is known to his friends and colleagues, saw an opportunity to make Hutton a first-class retail brokerage with a small but profitable investment banking arm. He says that when he agreed to join Hutton, "I had no idea that the firm was in such bad shape."

He began to get the picture the first day. Fomon told him that a client of Hutton's most productive broker, Houston's Don Sanders, had bounced a check for $48 million but had been allowed to resume trading in another account he had with the firm. "I told Fomon that if it were up to me, I'd close the account today," says Ritt. "And I wondered why he hadn't." But the decision had already been made to let Sanders's client keep trading. Rittereiser was powerless to do anything more than shake his head.

Rittereiser spent his first six months soothing state regulators who wanted to close Hutton down and bankers who wanted to pull the firm's credit lines. "Because of the check-kiting scheme, he had to cash in a ton of chips with insurance commissioners, regulators, and banks or Hutton would have gone down the tubes a lot sooner," says one of Rittereiser's closest aides.

On New Year's Eve, for example, the firm was in financial peril because institutional holders wanted to sell nearly $1 billion of Hutton's short-term paper to raise cash. Since Hutton was the sole market maker, and no other firm would bid at par, it had to buy the paper. Ritt to the rescue. "I arrived at 7 A.M. with a small team and $800 million in fed funds. Over the next twelve hours we masterminded the settlement of every security transaction Hutton had made so that we could stay within our bank limits. If we had overdrawn, some banks would have pulled their lines of credit. It was a question of the survival of the firm." Rittereiser left the building at 7 P.M., and before going home he stopped at Our Lady of Victory church to offer a prayer for having survived his first half year.

By mid-1986, Rittereiser had the nucleus of his new management team in place. They erected legal and financial controls to prevent a repeat of the F matter. They also organized Hutton's relocation from downtown buildings to expensive new headquarters in midtown, a move Fomon had spent years planning. But they proved singularly unsuccessful at capping costs. For a fear of losing its best account executives, Hutton still paid them such large commissions that many, especially those whose clients traded commodities, were unprofitable.

The relationship between Fomon and Rittereiser began to deteriorate in late 1986. Fomon, perhaps realizing that he was losing control of his firm, actively tried to sell it. Several companies, including Chrysler, seemed interested but backed off when they realized the extent of Hutton's problems. Fomon frequently complained about Rittereiser behind his back. "I wanted to sell the firm because I could see that he was a consensus guy, not a leader," says Fomon. A blowup between the two was inevitable.

In October 1986, Shearson Chief Executive Peter Cohen set off the explosion. He flew to Bermuda to meet with Rittereiser, who was vacationing with his family, and proposed a merger between Shearson and Hutton. Rittereiser was ambivalent, but over the next six weeks he and Fomon met twice with Cohen and once with James Robinson III, the chairman of Shearson's parent, American Express. Rumors of a takeover swept Wall Street, and once again turmoil swept Hutton. During a management committee meeting, one of the many Hutton officers who opposed a sale almost came to blows with Fomon. "I had to break it up," says an investment banker who was there.

At an all-day meeting on November 6, Fomon and Rittereiser told the board that Shearson was floating a $50-per-share offer for the firm. But the head of the retail brokerage, Jerome Miller, warned the directors that many brokers would quit if the firm were sold. The board asked Rittereiser for his position. He said that he opposed the sale and argued for more time to turn Hutton around. Fomon maintains that Ritt was just trying to save his job.

The differing positions of the chairman and president perplexed Hutton's board. "These two guys had created the interest in selling," says a director. "Then whoa, they split." The outside directors caucused and concluded that Hutton's investment bankers at Salomon Brothers should ask Cohen for $55 a share. But by now Cohen had sized up the antipathy of Hutton's brokers, and he called the deal off.

With Cohen out of the picture, the board had to decide who was going to run its company: Fomon or Rittereiser. Clearly the two could not work together any longer. Before it acted, the board wanted assurances that Hutton could survive on its own. Peter Ueberroth, the commissioner of baseball and a board member since 1984, put the question to Rittereiser. Ritt told the directors that he and his team would have Hutton earning money by 1988. At the initiative of Ueberroth, the board directed Fomon and Rittereiser to decide who was in charge. But the members left little doubt that they preferred Rittereiser. The next day, Fomon bought Ritt lunch at an Upper East Side hotel and in a tense meeting said, "You want to be CEO? Okay, I'll do it."

Although Fomon was as good as his angry word, he remained chairman for six months while he negotiated an $11 million golden handshake. At his final appearance before the board, Fomon took one more swipe at Rittereiser by nominating Ueberroth as chairman. According to Hutton officers, Fomon hoped Ueberroth would take the job and sack Rittereiser. When Ueberroth refused, Fomon said, "I'm going to put Hutton in play," and left the room.

Now that Rittereiser was chief executive, he had the power to shake Hutton to its bottom line. Despite the bull market, the firm was still losing money and investor confidence. But instead of acting quickly, Rittereiser set up committees to study Hutton's problems and come up with solutions. In the summer of 1987, his marketing team produced a remarkably simple-minded coloring book to tell employees what had to be done and why it had to be done quickly. Though it was meant to dramatize Hutton's desperate plight, the book simply offended people. "It was an insult to our intelligence," says one broker. "We couldn't believe that headquarters had put it out. These were the guys who were going to save the firm?"

Confidential Hutton documents show that Rittereiser told the board Hutton would earn $74 million during the first nine months of 1987; in fact, it made only $15 million and lost money in September. Then came October 19. All the brokerage stock prices sank, but none more than Hutton's, which cratered at $15 a share, vs. $35 two weeks earlier. "When Hutton stock got below $20, the firm was history," says Kendrick Wilson III, former head of corporate finance. "It was only a matter of time before some bargain-hunter snapped us up."

Fomon, who had been trying unsuccessfully to shop Hutton all summer, seized the moment. In a bitter act of revenge, he fomented a bid from former Shearson chairman Sanford Weill. If Weill were successful, Fomon stood to collect a $3 million finder's fee, in addition to whatever he could get for his 250,000 shares of Hutton stock. At a series of dinners Fomon held in his apartment, he introduced Weill to the directors. Having lost confidence in Rittereiser, they saw Weill as the take-charge guy who might rescue the company. But when Weill demanded an exclusive deal with Hutton without offering a firm price, the directors demurred. On November

23, Ueberroth and the board reopened discussions with Cohen. Nine days later, they agreed that Shearson would buy Hutton for $29 a share. Though the price came close to $1 billion, it was far short of Cohen's $50-a-share proposal the year before.

After the Shearson takeover, Hutton's board voted itself more than $2.5 million in retirement benefits. Ueberroth alone would pocket almost $1 million, including $500,000 for leading the negotiations with Cohen. Rittereiser, who did not request an employment contract, will get about $3 million if he leaves the newly named Shearson Lehman Hutton. Some members of his management team, who refused to join Hutton without contracts, will do better, collecting from $1 million to about $5 million each. Just about forgotten in the rush to divide the spoils were Hutton's other employees. Because of the way the board structured the company's profit-sharing plan, they will not be permitted to sell the Hutton shares held for them in trust. Most will walk away with little more than the right to collect unemployment checks.

Although the directors' special treatment of themselves seems unfair, it is in keeping with the long tradition of me-first-manship at Hutton. Robert Fomon was the exemplar of that spirit." People around here believed that if they could get away with something, they should do it," says a former Fomon associate. At Hutton, selfishness was a way of doing business. The company lived—and died—by it.

Candlelight Wedding Joins Two Billionaire Families

Georgia Dullea

April 19, 1988, the *New York Times*

When the New York Times *reported as a news story the wedding reception of Laura Steinberg, daughter of billionaire speculator Saul Steinberg, to Jonathan Tisch, son of billionaire Preston Tisch, you knew things were getting totally out of control. This was truly a predators' ball in which the newly rich celebrated their good fortune in one of the decade's most vulgar displays of consumption. Over five hundred guests took over the Metropolitan Museum of Art, heretofore a bastion of old-line New York WASP society. They gorged themselves on poached salmon with champagne aspic; trio of veal, lamb, and chicken, orzo with porcini; spring vegetables; and spun sugar sprigs of sweet peas that were served with the seven-foot-high wedding cake.*

The guest list was a rogues' gallery of hot money players and their socially ambitious wives, from the notorious Henry Kravis and his wife to such relative nobodies as Frank and Nancy Richardson. This was the kind of wedding where the bride's stepmother, Gayfryd Steinberg, in one of the great disingenuous utterances of a disingenuous decade, said, "You can really describe this as very much a family party and a young people's party."

IT WAS A POWER WEDDING. Laura S. Steinberg and Jonathan M. Tisch were married last night at the Central Synagogue in Manhattan in a candlelight ceremony joining two billionaire families that in one generation have carved a place in New York's world of high finance and society.

Mrs. Tisch is the twenty-five-year-old daughter of Barbara Steinberg and Saul P. Steinberg, chairman and chief executive of Reliance Group Holdings Inc. Mr. Tisch, thirty-four, is president of Loews Hotels. His parents are Joan and Preston Robert Tisch, who is president and co-chief executive officer of the Loews Corporation and former Postmaster General of the United States.

It was a Wall Street wedding, with names from the "smart money crowd" studding the guest list. Mr. Steinberg and Tisch family members are major stock market investors, notably the bridegroom's uncle, Laurence A. Tisch, who is chief executive of CBS. At the bridal couple's engagement party last year, a Tisch family member said, "If they get married, it will have to be cleared by the SEC."

It was a stylish wedding, white-on-white, with all the women's dresses designed by Arnold Scaasi. The bride's aunt, Lynda Steinberg Jurist, was matron of honor and the bridegroom's brother, the movie producer Steven Tisch, was best man.

The bride wore an off-white taffeta dress, delicately embroidered in gold, with a seven-foot train. Her tulle veil was held in place by a diamond and pearl tiara that may have been something old, something new or something borrowed.

Dressed in off-white moire shot with gold were her ten attendants. The men were in white tie and tails while children from both families were done-up as flower girls and ring bearers.

It was a wedding that blended tradition and contemporary mores. The bride's divorced parents were at her side during the ceremony, which was performed by Rabbi Stanley Davids, senior rabbi of the synagogue, under a chuppa fashioned of bronze palms from Mr. Steinberg's collection of antiquities.

Barbara Walters, Helen Gurley Brown and others hiked their bouffant skirts as they climbed out of limousines and ran to the synagogue steps, where a canopy shielded them from the rain. Most of the limousines could not reach the entrance because the wedding party's burgundy Rolls-Royce was blocking it.

Spotlights illuminated the East 55th Street side of the synagogue, a landmark Moorish-style building. Guests said the effect inside was of sunlight on the stained glass windows. On the altar, banked with flowers and glowing candelabra, were antique pieces from the Steinberg home.

"We tried very much to respect the integrity of the synagogue by using period pieces," said the bride's stepmother, Gayfryd Steinberg, who was described recently in *U.S. News & World Report* as "the queen of nouvelle society."

The families declined a request by *Life* magazine to document what was being called the wedding of the eighties. Interest was keen, however, as news photographers scrambled in the rain to catch the bridal couple before they sped off to the Metropolitan Museum of Art, where a gala dinner was held.

Passing through the receiving line in the museum's Great Hall were more than five hundred guests, including Norman Mailer and Norris Church, Lord Weidenfeld, Beverly Sills, Carolyne Roehm and Henry Kravis, Donald and Ivana Trump, Georgette Mosbacher, Alex Papamarkou, Lewis Rudin, Laura and John Pomerantz, Vernon Jordan, Nancy and Frank Richardson, Hillary and David Mahoney.

"It was a fairy-tale wedding," Blaine Trump was saying to her husband, Robert.

"You can really describe this as very much a family party and a young people's party," Gayfryd Steinberg said, levelly, in an interview before the party.

Her presence had excited the gossip columnists. Caterers, florists and other workers were required to sign confidentiality agreements, which could have subjected them to lawsuits for leaking details.

In designer beige were the bridegroom's mother, the bride's mother and stepmother. The bride's mother, owner of an antiques shop, Barbara Steinberg Unlimited, was escorted by Justin Hornik, whom she introduced as "a man I've been seeing for some time."

As for her daughter and son-in-law, she said they began dating about three years ago. "It just clicked. I hope they will always be as happy as they are today."

The bride, a graduate of the Dalton School and the University of Pennsylvania, has an M.B.A. degree from New York University. Until recently she worked as a story analyst for Warner Bros., Inc. in New York.

The bridegroom, who graduated from the Gunnery and Tufts University, is a trustee of both institutions.

After the reception, guests drifted past the Greek and Roman antiques to the museum restaurant, decorated in French Directoire, with swags, rosettes and tassels. On the tables were centerpieces of gilded magnolia leaves and spring branches.

Between courses of poached salmon with champagne aspic, trio of veal, lamb and chicken, orzo with porcini, and spring vegetables, guests danced to Hank Lane's orchestra.

The wines, from the Steinberg cellar, were Corton Charlemagne, Chateau Latour and Roederer Cristal Champagne.

A spun sugar sprig of sweet peas decorated each dessert plate. Dessert was wedding cake.

The New Greed Baiting

Edward Jay Epstein

August 1988, *Manhattan,inc.*

It may be a bit unfair to include Edward Jay Epstein's "The New Greed Baiting." But I did because this was one of the few times that a serious journalist tried to make the absurd case that Michael Milken and his junk-bond machine were getting a raw deal from the press. You have to laugh at lines like this: "The irony that may be lost in this frenzy of greed baiting is that the economy, rather than collapsing under the weight of junk-bond financing, is booming."

THE SPORT OF greed baiting businessmen, while still not as popular as baseball in terms of a spectator event, is rapidly finding its place as a national pastime in Media America. Its appeal derives from the incredible spectacle of successful money-makers in the colosseum of public opinion, being put to the ultimate test of defending themselves against the charge of making money. The richer they are, the better. The whole idea is to induce the maximum writhing, squirming, and pandering to the press before inflicting the coup de grace in the form of a moral sermon about the evils of money. Anything goes in the arena, with one exception: money-makers are not allowed to defend moneymaking as a virtue (since that would be ungladiatorial—and far too easy).

The blood sport usually commences with the media reporting that a heretofore-unknown money-maker has made a fortune. The amount may be artfully exaggerated to any high number of using the modifier "reportedly as much as" and then filling in the blank with a cascade of zeros. After their subject's wealth is publicly established, the media then stereotype him by religion, life-style, or some other category that will make him instantly recognizable to the crowd. To excite even more interest, the media can portray the money-maker as some kind of ultrasecretive "recluse" (which means, in journalistic parlance, that he refuses to give interviews on how much money he has made). Finally, like picadors in a bullring, they stick the anonymous allegations into him in the most embarrassing way—producing allegations that he cannot deny without seeming guilty. From that point on, he is fair game for greed baiting.

My objection to this kind of spectator sport lies less in the pain it inflicts on the money-makers (who can afford it) than in the distorted picture of reality it foists upon the audience. Consider, for example, some recent popular explanations of how big business is conducted in America.

First, there is Oliver Stone's movie *Wall Street*, which was backed and distributed by Twentieth Century Fox Film Corporation, an enterprise owned by Rupert Murdoch, who is certainly one of the world's great capitalists—and assessors of public opinion.

Although fictive, this film goes right to the heart of greed baiting. Its chic values are summed up when the hero, Martin Sheen, playing a dedicated blue-collar unionist, tells his son Charlie Sheen, playing a red-suspendered Wall Streeter who is headed for jail, "It's gonna be rough on you, but maybe in some screwed-up way, that's the best thing that can happen to you. . . . Create; don't live off the buying and selling of others."

The message here is that it is better to be in the slammer than to work on Wall Street. What is condemned by this moral equation is the very essence of commerce: "living off the buying and selling of others." Since this is purely an antigreed film, other crimes that occur—such as the conspiracy that the blue-collared trade unionists engage in to get control of the airline for which they work, a scheme that involves extortion, industrial sabotage, market manipulation, and insider trading—are ignored.

Then, in the realm of nonfiction, there is *The Predators' Ball*, Connie Bruck's entertaining investigation of junk-bond king Michael Milken. It is published by the *American Lawyer* magazine and Simon and Schuster—the latter, part of the Gulf + Western conglomerate, a major client of Milken's.

Bruck, to be sure, has done some fine investigative reporting about the $100 billion junk-bond market, but right at the beginning of the book, she comes up with an extraordinarily sexy picture of what makes it work: an orgy.

In the prologue, she suggests that Milken and his associates at Drexel Burnham Lambert played on the sexual lust of multibillion-dollar corporate raiders to get them to buy their junk bonds, recruiting paid women for a wild party that took place every year at a bungalow in the Beverly Hills Hotel. Bruck vividly describes one that occurred in March 1985. Those in attendance included such superpowers as Rupert Murdoch, Sir James Goldsmith, Carl Icahn, T. Boone Pickens, and Carl Lindner. Although it turns out that the author did not herself witness this event, she provides a vivid description. For example, she says that she confirmed that the women were paid by Drexel, with the amount "depending on how pretty they are and what they'll do." She quotes, albeit secondhand, the alleged organizer of the party, who asks, "How could I get all these guys to come if I didn't have the girls?" As the raiders partied late into the night, Bruck suggests, without drawing a diagram, that "things just got out of hand." She then explains how the courtesans fit into the grand scheme of things. "They were seen as necessary bait for clients" in earlier years when Milken had difficulty getting financiers to take his junk bonds seriously. This conjures up the spectacle of some of America's largest financiers being lured into the junk-bond business by a few well-baited hookers rather than by less prurient calculations about the relative cost of the bonds and the comparative risks.

This orgiastic view of junk-bond financing dovetails nicely with much of the 1985–86 op-ed-page wisdom exemplified by Felix Rohatyn's apocalyptic piece in the *Wall Street Journal* called "Junk Bonds and Other Securities Swill." These articles, written mainly by financiers and lawyers who specialize in traditional bonds, warn that nontraditional bonds are irrational and could lead to an economic catastrophe (unless Congress intervened by passing a law). But if it is assumed that Milken's nontraditional bonds are the equivalent of corporate pig swill, as Rohatyn suggests, why do otherwise-savvy investors buy them? Bruck supplies a novel answer—seduction—and converging with Oliver Stone's view on Wall Street, notes that junk-bond financing "would introduce terror and mayhem into countless corporate boardrooms. . . . It would cause the loss of jobs, as companies were taken over and broken up."

Their views of Wall Street are, if anything, prosaic compared with the putative view of sinister Wall Street machinations held by the leaky U.S. prosecutors attempting to build a case against Drexel. Although Rudolph Giuliani and his G-men say that they never comment on such cases, the theory of the prosecution periodically appears in the *Wall Street Journal*. On September 11, 1987, the "government's apparent hypothesis" was divulged in considerable detail by reporters James B. Stewart and Daniel Hertzberg, In their article, they note that "Milken is the master strategist, and he works this way: From his X-shaped desk in Beverly Hills, he directs clients to take investment positions that enable them to earn large trading profits. And he asks the clients to reciprocate by buying junk bonds to help finance Drexel-backed transactions. He identifies potential target companies. He raises money for raiders who threaten or launch the takeover bids, and he finds the financing for the leveraged buyouts he proposes. He protects the buyers of junk bonds by making a market in the bonds, but by then some of the buyers are largely in his control anyway."

This master-strategist-conspiracy theory is even less satisfactory than the bungalow-8-orgy theory in explaining why there is a $100 billion junk-bond market. It is true that Milken sits at an X-shaped desk (as do many editors in newsrooms). But does that give him the power to "direct" multibillion-dollar players to make investments? How does Milken order men like Carl Lindner, Henry Kravis, or Saul Steinberg to buy junk bonds? Why should they even act on his advice—unless they believed his junk bonds were more profitable than the wide range of other investments available to them. If the prosecutors changed the word directs to persuades or even begs, their theory might have more explanatory power (but then it would make Milken into just another bond salesman instead of a master conspirator). Of course, with more dredging through the records, they might come up with an even more titillating "apparent hypothesis." And why shouldn't they do their share of theorizing? Everyone else has.

The irony that may be lost in this frenzy of greed baiting is that the economy, rather than collapsing under the weight of junk-bond financing, is booming. There has never been a period with as much takeover activity as the past five years, and yet, rather than the predicted massive unemployment from corporate breakups, there is record employment in the United States. Productivity and personal income are also at record highs. And many of the old-line financial institutions, such as Morgan Stanley & Company, Inc., rather than calling nontraditional financing swill, are quietly taking over a large share of the market. Is it possible that a case could be made for greed?

RJR Nabisco Takeover

John Helyar and Bryan Burrough

December 2, 1988, the *Wall Street Journal*

How can you tell the story of the Gaga Years without including the Wall Street Journal *piece by John Helyar and Bryan Burrough that was the basis for their best-selling book about the RJR Nabisco takeover,* Barbarians at the Gate? *You can't.*

IT SHOULDN'T HAVE BEEN any contest. RJR Nabisco Inc. President F. Ross Johnson, his management team and his Wall Street partners had not only made the highest bid for RJR by nearly $700 million. Mr. Johnson's management group was RJR. Its members had the intimate knowledge of the company that comes only from years of experience. They were cozy with the members of the board that would ultimately decide the winner. The five-member special committee considering the bids seemed stacked heavily in their favor.

Today, the Johnson camp is licking its wounds in defeat. In a stunning climax to the highest-stakes takeover battle ever, RJR's board awarded the nineteenth-largest U.S. industrial company to Kohlberg Kravis Roberts & Co. despite its lower bid of $25.07 billion. It was a remarkable repudiation of Mr. Johnson, who, over the course of the six-week imbroglio that he himself had set in motion, alienated his own board and became a national symbol of greed. And it vividly dramatizes how important nonfinancial considerations may become in mega-takeovers, touching the lives of thousands of stockholders, employees and people in the cities and regions where target companies operate.

Members of the management bidding group, which included Shearson Lehman Hutton Inc. and Salomon Inc., are bitter; they believe they were discriminated against. None of them

167

would comment on the record, but one top management-group aide says, "We were cheated."

Late yesterday, the group left the door slightly ajar for another run at the company, saying in a statement the partners were "evaluating their options." But Mr. Johnson also made a conciliatory gesture in saying he would help Henry Kravis of KKR make a "professional and smooth transition."

But how the RJR group lost the prize when it seemed within their grasp is a complex tale. By the end of its grueling all-day meeting Wednesday, the RJR board became convinced KKR would give a better shake to employees, grant a bigger stake to shareholders and keep RJR from being totally disassembled.

Strategy also played a part. The Johnson group simply was outfoxed by KKR. The buy-out firm had been the low bidder in the first round of the auction. But by a complex bluff, it may have lulled the management group into thinking that it was no longer a threat. Then, KKR stormed back to raise its bid $12 a share, while management was lifting its offer only a dollar. After a circus-like day of bidding Wednesday, KKR won by turning the tables on RJR's directors and set its own final, last-minute deadline.

Yesterday, a tired but satisfied pair of cousins, Henry Kravis and George Roberts, soon to own such well-known brands as Planters peanuts and Del Monte fruits, sought to calm RJR's worried shareholders, employees and suppliers. "Oreos," the powerful Mr. Kravis assured, "will still be in children's lunch boxes."

For Messrs. Kravis and Roberts, the real work begins now. The pair will probably manage RJR for seven years or more before selling it or taking it public again. They are especially eager to do well in the wake of their disappointing breakup of their largest acquisition, Beatrice Cos., and charges that ego rather than concern for their investors propelled their RJR quest. "This was not a knee-jerk bid," Mr. Kravis says. "This was not an ego trip. This was not an impetuous decision."

In the end, the rival bids were so close that the board's own Wall Street advisers described them to directors as "substantially equal." That allowed the board to break the tie by considering factors other than dollars and cents. According to board advisers, the most critical ones were:

— The breakup factor. RJR directors want to keep the company as intact as possible. KKR promises to sell only $5 billion to $6 billion in RJR assets, primarily food companies, in the near future, while the management group intended to sell the entire food company for an estimated $13 billion. KKR hasn't disclosed which assets will be sold, nor has it revealed its longer-term plans.

— The equity factor. Directors wanted to allow stockholders to share in any KKR profits as much as possible. KKR proposed to distribute 25 percent of the equity in the future company to shareholders, compared with the management group's 15 percent offer.

— Bid structure. When directors cut through all the arcane details of preferred stock and debentures in the two packages, it became clear that KKR was offering $500 million more of equity than the management group was. Directors believed that this strengthened the KKR bid and reduced the debt payments that the future company would have to meet.

— Job commitments. Directors believed that KKR was more firmly committed to saving jobs at RJR than the management group was. In an interview published a few days before the bidding deadline, Mr. Johnson had shrugged off his group's planned firings. He said that the company would offer generous severance agreements and that most of the people who would leave had "portable" jobs.

KKR has committed to paying such benefits as severance pay and moving expenses, over the next three years, for RJR employees who worked for businesses that would be shed. "Those kinds of thoughts were absent on the other side," one director says. "They viewed it as a cost. It gets into the greed thing."

An RJR executive maintains that management would have paid those benefits, albeit for a briefer period, and would have provided generous severance packages for terminated RJR employees. But other directors shared the sense that top management cared little about the rank and file. "Employees are assets, and any manager who doesn't see that is a fool," one director says. "We could see Johnson didn't."

It was the last straw for a board increasingly disenchanted with Mr. Johnson. Not only were directors irate over his handling of the buyout, but also their review of the company's operations during the bidding process left them appalled. Management was spending huge sums on lodgings in Palm Springs, Calif., on security measures for Mr. Johnson, on a fleet of corporate jets so large that some directors dubbed it the "RJR Air Force."

Although the directors had benefited from this lavish style, they hadn't known the total extent and cost of it. That belated realization helped convince them that KKR could run the company better than Mr. Johnson, and without stripping it down to just the tobacco operations. Directors figured that KKR could save millions just by excising Mr. Johnson's excesses.

Of the factors influencing the board, KKR's promise to keep more of RJR intact may have been most important. Selling most of the company, as was proposed by the management buyout group, could trigger debt indentures and result in complications with the company's bondholders, who are already furious with what the buyout has done to the value of their holdings.

In addition, the board liked the features of KKR's preferred stock more than the management group's. It is convertible to common stock over a four-year period, compared with two and a half years for the management bid. That gives the company more time to build its value back.

The KKR plan appeared to assure the company at least a chance to preserve its identity and culture. KKR said it plans to name J. Paul Sticht as the company's chairman and chief executive. The seventy-one-year-old Mr. Sticht had held those titles at RJR in the 1970s and early 1980s, and he is known to pontificate about a company's responsibility to "stakeholders": its employees and communities. By enlisting Mr. Sticht, KKR had also snagged a credible manager and defused arguments in the Johnson camp that only it had the management expertise to run the post-buyout company.

Moreover, KKR has indicated it is "considering" moving RJR's headquarters back to Winston-Salem, N.C., from which Mr. Johnson moved to Atlanta last year. Mr. Sticht, who still maintains a residence in Winston-Salem, is believed to be urging that it do so.

The current Atlanta headquarters is, in any event, considered by many an expensive albatross ripe for closing by KKR. In recent weeks, its approximately 350 employees have been bracing themselves to lose their jobs or face another move. The mood of top tobacco executives in Winston-Salem also was said to be sagging yesterday; some of them had aligned themselves with the Johnson group.

But for many of R. J. Reynolds Tobacco Co.'s 12,400 employees, the winning bid of KKR was greeted with whoops because it brings back Mr. Sticht, a representative of the good old days. Some former employees have even contacted him about working for him "gratis," on an interim basis.

There is concern about how many jobs will have to be cut in tobacco, in view of the towering price KKR paid for RJR. Messrs. Kravis and Roberts said in an interview there will be layoffs but not "massive" firings. The two men will go to Winston-Salem and Atlanta today and tomorrow to meet with company executives and possibly community leaders.

One message: their hope for a swift return to normality. "We want everything to settle down and everyone to get back to work," Mr. Kravis said.

KKR's drive to acquire RJR never would have succeeded if not for a canny strategy hatched by Mr. Kravis. His plan to lull the management group involved an initial, low-ball bid, a disinformation campaign and a diversionary ski trip. It succeeded even beyond KKR's hopes.

The outline of the strategy took shape before the first round of bidding three weeks ago. Mr. Kravis was certain that the bids to be submitted wouldn't be final, reasoning that either KKR would be allowed to sweeten its bid or a second round of bidding would be held. So, he saw no reason to lodge his best bid, and KKR's $94-a-share offer was badly eclipsed by higher bids from the management group and from another group led by First Boston Corp.

At that point, KKR begun to spring its trap. It issued a statement suggesting that it might drop out of the bidding. A public-relations consultant from Kekst & Co. elaborated on the message to the press.

During Thanksgiving week, Messrs. Kravis and Roberts told dozens of Wall Street contacts that they were uncertain whether KKR would enter the second round of bidding. As the holiday approached, KKR spread word that Mr. Kravis was heading to Vail, Colo., for a long weekend of skiing and that Mr. Roberts was returning to his home outside San Francisco. Both did leave New York, but a cadre of KKR officials and lawyers kept working through the long weekend.

The strategy worked. The management group increased its bid only $1, to $101 a share, while KKR came back with a $106-a-share bid. Three hours after the bidding deadline late Tuesday afternoon, Shearson Lehman executives, ignorant of the buyout firm's higher bid, were still writing off KKR's chances. "Our information is that they won't be competitive," crowed an RJR group official Tuesday evening.

Meanwhile, the board's special committee was doing some cagey strategizing of its own. It prolonged the auction process into a second round of bidding, whipping the rival groups into a bidding frenzy and driving up the price. It was emboldened to do so because a study of the value of the businesses and the behavior of the bidders convinced some members that they had a good fall-back position even if the bidders dropped out: performing the breakup of RJR on its own.

Special-committee member Martin Davis had done a major restructuring of Gulf & Western Inc. in recent years, as its chief executive, and was a leading advocate of that aggressive strategy. He was backed by another member, John D. Macomber. They were influential in setting up the second round of bidding.

This approach made some other directors nervous, including special-committee Chairman Charles Hugel, who argued for a quick, orderly conclusion. It stirred up some friction in the latter stages of the auction. Some directors feared the whole thing could fall through, leaving RJR's stock in a free-fall and the board open to huge legal liabilities.

But the more aggressive faction prevailed, and it all came to a dramatic conclusion as the second round of bidding came to an end Wednesday. The critical moments of KKR's victory came around 9 P.M. Wednesday. Advisers to RJR's board, meeting at the midtown-Manhattan offices of Skadden, Arps, Slate, Meagher & Flom, emerged from a continuing board meeting to ask the KKR group whether it wished to increase its bid once more. After receiving assurances that no member of RJR's management group would see the bid, KKR's Mr. Kravis handed Skadden's Peter Atkins a signed merger agreement and a final deadline.

"If we don't get it back in thirty minutes, we are going away," Mr. Kravis told the advisers.

After twenty-five minutes, the board asked for and was granted an additional ten minutes to consider the offer. After nine minutes, one of the senior advisers, Felix Rohatyn of Lazard Frères & Co., called Mr. Kravis, Mr. Roberts and a senior KKR attorney, Richard Beattie, into a nearby conference room. There, Mr. Atkins handed them the completed merger agreement.

KKR had won the biggest victory in corporate history.

Power Broker

Joanne Lipman

December 5, 1988, the *Wall Street Journal*

"Power Broker" is a delightfully nasty profile of
Linda Robinson, head of the decade's hottest
PR boutique and the spin-control mistress who
represented RJR Nabisco CEO Ross Johnson in the
takeover. For Robinson, as for many of her ilk in
the eighties, there was no difference between a
paying client and a dear friend.

THE *NEW YORK POST*'s gossip columnist, Aileen "Suzy" Mehle, anointed it "the most perfect private party in recent memory." The setting was the Metropolitan Museum of Art, the dinner by haute caterer Glorious Food, and the hosts that glittering nouvelle society duo of the moment, buyout king Henry Kravis and his fashion designer wife, Carolyne Roehm.

There, too, mingling among assorted Tisches and Trumps, was one of Ms. Roehm's dearest friends, Linda Gosden Robinson, resplendent in "spring-green taffeta," Suzy confided.

But those in the know—and who at this power gathering wasn't?—would soon be buzzing about Ms. Roehm and Mrs. Robinson in an entirely different context. Mrs. Robinson is a powerful public-relations counselor; one of her clients is RJR Nabisco Inc.'s president, F. Ross Johnson, who is another close friend.

So it was more than a bit awkward when, just two weeks after the party, Mr. Kravis spoiled Mr. Johnson's proposed $20 billion-plus buyout of RJR with his own higher bid for RJR. Worse, Mr. Johnson's main financial adviser in his bid was American Express Co.'s chairman, James D. Robinson III, who just happens to be Mr. Linda Robinson. Mrs. Robinson and her husband suddenly found themselves on opposite sides from the Kravises in an acrimonious battle with far higher stakes than anything on the charity-ball circuit.

"It is a very difficult and very awkward situation when friends are pitted against each other," Mrs. Robinson says, but the Kravises "are still good friends and will always be. I sure wish we could all be on the same side. Unfortunately, it's a small world. In the end, you have to be a professional."

A professional she is, spring-green taffeta notwithstanding. Though Mrs. Robinson's name appears more often in the society columns than the news pages, she is one of the country's emerging power brokers. At thirty-five, she appears poised to wield a degree of behind-the-scenes influence approaching that of a few superlawyers and image makers, invariably men. Her reputation has grown so quickly that executives now mention her name barely a breath after that of acknowledged merger-PR guru Gershon Kekst.

Besides her involvement in the RJR Nabisco buyout, the biggest ever, she has been instrumental in some of the other most important recent corporate transactions, including Grand Metropolitan PLC's hostile $5.23 billion bid for Pillsbury Co. and Texaco Inc.'s proxy battle with Carl Icahn. She sits on the boards of two major corporations, SmithKline Beckman Co. and Ronald Perelman's McAndrews & Forbes.

Now, she confronts what may be her most challenging assignment: representing junk-bond king Michael Milken, who is expected to be indicted soon on securities charges.

Unlike ordinary PR people—often dismissed as "flacks" by reporters—Mrs. Robinson, a former debutante, insists on being part of major decision-making sessions. At Texaco, she was even included in meetings with financial advisers to decide on the size of the company's restructuring, announced in January. She advocated the figure ultimately chosen, $3 billion, arguing that anything smaller wouldn't be dramatic enough to satisfy stockholders.

James Kinnear, Texaco's chief executive, considers Mrs. Robinson one of his four closest advisers. "Linda is one of the clearest strategic thinkers that I have ever known," he says.

She is paid well for her talents. Counseling by Robinson, Lake, Lerer & Montgomery, the firm of which she is chief executive, can cost a monthly retainer of more than $25,000. People in the business say Mrs. Robinson herself bills about $300 an hour for her time, three times the rate of ordinary publicists and comparable to the rate charged by top corporate lawyers.

Yet despite her rising influence and reputation, Mrs. Robinson's efforts have sometimes backfired badly. RJR is generally considered to be a PR debacle, right down to last week's *Time* magazine cover picturing Mr. Johnson beneath the headline "A Game of Greed." In the end, the Kravises—and not the Robinsons—triumphed.

The press has also ridiculed her attempts to defend Mr. Milken by playing up his charitable contributions. "She generates ink, sure, but I question how effective that exposure really is for her clients," says Len Kessler, president of LMK Communications, Inc., a competing financial-PR firm. "You have to question whether she put out a fire or actually fanned the flames."

Other critics contend that Mrs. Robinson is inexperienced at best or is riding the coattails of her powerful husband. Steven Brill, the president and editor-in-chief of *American Lawyer*, ran up against Mrs. Robinson when his company co-published a book, Connie Bruck's *The Predators' Ball*, critical of Mr. Milken and his securities firm, Drexel Burnham Lambert. Her efforts to discredit the book spurred considerable additional publicity, which helped lead to a doubling of its press run. Says Mr. Brill, "She's out of her league."

Mrs. Robinson's foray in the image-shaping business was perhaps inevitable, given the careful tutelage of a series of mentors, beginning with her late father, Freeman Gosden. Mr. Gosden played Amos in the popular radio show of the 1940s, "Amos 'n' Andy." The Ronald Reagans are longtime friends of the politically active Gosden family. So was President Eisenhower. "There were always [political] discussions at the dinner table," says Mrs. Robinson's mother, Jane Gosden. "We talked about the strategies you could do to help get your friends elected."

Mrs. Robinson arrived at the University of California at Los Angeles in 1970 in the midst of the hippie counterculture, but she remained a flag-waving Republican. She dropped out of college for a few years and worked in an acupuncture clinic, among other places, but soon returned to the social and business mainstream when she married Stephen Dart, son of her parents' friend Justin Dart, the late chairman of the former Dart & Kraft Inc. The couple divorced four years later.

After a year in law school, she headed east in 1979 to become deputy press secretary for Mr. Reagan's presidential campaign, working with a small team including James Lake, now chairman of Robinson Lake, and campaign strategist John Sears. She joined the Republican National Committee the next year. When the committee's vice chairman, Drew Lewis, became transportation secretary in 1981, she followed him as the department's director of public affairs. She was credited with helping the Transportation Department maintain a relatively favorable image during the 1982 air-traffic controllers' strike.

Mr. Lewis became an important mentor. When he left the cabinet in 1983 to become chief executive of Warner-Amex Cable Communications Inc., Mrs. Robinson followed, and was named senior vice president for corporate affairs. She met Mr. Robinson—at the time, American Express owned half of Warner-Amex—and they married a year later in a private ceremony attended only by their mothers. ("I made a little speech and the mothers, the minister, everybody was crying," Mr. Robinson recalls). When American Express sold its Warner-Amex stake in 1986, Mrs. Robinson and six other Warner-Amex executives reaped windfalls of $1.07 million each pursuant to a deal they negotiated when they joined the company.

Shortly afterward, Mrs. Robinson, Mr. Lake and Kenneth Lerer, another Warner-Amex colleague, launched their own public-relations firm with offices in New York and Washington. After just three months in business, they sold to ad agency Bozell, Jacobs, Kenyon & Eckhardt, whose chairman, Charles Peebler, was an acquaintance of both Robinsons. Mrs. Robinson now heads up not only Robinson Lake, but Bozell's separate PR business as well.

Four of Robinson Lake's major clients were introduced to Mrs. Robinson through her husband. Among them are Commercial Credit Group Inc., whose chairman, Sandy Weill, is a former American Express president, and Squibb Corp., whose chief executive, Richard M. Furland, is an American Express director. One of Mrs. Robinson's partners, Walter Montgomery, had headed up American Express's PR department.

But Mrs. Robinson bristles at suggestions by some competitors and takeover specialists that she is capitalizing on her prominent husband's connections. She says the firm has one hundred clients, most of whom have never met Mr. Robinson. For every client she has met through her husband, she says, "there are people who won't hire us because of perceived conflicts with American Express."

Besides, Mrs. Robinson has introduced her distinguished husband to a few famous and powerful people herself, particularly in Washington circles. "I met the President through her—how about that?" Mr. Robinson says. He recalls tagging along with her to the 1984 Republican convention, where she was helping out the Reagan-Bush campaign. "When I checked in," he says, "they teasingly gave me a [nametag] that said 'Jimmy Gosden.' "

Mrs. Robinson also meets prospective clients on the social circuit, and seems to effortlessly mix business and pleasure. She and her husband attend dinners or parties almost every night. They also give a few parties of their own, like a surprise fiftieth birthday bash Mrs. Robinson orchestrated three years ago for her husband which included treating two hundred guests to a Broadway show followed by a lavish dinner dance.

At an Advertising Council dinner honoring her husband, she introduces him by exclaiming, "Isn't he cute?" and insists that this reporter feel his biceps, the product of daily dawn workouts. (Mr. Robinson smiles adoringly at his wife and flexes.) But she abandons dinner partners like International Business Machines Corp. Chairman John Akers and his wife, to spend most of the cocktail hour on the phone with RJR advisers. After dinner, she dashes out to a late-night RJR meeting.

Her social and business connections aside, few people deny her intelligence and determination. "She's the best I've ever met at what she does," says former Labor Secretary William Brock, who hired her as director of public relations of the Republican National Committee in 1980, when he was chairman.

Among reporters, Mrs. Robinson is known as a shrewd advocate. She earns good will by doling out exclusive bits of information, recognizing that reporters are especially grateful for information that doesn't surface in competing publications. She gains credibility by not whitewashing her clients' problems. She often cross-examines reporters, trying to prod them into "logical" conclusions favorable to her clients. She makes reporters feel important, breathlessly informing them that she is dropping all other pressing matters to take their call. And she is legendary for her ability to return phone calls promptly.

But reporters say there is a price. She often gains remarkable influence over how stories are written. Reporters may be fearful to alienate her, knowing the scoops she passes to them could stop or be transferred to a competitor. And they are aware, even though she doesn't tell them, that she has access to top editors and media executives—in many cases, a reporter's boss. Among her friends are television newscasters Tom Brokaw, Diane Sawyer and Barbara Walters, *Washington Post* Editorial Page Editor Meg Greenfield, and *New York Daily News* Publisher James Hoge. She was a guest at the recent wedding of *Wall Street Journal* Managing Editor Norman Pearlstine and author Nancy Friday.

Mrs. Robinson says she is careful not to use her connections to threaten reporters or go over their heads. "I bend over backwards not to take advantage of friendships of anybody in the media," she says.

Among reporters as well as clients, Mrs. Robinson is known for her persistence; she repeats her points again and again, and talks so fast she sometimes stumbles over her words. "She's enough sometimes to drive you right up the wall," says friend and client Drew Lewis, now chairman of Union Pacific Corp. "You get tired of being pestered by her, you get tired of her calling you at eleven at night, and you get tired of her telling you the same thing twenty times, because she does," he says. Her persistence was evident in the three solid hours she spent trying to persuade this reporter not to write this story.

She is also known for her hyperactive energy; she is virtually always moving, and keeps going at a fever pitch even when working all night. Her tireless work habits are a good fit with the workaholic culture of the bankers and lawyers she deals with. "Other PR firms tend to be nine-to-fivers," says Philip Keevil of S.G. Warburg & Co., Grand Met's investment bank. "But she's there [nights] and Walter [Montgomery] is there. You feel they're more a part of the team if they're alongside you."

Corporate clients say she is at her best when giving instruction on how to present themselves to the press, shareholders, the government and other audiences. In early August, two months before Grand Met made its offer for Pillsbury, she presented a forty-page communications plan to Grand Met's chief executive and his entourage. She suggested that Grand Met executives launch their bid from Minneapolis, where Pillsbury is based, so that they wouldn't seem like hostile invaders from afar; the day of the bid, she orchestrated meetings between Grand Met executives and dozens of local reporters and politicians.

Her efforts apparently worked. The day after the bid, a front-page *Minneapolis Star Tribune* headline blared, "Grand Met vows to keep up Pillsbury's very charitable ways," while a companion story was headlined, "Analysts say bid may be irresistible." Another newspaper story said that Grand Met executives had met with more state politicians than Pillsbury had, concluding that the trip "was a marvel of public relations."

She was similarly effective in the Texaco case, advisers say, partly because she wasn't afraid to stand up to Texaco's executives or their advisers. She pressed some Texaco executives, for example, to run ads and write shareholder letters casting Mr. Icahn as a "greenmailer" and an incompetent in his management of TWA Corp., the parent of Trans World Airlines. "Is this the man you want piloting your company?" read the headline on one ad, which went on to outline TWA's "crushing debt burden" and its aging fleet of planes.

Some Texaco executives were horrified, a meeting participant says, because that ungentlemanly approach "wasn't a Texaco-like thing to do." But she won out. "There were a lot of very strong-willed people with very strongly held positions," says the participant. "And she really had to knock a few heads. She had to verbally and intellectually dominate a lot of strongwilled people."

Yet two of her biggest efforts to date have had less than brilliant results. One aide to the RJR camp laments that Mrs. Robinson didn't have sufficient influence or ability to stem the torrent of bad publicity about Mr. Johnson. (The aide is, however, hard-pressed to name any public-relations adviser who would.)

Mrs. Robinson won't comment on her efforts on Mr. Johnson's behalf. But she says of the bad publicity surrounding Mr. Johnson, "Pioneers take a lot of arrows. Ross Johnson did a very innovative thing that ultimately was of great benefit to the shareholders."

Many believe Mrs. Robinson has also hurt her own efforts to defend Mr. Milken. When attacking *The Predators' Ball*, which was critical of Mr. Milken, she and some colleagues seized on alleged factual errors in a pre-publication copy and saw that key journalists were alerted. Drexel says her attempts to discredit the book were "consistent" with a strategy the firm had agreed on. But dissenting executives, and journalists who wrote about the mudslinging fest, say the effort was overzealous and generated far more publicity for the book than it otherwise would have received.

Mrs. Robinson concedes that the attack brought the book more publicity. "But we were willing to take that risk," she says. "In the extra inches of ink, there was more space devoted to factual errors."

More recent attempts by Mrs. Robinson and her firm to play up Mr. Milken's charitable activities have drawn derisive laughter from some quarters. After Mr. Milken made a surprise appearance at a Drexel breakfast and let slip that he was taking seventeen hundred poor kids to a Mets game, *New York* magazine ran a snide item about the "heavy-handed attempt at damage control." A local publication, *7 Days*, lampooned Mr. Milken in a cartoon showing him with a New York Mets pin and a halo. (The *Wall Street Journal* reported on Mr. Milken's image-burnishing activities in a page-one story on October 12.)

Perhaps more ominously, some people say Mrs. Robinson's vigorous defense of Mr. Milken has sparked suspicion among some Drexel executives, who are worried that she is putting his interests ahead of the firm's interests. "When there are separate representations, some amount of tension is inevitable," Mrs. Robinson concedes. "But we believe that Michael Milken's interest and Drexel's interests are ultimately one and the same."

Still, Robinson Lake's efforts have played a role in some positive stories about Mr. Milken, including recent articles in *Business Week*, the *Washington Post*, and the *Daily News* of Los Angeles. Mrs. Robinson's colleague Mr. Lerer handles the day-to-day responsibilities as spokesman for Mr. Milken, and some reporters say he has generated good will by setting up one-on-one sessions with the once-elusive Mr. Milken.

But Mrs. Robinson has little time to reflect on either her successes or failures. Most of her waking hours are spent on the phone, her trademark. At the Transportation Department in 1982, coworkers surprised her with a birthday cake that depicted her on the phone, saying, "I'll put you on hold." Her partner Mr. Montgomery recalls that last March her cab was blocked by New York's St. Patrick's Day parade—so she got out and began plowing through the crowds, still engrossed in conversation on the portable phone she takes everywhere.

With their busy schedules, the Robinsons almost never can spend a full weekend at their thirty-five-acre country place in Connecticut, the former home of the late designer Angelo Donghia, where Mrs. Robinson keeps five horses. They have little time for their stables and swimming pool; their tennis court, putting green and gym are often empty. Says her husband: "We try to be at home alone an average of one and a half nights—every two weeks."

The Man From Wall Street

David Vise and Steve Coll

February 8, 1989, the *Washington Post*

---

*Washington Post writers Steve Coll and David Vise
won a Pulitzer Prize for their even-handed series
on the SEC under chairman John Shad. I include
this piece from their four-part series because it is
one of the few that addressed an obvious, but
unanswered question: Who was the government's
top regulator in the Gaga Years and why did he
refuse to believe until very late in the game that
Drexel was a corrupt firm? Their answer is more
than a little disturbing.*

O N THE WEEKEND OF JANUARY 7, Drexel Burnham Lambert
Inc. Chief Executive Fred Joseph boarded an airplane in
New York bound for The Hague, capital of the Netherlands.
Only a handful of Joseph's colleagues at Drexel knew of his
trip, which came just weeks after the firm had agreed to plead
guilty to criminal fraud charges and pay a record $650 million
in penalties.

Joseph was flying to see John Shad, the U.S. ambassador to
the Netherlands. Shad had hired Joseph out of Harvard Business School twenty-six years earlier, and for more than a
decade on Wall Street had been Joseph's boss, mentor and
friend.

But their relationship had changed dramatically during the
1980s, when Shad became chairman of the Securities and
Exchange Commission, Wall Street's top cop. Joseph was running Drexel, the target of the biggest and most widely publicized securities fraud investigation in the SEC's history.

Now that Drexel was near an agreement with the government, Joseph wanted Shad to become Drexel's chairman and help save the firm.

It was surprising to some people that Shad, who had left the SEC in 1987, was interested in the job. But Shad liked challenges, and besides, he thought it would be good for the country if Drexel survived.

Though the commission had wide powers, Shad had done little as SEC chairman to restrain Drexel's junk-bond financed corporate raiders as they rattled the executive suites and shop floors of the country's largest companies with hostile bids during the mid-1980s.

Shad's views about takeovers and Drexel's role in financing many of them were complicated. But overall, he believed that takeovers were good for the economy because they rewarded shareholders and forced corporate managers to be more productive. The SEC finally acted to rein in Drexel after the agency staff found evidence of fraud late in 1986.

At the center of Drexel's rise was Michael Milken, its innovative and influential junk bond chief. Shad deeply admired Milken. During his own long career on Wall Street, Shad had engaged in some early junk bond financings and friendly mergers and acquisitions, though his use of these techniques was relatively conservative.

Milken should be punished if he were guilty of any wrongdoing, Shad thought. Drexel agreed to admit that Milken had rigged corporate takeovers and manipulated stock prices. But that didn't change Shad's feeling that Milken was a genius. If Milken, who has vigorously denied any wrongdoing, cut any corners, it was incidental to Drexel's success, Shad believed.

There was one other factor in the SEC's decision not to regulate takeovers aggressively that has gone unreported: At a key moment when some in the Reagan administration feared Shad was about to push for takeover restrictions, officials and economists privately told him that he was deviating from the free-market philosophy of the administration. Although the SEC is an independent agency, and not part of the administration's economic policymaking apparatus, several conservative economists in the administration lobbied Shad steadily to make sure he did not intervene.

The Leveraging of America

In June 1984, with Wall Street engulfed in a frenzy of junk-bond financed hostile takeovers led by Drexel, John Shad delivered a remarkable speech to the New York Financial Writers Association. For the first time since becoming SEC chairman, Shad spoke out about the dangers of corporate takeovers.

Shad warned that heavy borrowing to finance corporate takeovers had long-term economic and social consequences. Companies burdened by takeover debt would not be able to invest in plant, equipment, research and development of new products. Contrary to popular wisdom, he went on, many of the U.S. companies that were targets of takeovers had strong managements, not weak ones. When the next economic recession struck, many heavily leveraged companies would be pushed into bankruptcy, Shad predicted.

"In today's corporate world, Darwin's survival of the fittest has become, 'Acquire or be acquired,' " he said. "The more leveraged takeovers and buyouts today, the more bankruptcies tomorrow."

"The Leveraging of America" was the title of his talk, and it was a speech of which Shad was proud. After he delivered it, he asked one of his legal assistants to distribute copies to the chief executives of the Fortune 500—the largest corporations in the United States.

The speech, which made news worldwide, marked a potentially important turning point in the SEC's approach to the regulation of corporate takeovers.

Until 1984, the SEC had studied takeovers without advocating that anything be done about them. For two years the SEC had been under pressure from Congress, corporations and labor unions to take a stand on controversial takeover tactics, including the heavy use of high-risk, high-yield junk bond financing.

And perhaps most important, some of Shad's old friends from his three decades on Wall Street, including takeover attorney Martin Lipton and former SEC commissioner A. A. Sommer Jr., privately urged him to crack down on junk bonds and hostile takeovers. Shad defused the pressure temporarily by appointing a committee of experts, consisting mostly of Wall Street takeover professionals, to give the SEC advice about what to do.

The committee suggested tinkering with the takeover process, but recommended no fundamental change in regulations. But Shad grew more concerned as the use of debt to finance takeovers spiraled—in his days on Wall Street, he had been more cautious about the use of such leverage.

Now, in deciding to speak out, Shad had a wide impact; as SEC chairman, he was Wall Street's chief regulator, and he seemed to be taking a definite stand on a major economic policy issue. He heard warm praise from Wall Street friends who were growing worried about the aggressive, debt-driven takeover practices of Drexel's stable of corporate raiders.

Inside the SEC, Shad's speech alarmed Gregg Jarrell, the commission's recently hired chief economist. A self-described former hippie, Jarrell had come to the SEC to promote the free market doctrine championed by the school where he was trained, the University of Chicago. Young, possessed of a sense of humor, and unconcerned about how long his career in Washington would last, Jarrell wanted to shake things up at the SEC.

On takeovers, his views were radical. "The best of all worlds is the termination of federal regulation," he wrote in a dissent to the report of Shad's committee of takeover experts. His views attracted the attention of raider T. Boone Pickens Jr., who like Jarrell was an avid racquetball player. When in Washington, Pickens would come by SEC headquarters in his stretch limousine and pick up Jarrell for a game.

When Shad provided him an advance copy of his "Leveraging of America" speech, Jarrell reacted strongly. "B.S.!" he wrote in the margin, making so many marks on the page that he turned his copy red. "You've got no evidence."

Others felt as Jarrell did. SEC Commissioner Charles Cox, a free-market economist who had earlier held Jarrell's job and who had received his commission seat with Shad's help, said he was "surprised" by Shad's speech. Douglas Ginsburg, then head of the regulatory section of the Office of Management and Budget, also expressed concerns, as did other economists and officials at OMB, the Council of Economic Advisers, the Justice Department and the Treasury Department.

The conservative economists' critique was something Shad had said he wanted. One of Shad's goals when he became chairman was to transform the SEC's approach to problem solving by de-emphasizing legal reasoning and promoting an economic-based approach. He wanted all regulatory proposals analyzed by a method known as cost-benefit analysis, in which the goals of regulation are measured against predicted cost. He wanted to get rid of "burdensome" regulations.

Above all, Shad wanted to address complaints from Wall Street—which reflected his own views—that some SEC lawyers who had limited knowledge about how markets worked were making decisions about new rules with no appreciation for the economic consequences.

Jarrell and the others saw Shad's speech as a betrayal. "The administration's view was that Shad was off the reservation," Jarrell recalled. "Number one, they wanted some communication with him, and number two, they wanted to get in there and influence" Shad's approach to takeovers.

Since coming to Washington, Shad had developed little intimacy with the White House. Once, when Shad wanted to discuss financial regulation with Vice President Bush, he had to dial 411 to find the White House phone number. When he reached Bush's office, he had trouble persuading the aide who answered that he was the chairman of the SEC.

Jarrell's concern was that Shad didn't understand what the administration wanted the SEC to do on takeovers. "I tried to move him [Shad] wherever the administration wanted to go," Jarrell recalled.

To do so, he set up lunches, meetings and other lines of communication between Shad and certain administration officials, including Ginsburg, whom Shad had met before he knew Jarrell. At the same time, Jarrell worked with other economists inside and outside the SEC to develop studies that would support the administration's position that takeovers— even the Drexel-sponsored hostile takeovers mounted by corporate raiders who had little cash to finance their bids—were good for shareholders, the economy and the country.

Jarrell said one of his tactics was to leak his pro-takeover studies to the press before Shad or the other SEC commissioners had a chance to review them. "Getting the reports out to the press in advance of their publication worked like a charm," Jarrell said. "We pushed Shad right to the limit."

When Shad confronted him, Jarrell recalled, "I had to deny, deny, deny that I had leaked my studies. . . . Our studies changed the nature of the debate." Jarrell was criticized for the leaks by Shad and others, but he didn't seem to care.

In other quarters of the administration, a similarly aggressive push was on. One official at OMB kept a big chart on his wall showing all the bills in Congress that would restrict corporate takeovers; the official's job was to stop the bills before they got too far. On May 20, 1985, OMB's Ginsburg appeared at an SEC meeting and said the administration was dubious that takeovers had reached the point where "public confidence is implicated or the financial markets threatened." Ginsburg urged that the SEC do nothing.

Those who had liked Shad's "Leveraging of America" speech hoped that it was merely the first salvo in a war that would end with new restrictions on takeovers. But Shad led no such effort.

Late in 1985, Jarrell and Ginsburg helped engineer the appointment of Joseph Grundfest, a free market economist, as an SEC commissioner. A lawyer and Democrat, Grundfest had written a chapter in the 1985 Economic Report of the President lauding the benefits of takeovers. His appointment tipped the balance of the five-member commission in favor of the free market approach.

SEC Votes to Back Down

In January 1986, a month after Grundfest's appointment, the SEC voted to back down from nearly all the legislative proposals on takeovers it had earlier submitted to Congress. Shad, Cox and Grundfest agreed that market forces and other legislative changes had substantially cured the perceived abuses.

Shad's opponents said the commission before Shad—the SEC of Stanley Sporkin, who was the commission's enforcement chief before being pressured out of the agency in 1981—almost certainly would have attacked junk bond-financed takeovers as manipulative ploys. They felt Shad should have used the SEC rules to protect investors by forcing the raiders to disclose evidence of secure financing before launching their hostile bids.

"Lawyers in billion-dollar deals will make a close call about [takeover] disclosure and say, 'So what' about the SEC," said Ted Levine, formerly associate director of the SEC's enforcement division. "I know because I hear those kinds of conversations in transactions all the time. There's a loss of discipline."

By 1986, the shouts Shad heard about Drexel and the hostile corporate takeovers it financed had become louder.

Enormous, venerable companies such as Gulf Corp., Walt Disney Co. and others had been threatened by upstart raiders with bold plans but little money. There were allegations that Drexel had formed secret alliances with raiders and professional stock speculators called arbitrageurs to rig the process so that no target could defend itself. The SEC's enforcement division had looked into it, but it was unable to develop the kind of evidence that would stick in court.

Shad thought it would be dangerous for the SEC to attempt to slow takeovers—such regulation might have unanticipated and disastrous effects on the economy. Moreover, the 1968 federal statute governing corporate takeovers, called the Williams Act, was intended by Congress to be neutral; the SEC wasn't supposed to take sides in takeover fights, as Shad read the law.

Shad considered Fred Joseph, the man at Drexel's helm, to be a person of high integrity. They had worked together on Wall Street for almost a decade, and they were similar in many ways. Both were outsiders to the Street's blue-blooded establishment—Shad the son of a launderer, Joseph the son of a cab driver—and they shared an intense ambition to prove themselves.

Shad hired Joseph in 1963 to work with him in the corporate finance department of E. F. Hutton. During the job interview, Shad asked Joseph what his father did, what kind of name Joseph was, and what his favorite sport was. Joseph fired back: Cab driver, Jewish, boxing. It was exactly what Shad wanted to hear: He knew that Joseph was as hungry as he was, and he was impressed by Joseph's academic record, too.

Not only did Shad admire Joseph personally, he shared his views about Wall Street and investment banking. They made their mark at Hutton because they were willing to take risks, to step outside the boundaries of traditional investment banking. They concentrated on advising midsized, growing companies whose credit was not as sound and whose banking needs were not as predictable as the big blue-chip corporations.

Shad broke ranks with Wall Street by raising money for Caesar's, the casino company, a deal that others credited with making casino financings acceptable on Wall Street. Later, after Joseph became Drexel's chief, that firm became the investment banker not only to Caesar's but also to nearly every major casino operator in Las Vegas and Atlantic City.

"You sure don't look like an investment banker" was the line Joseph always used to tease Shad, who was overweight and far from dashing. The line captured the identity that Shad and Joseph shared: They were upstarts, fighters, climbers.

Shad hated more than anything to waste time in cars, and he pushed cab drivers relentlessly to pick up the pace. In one trip with Joseph to the airport, Shad demanded that the cab driver move first into the right lane, then the left lane, then told him to take an exit and get back on the highway at the next entrance. The driver hit the brake, got out of the cab, and opened Shad's door. He told Shad: "If you can drive better than me, sir, you drive." So Shad took the wheel and chauffered Joseph and the cabbie to the airport.

In 1970, Joseph backed Shad in a fight for Hutton's top job. Shad lost. Afterwards, Joseph left the firm, landing eventually at Drexel, while Shad settled in as Hutton's vice chairman. Though they saw each other less frequently, Shad and Joseph continued to pursue the philosophy they had shared at Hutton. While Shad initiated a handful of junk-bond financings and many friendly mergers, Joseph and Drexel went on to pioneer a $100 billion evolution in junk bonds and fostered numerous hostile takeovers.

So when Shad was deluged at the SEC with criticism that

Drexel and its junk bond genius, Michael Milken, weren't abiding by Wall Street's traditional rules, he was not easily persuaded. Intellectually and viscerally, he admired the work of Milken, partly because Milken had extended into a multi-billion-dollar business some of the same approaches to investment banking Joseph and Shad had taken while at Hutton. Drexel, in many ways, was the kind of investment bank that Shad might have built himself.

Advice From Boesky

On February 19, 1986, Ivan F. Boesky was among the guests John Shad invited to SEC headquarters to discuss the problem of takeover rumors in the stock market.

Shad enjoyed his power to convene panels of experts to discuss the issues of the day. He was drawn to the ebb and flow of what he called "roundtable" dialogue, and he depended on his panels to suggest solutions to problems the commission faced. The panels were a facet of Shad's attempt to ease the traditionally adversarial relationship between the SEC and Wall Street.

Shad knew Boesky by reputation as one of Wall Street's boldest professional stock speculators. The son of a Detroit restaurateur, Boesky had accumulated a fortune of more than $100 million in just a few years on Wall Street by trading the stocks of companies involved in corporate takeovers.

Suspecting that Boesky's incredible success was based on illegal, inside information, the SEC had launched numerous investigations. The Boesky probes, along with numerous other prosecutions, reflected Shad's vow to come down on insider trading "with hobnail boots." But the commission had never been able to prove a violation.

At the February 1986 roundtable, Shad asked Boesky and other Wall Street professionals what the SEC should do about the plethora of rumors and at what stage companies should disclose merger negotiations. The earlier such disclosure, the less time there is for insiders to trade while the public is unaware of negotiations.

"I think that the goal should be the most disclosure as soon as possible for the marketplace to have a more orderly system," Boesky said.

What Shad didn't know that day was that Boesky secretly

was involved in several illegal trading arrangements, including some with key Drexel executives. On May 12, 1986, one of those Drexel executives, Dennis Levine, was charged with insider trading in a scheme that had netted him about $12 million in illegal profits.

Within weeks, Levine agreed to plead guilty and began to tell federal prosecutors and SEC lawyers in New York everything he knew. Among others, Levine fingered Boesky.

Shad feared that Boesky would take his millions and flee the country. But instead, Boesky decided to cooperate, trading his knowledge for leniency. He confessed a multitude of fraud schemes to the government, including an illegal stock trading arrangement that he said he had entered into with Drexel's Milken. The arrangement, Boesky said, rigged corporate takeovers, manipulated stock prices, and evaded a host of other securities and tax laws.

As the details of Boesky's confessions about Drexel became known, several congressmen asserted that Drexel's role in the takeover boom of the 1980s had been fundamentally corrupt.

John Shad didn't believe that—Fred Joseph, he thought, did not run a corrupt firm. It appeared that Drexel might have a problem with a single branch office, its Beverly Hills, California-based junk bond operations headed by Milken. Was it possible, as SEC attorneys had alleged, that Milken's group had become a runaway operation, that Milken had become bigger than Joseph or even the firm?

In June 1987, with the Drexel investigation in full swing, Shad left the SEC to become ambassador to the Netherlands, amid praise from some members of Congress who earlier had been his opponents.

Six years at the commission had made him the longest-serving chairman in SEC history. He oversaw the biggest investigations of Wall Street since the agency's creation. One investigation focused on a massive check-kiting scheme at his old firm, E. F. Hutton, a probe in which Shad declined to be involved because of his past connection with the firm.

Shaken by these scandals, Shad decided in 1987 to donate most of his fortune, about $20 million, to establish an ethics program at the Harvard Business School.

Shad had come to the SEC hoping to ease the fifty-year

adversarial relationship between Wall Street and the commission. Despite resistance from the commission's bureaucracy, he succeeded in reducing restraints on stock trading, including the highly speculative stock index futures.

He had shifted the SEC enforcement division's top priority from attacks on corporations to the pursuit of cheating by individuals on Wall Street. Shad transferred more responsibility for policing stockbroker sales practices to Wall Street, believing it would be more effective.

On Shad's watch, the stock market rose to the highest level in U.S. history. Soon after his departure, the market crashed, but stock prices remained higher than they had been when he came to the SEC. Corporations raised billions of dollars in new capital, aided by his elimination of "burdensome" regulations.

By the end of Shad's tenure, however, the Street's traders and bankers lived in greater fear of the government's scrutiny than they had before he came to Washington.

On his last weekend at the SEC, Shad received an honorary degree from the University of Rochester, where economist Gregg Jarrell had gone to teach.

Shad told Rochester's graduating business students, "Wall Street has long been a favorite target, and yet Wall Street's ethics compare favorably with other professions and occupations. . . . By the highest conjecture, securities fraud is a tiny fraction of one percent of the enormous volume of securities transactions. . . . The few robber barons who existed were born over a century ago, and were buried in the debris of the 1929 crash. Today, the bulk of American industry and finance are managed by a generation of giants."

Weighing an Offer

Last month's meeting between Shad and Joseph at the embassy compound in The Hague was simple and direct—a negotiation between old and trusted friends.

They scratched on a single piece of paper the outline of a proposed deal that would make Shad Drexel's chairman.

Shad, who had lived by the credo that he would spend one third of his life learning, one third earning and one third serving, was concerned that any move to Drexel would be perceived as an ethical compromise.

He wanted a new job in the Bush administration, but had learned that no acceptable post would be forthcoming. Before accepting the Drexel chairmanship, Shad wanted to know more about the circumstances surrounding Drexel's guilty plea.

He told Joseph he would have to consult with his former colleagues at the SEC and with Justice Department prosecutors. Former Manhattan U.S. attorney Rudolph W. Giuliani, who spearheaded the criminal probe of Drexel, expressed enthusiasm for the idea. After Giuliani's endorsement, Shad indicated he would not announce his final decision until after he resigns as ambassador late this month.

In 1981, Shad had come to Washington from Wall Street. When he needed expert advice, he turned to Wall Street. When he considered the larger issues of economic policy, he relied on his experiences as an investment banker. Wall Street was what he knew, it was in his bones.

When Joseph offered him the Drexel job, Shad was inclined to accept. Eight years had passed since he left Wall Street. It was probably time to go home.

The Second Wife

Jane Lane

March 1989, *M*

---

*M magazine's "The Second Wife" was the first
story about some eighties women who made their
living by being geishas for the horny tycoons of the
decade. It tells you which dame bagged which
billionaire, how she went about it, her traits, her
psychological profile, her duties, and what it is
going to cost her sugar daddy if he wants to dump
her like wife number one. The article is bitchy, a
tone I think appropriate given the subject.*

OVER COCKTAILS, one socialite was comparing notes with
another on the splendid fortune of Mrs. X, who'd just
bagged a huge divorcé tycoon. "I should have taken down that
score," she sniffed. "She just got lucky." Her older and wiser
friend eyed her skeptically. "You wouldn't have lasted fifteen
minutes with him," she observed. "Honey, you're not quali-
fied for that job."

It's a tough way to make a living, being second wife to a
world-class tycoon. But somebody's got to do it, so it might as
well be the hearty breed so eminently suited to the task: tall,
thin, dizzyingly energetic, she is the contemporary *femme du
monde* who jockeys the roles of courtesan, social secretary
and *saloniste*. Unscathed by feminism, this flower of the free
enterprise system brings an exuberantly entrepreneurial spirit
to marriage only another free-market fan could appreciate.

And when the real pros hit, they hit like tidal waves.

"It's a total sweeping off of feet, a mortar shell hitting
these guys," observes one prominent social stateswoman.
"When it comes to finding a second wife, they want a total

change, a totally different type of woman, and not always from the *crème de la crème*. It's a whole different world for these men: They're dealing with highly ambitious women seeking money and power. They're all pushers."

If you subscribe to prevailing wisdom, the currency second wives deal in is sex, not dollars. This is only partially true, although the appearance of passion counts for immeasurably more than reality.

"If you believe Mercedes [Bass, who just became the new Mrs. Sid Bass after the conclusion of a raging divorce battle between Sid and his first wife, Anne], Sid is the greatest lover in the world, unlike any man she has ever known. Which is doubtful," says a friend.

"The fact is, he was fed up with ball-breaking American women, and wanted a European geisha, and Mercedes [an Iranian by birth] qualifies as an honorary French or Italian," he continues. "Sid was tired of criticism and carping; now he wants someone who massages his psyche. Not to belittle her, but there are so many Mercedeses in Paris; that kind of psyche-stroking doesn't exist here."

Does that mean a woman need only polish up her French and be nice to her man, to get his millions and billions? Whoa, there, Nellie; not so fast.

Try this on for a day's work: up at eight, read the papers (gossip columns and business section especially); trainer arrives for hour's workout; extensive telephone conversations with friends and florist; negotiations with cook or caterer, depending on complexity and sophistication of household; dress for lunch; go to lunch but don't eat; meet with decorator for shopping or hurling abuse; meet with designers and jewelers for same; hairdresser and manicure, makeup for the intensely committed; dress for dinner; go to dinner but don't eat; pretend to fend off paparazzi; talk nonstop and with faux authority about everything. Home by 11:30. A night of scorching sex is almost too painful to contemplate after such a schedule.

"There's no reason why they'd need to look for a second wife if they're looking for you-know-what," says a man who walks plenty of those women. "Any man who is the R word [rich] could have hot and cold running sex twenty-four hours a day. These men want to build a real life, an amusing life, with parties, society, F-U-N and glamor.

"The ladies are fairly impressive creatures," he adds. "It's exhausting work. These are the women who keep charity going. They're very hard-working and good at their jobs."

The intensity of their glow is directly proportionate to the quantity of money and power on the market, and we are most distinctly in a boom time. These women are rich enough, and influential enough, to establish and maintain their own order: Nouvelle Society.

"It isn't High Society," reminds one walker. "There isn't any High Society; or else it's pretty rare, and people aren't terribly interested. Nobody in the press cares about people in Newport working on their rose gardens."

What about the utterly moldy idea of marrying for love?

Well, for these couples, purpose has superseded passion. They want to *accomplish* something—the Rohatyns with their social consciousness-raising, the Gutfreunds with their glamorous fantasies, the Roehm-Kravises with their neo-imperial aggressions, the Hallingbys with their relentless search for the perfect high profile. Marriage for them is a synergy of ends and means.

"They can be divided into two categories," observes one walker. "Women who are not really of any importance by themselves, like Gayfryd Steinberg, Mercedes Bass or Susan Gutfreund, and complement their husbands."

Then there are women like Julie Kosner (the writer who is the second wife of Ed, editor and publisher of *New York* magazine) and Claudia Cohen (the television personality and second wife of Revlon's Ronald Perelman) who accomplish something on their own. In either case, they are remarkably well suited to each other."

They are bound by the silken cord of dependency. The well-disciplined air hostess finds her ultimate passenger, and the tycoon makes his most titilating purchase.

"The first time, these men marry the girl they're supposed to marry, and split moments before cellulite," says a social commentator. "Then they find the type of woman who never competes, who never harangues. She's like a shiny medal. The glamor of the second wife is that she's not the first."

Traits of the Second Wife

• She'll be younger, sexier and usually prettier than the first one. When you get to number three or four, it could be a different story, but probably not.

• She's likely to be more worldly than the first wife. A second language is a common feature, as, increasingly, is a background as a career woman.

• She's taller than her husband, if he's under 5′ 9″.

• She's socially determined, and is not prone to feeling demeaned by her role as ornament.

• She's sexy enough to make her husband's friends envious, but not so sexy that their wives hate and shun her.

• She's clever, clever, clever, but not a boring rocket-scientist type.

• She's not prone to sulks, unless they're part of a routine that he finds endearing or exciting.

• She's tough as nails when it comes to dealing with tradesmen and the help.

• She's outwardly disdainful of attractive young men.

• If she fools around, she's exceedingly discreet.

Shrink's View: Bad News

"Men who would be objectionable under any circumstances except for the fact that they have a lot of money." That is psychoanalyst Dr. Roberta Jaeger's blunt assessment of magnates who make their money with one wife and then find a second wife to help spend it.

"They're looking for a wife who will help them to make it in society," says Dr. Jaeger of the nuptial motivations of the parvenu powerful. "A lot of these guys, I think, are boorish and losers. They're not very interesting, they're highly unattractive, they're very self-centered. For wives they want the kind of women who are attracted by power and money, who are very impressed with that, and who like going to all these charity functions and parties.

"And that's what their relationship consists of—the wife is like a new building or a new business," continues Jaeger, training and supervisory psychoanalyst at Columbia University's Psychoanalytic Center. "The prettier, the more flamboyant, the better. These are not people who are interested in relationships, or even capable of relationships."

The obsession with business and the self—and the wife as extravagant chattel—she calls "pathological. I think that very often these people have very pathological sex lives. As a matter of fact, I know that from experience.

"I've been particularly impressed by the number of people in important positions who are incapable of having any sort of reasonable sex life. But the wives make adjustments, too, in return for the jewels and the trips and the villa in Monaco."

Second and succeeding marriages are not likely to work, she says, when the partners haven't learned from their previous experiences. "Someone can make the same mistake two, three, four times," she says, and she counsels people who have. "When people go into this for the second time, there's more cynicism, there's a little bit more demandingness. Often, there's a lot of resentment on the part of the woman, who feels she's being asked to pay the price of the first mistake.

"However, with time, if things really are compatible, those things are forgotten. It's not been uncommon in my experience to see a pre-nuptial agreement, which in my opinion is like starting off a marriage with a divorce, put aside."

The High Cost of Cutting Loose

When Raoul Lionel Felder started practicing matrimonial law in Manhattan three decades ago, "men were entirely subject to blackmail," he says. "It was terrible. With

New York having only one ground, of adultery (for divorce), men would have to pay exorbitant prices to buy out of a marriage."

Things have been improved, says the flamboyant attorney best known for the expensive settlements he's won for various celebrity wives; but for the well-to-do husband who's decided to junk his helpmeet for a newer, possibly flashier model, nothing is going to be cheap.

To begin with, divorce lawyers like Felder, who service the upper strata of society, have pushed their meters out to as much as $450 an hour for representation. "But it's not the lawyer's fees or the court costs," explains attorney Samuel Fredman, who represented the ex-wife of Bess Myerson paramour Andy Capasso; it's the "equitable distribution" of marital property that will put the largest, most painful dent in a departing husband's net worth.

In the forty-two states that have adopted some form of "no-fault" divorce, community property is all property acquired or substantially enhanced in value during the course of the marriage, and is divided equally between husband and wife. New York, however, is still a fault state, and "its equitable distribution laws are more amorphous," says attorney Peter Bronstein, who made a free woman of Mercedes Kellogg prior to her recent marriage to Texas magnate Sid Bass. "Equitable is in the mind of the beholder. What is legitimately marital property and what is equitable can be the issue. With a top level investment banker/entrepreneur, who's put together $100 million, it's highly unlikely that the woman would get anywhere near 50 percent of the marital assets even if it has been a relatively long marriage."

He mentions that a client "worth hundreds of millions of dollars" recently deposited $50 million in the account of his estranged wife, prior to any negotiations. Would the wife be entitled to more than $50 million in an equitable distribution settlement? the client asked Bronstein. "Frankly," he says, "I advised that she would not be."

Faced with the prospect of a serious financial scalding, why, then, do men do it? "The man is looking for something more exciting," theorizes Fredman. "A rejuvenation,

'I didn't know people like me could feel like this again' kind of thing. It sounds dime-novelish in its context, but that's what's been happening."

Felder agrees. "The second wife can be a trophy of success," he says. "You know, you want all the accoutrements, you want a Rolls-Royce, you want several homes—and you want to have this blond nitwit who looked the way Peggy Lee did forty years ago on your arm."

Duties of the Second Wife

• To wear serious jewelry like she means it, which may mean reaching a deep understanding with mega-jeweler Fred Leighton.

• To devote herself to good works for causes that give big parties, attract the right crowd, and require large annual cash infusions from their patrons.

• Only sometimes, to bear children (if he genuinely wants another set of brats). More often, the greater duty, and burden, is to bear with his original-equipment children.

• To train her husband to check his imperious boardroom manners along with their coats at the door of social events.

• To identify and lure the right interior decorators into her employ to feather the suitably ravishing love nest and auxiliary residence.

• To illuminate for her husband the erotic possibilities that might arise from a high-priced score in the auction room.

• To goad her husband into upgrading the quality and downplaying the blandness of his wardrobe—sometimes disastrously.

• To do whatever it takes to keep sparks flying in the boudoir.

• To spend money with abandon, but not reckless abandon. He should feel the dough is well-spent.

• To make him feel sure he's loved for his own wonderful self, even if his most distinguished physical asset is his bulging wallet.

• To worry visibly about his physical condition and health, but only in private with him.

• For a tycoon, to develop a new and upscale social entourage.

• To know which is the hot Caribbean island of the moment; and, to know when to relent and accompany her husband back to Casa de Campo—again—for the golf.

• To learn enough about his business so that his business associates won't think she's a bimbo.

The CEO's Second Wife

Julie Connelly

August 28, 1989, *Fortune*

"The CEO's Second Wife" by Julie Connelly generated an enormous amount of controversy when it was published. First, because the folks at M thought the piece bore a striking resemblance to their "The Second Wife" which appeared six months earlier. And second, because many Fortune writers and editors were appalled by the admiring tone of the article. After all, this was essentially the age-old story of rich men discarding the women who brought up the kids and replacing them with sexier, younger dames. But good journalism or not, the story reflects the mood of the times and reminds us that the press bought into the crass enthusiasm of the decade as much as anyone.

His temper might perhaps be a little soured by finding, like many others of his sex, that through some unaccountable bias in favor of beauty, he was the husband of a very silly woman; but she knew that this kind of blunder was too common for any sensible man to be lastingly hurt by it.

—Jane Austen, *Sense and Sensibility*

ANY AMBITIOUS MANAGER with the top job in his sights used to know better than to ruin his chances with an untimely divorce. From the Duke of Windsor to William Agee, marrying The Woman I Love has made it tough to hang on to The Job I Love. Though half of all American marriages contracted since 1970 will end in divorce, the man who would be king in the business world was expected to remain wed to the princess who floated down the aisle, a white cloud on her father's arm, the day after graduation.

Not anymore. Gusty change is finally rattling the windows of the nation's most conservative secular institution, the corporation. Chief executives set the tone for acceptable behavior in their companies, and though the majority are still on their first marriages, a growing minority have discovered serial monogamy. Eugene Jennings, a Michigan State University professor and an expert on managerial life, estimates that in the 1980s, 12 percent to 15 percent of CEOs have been divorced, versus 6 percent to 8 percent in the 1960s.

In the corporate world, as in much of the rest of society, it took the roaring Eighties to make divorce fully respectable. As the decade began, Americans inaugurated their first divorced President, a man who somehow managed to convince a nation that he was the embodiment of old-fashioned family values. If the CEO of the United States should shed and rewed, why not the CEO of a FORTUNE 500 company? Says Linda Robinson, thirty-six, who is both the second wife of American Express Chairman James Robinson, fifty-three, and the chief executive of Robinson Lake Lerer & Montgomery, a public relations firm: "How can the board of directors pass over a divorced candidate for CEO? The board consists of other CEOs who are getting divorced too."

"The change has been radical," observes Helen Singer Kaplan, sixty, a psychiatrist and the second wife of Charles Lazarus, sixty-five, founder and chairman of Toys "R" Us. "There's no longer a prejudice against divorce and re-marriage—almost the reverse. In some cases the man with the old, nice, matronly first wife is looked down on. He's seen as not keeping up appearances. Why can't he do better for himself?" (It should be mentioned that in the corporate stratosphere, the phenomenon of divorce still pertains largely to men: The two women CEOs of FORTUNE 500 companies, Kathleen Graham of the Washington Post Co. and Linda Wachner of Warnaco, are both widows.)

Powerful men are beginning to demand trophy wives. "The culture of self-indulgence has just crept up to the CEO level," says Boston psychologist Harry Levinson, a longtime counselor to top management. "Indulgence is an issue for people who have worked very hard to get where they are. They feel they've earned it, they're entitled to it."

The Eighties have seen the rise of the celebrity CEO, who owes his fame to his fortune. Management buyouts have made new millionaires and billionaires of people like John Kluge, Ronald Perelman, and Saul Steinberg. "What's a man going to do with $3 billion?" asks Michael Thomas, the social critic and author of *Green Monday* and other Wall Street romans à clef. "If you're so rich, why aren't you glamorous?" The more money men make, the argument goes, the more self-assured they become, and the easier it is for them to think: I *deserve* a queen.

Enter the second wife: a decade or two younger than her husband, sometimes several inches taller, beautiful, and very often accomplished. The second wife certifies her husband's status and, if possible given the material she has to work with, dispels the notion that men peak sexually at age eighteen. This trophy does not hang on the wall like a moose head—she works. Hard.

For starters, she often has her own business, typically an enterprise serious enough to win respect for her but not so large as to overshadow her husband. Says Audrey Butvay Gruss, "thirty-nine and holding," whose Terme di Saturnia cosmetics company grosses nearly $3 million a year: "My success is not a major financial factor in our marriage." Her husband, Martin, forty-six, runs Gruss & Co., a private investment partnership founded by his father, Joseph; the Gruss clan is reportedly worth in excess of $400 million. Carolyne Roehm's flourishing dress business has revenues of about $10 million. Its sole backer is her husband, Henry Kravis, forty-five, whose share of Kohlberg Kravis Roberts, the leveraged-buyout firm, is reportedly worth at least $300 million.

In addition to her business, there is the time-consuming process of looking good. These women have a finish to their appearance that usually bespeaks facials, religious application of expensive skin creams, and an actress's skill with the paint box.

They are also thin, the real-life social X-rays Tom Wolfe described in *The Bonfire of the Vanities*. First wives invariably think their husbands were lured away by hot tomatoes proficient at the kind of sex formerly banned in most states. One look at those desiccated bodies, the knees and elbows sharp enough to puncture a tire, might suggest that sex is the last thing on men's minds.

If you've ever wondered why Carolyne Roehm's $2,000 evening gowns don't look the same on your spouse as they do on her, the answer is that she fits every piece of her collection on herself. At thirty-eight, Roehm is five feet nine and three-quarter inches tall, wears a size four, and aims for what she calls "the long drink of water" look. As Nancy Brinker, forty-two, size ten and six feet tall with her boots on, puts it candidly: "Trying to stay precious is not easy. I work out one hour a day at aerobics, I diet rigorously, and I play polo with my husband. This stuff gets harder as you get older, but Norman likes me to look good." She is the third wife of Norman Brinker, fifty-eight, who founded the Steak and Ale and Bennigan's restaurant chains. He is now CEO of Chili's, a Dallas-based fast-food outfit that peddles what you'd guess.

The second wife's most important duty, however, is to help her husband build a new life. Because a man often finds he divorced his friends when he divorced his first wife, the current spouse must fill the void and create a new circle for her husband. For example, Linda Robinson and Laurie Johnson, thirty-seven, the second wife of Ross Johnson, fifty-seven, the former chairman of RJR Nabisco, talked their husbands into a vacation together four years ago, a ten-day cruise through the Greek islands on a chartered yacht. Carolyne Roehm showed her spouse the treasures of India for nearly two weeks last spring in the company of her friends Oscar de la Renta, the dress designer, and Annette Reed, the daughter of Charles Engelhard, founder of Engelhard Minerals & Chemicals.

In essence, a second wife takes charge of her husband's life after five o'clock, for unlike their hardworking subordinates, men worth millions often don't have much to do after five.

She totes him to small dinner parties, opera galas, museum benefits, and auctions for worthy causes, having secured the invitations by serving on various committees and getting her husband to cough up something suitable in the way of a donation. Through her fund raising on behalf of PEN, the international writers' society Gayfryd Steinberg, thirty-nine, has helped improve the reputation of her husband, Saul, fifty, the chairman of Reliance Group Holdings. A huge oil painting by Rubens dominates the living room of their Fifth Avenue apartment, and Gayfryd's chunky mate has become a deep-pocketed pillar of New York's Metropolitan Museum of Art.

Few have been as successful at showing their husbands a good time as Susan Gutfreund, forty-one, the onetime airline stewardess who married John, fifty-nine, the CEO of Salomon Inc., eight years ago. The second Mrs. Gutfreund's extravagance is legendary. Her chauffeur sometimes hand delivers her dinner invitations. Her Paris town house on the rue de Grenelle features an underground parking area that a pal describes as "the most luxurious garage I've ever seen—it looks like a ballroom" Susan's ability to spend serious money has helped bring the Gutfreunds into the orbit of such people as Jayne Wrightsman, the widow of Charles (who made enough in oil to donate rooms full of French eighteenth-century furniture to the Metropolitan Museum), and Marie-Hélène de Rothschild, wife of Baron Guy and a mainstay of French café society. John Gutfreund is said to brag—perhaps for the benefit of the IRS—about the international business heavies who frequent his wife's *hôtel particulier*, types he probably doesn't stumble over all that often in the Room at Salomon Brothers.

The part of the second wife's job that may require the most finesse, though, is convincing the chief executive that he targeted her, rather than the other way around. In reality, the women usually know the men are available—or at least unhappy in their marriages—and they call in as many chits as necessary to arrange discreet introductions. Because a corporate mogul has a lot to lose—respect, credibility—if he is seen with a succession of young dates, an enterprising woman may usually find that the best way to meet him is through friends: Kathryn Wriston, Walter's wife, introduced Jane Beasley, thirty-seven, to her future husband, GE Chairman Jack

Welch, fifty-three; the Gutfreunds are said to have met at a party arranged by acquaintances of Susan's.

Georgette Mosbacher, forty-one, is an exception in that she has always been surprisingly frank about how she reeled in Robert, sixty-two, the Houston oilman who is now Secretary of Commerce. In the early 1980s, the recently divorced Mosbacher was considered the second most eligible man in the world after Prince Rainier—or so it was said in Texas. Having looked him up at the suggestion of a mutual friend, Georgette pursued him vigorously. When Bob tried to cancel dates, she told *Texas Monthly* magazine, "I'd have to intimidate him."

While divorce no longer spells trauma for the executive's career, the breakup of a marriage remains a personal blow, and the big loser is usually the first wife. Her fate is sealed in these four words: She Didn't Keep Up. The mistake the first wife too often makes is allowing her children to become the focus of her life instead of her husband. In the process she loses touch with him and his concerns. Says one CEO: "My first wife was unsupportive of the demands of my professional life. She thought my day could be divided neatly into nine-to-five business, five-to-nine family time, nine-to-eleven private time, and then to bed. This is difficult to arrange if you are serious about your career."

As their husbands rise in the corporation, first wives may become convinced that power is corrupting the presumably wholesome lads they married. "They become self-appointed critics and consciences," says Manhattan psychiatrist Clifford Sager, who specializes in marital therapy. "They try to cut their husbands down to size." This was what happened to John Rollwagen, as he told the story to Jan Halper, the author of *Quiet Desperation, the Truth About Successful Men.* Said Rollwagen, now CEO of Cray Research: "Mary would subtly judge me, usually quite negatively. My former wife was controlling and competitive . . . She'd say things to me, such as 'Don't think you'll ever be head of a company.' " Sometimes the woman belittles the man's accomplishments; other times, the man himself. In the acid words of the angry first wife of a CEO: "I wish husbands would ask themselves if their young wives would have married them if they were not successful and rich."

Keeping house and raising the kids seem to earn women fewer points in the great world nowadays, and they may begin to ask what they have sacrificed their own potential careers for. But as his wife is waking up, the CEO is wanting out. Typically he has begun asking a few questions of his own. Says Maryanne Vandervelde, an organizational psychologist and author of *The Changing Life of the Corporate Wife*: "Chief executives got to the top by being single-minded about their careers. But they neglected their emotional growth. Then they hit their fifties and find themselves thinking, 'Is *this* all there is?' " When there don't seem to be any more challenges left, it may be easier to find a new wife than a new job.

Ideally, this would be the time for longtime partners to repair their marriage, but often too much damage has been done. Says Roslyn Bremer, the first wife of Carl Spielvogel, CEO of the Backer Spielvogel Bates Worldwide ad agency: "Carl and I were in love, but our interests changed. He became more interested in cutting a figure in society." Spielvogel's second wife, Barbaralee Diamonstein, is an art critic. In most cases the husband has already been tempted by the younger, independent women he finds out in the workplace. It's a truism that women leave men for other lives, and men leave women for other women. Says a wiser ex-wife: "I should have insisted that he wear a wedding ring."

When a top executive's marriage breaks up, the first wife is not exactly left penniless. Says Raoul Lionel Felder, a New York City matrimonial lawyer who usually represents wives in divorce actions: "Let's say the husband's net worth is $1 million, figuring the present value of stock options accrued during the marriage, and he makes $500,000 a year. The marriage is ten years old and there are two children. You should aim for a $500,000 settlement, under equitable distribution, and be prepared to take $350,000 for a quick decision. For the wife's support, I'd settle for $200,000 for ten years." The lady gets pensioned off, in other words, with at least $2.35 million over time. If the husband is worth $2 million or more, says Felder, "use multiples."

What the first spouse really loses is the life that went with her position as the boss's wife—the status, travel, and social life. These were going to be the good years: The children were grown, there was finally plenty of money, and she was free again to be a companion to her husband—only to have another, often younger woman come in and skim it all off. Says one of these young women: "If I had a daughter, I'd tell her never to be a first wife."

As long as the divorce is not messy, the corporation will ignore it. Ironically, the company may even benefit: To escape the pain of divorce, unattached executives tend to throw themselves into their work. "I'd screwed up my personal life, and I wasn't going to screw up my job," says a Midwestern CEO. "I directed all my anxieties and tensions into the job, I went on the road, I poured ten, twelve hours a day into work." Gradually this effort may taper off as the men start to reorganize their priorities. They may feel they cheated themselves in their first marriage by spending so much of their energies at work, and thus they become more interested in dating and the social activities that lead to remarriage.

Most executives report that they have become better, more thoughtful managers because their marital problems made them conscious of the personal lives of their employees. Faye Crosby, a Smith College psychology professor who has studied the effects of divorce in the corporation, describes a manager who told her he had always assumed that if a subordinate said he had to go to the dentist, that's what he meant. Then, when the manager was getting his divorce and needed to show up in court, he found himself telling his office that he had dental appointments. Says Crosby: "It never occurred to this man before that people needed privacy for private matters."

James Fifield, the chief executive of EMI Music Worldwide, believes that as a result of his divorce, "I'm definitely more sensitive to how the demands I put on people affect their families. I tell someone, 'Take your wife and stay over the weekend in L.A. Then on Monday go where you have to go.' This way I'm not some ogre driving people into the turf."

In creating a new life after his marriage founders, the executive must be discreet. Says one astute CEO: "After my divorce I went alone to business dinners where the other men brought their wives. I began bringing my girlfriend only when she became a serious interest and it was obvious that we were going to get married." Even when they were living together, the man never took his fiancée to overnight business conferences where they might run into his colleagues' wives.

It can be troublesome, of course, if a CEO on the loose starts an affair with a subordinate. "What people object to is pillow talk," says Kenneth Olshan, the chairman of the Wells Rich Greene advertising agency. "One person then has access to the CEO that is unusual, and that person's opinion seems to be more valued."

This was the experience of Charlotte Moss, thirty-eight, who when she was a vice president in the tax investment marketing department at Merrill Lynch began seeing Barry Friedberg, forty-eight, who runs the firm's investment banking operations. "Barry and I were very open about our relationship, and we kept it out of the office," she says. "But people were afraid to tell me things because they thought I might tell him." Shortly before the pair were married in 1985, Moss left Merrill Lynch, went to England with her $75,000 bonus to buy "a truckload of antiques," and set herself up in Manhattan as a decorator and retailer.

The union that rises from the ashes of the first is very different from its predecessor. The most obvious difference is that this marriage starts at the top in terms of money and power. Carolyne Roehm manages a staff of four at the couple's apartment in Manhattan and five at their Connecticut weekend home. The two who work in the Southampton summer place also travel with Roehm and Kravis to their Vail, Colorado, ski lodge in winter. It's axiomatic that first wives shop at Loehmann's and seconds have charge accounts at Neiman-Marcus, firsts stay at home with the kids while seconds have nannies, firsts cook their husband's business dinners but seconds have the caterers in. "This isn't the husband's fault," says Roslyn Bremer. "The first wife doesn't feel free to spend money so lavishly, and she doesn't know how." Seconds who have been earning their own keep for a while definitely know how.

The money is less important, however, than the power conferred on a woman by her connection to someone who has become a Very Important Man. This is why Bonnie Swearingen, fifty-ish, who married the former chairman of Standard Oil of Indiana twenty years ago, gently reproved an interlocutor with: "I didn't just marry a CEO. I married one of the world's outstanding business leaders." And why Esther Ferguson, forty-six, who is married to James, sixty-three, the former chairman of General Foods, brags, "I'm the only woman in America to have been married to two CEO's of FORTUNE 500 companies." Her first husband was G. William Moore, who ran Fieldcrest Mills.

When she traveled with her second husband, who just retired from General Foods, Ferguson was able to corner the likes of Henry Kissinger and William Simon and get them to serve as directors of her National Dropout Prevention Fund. Nancy Brinker, who started the Susan G. Komen Foundation for breast cancer research seven years ago in memory of her sister, who died of the disease, admits, "People turned out for our first fund-raising event on the strength of Norman's name, but I was able to take it from there." She and several thousand volunteers have raised $5 million so far.

The women are usually careful not to abuse their power, which is why exceptions like Georgette Mosbacher provoke such mixed reactions. The thrice-married, Indiana-born Georgette, tagged the Happy Hoosier by the *Washington Post*, reportedly crashed an exclusive Washington brunch preceding the annual Kennedy Center Honors Gala last December. She followed this by boldly upstaging Marilyn Quayle, the Vice President's wife, at an inaugural event.

Second marriages appear to be happy—a real departure from the first—but then why shouldn't they be? Many of the women have a fast mistake in their past—married at twenty-three and unmarried at twenty-six—and they are determined not to be divorced again. They've seen what went wrong in first marriages, both their own and their husbands'. Not for them losing sight of the main chance: They speak of their men in ways that would bring the blush to the most egomaniacal CEO's cheek. In the middle of a conversation,

Audrey Gruss leaps out of her chair, grabs a photograph of her husband in his polo duds, and kisses it, cooing, "Isn't he adorable? He is my Prince Charming."

Betsy Fifield, thirty-four, says firmly: "My husband is my number-one priority." She married record company executive Fifield, forty-eight, in 1984, and quit her job as a vice president at McCann-Erickson two-and-a-half years later because "Jim and I want to be together as much as possible, and I didn't have much flexibility to do the things I like to do with him." She has started her own marketing business and gives her husband what she calls one "wife day" a week during which she'll do errands for him. Nancy Brinker observes, "Men want to be entertained. So I'll tell Norman stories about what is going on, tidbits from the day, and talk to him about movies and books." Dinner chez Brinker is often a candlelight affair with no phone interruptions and a low-fat menu that Mrs. B. plans carefully with her cook in order to make it delicious. "Of course these women feel this way about their husbands," says Helen Singer Kaplan, the psychiatrist. "I feel that way about mine." What's important about a second marriage, she believes, is that it compensate for the pain of the last. She adds, "If a wife was cold or unresponsive, a man will look for her opposite, who is supportive and sexy. I really see happy people, they've corrected for past mistakes."

But even as the second wife gives her husband pride of place, she maintains an independence that eluded many first wives. Charlotte Moss's decorating business has annual revenues of seven figures and requires several ten-day trips to England each year. Raised in Virginia, Moss took on the traditional housewifely tasks in her first marriage—"I was still so Southern I even cooked"—only to have her husband ask for a divorce after five years of marriage that included four moves for his business. "From that marriage I learned never, ever, to put my well-being totally in the hands of another person," she says. Linda Robinson feels guilty "that I can't attend all of Jim's business functions," and she feels worse when she's working almost around the clock for a client and can't spend the weekend with her husband.

With both careers going gangbusters, what couples spend the most time doing together may be harmonizing their calendars. In the traditional first marriage, the wife serves as social secretary, but one hostess, herself the second wife of a prominent Wall Streeter, was appalled to discover how that nicety has vanished in succeeding marriages. She and her husband were scheduled to dine with another couple and when she called her opposite number the day of the dinner to confirm, the other wife replied, "Well, it's in my book, but you'd better phone my husband also and confirm it with his secretary." Says Carolyne Roehm, who spends weeknights out with her husband or entertaining their friends at home: "Henry and I get our wires crossed all the time." The Robinsons leave the juggling to their respective secretaries, who call each other several times daily to coordinate events as far as a year off. Conflicts go on little slips of paper for the couple to resolve.

The way that a second marriage differs most dramatically from the first, though, can be summed up in one word: children. There usually aren't any. Says Chérie Burns, the author of *Stepmotherhood*: "Some men have outgrown their family lives. They want the fantasy life with a beautiful young thing, and they don't want children messing it up." Having taken care of his dynastic ambitions with his first wife, the CEO now wants a playmate, someone who is free to travel with him and have fun. The women, for the most part, are terrified that kids would upset the apple cart. Says one: "It's hard to risk this stress on the marriage." Another adds forthrightly, "I don't see room for children in our life. I just don't know how you can combine a marriage and kids."

Second wives also find their desire for children affected by the presence of stepchildren. Nearly fifteen years ago, when Laura Pomerantz, now forty-one, married her husband John, fifty-six, chairman of Leslie Fay, the women's clothing manufacturer, they already had three girls, ages nine, seven, and five, from their previous marriages. "I wanted more children, but John didn't," Laura says. "Now we're both sorry." Initially they were uneasy about how a new baby would affect their children as they worked to unify the family. As time went by and the girls adapted, the parents found themselves reluctant to disturb the balance when everyone seemed so happy.

The sad fact for most men is that divorce and remarriage fray the ties to their children. Says Robert Weiss, a research professor at the University of Massachusetts in Boston, who is studying achieving men: "In the process of leaving their first families, men believe they can make it up to the kids in quality time. Then they discover it is extraordinarily difficult. So much of being a good father is being on the scene."

Having pots of money may ease the burden of not being there because the CEO can afford to fly the kids out to see him and go on exciting vacations with them. But too many men made the mistake of allowing their first wives to "take care" of the relationship with the children while they concentrate on getting ahead. When the couples part, the men find they have no connection to their children.

Listen to one remarried father who now lives about a thousand miles away from his daughters: "It's not that I didn't care about the kids, but I was not like typical fathers. I couldn't be at the softball game because I had to be in London. My first wife had to make it clear that I had this important job—it wasn't that I didn't want to be with them. I was not going to divorce myself from the kids, but it was naive of me to think I'd have the same relationship as I had before the divorce. It's another price you pay. You hope for some relationship with your first wife as it affects the children, but it just doesn't work out that way. Animosity and friction are always there, even if she remarries. You just don't have the relationship with the kids you'd have if you lived there."

The stepmother's relations with kids whom she usually sees for a few weeks in summer and one or two weekends a month are a bit delicate. Says Carolyne Roehm of her three stepchildren: "I'm here for them if they need my help, but I'm not trying to replace a parent in their lives." Occasionally a stepmother will take an active role in ensuring that her husband maintains ties with his progeny. Laurie Johnson gave her husband's son a diamond and tourmaline ring that Ross had given her on their first Valentine's Day. The boy was getting engaged and wanted a jewel to present on the spot. "I told both Ross's boys that I had rings for them," Johnson says. "This family needs tradition."

It's easy to resent the second wife as an interloper, and she certainly garners her share of ill will. "Those first wives, boy they really stick together and support the one who was left," complains a second. Says Beliza Ann Furman, a second wife who is the founder of Wives of Older Men, an organization for women who are at least eight years younger than their husbands: "The social invitations don't come so quickly. The wives of my husband's friends thought I was a threat."

When Laurie Johnson was first married to Ross, then the CEO of Standard Brands, she was twenty-six and very anxious to please. "I'm sure a lot of people didn't like me," she says. "Those women could be back-stabbing. We'd be invited to a party and the hostess would tell me it was casual, and then everybody would show up dressed to the nines. I'd come in blue jeans or something and feel like a jerk."

But the time comes when the second wife does have to pay her dues. He retires, or loses his job, as Ross Johnson did. She's still going strong when he just wants to play golf. She may enjoy it at first. "In the beginning after Ross left RJR, we went to the movies a lot," says Laurie. "We never went to the movies in the first ten years we were married." But after a while it can become a drag.

Even for him. The Canadian-born Johnson is on eight boards, and in May he opened an international management consulting firm in Atlanta called RJM Group, which employs six people. Laurie, who worked only briefly during her marriage, is the vice president for administration and finance. "We have an office. Ross can go to work, so he's not staying home and invading my time," she says. "I was afraid people would drop us, but right after Ross left RJR we were invited to the Canadian Prime Minister's fiftieth birthday party."

Serious retirement can be an eyeopener, though. It's particularly tough on the executive whose personality erodes with his power base. One second wife was overheard complaining, "After my husband stopped being CEO and didn't have the company plane anymore, he just wasn't the same person."

A spouse can't help but suffer from her husband's loss of

status. Observes Jane Ylvisaker, forty-three, whose husband, Bill, sixty-five, retired from Gould Inc. in 1986 to start a venture capital firm: "Some people seem to be devastated when they lose the chauffeur, the company flat, the private plane. A lot of others change their attitude toward you—it's noticeable certainly. Even though you thought you knew them for what they were, it can be a great shock when they don't pay attention to you." Adds Bonnie Swearingen: "Retirement is bittersweet. When we had to give up traveling by private plane and join the rest of humanity in airports, I was spoiled to the point that I don't like to travel anymore."

And retirement may be just the start. What happens when life in the fast lane starts pulling over to a slower track in deference to Harry's pacemaker? True, this may not happen for a while: "My husband has a heart rate of fifty-one. Mine is ninety-eight or so," exclaims the youngish wife of a fifty-three-year old. "He's so physically fit—he's got more energy than I do, and I've got a lot." Ah, but when she faces the prospect of pushing him around in a wheelchair, what's to prevent her from leaving him? A prenuptial agreement, limiting what she might get in a settlement? Perhaps—most second wives sign them. What it comes down to finally may be love, love sufficient to withstand the "for worse" now that she's had the "for better."

Why Won't the Caged Bird Sing?

Rachel Abramowitz

June 1989, *Manhattan,inc.*

"Why Won't the Caged Bird Sing?" tells the sad but riveting tale of a former teenage runaway named Lisa Jones who found a home in Michael Milken's junk bond shop as a lowly trading assistant. Jones made more money than she had ever dreamed of. But when the Feds busted Drexel, she lied to government investigators. Rachel Abramowitz does a nice job explaining why Jones lied and was willing to go to prison for Michael Milken. And go she did—to a federal penitentiary.

O N DECEMBER 17, 1987, TOM DOONAN, a longtime criminal investigator for the U.S. attorney's office in New York, climbed on a plane and flew to Los Angeles. Compact and well muscled, with cropped blond hair and small slit eyes, Doonan was heading West to interview Lisa Ann Jones, a twenty-four-year-old Drexel trading assistant. She wasn't a very important part of the junk-bond juggernaut, but she had worked for trader Bruce Newberg, one of the prime targets of the government's ongoing investigation of Drexel. The government thought that she could shed some light on an illegal activity known as "parking," a way of concealing stock ownership. Earlier the same day, Feds had raided Princeton/Newport, a securities firm the government suspected had participated with Drexel in a stock-parking scheme.

Lisa wasn't home when Doonan arrived at her Sherman Oaks apartment at 6:30 P.M. He left and came back three more times before he finally saw a light shining through the drawn blinds. He knocked on the door and showed his credentials. Lisa was hesitant but nonetheless invited him in, and they sat facing each other in her modest living room.

At first Lisa answered his questions about Drexel and Princeton/Newport, though Doonan felt that she was uneasy and evasive. And when he zeroed in on the questionable trades, Doonan remembers, she drew back.

"Now a number of these sales by Princeton/Newport to Drexel are then sold back within thirty, thirty-one, thirty-two days? Drexel parks them for Princeton/Newport?" asked Doonan.

"We do trades like that, but they're not parks," Doonan remembers her saying, though Lisa remembered the conversation differently.

"Are they for tax purposes?" he asked.

Lisa then declared that she would not answer any more of his questions without having a lawyer present.

So Doonan handed her a grand-jury subpoena. "We were hoping you would be willing to cooperate with us in this investigation," he told her, and cautioned that, if Drexel hired the lawyer, the lawyer would be looking after Drexel's interests.

"I know you're just an Indian like me," said Doonan. "The government is just interested in the people who told you to do this."

The government was soon to become very interested in Lisa Jones. They have systematically built their case against Drexel by getting employees to confess the crimes of their bosses, but Lisa wouldn't cooperate. A runaway who never even finished junior high school, she had been fending for herself since she was fourteen years old. Ten years later, when Doonan arrived on her doorstep, Drexel was paying her more than $100,000 a year: success by almost any measure save that of Drexel's junk-bond department, where million-dollar salaries were common. To arrive there, Lisa had invented a background for herself. At various times, she had lied about not only her birthdate but her birthplace; she claimed she was married; she claimed a college degree; and she invented a prep school out of whole cloth. Even under ordinary circumstances, the untruths would perhaps be understandable; a fourteen-year-old has to lie about her age to get a job. And once she had created a past, it became extremely difficult to give it up.

But perjury became the issue. Before a grand jury in January 1988, Lisa denied knowing about the trades Doonan said she discussed with him, trades that, according to tapes seized in the Princeton/Newport raid, she had conducted regularly. And what haunted her when she was indicted and brought to trial were not the facts she had gone to such lengths to conceal but the fact that she had concealed them. On trial, she became not the success she had striven so hard to be but a liar.

On March 22, 1989, Lisa Jones was convicted of five counts of perjury and two counts of obstruction of justice. She is the first to fall in the government's massive probe of Drexel's activities, the only junior-level employee to be indicted, and according to the lawyer who defended her, the only junior-level employee even to be targeted for indictment. On the stand at her trial, she hardly looked capable of thwarting a major government investigation. Plump and self-conscious about it, she has a placid face framed by curly brown hair; her most notable feature was a doelike quality, an almost archaic sweetness. Says one insider, "She looks how your mother must have looked twenty-five years ago."

As Drexel rocketed into prominence in the 1980s, it pulled Lisa in its wake. And like that of many of the firm's Beverly Hills employees, her life and the life at the office were inseparable. But many of her colleagues had a safety net—an education, a family—Lisa didn't. "Her life is that place," said her defense attorney, Brian O'Neill, after the trial. "She had no main squeeze, no support. It was really important to her that she worked there. She was very proud of it." It was so important to her, apparently, that when Tom Doonan knocked on her door, her instinct for self-preservation failed her.

Lisa Jones is the sort of young woman who could easily have fallen through the cracks in this country. She was born in Atlanta, Georgia, to a waitress who later resettled in Woodbury, New Jersey. She never knew her father and lived with her mother and stepfather and two younger sisters, one of whom she adored. She later spoke with particular bitterness about her mother, complaining to friends that she allowed her stepfather to spank her.

In 1977, when Lisa was just past fourteen, she found an unlikely ticket out of the situation, an unemployed nineteen-year-old named Doug Gordon. Shortly after they met, Lisa secretly packed her bags and set out to become an adult, driving across country to California with Gordon and his father. Her mother was distraught. She advertised Lisa's disappearance on TV, but Lisa didn't contact her for some five years, until she was firmly ensconced at Drexel.

She and Gordon pretended to be married—Gordon used her name—and found an apartment in the San Fernando valley. Claiming she was eighteen and a graduate of "Fernlyn Prep," Lisa found a job as a teller at Bank of America. With an annual salary of $5,000, Lisa paid the entire rent on their apartment and seemed to support them both.

Gordon spooked some of her friends. "He was kind of a shady character, the kind of guy you didn't want around. You didn't know what he was going to do," said a former Bank of America employee who once lived with Lisa for several months. Within a year, Lisa found herself unable to meet the payments on the apartment. At her trial, she testified that Gordon stole money from her and sometimes hit her when they argued. One night in August 1979, she disappeared again, creeping out of the apartment to move in with her friend from the bank.

"She was very street smart," remembers the roommate. "She was always motivated. She got an idea in her mind, and she followed it. . . . She was not afraid of anything." Yet Lisa also craved affection. "She wanted to be loved. She was always giving gifts, hugging. I think that, by trying to extend her love, she was trying to get you to go out of your way for her, so she would feel loved. She pitied herself. Her needs were more than the average person. She was manipulative about getting her needs fulfilled," says the roommate.

Lisa met her next boyfriend, Stephen Gurewitz, at a party. Dark-haired and gangly, the twenty-two-year-old Gurewitz studied computers at the local community college. He was also addicted to PCP, a fact that Lisa learned the day they met. But Lisa liked him, and she needed a place to stay. When she told him she was twenty, he believed her, and within a month they were living together in an apartment in Encino.

Lisa quickly became almost a member of the Gurewitz family, which paid most of the rent on their apartment. She called Stephen's father "Pops" and became particularly close to his mother, Rosemary, whom she called every day and often sent affectionate cards to, one of which read: "You are the only women I ever *really* loved. You are like my mother." She impressed the Gurewitzes as someone who was going places, focused and directed. "She set goals for herself and attained them," says Rosemary Gurewitz. Adds her husband, Arthur, "She's tough and streetwise. She was very mature for her age. Very forward in presenting herself. She was not bashful."

In 1981 Lisa was referred to Drexel Burnham by an employment agency. On her job application she further embellished her education, writing that she was enrolled at Pierce College, a local community college, although the only course she had ever finished at Pierce was Philosophy and the Occult. Drexel hired her as a sales assistant in the junk-bond department. She was seventeen.

Lisa began to live by Drexel time. She started work at 5 A.M. and worked until 2 or 3 P.M., when Stephen would come and pick her up at Drexel's offices in Century City. She manned the phones, opened new accounts for institutions, and wrote up tickets on executed trades. She was meticulous, a trait that wasn't lost on her superiors. For her efforts, she earned $13,000 a year—it was the first time she had ever made a five-digit salary.

Her work at Drexel was much more exciting than counting money at the Ventura branch of Bank of America. She soon started coming home gushing to the Gurewitzes about the catered lunches and the huge salaries made by the bondsmen. And she raved about Milken. "She thought the sun rose and set on Milken," says Gurewitz, remembering how Lisa would talk about him. The Gurewitzes and Lisa once ran into Milken in a restaurant, and Lisa brought the whole family over to meet him. "She was so proud of him."

At the end of 1981, Lisa had a scare when the Drexel

personnel department called her. In a background check, they had discovered that Fernlyn Prep did not exist. Lisa told personnel that she was studying for her high-school equivalency exam, and Drexel let her stay.

Lisa, secure in her new life, tried to reestablish contact with her mother, with whom she had not spoken in five years. She was shocked by the response. "You wounded me greatly," her mother wrote back. "A scab has finally begun to close over the wound. I don't want it reopened." Finally, on Christmas of 1982, Lisa spoke to her mother for the first time in five years and eventually flew back to see her.

In 1982 Stephen moved into a nine-month live-in rehab clinic. Lisa stayed in the apartment and planned on marrying him when he got out. But by the time he was released, Stephen had changed his mind. He felt that Lisa was too domineering. Lisa was understandably bitter. When she moved out, she took much of the furniture, pots and pans, and china that the Gurewitzes had given to their son, as well as the couple's sports car, which the Gurewitzes had made payments on. "Lisa can be nice and sweet, but she can be cold and calculating," says Rosemary Gurewitz. "She'd drop you when she had no more use for you," adds the former roommate, whom Lisa never spoke to again after she went to work at Drexel. Rosemary Gurewitz kept up with Lisa for several months after she broke up with Stephen. The last time they saw each other, she took Lisa out for her birthday, and Rosemary remembers Lisa giving her a bizarre ultimatum: "I can't continue seeing you if you remain friends with Steve and Art."

A year later, Stephen Gurewitz committed suicide. His sister called Lisa to tell her, but, says Rosemary Gurewitz, "Lisa never called or wrote." Nor did she attend the funeral.

By 1983 Drexel had moved from Century City to the corner of Wilshire and Rodeo Drive, one of the most valuable and ostentatious pieces of commercial real estate in Los Angeles. In it, Milken installed his famous X-shaped desk, with him in the center and his minions radiating outward in order of importance. Lisa sat at one of the desks that ringed the main X, because she was rising, too. By 1983 she had become trading assistant to Bruce Newberg, a twenty-six-year-old summa

from Wharton and a trader in the convertible-bond depart
ment. Tall and balding, with darting eyes and a kinetic, intense manner, Newberg would bark orders to her all day,
barely ever breaking to talk to her. "I was trying to keep my
head above water, to be, you know, just to keep up with the
flow of things," Lisa said on the stand. "It got busier and
busier."

Her main job was to write trading tickets and to give
information to clients. She did not have the authority to buy
or sell on her own, although she very much wanted to become
a trader. Three times she failed the series seven exam, the
basic exam that all traders must take to become licensed.
(Many trading assistants are also licensed.) Even so, she wrote
on her W2 tax form that she was a stockbroker. Asked on the
stand why she kept taking the exam, she said, "I just wanted
to be like everybody else."

Indeed, after Lisa broke off with the Gurewitzes, it had
become more and more important for her to be like everybody
else. "That place took on all aspects of family," says Brian
O'Neill. She hung out with a clique of fellow trading assistants, and often baby-sat and cooked for the divorced men in
the office when it was their turn to take care of their children.
Lisa took pains to hide her background from her Drexel
friends, who sometimes found her shy and difficult to get to
know. One friend told a reporter, "She was the kind of person
who, if she was ever put in the spotlight, she'd just melt. She's
very self-conscious. She's overweight. She's had loser boy-
friends. And she's obviously a person with very low self-
esteem."

According to O'Neill, Lisa grew close to Newberg. She
often baby-sat for his children, and even after he moved to
another department, they continued to talk on the phone and
occasionally had dinner together. Newberg's power in the
firm abetted Lisa's rise. Her salary began to skyrocket, jumping from $32,500 in 1984 to $103,685 in 1986. There were
other perks too—business dinners, trips to New York, where
she stayed at the Parker Meridien, Raiders tickets. She lived
in a small $400-a-month two-room apartment and sent mon-
ey home to her mother and sister, with whom she had managed to reestablish contact.

From the very beginning, Lisa was involved in some unusual activities at Drexel. One of her occasional duties, say the Gurewitzes, was to collect from employees and pay bookies in the Drexel lobby. Arthur Gurewitz told a postal investigator that Lisa claimed that sometimes she wouldn't write down sales and that she often postdated them. She sometimes held back information from clients about a buy or sale of a security, and she hid sales. (Lisa denied saying these things.)

According to William Hale, who brought the Princeton parking scheme to the government's attention and was a central witness in Lisa's case, the chain of events that led to her conviction began in late 1984, when the members of Princeton/Newport investment partnership met to discuss how to cope with the new tax codes. Located in both Princeton and Newport Beach, the investment partnership was run by Jay Regan, a longtime crony of Mike Milken's and partner in several of Milken's private-investment partnerships. According to Hale, Regan and his associates Paul Berkman, Jack Rabinowitz, and Hale held a meeting with their accountants by conference call and discussed ways to generate short-term capital losses that they could write off on their taxes. Then, says Hale, they disconnected the conference call, and the partners talked about stock parking. Parking securities is selling them with a secret understanding that they will be bought back at roughly the same price after thirty-one days, the time needed to establish them as a tax loss. A company could in this manner retain ownership of a security while realizing paper tax losses. Parking can also be a useful tool during takeovers, allowing a raider to conceal how much stock he actually owns. It also facilitates insider trading, allowing an investment bank advising a raider to accumulate stock secretly in the takeover target.

According to Hale, Regan established a parking structure with Drexel, as well as with Merrill Lynch and a London firm. As part of the deal, Hale testified, Drexel was also permitted to park stocks at Princeton/Newport. (Newberg, Milken, and Berkman have been indicted for this offense and have pleaded not guilty.) Paul Berkman began to do the tax parks with Bruce Newberg, but by March of 1985, he had shunted the task off to Hale, a junior assistant trader. And after a couple months, Newberg also got fed up with the busywork of doing the tax trades. He told Hale to do the trades with Lisa Jones, his trading assistant. According to a recantation letter written by Lisa's attorney, Newberg pulled Lisa aside one day and told her that they were going to do a special kind of "programmed trading" with Princeton/Newport, though at the time she wasn't informed of its purpose.

Hale and Lisa spoke two or three days a week, sometimes many times a day, for over fourteen months. Parking was a transaction that required meticulous attention—bookkeeping, accounting, keeping securities straight, and not accidentally selling securities they were supposed to keep. Drexel charged Princeton/Newport a cost-of-carry fee: the amount it would cost Drexel to maintain a position in the stock; the formula for computing this figure was by her calculator. To hide the fact that they were parking securities, said Hale, he would artificially change the buy-back price. If the stock cost $90 a share, Princeton/Newport might buy the shares back at $85, thus creating a pool of money that either Drexel or Princeton/Newport owed the other party at any one time. At the end of every month, Hale and Lisa would settle their accounts—clean up the "parking lot," as Hale called it. Hale and Lisa quickly became phone friends.

By the middle of 1985, Hale and Lisa began to feel concerned about the situation. They talked about how they had to take care of these transactions for the bosses, the benefit of which they would never see. "We said that they were illegal and that we were uncomfortable doing them," testified Hale. Hale said he complained to Berkman about the illegality of the trades; he was fired soon after. In 1987 when Newberg was switched off the trading desk, he left it to Lisa Jones to explain the scheme to his successor, Peter Gardiner, according to Gardiner's grand-jury testimony.

On November 14, 1986, Ivan Boesky pleaded guilty to insider trading, sending shock waves through Drexel that continue to reverberate. Within two weeks, it had become apparent that the firm was under investigation by both the SEC and a federal grand jury, but it took a little more than a year for the shock waves to reach Lisa. She spent much of that year in

London, where Drexel had sent her to help open a trading desk and train the trading assistants, and where she lived exceedingly well on a company expense account.

Morale at Drexel had risen cautiously throughout the summer when the expected indictments did not materialize, but when Lisa returned in September it had begun to fall again. By December of 1987, when Doonan knocked on Lisa's door, there was a gloomy certainty around the office that things would get worse before they got better.

Doonan's visit scared Lisa deeply. She waited a few minutes to make sure that Doonan was gone. And then, convinced that the government was bugging her phone, she got in her Volkswagen and drove to a pay phone in a nearby shopping mall. She called Kevin Madigan, Drexel's in-house attorney. A crony of Milken's and active in his investment partnerships, Madigan was handpicked by Milken to make sure that Drexel complied with the rules governing security houses. On the stand, Lisa kept calling Madigan "a friend" of hers. "I told him I was scared, that someone was here asking questions, and he told me to go back home and try to calm down, and I told him I didn't want to. Because I was scared that this person was there."

Lisa stayed up that night and, as Madigan suggested, tried to write down everything that had happened in her encounter with Doonan. In Lisa's version, she denies ever doing the trades for Drexel. Concerned, perhaps, about what the government would uncover, she admitted to Drexel that she wasn't as old as she had claimed she was. Soon after Doonan's visit, a Drexel lawyer called the U.S. attorney's office and yelled at them for questioning their ability to represent Lisa fairly.

The only person Lisa told about the subpoena was her mother. Many of her friends had been subpoenaed or were about to be, and her lawyers told her that to talk about the case could make them critical witnesses against one another. She flew off for a two-week vacation in London before going to New York on January 9 to prepare her case with Drexel's lead lawyers, Thomas Curnin at Cahill Gordon & Reindel, Peter Fleming of Curtis, Mallet-Prevost, and Eliot Lauer, the Curtis partner who was to accompany her to the grand jury.

On January 13 she finally appeared before the grand jury

and immediately took the Fifth. The government responded by serving her with an immunity order, which protects a witness from prosecution as long as she testifies truthfully.

The prosecution questioned her about her background (she lied again, even about where she was born), about what she did for Newberg, and most notably about the trades with Princeton/Newport. Frequently they stopped to remind her that she was under oath. Nervously, Lisa continued to deny her knowledge of the trades, sometimes just mutely shaking her head. The prosecutors began to get visibly frustrated. At one point, one of them left the courtroom and began yelling at Lauer in the hallway, "She's perjuring herself!" in a voice loud enough to be heard by everyone in the grand-jury room, including Lisa. She began to cry.

At two more sessions, Lisa told the same story. As each session closed, the government reminded her of her right to recant. She told them that she thought her testimony had been accurate.

Soon after Lisa finished testifying, the government discovered that her voice was on the Princeton/Newport tapes. Hale and Lisa were cleaning up the parking lot. On February 23, the government sent Lisa a target letter, informing her that it was likely that she would be prosecuted for perjury.

Many of Lisa's problems on the stand clearly stemmed from her continued attempts to hide her past. But since the trial, legal-ethics experts and defense lawyers have questioned whether it was in Lisa's interests to use Drexel lawyers, who may have had trouble seeing Lisa's interests as distinct from those of Drexel. "Frequently a client has guilty knowledge and is reluctant to talk about it to her lawyer, so she says she didn't know anything," says Monroe Freedman, a law professor at Hofstra University who has followed the case closely and may become involved in it himself. "They say, 'Great! We were hoping you would say that.' " It is possible that Lisa was afraid to tell her lawyers the truth, afraid it would get back to her superiors. Lisa, according to a Drexel lawyer, was told she could retain her own attorney at Drexel's expense, though a continuing question in the case has been how much she understood of legal procedure. It is also possible that the Drexel team didn't take the perjury threats as seriously as they should have, or that she was lost in the shuffle among the eighty-five employees also represented by the company's lawyers before the grand jury. Curnin has denied that there was a conflict of interest. Eliot Lauer and Peter Fleming have refused to comment on a pending case.

If Lisa had changed her testimony after receiving the target letter, it is possible that she would have escaped the indictment. In any event, Drexel insisted that she find her own attorney, whom they would pay for. Curnin and Fleming gave her a list of possible lawyers, whom she interviewed, choosing Brian O'Neill, a prominent California trial lawyer who has represented some of the most notorious defendants to sprout on the West Coast, from *Fatal Vision* killer Jeffrey MacDonald, convicted of murdering his family, to the Bhagwan Rajneesh.

On August 2, 1988, O'Neill arranged for a meeting with the U.S. attorney's office to discuss a possible plea or settlement. It was the first time that Lisa got to hear the incriminating tapes. Although on the stand Lisa denied there was any formal bookkeeping method for the parking, on the tape she seems to be confidently going through a stack of securities:

WH: Now on the Lear, on the Lear Pete.

LJ: Who?

WH: On the Lear Petroleum.

LJ: I have to bust the trade. I'm restricted. [She can't trade in it, because Drexel has a corporate-finance relationship with the firm.]

WH: You can't do that trade unsolicited?

LJ: I, how can I do an unsolicited that you came in to me?

WH: Yeah, sure.

LJ: But the problem is on an unsolicited trade, I can't position it.

WH: Oh, you got to puke it out to the street.

LJ: Yeah, that is what an unsolicited trade is, when you're restricted in something.

WH: That's right. You got to puke it out to the street as an agent.

LJ: Yeah. And I don't think you want me to do that.

WH: Oh, shit.

Sometimes, as in the above conversations, they followed

the rules. But on most of the tapes, they seem to be parking Lisa claimed on the stand that she first heard the term after Boesky Day, but the tapes reveal otherwise. At one point she mutters to someone in the background, "Oh, I don't know. I thought you were buying it for somebody else. I gotta pick up. I told him . . . Park . . . Park? . . . All right, thanks, Mike."

Lisa listened to the tape and then took a little walk with Brian O'Neill around Foley Square. When she came back, she said her memory was refreshed about the so-called "program trading" and she was now willing to go back to the grand jury and testify about it. That day, from the airport, O'Neill dictated a letter reaffirming these facts, maneuvering to create a legal defense that would require the government to drop the case because his client had the right to recant.

It was too late. The government already had prepared a case against Newberg and Princeton/Newport's people without her help and two days later indicted them under RICO on thirty-five counts of conspiracy to commit tax-and-securities fraud. On November 9, 1988, they indicted Lisa Jones for perjury.

"The government wasn't trying the Drexel case through Lisa Jones," says prosecuting attorney Mark Hansen, who is also prosecuting the Princeton/Newport defendants. "It didn't plan to go after Lisa Jones; it was always meant that she should be free of prosecution, although the evidence was overwhelming that she was knowingly involved in an illegal scheme." But going after her for perjury was a different matter. Prosecuting Jones would send a clear message to others considering hampering the government's investigation by stonewalling, and, of course, there was always the possibility that Lisa still knew more than she was admitting. Hansen admits ruefully that the prosecuting team has fielded many phone calls from friends and relatives asking why they are pursuing a mere trading assistant. "There's a place for big fish and a place for little fish," he says.

Once she was indicted, Drexel put Jones on leave of absence, though they continued to pay her a $90,000 salary and a $45,000 bonus—her biggest bonus ever. They also continued to pay travel and hotel expenses (she took the super-luxurious MGM Grand Air to her arraignment and stayed in a $450-

a-night suite at the Stanhope during her trial). They did not stint in helping her prepare her defense. They did videotapes of her. They hired a ballroom in which they held mock trials with sample juries. Of course, it wasn't purely altruistic. If Lisa Jones had been acquitted, it would have been a blow to the government's case against Drexel. In a sense, she was the first skirmisher the company sent into battle.

When Lisa came East for trial, she came alone, save for her lawyers and whichever of the Drexel lawyers she recognized in the stands. Attorneys for Drexel, Milken, Newberg, and the Princeton/Newport defendants packed the court gallery. Richard Sandler, Milken's personal lawyer and longtime intimate, told one reporter that he had come to the trial to show his sympathy, because, "[Lisa Jones] is a person that I care about." Before the trial, her friends in Drexel's Los Angeles office had sent her an eight-foot-high poster of good wishes.

When she finally took the stand on March 16, she spoke in a barely audible voice and often broke down crying. She seemed disoriented, and her speech was considerably more childlike than it had been before the grand jury. Brian O'Neill and his associate Eileen McDevitt often seemed to be shepherding a sleepwalker through her paces. Lisa Jones had spent her life pretending to be older than she was; on the stand she seemed younger.

The first day, Lisa almost perjured herself again. After the tapes had been played, prosecuting attorney Mark Hansen asked her whether she had had other conversations like the taped one, and she responded, "I don't know," later to be expanded to "I have conversations like those but was not aware they were parking" and "I don't know all the conversations I had with Mr. Hale." In the recantation letter, however, she had distinctly said she had talked to Hale several times about programmed trading. Hansen began to get irate. In chambers, he raised the possibility of continued perjury, and the next day Lisa changed her story and admitted that she had had the parking conversations with Hale.

Hansen built his case on a financial motive: she lied so as not to derail "the gravy train called Drexel Burnham Lambert, a place that, as she got ready to be tried before you, gave her a

$45,000 cash bonus." It was, said Hansen, just one part of a larger pattern of deception. "She got herself to lotusland by making up fictional stories about herself," he said.

At times during her trial, she seemed to have come to terms with her past, to have understood her life. "I lied on this [job] application, Mr. Hansen, because I needed to support myself," she said at one point. "I was a young girl, and there was no one to support me."

Yet at other times, she still seemed to be living in the past she had created. Precisely what she was protecting was unclear. "Do you have a recollection of whether you ever went to California State University at Northridge?" asked Hansen at one point.

"I don't know," Lisa said.

"You can't recall whether you ever went there?"

"I have been to the school there. I just don't remember when."

After five minutes of agonized haggling, Hansen produced a record from the school, and Lisa finally backed down.

But later he asked, "Did you or did you not know that you hadn't gone to school at Northridge at the time you told the grand jury that you did?"

"I guess I thought I did. I don't know."

O'Neill attributed her confusion to fear. Lisa testified how Doonan had scared her, and how the grand jury had scared her, and how the courtroom, that very day, scared her. O'Neill also tried to show that Lisa had conducted so many transactions that she couldn't possibly remember these few. Toward that end, he had a paralegal count out all the sixty-thousand-odd trading tickets that Lisa had filled out. The tickets filled twenty-eight cartons, and O'Neill had them brought into the courtroom, where they sat as a peculiar monument to the glory days of the junk bond.

Toward the end of the case, after Lisa's testimony, O'Neill attempted to find a psychiatrist who would testify that, because of Lisa's background, she had difficulty remembering painful events. The theory was as plausible as any, but he couldn't find one in time.

Throughout the case, he hammered away at the idea that Lisa was a foot soldier, following orders wherever they led.

And in the end, in his closing statement, he relied on sympathy. "In the Old Testament," he said, "they had a book of Leviticus, and the book of Leviticus is a good book. It talks about sin and atonement. What the Jews did was symbolically try to take care of guilt, take care of atonement for sins, and they had this notion of symbols, the wonderful notion, and they created something called a scapegoat.

"What they did was symbolically invest this goat with the sins of the community and, to atone for the community's sins, they moved the scapegoat out and turned him loose in the desert to bear the guilt for others.

"Don't let the government send Lisa out into the desert to atone for the others' sins!" His voice cracked. Tears welled in his eyes. A juror cried.

The jury deliberated for three and a half hours before returning a verdict, finding her guilty of five counts of perjury and two counts of obstruction of justice. As she cried at the defense table, she was comforted by two other Drexel assistants who had sat in the gallery on the last day of the trial. They appeared older, more sophisticated than Lisa. They were crying, too.

Not surprisingly, Lisa was devastated by the verdict. O'Neill convinced her mother to fly out and see her and had Lisa see a psychiatrist. One friend told *Newsday* after the trial, "I don't think she's going to be resilient at all. She feels she was a victim. I don't think she feels she's to blame at all." Another close to her added that she was extremely upset about having lied to her friends about her background.

Drexel soon released a statement to the press: "Among the people she worked with, Lisa Jones was fondly regarded as a warm and highly industrious individual. The verdict today therefore is a very sad event which causes us a great deal of sorrow." Lisa was freed on $100,000 bail, and more than a month after the verdict, a spokesman for Drexel said the firm was still paying her salary and her legal fees. Lisa has never told the government anything that it didn't already know.

Soon after her verdict was announced, Drexel settled civil charges with the SEC and pleaded guilty to the Princeton/Newport tax-trade scheme. On March 29, Milken was indicted. In the days since the verdict, Lisa has been inundated with TV and movie offers, from people who want her life story.

In the meantime, O'Neill has told friends that some of Lisa's coworkers questioned whether she had been sufficiently prepared for her grand-jury testimony by Drexel's lawyers. She is currently seeking a new trial, alleging conflict of interest. O'Neill, who represented five other Drexel employees, left the case in early April. Lisa is now represented by Daniel Bookin, a former prosecutor in the U.S. attorney's office for the Southern District of New York.

On June 7 Lisa Jones will be sentenced. Under federal sentencing guidelines, she could receive at least ten months—and as much as five years—for each count. She could be sentenced to thirty-five years, which is far more than Boesky and Levine combined.

Making the Club Concorde Connection

Lyle Crowley

November 1989, *Manhattan,inc.*

In the eighties, the Concorde was the transatlantic chariot of choice for big-time investment bankers and speculators. "Making the Club Concorde Connection" tells you everything you ever wanted to know about life at Mach 2. As Lyle Crowley puts it, in the eighties, if you weren't supersonic, you were nothing.

"HALLO, SIR, BACK AGAIN SO SOON?" inquires the uniformed host, a red carnation pinned to his lapel. Inclining slightly in the merest shadow of a bow, he ushers in the gentleman he had seen off only that morning. A club regular, no doubt. The Club Concorde, that is.

"It's good to see you again, sir," he greets another passenger in his crisp BBC accent. The portly gentleman nods and steps past him into the plush, silver gray interior. The strains of soothing classical music fill the air. Removing his jacket and handing it to a flight attendant, he ignores the iced bottles of Mumm's champagne and Puligny–Montrachet and makes straight for a cushy leather seat, disappearing behind the salmon-color pages of the *Financial Times*. A thick sheaf of British newspapers lies folded on the floor by his Hermès briefcase.

It's 6:30 P.M. London time, and the Club Concorde's members are steadily arriving. They come alone and in groups of two or three, some straight from the office in their Savile Row suits and Burberrys, while others, with no need to impress, sport chinos and polo shirts. The loud din of chatter echoes in

235

the narrow chamber, while businessmen bellow greetings to friends, trade stock tips, brag about deals, and instruct their favorite flight attendants to get their drink orders in before the dinner service begins.

"Welcome, sir, how are you?" The host greets a top executive of Glaxo, the largest British pharmaceuticals company. The morning paper carried a front-page story on Glaxo projecting a £1 billion profit for 1988. But the staff is blasé about billionaires. "It's always the world of John Galbraith and Lord Carrington," demurs Captain David Ross.

"We are very conscious of the ego of our travelers," says Julie Sondhi, a British Concorde spokeswoman. "They are captains of industry. Personal recognition is stressed. Service is stressed. We treat them the way they expect to be treated."

Really it's the sort of thing the British do best. It comes from a long tradition of fine service that began with catering to royalty and continues today in the legacy of fine hotels and venerable men's clubs that is still the envy of the civilized world. It is the quiet calm of good British service, the efficiency, the attention to detail that make the trains run on time and the tea arrive hot.

These days, the British Concorde is an elite aerial club made up of the growing cadre of corporate titans, financiers, and lawyers who have decided there is but one way to travel to Europe: to fly faster, literally, than a speeding bullet in the muzzle of a gun. For that privilege they—and their companies—willingly pay $6,934 round-trip (BA gives roughly a $1,000 break to those who go back and forth the same day.) British publisher Lord George Weidenfeld has crowned it a new type of entente cordiale. A meeting of gentlemen who have, shall we say, a common understanding that time is money. Concorde *cordiale*. The clientele are international players who might scoff at a three-hour meal at Le Cirque; so much time, they would say, and so little progress. Once airborne, however, they are willing to linger over their lamb chops.

"I think the people who meet and use the Concorde regularly are very club-minded people," maintains entrepreneurial British publisher William Davis. "You initiate things. I have known the starting point of incidents where people have sat near men like Robert Maxwell. The only time he sits still for five minutes is on the Concorde. It's probably the best opportunity many will get in their lives to talk to him." Recently Davis raced to New York to lunch with Donald Trump on behalf of Maxwell. "It's much more likely that a man like Trump will give you two hours if you arrive on the Concorde," says Davis. "He feels if you've made that effort, then it's worth his time. It's quite flattering."

The "Club Concorde" is actually BA's quaint term for its regular customers—approximately thirty thousand repeat flyers—executives who travel the New York–London route so often they no longer notice the amenities, the pricey silver souvenirs and leather wallets that British Airways dispenses. While famous figures from Pavarotti to Prince Charles line the aisles regularly, there is little question who dominates the plane: a full 40 percent of Concorders are chairmen, managing directors, or board directors of large corporations. Their average age is forty-three. More than three-quarters are male. To be considered members of Club Concorde, they must average more than five flights a year.

The top thousand executives are selected as members of the Premiere Club—the ultimate accomplishment. Members in this elite corps qualify for privileges for which Club Concorders do not—such as the much coveted priority check-ins, special limo services, and other perks. The top sixty travelers in this group all do the New York–London route a minimum of twenty-two times a year.

The Concorde Club roster reads like a Who's Who in world finance: Sir James Goldsmith; Jeffrey Rosen of Wasserstein Perella; Henry Kravis of Kohlberg Kravis Roberts & Co.; John Gutfreund, chairman of Salomon Brothers; and Morgan Stanley president Richard Fisher. There are also the publishing giants Rupert Murdoch and Robert Maxwell; advertising tycoon Martin Sorrell; Thomas J. Cunningham III of Kissinger Associates; and Robert Bauman of SmithKline Beecham; as well as the assorted vacationing millionaires and their wives, all of whom wish to reach the other continent in the best possible shape in the least possible time. Three hours and eighteen minutes, the weather permitting.

Staying in one place does little to bring profits in the high-speed world of international finance. And sometimes being in the right place is all it takes for a payoff. Whether on the plane or in the lush Concorde lounges before takeoff, tales abound of executive wheeling and dealing. The physics of finance apply: densely pack power brokers in a small, warm tube for three hours and they will tend to interact. The end result equals greater profits. "You rub shoulders with rich and powerful people on the Concorde," explains British business author Robert Heller, "and if you rub long enough, some of the gold dust may come off onto your shoulders."

Not surprisingly, the Concorde's fortunes are inexorably tied to Wall Street—as the Dow Jones goes, so follows the Concorde. "Those planes were empty in October, November, and December following the crash of '87," says Sondhi, with an audible sigh. But the fiscal skies have cleared, and the jet has once again become Wall Street's shuttle to London's financial world—in fact, now more so than ever. Because of the weak dollar, the British have been busy buying companies in the U.S. At the same time, an American invasion of Europe is under way, fueled by the plan for a unified European market in 1992. England in particular seems ripe for the picking. The British lag behind the Americans in takeover expertise, and an abundance of weakly defended companies with nicely dividable assets are begging to be snapped up.

Many top U.S. investors are racing to harvest the motherland. In one period last year, for example, buyout king Henry Kravis and his attorney took six Concorde flights in eight days, juggling British executives at one end and American bankers at the other. "There's no question that there's a lot more going on in London than in Paris or anywhere else in Europe," says Kravis's adviser, Richard Beattie of Simpson Thacher & Bartlett.

Takeover specialists Joe Perella and Jeff Rosen can vouch for that. One night last fall they learned of a hostile raid against British mining giant Consolidated Gold Fields. Caught out of the office, Perella had only hours to locate Rosen and hash out a plan. But there was a chance: Perella was in good standing with the chairman of the target company, Rudolf Agnew. So at 4:00 A.M. New York time Perella reached Agnew by phone in London. "This is an important assignment to us," Perella said. "Are you free for dinner tonight?" The chairman pondered a moment, no doubt glancing at the clock, then told Perella, "If you're here, I'll have dinner with you."

At 9:30 that morning Perella and Rosen took off on the Concorde. Hours later—while other flights still lumbered across the Atlantic—the two bankers were in an elegant private dining room on St. James Square, toasting Agnew. By the end of the meal they were hired.

Even before takeoff it is clear who rules the aisles on the Concorde. As one would expect, there are the crowd-shy stars (Robert Redford) and rock musicians (Billy Joel and his wife, Christie Brinkley), and exhausted athletes, especially after major tennis tournaments, when Chris Evert, Ivan Lendl, and others are returning home. But any observer of a Concorder's activities can sense the thrust of activity by looking at the busy phones and listening to the urgent buy-sell conversations. In the Concorde lounge at Heathrow Airport there is a long table lined with colorful hors d'oeuvres, caviar, and cold shrimp and an impressive bar that goes largely ignored; despite the temptations, most passengers have their mind on business. Dotted around the lounge are small, intense gatherings of executives, their heads close together, their words impossible to overhear.

"The trip coming back to New York on the Concorde is what I call the aura trip," says Miles Slater, president of Slater Associates, who last year took the Concorde back from London once every week and a half. "It really is as concentrated a group of high-powered professionals as you'd want to see."

"The 9:30 A.M. Concorde to London is the most valuable transatlantic flight in Europe," insists a prominent Manhattan travel agent. British Airways also flies a Concorde to London from Washington and Miami, while Air France runs the Concorde to Paris with its fleet of seven planes. "You have connectors out of London to all the major European capitals," the agent explains. "That plane is the key, I guarantee you. Every time I've flown it, it staggers me to see who's on board."

But Concorders find themselves surrounded by influence

to and from London. "I think there's very definitely a special camaraderie among frequent flyers on the Concorde," says one merchant banker and Concorde habitué. "At any point in time the plane is always full of investment bankers and potential clients. Think of it like this: when you get on a regular plane, who are you likely to end up next to? On the Concorde you are likely to be seated next to someone whose business card you are glad to have and whose acquaintance you are glad to make."

"It's true to say it's a sort of club," agrees British television host David Frost. "It's very rare that there isn't someone on the flight that you find you know. There are all sorts of friends and acquaintances. The phrase that you hear frequently is 'We've never met, but we've spoken on the phone,' " he says, adding that he finds the networking habits of Concorders amusing, if somewhat puzzling. "I've noticed—it's illogical—but people say, 'We must get together for a drink in New York.' Theoretically, they could have the drink right there for three and a half hours. But they don't want to do that," Frost chuckles.

Of course Frost probably knows the flying habits of more Concorde regulars than most: since taking the maiden flight from Paris in 1976, Frost has become one of the most experienced "Conckers." For meeting tight interview deadlines across the Atlantic, the Concorde is indispensable, according to Frost. After more than three hundred trips, his inflight social habits are well known to the crew: "Mr. Frost just pops a sleeping pill and orders a salad," reports one veteran BA attendant. "He doesn't like to be disturbed."

There are those who get down to business before deplaning. Publisher Lord Weidenfeld ran into Social Democratic Party head David Owen a year and a half ago. On that flight, the two structured a book to be published on geopolitics. "I can't remember a single trip when I haven't met either a European or an American," says Lord Weidenfeld, "and it's been very helpful. Usually the operative time to exchange meaningful talk is five to seven minutes. That allows for a great number of conversations in the lounge or seat hopping during the journey."

On a typical journey last week, Weidenfeld found himself

sandwiched between former assistant secretary of state Thomas Enders and James Sherwood, chairman of Orient Express Hotels and Sea Containers. Nearby sat a coterie of merchant bankers "working on a dawn raid," mutters Weidenfeld ominously. On the trip back, he shared his two-seater with Murdoch.

"It's a contact," says Kravis lawyer Richard Beattie of the Concorde experience. "You see somebody you may not have talked to in a while and you share some things and that will provide a basis for getting together later on. Someone will use that as an opportunity to call Henry. There's also a lot of gossip picked up. As you know, in this M&A world there's sort of a thriving gossip side-business."

None who have buckled up for takeoff will ever wonder why the British call it "the Rocket." The departure more closely resembles blasting off: the plane accelerates from 0 to 250 miles per hour in thirty seconds. On takeoff from Kennedy Airport, a dramatic bank turn begins as the wheels pull off the runway, instantly affirming capabilities closer to *Top Gun* than to a conventional jet. "If you did that with a 747, the wing tip would hit the ground," says Concorde Captain Peter Horton. Heading ten miles high—fifty-eight thousand feet— the plane will take most flyers as close as they will ever come to outer space.

British Airways pitches its dashing plane as a seminal experience: "The Rise of Civilization." Gone are the days when Brits harrumphed that BA stood for "Bloody Awful." English pride has returned to the Concorde, perhaps with a smattering of French prejudice. "The British feel incredibly xenophobic or patriotic," says author Robert Heller. "They love the fact that it's a British plane. They forget the French Concorde altogether." During the creation of the Concorde through a French–English consortium, there was a typically Anglo-French battle over whether Concorde would be spelled with an *e* at the end, as the French demanded. When the British finally conceded the point, the prime minister reportedly declared, "The *e* shall stand for England!" to the cheers of his countrymen.

The British have been far more successful than the French

at marketing their bird. British Airways Concorde amenities include helicopter service to and from JFK, as well as a Learjet that waits beneath the Concorde wing in New York, ready to whisk passengers off to Boston—for a fee, of course. Occasionally the big bird is used as a pricey perk. During Drexel Burnham Lambert's heyday no expense was spared: once in the late 1980s the firm chartered a Concorde to send clients and executives over to London, complete with hotel rooms and tickets to the Wimbledon tennis tournament. But Drexel had some sense of proportion—everyone had to pay his own return fare.

British Airways has also concocted promotional round-the-world journeys, holiday excursions, trips to witness the flight of Halley's comet, and various mind-boggling one- and two-day trips. An early flight to see the Pyramids in Egypt, for example, could return a traveler to London for dinner. Or one could take the kids up to Lapland to visit Father Christmas for the day. Perhaps the Bolshoi Ballet in Moscow for the night? Or maybe Concorde down to Venice and travel back on the Orient Express? The list goes on.

Few have escaped hearing about the round-the-world trip hosted by William Buckley this past April. Buckley, who spoke to a reporter on the condition that his long-winded *National Review* articles on the excursion be read first, takes a somewhat unglamorous view of the plane. "Mostly it's invisible businessmen," complains Buckley. "I tend to find people are intentionally nongregarious. I don't find the airplane's ambience conducive to work." Perhaps Buckley has been less enthused with the Concorde ever since the plane dropped a nine-foot tail section into the South Pacific during his transcontinental jaunt.

But Buckley's seems to be a minority opinion. Jeffrey Rosen of Wasserstein Perella is among the most frequent flyers. Virtually every other week (four round trips a month, to be precise) he can be seen racing to Kennedy airport. ("He's never off that plane," say many of his peer travelers.) He is well aware of the values of Club Concorde. "You find in the cabin a lot of people with whom you may have business in common at that time, bankers or lawyers on either side of a transaction," says Rosen, finally tracked down in a Geneva hotel. "People aren't racing up and down the aisles initiating or concluding deals right and left, but you do spend time getting caught up with what is the latest step in a deal or development in a company."

Rosen is one of those whose ability to do business has been transformed by the Concorde. "The plane has clearly created many new travel possibilities," he says. "It's very wearing physically. In the long run, maybe it's not so good for you." Rosen should know: in many cases he dashes out of meetings in New York and jets to London for a night to deal with client matters. "It's an expensive way to travel, no one will deny that. To some it seems to often border on frivolous, but it obviously has its advantages."

Certainly, to those concluding high-powered transatlantic deals, the flying premium of the Concorde is a mere drop of red ink. "We have a thousand people in London right now," says Richard Fisher, president of Morgan Stanley. "I'd say time is worth spending money for."

To some high flyers, seating is of paramount importance on board the Concorde. Rupert Murdoch would no sooner be found behind the first few rows than would Henry Kissinger be found seated by the kitchen at the Four Seasons. What began as a harmless desire of passengers to be last on and first off the plane has turned into a system as symbolically significant as the seating in the Soviet Politburo. Exactly how the precious front-row seats are obtained is unclear. "It's not like a restaurant where we keep a few tables open for our best customers," grouses a BA staffer.

For such treatment one must seek out an industrious travel agent. "I used to be able to get front seats all the time," says the Manhattan travel agent. "Now I have to fight for the middle of the plane." There is special prestige attached to being visible up front, as well as the theory that one can network more successfully there, since, logically, the best string-pullers would be one's seating companions. Of course, others decide they want to sit in the back for the reverse snob appeal.

"Basically I like the first bulkhead seat, second cabin, in the middle of the aisle—14C," says merger defense whiz Marty Lipton cryptically. Some stars—or CEOs for that matter—

value their privacy enough to purchase both seats in their row. Others, such as renowned tenor Luciano Pavarotti, resign themselves to the physical necessity of two seats on the slim, tubular craft.

The stunning actress Michelle Pfeiffer is tucked innocuously in a window seat toward the back of the plane, her nose buried in John Le Carré's new best-selling novel, *The Russia House*. As with all true Concorders, her reading material is not incidental: she has just signed on to costar with Sean Connery in the upcoming film version of the cold-war thriller.

Sitting across the aisle from his associate, Jeremy Epstein, a litigator with Shearman & Sterling, digs into a thick wad of newspapers and begins poring over the *Wall Street Journal*. (True Club Concorders are media addicts. it is not unusual to see men boarding the plane with shopping bags crammed with journals and newspapers.) A tall, lean man in his forties, Epstein repeatedly shifts his arms and legs in search of a satisfying position. "It's not as comfortable as first class in a regular flight," he complains. "It's too cramped and much too loud." He has to raise his voice to make himself heard above the din of the four Rolls-Royce engines, comparable to the whirring roar of a monstrous air conditioner.

Besides the stress of cross-continental travel, Epstein finds doing business with the British creates all sorts of new problems. "The cultural differences are particularly acute," says Epstein, who studied at Cambridge and is versed in the ways of the English executive. "In our lawsuits, not only do we bore them to death with our legal detail but we insist on deposing everyone from the CEO to the entire board. It can be a wrenching experience for a British top executive who is unused to having his word doubted." Thus, meetings in person are often necessary to smooth ruffled feathers and keep legal proceedings on track. Often, British clients arrive in New York in the morning and go back in the afternoon "without even bringing a toothbrush," says Epstein.

Nearer to the front of the plane, a retired industrial executive, en route to Istanbul, selects a pack of Silk Cuts from the matronly stewardess. (Concorde air hostesses are selected for their experience, we're told.) Although well acquainted with the Concorde, he still finds the technology a kick and periodically reads off the speed, temperature, and altitude, which are digitally displayed up front. (Fortunately the digital computer display is not connected to the main controls, as the altimeter once went berserk and rolled up to ninety-eight thousand feet. "If we go any higher, we'll be in orbit," one executive remarked at the time.) "Just think," he exclaims, downing a swig of port wine, "here you are going twice the speed of sound, eating this brunch." He gives a Ronald Reagan–style nod. "Why, when I was young we didn't even have circular air-conditioning."

The one aspect of the technology that pleases travelers most, however, is that the high altitude avoids the turbulence suffered by most commercial aircraft. It makes dinner rather more digestible. Also, the Concorde is pressurized to about five thousand feet, considerably less than most jets, thereby cutting down on body stress and jet lag. Although the Concorde menu promises a movable feast compared to most airline meals—who wouldn't choose lobster terrine over limp macaroni salad?—a majority of regular flyers pass up the food. Indeed a recent BA study indicated that the most popular inflight libation was mineral water. This is a serious crowd.

Up front, the cockpit door remains open. From a jump seat behind the two pilots, passengers can look beyond the compact control panel and stare out the great, sloping beak of the plane—a mesmerizing view of the curvature of the earth. "She's a very sensitive aircraft," Captain David Ross explains, twisting around in his seat and facing backward. "Very slippery . . . a bit like a racehorse. You've got to hold her back all the time. If she gets away, she's off." Fortunately for everyone, however, the plane is flown by computer much of the time.

Morris Kramer, a lawyer at Kadden, Arps, has a penchant for supersonic travel. "The ability to be there that day is critical," says Kramer. "I can get a call from London that wakes me up very early—maybe 5 A.M. If someone thinks my appearance at dinner that night makes sense, they can get me." Kramer, who averages about forty flights a year, is not immune to the macho of Concorde Club regulars. "It's not like regular first class," he says. "If you don't know at least a dozen people in the lounge, you aren't a real player."

But many power shuttlers are low-profile and, it sometimes seems, would sooner swim to Europe than be stamped with the label "jetsetter." They are loath to speak of networking aboard the plane or in the Concorde lounges. "I don't fly it as a traveling social club," M&A attorney Arthur Fleischer Jr. explains. "I'm not saying it isn't, but happily I'm not one of those people."

"I never really speak to anyone on the Concorde," says Roland Franklin from his bathtub at the Savoy Hotel, where he conducts all his business (from the hotel, that is). Franklin is another who plays down his hobnobbing on the plane, though his face is by now quite familiar to those who regularly shuttle back and forth on the Concorde. For ten years the chief adviser to Sir James Goldsmith in the U.S., he now runs his own firm and is mounting a bid for DRG, a British paper company.

"Nothing interesting ever happened to me, except once when I exited through the chutes instead of the door," he says wistfully, splashing about in the tub. When he has the time, Franklin likes to fly to London by Concorde and return at a more leisurely pace on the *QE II.*

However, others may have more complex reasons for playing down their clubbing. "The whole point of the snob factor is inverse now," says author Robert Heller. "You get the factor by talking about it as if you just hopped on the local bus. If you make a big deal out of it, you're revealing yourself as one who is not a true Concorder."

But the playing field can be rough for novices. Woe to those who let a few assets go to their heads. Recently one overexuberant young executive was boasting aloud to a fellow traveler about the company he was about to purchase. Catching a snippet, the man seated in front turned around.

"You're doing an acquisition?"

"Yes. Six million dollars," the entrepreneur replied smoothly.

"Pleased to meet you," said the man. "My name's Hanson."

Familiar with Lord Hanson's $12 billion empire, the deflated executive shrank back in his seat. He had learned the crucial difference between first-class flyers and Concorde clubbers.

Perhaps the man most knowledgeable about the Concorde is Fred Finn, the future *Jeopardy* answer to the question: Who is the most traveled man in the world? Finn has flown the equivalent of four round trips to the moon on board the Concorde—657 flights. "I think I can safely say I know that airplane pretty well," he says with no small amount of pride. "I think it's gone through phases, from having top entertainers to being a businessman's express these days," Finn observes. "The big deal makers of the world are on it. It is a place you can catch top businessmen where they don't have to go through the usual procedures. All the fences are down and people are relaxed and it is quite an exhilarating experience to fly on it."

Finn, like every veteran, has his share of Concorde adventures and misadventures, as well as a few tall tales. Like the time lightning hit the plane. "There was a hell of bang," says Finn unfazed. One of the plane's better-known "characters," Finn, who is rumored to be a CIA agent, used to work for the Empire Pencil Company and is now an editorial consultant to *Executive Travel* magazine. Frost, naturally, has encountered Finn. "He certainly is opaque about what he does," observes Frost.

Each CEO has his or her own idiosyncratic travel preferences. Martin Sorrell, whose WPP Group owns the advertising agencies Ogilvy Group and J. Walter Thompson, prefers to FAX himself over to New York via Concorde, then take a regular jet home, assuming the day to be lost inevitably. "I think it a pity if and when it stops," says Sorrell. "It's rather like car telephones. You tend to take it for granted."

One trend that is cutting into the Concorde's passenger list is the growing popularity of private planes. "The corporate people are not on the Concorde as much anymore," contends Marty Lipton. "It's the investment bankers and lawyers." CEOs such as Shearson's Peter Cohen and finance kings such as Ted Forstmann favor the privacy of their own corporate jets and thumb their noses as those who squeeze onto the Concorde. Donald Trump prefers his private Boeing 727. "It's so-o-o-o much more comfortable," says his secretary.

Of course private jets can't approach Mach speed, and to a true Concorder, if you aren't supersonic, you're nothing.

"Frankly, why somebody would fly their own plane at subsonic speed, stopping to refuel, when they could take the Concorde is beyond me," says one banker. "It's just a total ego trip."

As far as his frequent flights on the Concorde are concerned, lawyer Jeremy Epstein shrugs and says, "You know what Lloyd Bentsen said last year about the future of Mach 2 travel? 'What's the point of another supersonic flight? So the investment bankers can get to Japan faster?' "

As for the future of the Concorde, the current life expectancy of the seven British Airways planes runs just past the year 2000. The original Concorde production facilities no longer exist, and there are no plans yet to pull together the massive funding required to develop a new prototype. "I don't think, oddly enough, that the Concorde ever really becomes prosaic," says Frost. "It maintains a certain glamour even when you've traveled it a great deal. And I suppose that glamour is heightened by the fact that it's something that, in a very Luddite way, may be taken away again."

For the younger generation of travelers, however, the Concorde may be a tough habit to break. Waiting in the Concorde lounge recently, British publisher Bill Davis smiled at a cherubic young face. "Is this your first trip?" he asked somewhat patronizingly. "No, it's my sixth," retorted the worldly little girl. Such junior jet-setters may be poised to inherit the earth, but alas, they have little hope of inheriting the Concorde.

ACT 3

A Wicked Hangover (1990–1991)

Self-Made Man

Bryan Burrough

January 22, 1990, the *Wall Street Journal*

By 1990, Americans had turned against Reaganesque financial excess and Wall Street. Bryan Burrough's profile of Jeff "Mad Dog" Beck, a minor Drexel investment banker, signaled the change in the national mood and is without a doubt the greatest hatchet-job of the decade. Beck was the reductio ad absurdum of investment bankers—a pathological liar who would do anything for a deal. He even ate a box of dog biscuits to get a chief executive's attention. This is one helluva read, nasty but good.

INSIDE WALL STREET's tightly knit takeover community, everyone knows The Mad Dog. At least they think so.

Jeffrey "Mad Dog" Beck of Drexel Burnham Lambert will go down as one of the top merger "rainmakers" of the Roaring Eighties. A well-connected, often outrageous investment banker who played key roles in the decade's two largest leveraged buyouts, Beatrice and RJR Nabisco, Mr. Beck, forty-three, may be the only banker in history to wolf down a box of dog biscuits to get a chief executive's attention.

Throughout his career, an outsized part of Mr. Beck's allure has been his rococo background; heir to a billion-dollar Florida fortune, decorated for heroism as a special forces platoon leader in Vietnam, rumored to have worked for the Central Intelligence Agency. No one, friends say, can make fighting in the steaming jungles of Southeast Asia come alive as can Mr. Beck, who has held many a Manhattan dinner party in thrall with his wartime tales. He likes to pull up his left shirtsleeve, point to a scar on his wrist and explain how it was shattered by a bullet from an AK-47 rifle during fighting in the Ia Drang Valley; only a bulky Seiko watch, Mr. Beck says grimly, saved his hand. For calling in napalm strikes on his own patrols and other exploits, he tells rapt listeners, he earned a Silver Star, two Bronze Stars and four Purple Hearts.

Mr. Beck's is a stirring story, good enough, in fact, to have drawn the attention of actor Michael Douglas, who paired the Drexel banker with a screenwriter to assemble a script based on Mr. Beck's life. Mr. Beck has served as the model for one popular novel's protagonist, and his Wall Street career is the centerpiece of a nonfiction book to be published this fall by Random House.

Filmmaker Oliver Stone, himself a Vietnam veteran, befriended and swapped war stories with Mr. Beck during the filming of the movie *Wall Street,* on which the banker served as a technical adviser and even took a cameo role. "Jeff was on the killing edge, the front lines, of the takeovers," Mr. Stone says in an interview. "To me, he really *was* the new Wall Street."

The only problem, as a handful of Mr. Beck's acquaintances now know, is that the banker's stories are almost all lies. A reporter's investigation into the star dealmaker's career reveals that much of Mr. Beck's "past" has been created from whole cloth, the product, friends and business associates say, of the banker's active fantasy life.

Army records and his first wife's family confirm that he never served in the special forces, never fought in Vietnam, never, in fact, came closer to combat than the Army reserves. Nor, apparently, is there any basis for Mr. Beck's repeated claims to associates over the years that he stood to inherit a family fortune he variously estimated at between $100 million and $2.5 billion, or that he owned a "small empire" of private businesses, as a major magazine once reported.

Confronted with evidence of his deceptions over lunch at a Manhattan restaurant, Mr. Beck first looks away, then stares at the ceiling for a moment. Under the table, his left leg begins rapidly bobbing. A thin mist falls over his eyes. "I can't talk about it," he says after a long silence. But he does, though his answers amount to riddles wrapped in questions, wrapped in lies. His explanation, broadly hinted at, is that for twenty years he has led a double life as an intelligence agent.

Later, in seemingly contradictory statements, Mr. Beck categorically denies telling most of the tales attributed to him by business associates, friends and others. "This is getting wilder and wilder," he says. "I am beyond shock."

In one sense, Mr. Beck's story is a parable of Wall Street in the 1980s, a time when virtually everything—old standards, morals, sometimes even the truth—was sacrificed in the almighty hunt for The Big Deal. Though over the years some doubted his truthfulness, none of his longtime clients, men like LBO magnate Henry Kravis, has openly questioned, much less unmasked, Mr. Beck's "past" or his other deceptions. At least in part, many of his colleagues acknowledge, this is because Mr. Beck's deals routinely made millions of dollars for his clients and partners. Investors like Mr. Kravis, who put up with Mr. Beck's half-truths and histrionics for years, kept him around for the simple reason that he had an incredible knack for sniffing out brewing takeovers. Mr. Kravis declined to discuss Mr. Beck for this article.

"To some extent Jeff was a product of the Wall Street environment," says Ronald Peters, head of Oppenheimer & Co.'s merger department, who has known Mr. Beck for twenty years. "He didn't have the brains or smarts of [top investment bankers like] a Bruce Wasserstein or Marty Siegel. What he's flying on is his promotional abilities. [The stories] gave him something to go on, when he really had nothing at all."

Mr. Beck was born in South Florida in 1946. His late father, he says, was a salesman, and friends confirm his mother remarried a well-to-do Miami businessman. As a student at Florida State University in the mid-1960s, Mr. Beck married a Miami woman named Sylvia Pfotenhauer. At various times, his former mother-in-law Edith Pfotenhauer recalls, Mr. Beck claimed his father was chief executive of a major paper company and that he was heir to the German family that owned and brewed Beck's Beer. The Pfotenhauer family doubted those and other of Mr. Beck's stories, but hoped he would grow out of his taletelling. "He was a very good-natured kid; at first we liked him very much," says Edith Pfotenhauer. "I don't know why he always needed to elaborate."

For a man who later claimed to be a war hero, his first wife says Mr. Beck evidenced an ironic desire to escape service in the armed forces. "He felt like everyone else; he didn't want to be drafted," recalls the former Ms. Pfotenhauer, who has remarried, changed her name and is now living in a Western city. "He was more interested in his education." Instead, she says Mr. Beck joined the Army reserves. Mr. Beck's former brother-in-law Ingo Pfotenhauer says he likewise joined the Coast Guard reserves after Mr. Beck told him it was the best way to avoid the draft.

Mr. Beck has claimed he did two tours of duty in Vietnam between 1967 and 1969; records at Florida State, however, show he enrolled in 1964 and, after two semesters at William & Mary in 1965, graduated in December 1968. Afterward, Sylvia Pfotenhauer says, she worked on her master's degree while Mr. Beck put in a few weeks in mandatory reserve training. It was as close as her husband ever got to military duty, she says. The Becks explored several career paths—they were accepted by the Peace Corps for work in Afghanistan—before finally deciding to pursue graduate studies at Columbia University in New York. "When we went to New York, I told him, 'Now Jeff, we're starting out fresh,' " Ms. Pfotenhauer recalls. " 'Please, let's leave all these wild stories behind us.' "

Ron Peters befriended Mr. Beck during the two students' first weeks at Columbia Business School in the fall of 1969. Mr. Peters recalls being immediately impressed with the ambitious young Floridian, who dressed in a coat and tie at a time other students wore scraggly beards and fatigue jackets. From their first meeting, Mr. Peters recalls, Mr. Beck regaled him and other friends with tales of his days fighting in the Vietnamese jungles. Occasionally Mr. Beck disappeared for a time, later explaining to Mr. Peters that he had been called to Washington to testify on his wartime "assignments," Mr. Peters says.

"The implication was that he had been in Cambodia when he wasn't supposed to, like he was on long-range patrols that were covert," Mr. Peters says.

Though Mr. Beck seemed careful never to tell the stories in her presence, Ms. Pfotenhauer was soon stunned to hear her new friends avidly questioning her husband about his recent tour in Southeast Asia. "I was in shock," she recalls. "I don't know if he expected me to go along with it, or what. I didn't want to say, 'What's going on? You didn't go to Vietnam.' I waited until we were alone to talk to him about it."

Confronted, Mr. Beck couldn't explain the new lies, his former wife says. At other times, Ms. Pfotenhauer says she had urged her husband to channel his active fantasy life into a writing career, to no avail. When others caught him in a contradiction, she adds, he would invoke national security, hinting that he had been involved in intelligence matters and shouldn't talk further. "That was the big coverup," she says. "He would tell people there were secrets he just couldn't talk about. That's how he got away with it."

Finally, Mr. Beck's wife had had enough. "I gave him an ultimatum: This has to be cleared up or else. For me, it all of a sudden got too weird. I literally said I want out of this as soon as possible. I wanted a very simple clean divorce."

After a postgraduation year at First Union National Bank in Charlotte, N.C., where he met the woman who would become his second wife, Mr. Beck returned to New York to work at the securities firm of Donaldson Lufkin & Jenrette. There he was introduced to an infant industry that he would find uniquely suited to his creative talents: mergers and acquisitions.

In January 1980, Ronald Reagan and his administration's loosened antitrust restrictions were only a year away from the Oval Office, and the financial world stood on the threshold of a new age in which its fee-hungry investment bankers would provide the impetus for an unprecedented restructuring of America's publicly held companies. On Wall Street, thirty-three-year-old Jeff Beck had just been hired to begin a merger department at a small firm named Oppenheimer & Co.

Senior Oppenheimer officials, eager to grab a piece of the burgeoning takeover business, felt Mr. Beck was ideal for the task, a young, aggressive rainmaker type with a network of corporate relationships already in place after eight years of apprenticeship at Donaldson Lufkin and, later, at Lehman Brothers Kuhn Loeb. Upon his arrival, however, they had second thoughts. Mr. Beck was a fine promoter, they discovered, but he knew next to nothing about financial analysis.

And his boisterous personality, including a penchant for off-color jokes, made him few allies.

"From the moment he got here, we knew this was going to be a turbulent experience," recalls a senior Oppenheimer executive who worked with Mr. Beck. "He alienated a lot of people right away. In fact, he alienated nearly everyone he talked to. He began every conversation by telling everyone what a big deal he was. It was all about his net worth, his contacts."

The complaints abated, however, when Mr. Beck, after hiring a handful of helpers, began pulling in a startling array of new business. Taking on jobs too small or too complicated for more-established firms, Mr. Beck's cadre of hustling young bankers quickly made a name for themselves, achieving a degree of notoriety with a favorable feature in the *Wall Street Journal* in early 1982.

"CEOs loved him," recalls Stephen McGrath, who as an executive vice president at Warner Lambert Co. in the 1970s grew close to Mr. Beck. Mr. McGrath recalls that the company's chairman, Ward Hagan, was so impressed with Mr. Beck that he channeled more of Warner Lambers's divestitures to him. "Guys from [blue-chip banks] know the right fork to use, they go to the right country clubs," Mr. Hagan once told Mr. McGrath. "Beck comes in here . . . he doesn't know how to eat, but he gets things done." Another client, Detroit real estate magnate Alfred Taubman, grew so fond of Mr. Beck's upbeat personality he once gave him a cheerleader outfit.

Mr. McGrath says he had long suspected his friend of harmless exaggeration, but after joining Mr. Beck at Oppenheimer in 1983 he says he quickly came to believe the bankers' problems were far more serious. His suspicion grew when, after Mr. Beck volunteered he had been captain of his college tennis team, Mr. McGrath invited him to his club for a match. Mr. McGrath, who considers himself an average tennis player, recalls that he thrashed Mr. Beck 6-0, 6-1. Afterward, Mr. Beck said only that he was "a little rusty."

At Oppenheimer Mr. Beck often told business associates how he stood to inherit a massive fortune at age forty; more than a dozen people interviewed for this story remember these stories in detail. At times he promised to bequeath hundreds of thousands of dollars to various secretaries and associates. At first no one doubted the stories. But as the size of the alleged inheritance grew over the years—sometimes during the course of a single conversation—and reached into the billions, many people came to believe Mr. Beck was lying, his associates say.

His Vietnam tales were no less vivid. Military phrases dotted his jargon: "Lock and load!" Mr. Beck was prone to shout before an important meeting. He acquired the "Mad Dog" sobriquet from his troops, Mr. Beck liked to say, after leading doomed patrols such as the one in which, he claimed, only six out of fifty-three men survived the defeat of an entire North Vietnamese regiment. His war wounds, he explained, weren't limited to a scarred wrist. "Know what shrapnel up your butt feels like?" he once asked a reporter. "It burns."

Despite his growing doubts about Mr. Beck, Mr. McGrath was amazed by his partner's deal-making abilities. Looking for a buyer for Chicago-based Esmark in 1983, Mr. McGrath compiled a bulky set of analyses that the two men took to Europe and reviewed with a pair of possible suitors, Unilever and Nestlé. They got nowhere. Afterward Mr. Beck suggested running Esmark past Mr. Kravis, who, Mr. Beck surmised, might be eager to bolster his reputation after having an overture to Gulf Oil rebuffed. Mr. Beck arranged a dinner between Mr. Kravis and Esmark chief Donald Kelly and, to the two dealmakers' amazement, a deal was struck. As they left Mr. Kravis's apartment following the dinner, Mr. McGrath turned to Mr. Beck and said, "You're a genius."

Announcement of the Esmark deal "broke Kravis into the creme de la creme," Mr. McGrath explains. "Jeffrey saw that, and I didn't. He was brilliant that way." Mr. McGrath pauses in his recollection. "We were a great team, you know. But it broke apart because he was . . ." Mr. McGrath pauses again. "He was crazy."

Another Oppenheimer banker, David Aaron, was so captivated with Mr. Beck that he used him as model for the Wall Street protagonist of his popular 1989 spy novel, *Agent of Influence.* Among the main character's more memorable lines was an excuse Mr. Beck, a ladies' man between his three marriages, concocted to break more than one date: If the woman objected too strongly, Mr. Beck simply told her his mother had died.

"I found him to be one of the most colorful fellows I've ever met," Mr. Aaron says. As an investment banker, "the thing I found most impressive was his insight. He really could create something where others would see nothing. He always understood the dynamics of the people involved. [In mergers] it's not how balance sheets go together that matters. It's how the people go together. Jeff always understood that."

Mr. Beck's talent for histrionics had endless uses. When Mr. Kravis's bid for Esmark was topped by Beatrice, a rival food company, Mr. Beck desperately wanted a fee for setting events in motion. "You've got to do something for me; you've got to do something for me," he moaned, spread-eagled on the floor of an Esmark office in Chicago. A mischievous Mr. Kelly, the Esmark chief, already persuaded to pay Mr. Beck, decided to play a trick. Called into Mr. Kelly's office and told he wouldn't receive a fee, Mr. Beck went berserk, walking to the office window, opening it and shouting: "I'm going to jump!" Mr. Kelly, breaking up in laughter, yelled, "Don't jump!" then revealed his charade and gave Mr. Beck a $7.5 million fee for Oppenheimer.

After the breakup of his second marriage, Mr. Beck began cutting a colorful profile on the Manhattan social scene. A car and driver whisked him around the city from his striking, antique-filled apartment on Manhattan's Upper East Side. One woman who dated him for more than a year during this period says that Mr. Beck, after introducing himself at a party, told her he was a German Lutheran from a small town in North Carolina. The woman also heard repeated stories about Mr. Beck's massive family wealth and detailed stories of Vietnam.

"He would wake up in cold sweats, shaking, and I'd ask him, 'Jeff, what's wrong?' " she recalls. "He'd, you know, grab his head and say, 'Oh my God, I was dreaming about Vietnam.' " She adds: "Sometimes it seemed he couldn't watch a war movie without crying or getting the shakes. He didn't hear a gunshot on TV that he didn't jump, [acting] shaken." Years later, the woman learned it was all an act. "The guy lied in his sleep!" she exclaims, still exercised by the memory. "Oh, he really had that one down pat."

When a woman named Stephanie Shuman broke up with Mr. Beck in 1982, she became worried enough about his resulting erratic behavior, including late-night phone calls, that she called Mr. Beck's sister. Explaining her concern that their breakup was complicating Mr. Beck's continuing effort to cope with his Vietnam experiences, Ms. Shuman said: "I want you to know I feel poorly about Jeff. He's really having a tough time about this whole Vietnam thing."

Ms. Shuman would never forget the sister's reply. "She said, 'Vietnam? Jeff was never in Vietnam. He was never even in the service.' " Dumbfounded, Ms. Shuman confronted Mr. Beck, who explained that he and his sister had lost touch for several years while he was in Vietnam. Mr. Beck's sister didn't respond to repeated phone messages.

News of Ms. Shuman's discovery eventually filtered through the Manhattan social set back to senior Oppenheimer executives, who began to suspect they had a bigger problem on their hands than previously thought. Short of concrete evidence, however, and in light of his increasing value to Oppenheimer, they took no action. But Mr. Beck was nevertheless headed for trouble: His "flame-out," in fact, was to be more spectacular than his rise.

In January 1985, Mr. Beck's team was poised to complete its most important deal, the billion-dollar leveraged buyout of Chicago-based Northwest Industries by a group led by Mr. Kelly and Oppenheimer. Just as the deal was to close, a key investor suddenly backed out, leaving Oppenheimer and Mr. Kelly roughly $75 million short of the needed equity. As panic spread through both camps, Mr. Beck, according to several people involved in the deal, stepped forward and pledged to supply the entire sum from his personal fortune.

Mr. McGrath, who like many of his colleagues didn't believe Mr. Beck had any fortune to speak of, confronted Mr. Beck, who stuck to his story. In the end, Mr. Kelly killed the deal. "I'm not sure that anyone took him seriously at that point," Mr. McGrath says of Mr. Beck's offer. "We were embarrassed by it." Mr. Beck acknowledges portions of this story, but says he proposed to borrow the money rather than personally pledge it.

If his colleagues were embarrassed, by all accounts senior Oppenheimer officials were horrified that what they viewed as Mr. Beck's fantasies had intruded into the largest deal in the firm's history. Rumors began flying that Mr. Beck's department would be shaken up—and that he might be fired.

For months Mr. Beck had been bragging—accurately, but against colleagues' advice—about how his department's growing income was "carrying" Oppenheimer. "We were really flying high [and] Jeff was really rubbing it in," says Mr. McGrath. "I said, 'Jeff, this business isn't going to always be this hot. You can't keep acting this way. As soon as you start tripping, you're going to get killed by everyone.' "

Now Mr. McGrath's warnings showed signs of coming true. As his political position inside the firm deteriorated, Mr. Beck began disappearing for long periods and, when at the office, often spoke of leaving the firm to found his own investment banking boutique. One day he invited Mr. McGrath and Mr. Peters, who had also joined the firm, to resign with him and form their own firm, which he said would be capitalized with his $2 billion family inheritance. "Sure," Mr. Peters said skeptically, "if you can prove it."

Both Oppenheimer executive recall that, at that point, Mr. Beck took out a note pad on which he had drawn a box labeled "J. P. Beck Enterprises." Below the box was an intricate, interlocking grid of businesses—cattle ranches, oil-and-gas firms, insurance companies and real estate—all supposedly owned by Mr. Beck. "Of course," says Mr. McGrath, "it was all XYZ Ranch, Acme insurance company" and other nondescript entities.

For Mr. Peters, who had named Mr. Beck the godfather of his oldest son, it was a heart-rending moment. "In many respects," he says, "I want to believe it was true. It was just too painful to believe it was all lies."

Nothing, of course, came of Mr. Beck's scheme. Distraught, his colleagues recall, Mr. Beck took to walking from office to office, often interrupting meetings, searching for someone with whom to commiserate. Mr. McGrath began locking his door, shouting at Mr. Beck to "go away" as he repeatedly knocked. "He was unbearable," recalls Mr. Peters. "The pillars that had held him up for so long weren't there anymore. He just wandered around with nothing to do and he wanted people to be with him."

Then, when matters were near their bleakest, Mr. Beck attempted what amounted to a last-ditch effort to regain his colleagues' sympathy. Walking into Mr. McGrath's unlocked office, he confronted his colleague with a bizarre tale. "You gotta help me," Mr. McGrath recalls Mr. Beck pleading. "There's somebody with pictures of my wife in compromising sexual positions. I've paid 'em $250,000 in a Swiss bank account. But they're still blackmailing me."

At once stunned and amused, Mr. McGrath says he told Mr. Beck he thought he was lying. At that point, the Mad Dog looked straight into his friend's eyes and said: "You wanna see the pictures?" Distraught, Mr. Beck took the same story to Mr. Peters and to Oppenheimer's chief executive, Stephen Robert. "You couldn't laugh," Mr. Peters recalls. "It was just one more story. You said, 'Jeff, that's awful,' then you walked out, shaking your head."

For some time Mr. Robert had discussed with friends like Mr. Kravis what to do about Mr. Beck. Now, finally, he acted. The final straw came when Mr. McGrath, disgusted with Mr. Beck's behavior, walked into Mr. Robert's office and laid before him a simple ultimatum: "It's either him or me."

Mr. Robert, choosing Mr. McGrath, called Mr. Beck in and fired him in July 1985. The Mad Dog took it well. After all, the two men had long talked about the banker's plans to form a firm to manage his wealth: Mr. Robert and others, including Mr. Kravis, assumed Mr. Beck would now retire or otherwise lead a leisurely life.

Several months later, Mr. Robert was surprised to take a call from his counterpart at Drexel Burnham, Fred Joseph. Mr. Joseph said he was thinking about hiring Mr. Beck, but had heard stories about his erratic behavior. "You gotta help me here," Mr. Joseph asked. "This is one of the most controversial guys I've ever checked references on. What's the truth?"

Mr. Robert detailed for the Drexel chief executive some of the problems Oppenheimer had with Mr. Beck, though he pointedly avoided going into his growing beliefs about the banker's truthfulness. "What are you going to hire him for?" Mr. Robert asked.

Mr. Joseph explained that Drexel, eager to hire high-profile "rainmakers" to team with its mammoth junk-bond network, wanted Mr. Beck to attract new business. (This effort would also lead Drexel to hire Dennis Levine, the first major figure identified in Wall Street's insider-training scandal, and Martin Siegel, the star investment banker indicted for passing inside secrets to fallen arbitrager Ivan Boesky.) "If that's what he does," Mr. Robert replied, "if he's not running people or processing deals, and you can control him, it might work."

Mr. Joseph thought he could, and hired Mr. Beck in October 1985. At that time, Mr. Kravis was in the thick of the fight to acquire Beatrice, a company first brought to his attention by an insistent Mr. Beck, Mr. Beck says he was "begged" by Messrs. Kravis, Kelly and Joseph to join the Beatrice fight. And indeed, when Mr. Kravis ultimately acquired Beatrice, he paid Mr. Beck a whopping $4 million fee.

Backed now by the most powerful investment house on Wall Street, Mr. Beck wasted no time setting his sights on snagging major new clients. Among those Mr. Beck began courting was F. Ross Johnson, chief executive of RJR Nabisco. When, after their initial meeting, Mr. Johnson and his wife were vacationing in the South of France, Mr. Beck sent the couple a bottle of Roder Cristal champagne and flowers. "Have a good vacation," the card read, "from The Mad Dog." At their second meeting, Mr. Johnson brought along a box of Milk Bone Dog Biscuits, a joke on the Drexel banker's canine nickname. Then, while discussing strategy with the Chief executive of one of America's largest companies, Mr. Beck ate the whole box.

The Drexel banker was among the first investment bankers to interest Mr. Johnson in a leveraged buyout, though Mr. Johnson ultimately chose to launch his LBO with a Drexel competitor. Mr. Beck worked for free, reckoning that Mr. Johnson would someday return the favor.

Some of Mr. Beck's most notable accomplishments now came outside the financial world. In 1987 he realized his ambition to work in films when he served as an adviser on *Wall Street.* Mr. Beck found a kindred soul in the movie's director, Mr. Stone, who remembers the investment banker vividly. "I sensed he was a man who was troubled," Mr. Stone says in an interview. "He was obviously twisted by what happened over there [in Vietnam]. It was something very repressed in his character. I sensed that with me, it was okay for him to talk about it."

As a fixture on the *Wall Street* set, Mr. Beck suggested the inclusion of a number of military flourishes, including use of the term "lock and load!" by an investment banker readying for battle. (Another of his dialogue suggestions involved an obscene act involving the human skull.) Mr. Beck's work on the film climaxed with a long cameo speech exhorting a group of deal makers on the eve of a hostile takeover attempt. "I thought he did quite a lovely job, for a non-actor," Mr. Stone says.

After his cameo appearance, Mr. Beck told friends he received several acting offers. Mr. Beck also said he had not only met Mr. Stone in Vietnam, but that the director, in a previous movie, *Platoon,* had modeled a central character, the macho jungle fighter Barnes, on a composite of Mr. Beck and others. Mr. Stone, who says he didn't meet Mr. Beck until *Platoon* was completed, denies both stories.

As his fame grew, Mr. Beck began rubbing elbows with a wide circle of high-profile friends. Among those captivated by Mr. Beck's jungle-fighting tales was Mr. Douglas. The actor introduced the deal-maker to a New York screenwriter named David Black and arranged for the two men to begin work on an autobiographical screenplay of Mr. Beck's Vietnam experiences. There was talk that, if the project reached development, Mr. Douglas might be interested in portraying Mr. Beck. After a contract was drawn up by Mr. Kravis's New York law firm, Simpson Thacher & Bartlett, in December 1987, Messrs. Black and Beck worked for months on the screenplay. A brief "treatment" outlining the proposed film was produced.

Exactly what happened next is unclear—both Messrs. Black and Douglas decline comment. But, according to several people familiar with the project, the two came to believe that Mr. Beck's stories were untrue. At that point, Mr. Douglas called one of Mr. Kravis's aides and, in a rain of invective, denounced Mr. Beck as one of the vilest liars he had ever met. "He was never even in Vietnam!" Mr. Douglas is said to have shouted.

That episode, however, apparently did nothing to quench Mr. Beck's thirst for recognition. His career on Wall Street is at the center of *Rainmaker*, a book scheduled to be released by Random House this fall. The author, Anthony Bianco, a reporter for *Business Week* magazine, says the book was initially to be Mr. Beck's first-person account of his Wall Street years. Now, Mr. Bianco says, the book has been "broadened," though he refuses to say to what extent he has accepted stories told by Mr. Beck, who has cooperated on the project for more than two years. "All the questions you're asking," Mr. Bianco says, "I've thought of."

In the last two years, Mr. Beck helped get Drexel hired in a series of major takeovers, including fights for Federated Department Stores, Pillsbury and, most notably, RJR Nabisco. Mr. Beck, in fact, was the first Wall Street investment banker to sniff out Mr. Johnson's brewing buyout plans, alerting Henry Kravis to suspicious goings-on at RJR a full month before the initial announcement of Mr. Johnson's preparations.

But the Mad Dog's long relationship with Mr. Kravis soured when the LBO magnate accused Mr. Beck of leaking to newspaper reporters his subsequent surprise bid for the company. In a fit of pique, Mr. Kravis exiled the Drexel banker from key meetings for a period of weeks and, while he subsequently forgave him, the pair's relationship has never totally healed, associates say.

In the wake of the historic RJR buyout, Wall Street grew quiet. Major takeovers all but abated. For rainmakers like Mr. Beck, 1989 was an unprecedented drought. For the most part, the Mad Dog dropped from sight. Longtime clients like Mr. Kravis asked where he had gone. Rumors flew that Mr. Beck was leaving Drexel, attempting to begin an LBO fund or his own boutique firm. Reality, it turns out, was even stranger than the speculation.

On a frigid December day, a month before the restaurant confrontation, Mr. Beck limps across his tastefully appointed apartment to take a visitor's coat. Outside, the view of the

Metropolitan Museum of Art and Central Park is panoramic. On a mantel are Christmas cards from the likes of Ross Johnson, Al Taubman, Drexel Chairman John Shad and Al Checchi, the investor who recently acquired Northwest Airlines. On a coffee table, a videotaped biography of Mother Teresa lies beside an engraved silver cigarette box filled with Merit filters. The inscription reads: "Jeffrey P. Beck. In Appreciation for Blood, Fear and Courage in the Vietnam War. There but for him, go I." Asked who gave him the box, Mr. Beck says, "Oh, some guy I saved."

Winter winds rattle the apartment's windows as Mr. Beck, between sips of apple cider, talks of how a severe horseback riding injury has laid him up for months and given him time to reassess Wall Street during the 1980s. "These major deal-makers will never admit it was all a big mistake," he says of the decade's merger frenzy. "Most have no idea what happened or what will happen in the nineties. They're too caught up in chasing after the next deal."

This, then, is a kinder, gentler Mad Dog, one who has emerged from the eighties to focus his attention on broader concerns. "Just look at the world today," he exhorts a visitor over a lunch of warm tea and finger sandwiches. "You have the advent of benign social democracies. China will see the light, I promise you. As I predicted two, three years ago, to several people, Eastern Europe is collapsing, and cuts will come in military spending.

"The world has basically awakened," he says, talking vaguely of future plans in the post-Wall Street world. "It's going to need creative, aggressive people. And how many people do you think these corporate entities trust?"

Is Mr. Beck one?" Absolutely," he says. "I mean, how many visionaries do you have?" He refuses to outline his future plans in detail, though he repeatedly suggests he is gathering "some of the country's best minds" to form his own firm.

While he spends much of his time at home these days, Mr. Beck is quick to disavow any suggestion he has time on his hands. He says he visits his Drexel office at least twice a week. "During my convalescence and physical therapy," he says later, "it's been very pleasing the number of, I guess you would call them important people, who have come by to ask my advice on things."

Like who? Beck thinks a moment. "I'm not sure I want to tell you the names, since they came by here in total confidence. But you can assume they're the top names in their fields."

A month later, when he is confronted at the restaurant, Mr. Beck's tone changes considerably. He backs off from his stories of having served in Vietnam, acknowledging that official records validating his claim don't exist. "Let me put it this way," he says. "I made trips to Vietnam. I also made trips to other places that were considered delicate . . . I was an adventurer. I contracted to do these things. And I did them for higher values. Not for myself . . . I did them for my country."

Time and again, he insists that, if this newspaper would delay an article, he would be able to prove his claim of years of unspecified intelligence work. "I'm in an incredible Catch-22 here," Mr. Beck says. "The whole thing has been constructed so that people like you would run into brick walls. . . . If you can wait two or three months, things will all come out."

Mr. Beck denies having claimed to anyone he stood to inherit a billion-dollar fortune or that he worked for the CIA. He is repeatedly asked if he can name any of the "little empire of privately held consumer products and insurance companies" that *Business Week* once reported he owned. "I can," he says, "but I won't."

After all he has said and done, longtime acquaintances like Mr. McGrath say they find it hard to dislike Mr. Beck. On one level, they remain deeply angry at his intricate deceptions; on another, they never forget how good his friendship, his kidding and caring, made them feel.

"No one wants to hurt Jeffrey," Mr. McGrath says. "Beneath all this, he's basically good. . . he made us all feel so good." Adds Mr. Peters: "In my mind most of his lies had no victims. It was just Jeff's imaginary world. You couldn't find out what was real and what wasn't."

Others aren't so forgiving. "There is no real Jeff Beck," Ms. Shuman, the former girlfriend, says. She laughs harshly. "He's not a real guy. You could work your whole life and not find this guy. He doesn't exist."

At Drexel Burnham, where Mr. Beck remains a senior investment banker, a spokesman says: "Jeff has been concentrating for us on new business and he's been very good at it. If there is something in his background, we're always interested in learning about it."

Faced with dozens of stories he continues to deny, Mr. Beck vacillates between angry outbursts and contemplative moments. "Know what's interesting?" he asks. "You can live life the right way or the wrong way. I've always lived it the right way." He pauses for several moments. "I know what the truth is."

The Last Days of Drexel Burnham

Brett Duval Fromson

May 21, 1990, *Fortune*

In "The Last Days of Drexel Burnham" I tell the story of how the rogue firm went bust. Did Drexel do itself in or was it done in by the business establishment? It was both. I came away convinced that Wall Street was far better off without Drexel.

D ON'T WEEP FOR MICHAEL MILKEN. Though he broke down in court when he had to admit he was a felon, he certainly cut a good deal for himself. In all likelihood he'll still be plenty rich when he gets out of prison. Contrast that to the dismal fate of his firm, Drexel Burnham Lambert—bankrupt within months of settling similar charges for a similar amount of money. How did so powerful a firm fall so quickly?

At year-end 1988, Drexel Burnham had a brawny $1.4 billion in capital and 50 percent of junk-bond underwriting. A year later its market share had dwindled to 38 percent, top executives were scrambling to roll over $300 million of the firm's own commercial paper, and Drexel was hemorrhaging—losing $86 million in one month alone.

Did Drexel do itself in? Or was it done in? The truth is that this was a case of suicide—and murder. So potent had the firm become that employees truly believed they could do whatever they wanted without fear of retribution. That's why they could threaten Fortune 500 corporations with takeovers and never expect political retaliation. And that's why they could leverage themselves and their clients to the hilt without preparing for the day debt would go out of fashion. Says a former officer: "You see, we thought, 'We are invulnerable.' "

Management was as misguided as it was self-confident. In the good times, CEO Frederick Joseph and the board of directors were lax supervisors, allowing the firm to be run like a Middle Eastern souk. Milken sat at the center of his X-shaped desk in Beverly Hills and was accountable to no one. Eager for Drexel to become an investment banking powerhouse, Joseph knew better than to tinker with the marvelous Milken money machine he needed to finance hostile takeovers. That led to abuses in Milken's operation, which created a backlash ending in federal felony charges.

Even after it settled with the government, Drexel had a chance to survive if it could slim down. But Joseph lost control over his top dealmakers, who, to prove that the firm could flourish without Milken, went on a disastrous spree at precisely the wrong time. Because the bright and hardworking staff had been motivated almost solely by making a buck, esprit de corps degenerated rapidly into every man for himself once the money slowed. The firm floated issues for marginal companies and then flogged them furiously to customers. What couldn't be sold—and this became fatal—had to be inventoried.

Although few participants are willing to speak on the record, the picture that emerges of Drexel's final days is of a firm thrashing desperately to avoid the inevitable. That was nowhere more evident than in the last ditch-efforts to raise cash. Although Joseph and his chief financial officer, Richard Wright, had been warned that a liquidity crisis would likely hit the firm, they failed to alert the directors and senior officers until a few days before the end. As the junk-bond market was tanking in the U.S. last fall, Drexel Chairman John Shad, the former chairman of the Securities and Exchange Commission who had railed against junk-bond takeovers, was in the Far East assisting Drexel's effort to raise money for the firm by selling junk that couldn't be sold domestically. Even after the onset of the credit crisis, Wright continued urging Drexel's reluctant salesmen to peddle the firm's own risky commercial paper.

Drexel's final throes obscure another story of how business really works when inexperienced outsiders try to wrest power from those who are used to having it. As Drexel's capital evaporated, its bank lenders quietly abandoned it. By February 1990, when regulators stepped in to stop Joseph from dissipating what capital remained, only the top officials at the Treasury Department and the Federal Reserve could have saved the firm. And they were not about to. Says a former Treasury official: "People down here said, 'Hell, no. There's no reason anybody should do anything. We don't like 'em.' "

The Outsiders

The story of Drexel's demise goes back to 1978, when Milken moved the high-yield bond department from New York to his hometown of Los Angeles. Milken's father was dying of cancer, and Mike's young children had health problems. Milken told his superiors that at least one of his kids was subject to epileptic seizures, and that he and his wife, Lori, wanted to be closer to their families on the West Coast.

The move paradoxically brought Milken closer to Fred Joseph, then head of the corporate finance department in New York, which had serious image problems. At the time the only Harvard business school graduates Joseph could recruit were those who had been turned down by other Wall Street firms. But the view of Drexel as an investment banking backwater began to change with Joseph's discovery that Milken's big junk buyers—companies like Rapid-American and Reliance Insurance—were also eager to be big junk issuers. They were the engine that propelled Drexel to fourth place among all underwriters by 1986 and enabled Joseph to hire attractive, personable bankers like Martin Siegel, who had made a name for himself in mergers and acquisitions at Kidder Peabody.

Milken and Joseph were a team from the beginning. Milken may have been the much-pampered genius with gleaming new offices in Beverly Hills, but Joseph was the smooth, articulate voice of the firm and the man who was building the institution around Milken. From their offices on opposite coasts, they spoke to each other five to fifteen times a day.

One former Drexelite describes the West Coast office that Milken ran as "structurally antisocial," entrepreneurship bordering on anarchy. Milken's Hobbesian style of management may explain much of the cornercutting that went on in Beverly Hills and caused so much trouble with the regulators. A former Drexel broker recalls hearing one of Milken's salesmen threaten a client over the phone: "If you don't buy these bonds from me, I'll burn your house down!"

Back in New York it was easy to ignore Milken's managerial weaknesses. Fees were rolling in like the waves at Malibu, and Joseph took his fair share of credit for them at the board meetings. Of every dollar the high-yield department made, close to two-thirds went to the firm, and the rest went to Milken and his group. Drexel's East Coast executives, many of them holdovers from the old Burnham & Co., the retail brokerage firm that had bought Drexel Firestone in 1973, had never seen such money.

An executive who joined Drexel in the mid-1970s recalls being shocked that a senior partner's interest in the firm was then worth only about $400,000—a pittance even by the standards of the day. By the mid-1980s, he said, a partner with this much equity was worth about $15 million. Another former officer recalls hearing Robert Linton, then chairman, say that one of his great motivations was watching the book value of his stock go up every month.

Sharp Elbows

When Joseph and Milken committed Drexel to the hostile tender offer financed by junk bonds, they enraged a powerful special-interest group—the CEOs of big corporations and their board members, lawyers, bankers, and political representatives. Drexel also made a dangerous enemy on Wall Street in Salomon Brothers, heretofore the top bond house and every bit as tough and sharp-elbowed as Drexel itself.

As early in 1984, Drexel was trying to monopolize the high-yield business. It refused to allocate any bonds on a deal it underwrote for Golden Nugget, the casino operator, to Salomon Brothers, which had customers for them. According to two eyewitnesses, Salomon's chairman, John Gutfreund, was in such a frenzy over these tactics that he warned Joseph that he was going to get Milken. Gutfreund's precise phrase, though his firm denies it, was "knee his nuts off."

The more genteel but equally direct reaction of big business came in 1985 when Drexel financed T. Boone Pickens's $8.1 billion raid on Unocal Corp., then the twelfth largest U.S. oil producer. Fred Hartley, who was Unocal's forceful CEO, had plenty of Washington connections. His investment banker was Nicholas Brady, then head of Dillon Read, a former U.S. Senator from New Jersey, and a good friend of the Vice President, George Bush.

While Hartley worked the press, equating Drexel to a terrorist group, Brady and other Washington insiders got Congress on the warpath. Says a former White House official: "Nick really hung Drexel out to dry. He put the firm in Congress's gunsights."

More specifically, in the sights of then-Congressman (now Senator) Timothy Wirth of Colorado and New York Senator Alfonse D'Amato, who chaired hearings on the dangers of takeovers and junk financing. Fred Joseph was called to testify, as were such Drexel-financed raiders as Carl Icahn and Boone Pickens. Among the chorus of Cassandras prophesying the doom of financial markets if junk-bond takeovers were not curbed was SEC Chairman Shad. Said he: "The more leveraged takeovers and buyouts today, the more bankruptcies tomorrow." Unocal ultimately bought Pickens off, and Congress never acted on the thirty or so bills that came out of the hearings, but Drexel had been warned.

Boesky Day

On November 14, 1986, Ivan Boesky, a longtime Milken client, pleaded guilty to SEC charges of insider-trading violations based on allegations made by investment banker Dennis Levine. Burnham & Co. founder I. W. "Tubby" Burnham, chairman emeritus, was the only board member to suggest that Drexel might throttle back on junk bonds. When Milken heard about Burnham's radical idea, he threatened to quit. Fearing they would lose their Midas, board members put Burnham's proposal to a vote and defeated it resoundingly.

Within two months of what became known as Boesky Day, Aetna Life & Casualty Co. notified Joseph that it would not renew Drexel's excess insurance protection, which guarantees replacement of securities in a customer's account above the $500,000 covered by the Securities Investor Protection Corp. According to sources at Drexel, Joseph was told that Aetna's decision not to renew had been made "at a very senior level" and was "not appealable." Drexel had to self-insure, and that cost the firm about $11 million more than it paid Aetna.

Senior Drexel officials were convinced that Aetna's blue-ribbon board of directors was behind the decision not to renew coverage. On the board were David Roderick, former chairman of USX, and Warren Anderson, former chairman of Union Carbide, both of whom had faced Drexel-financed raiders and been forced into painful restructurings. An Aetna spokesman says that the board was not involved in the decision but that, because of the Boesky scandal, it was made at a higher level of the company than normal.

The government began subpoenaing witnesses and preparing indictments against Drexel and Milken based on information it had obtained from Boesky. Throughout 1988 the competitive pressure on all Wall Street firms to do deals, even bad deals, was intense. Says one of Milken's key West Coast lieutenants: "The government investigation spurred us on to prove that we were still the most powerful. That's why the quality of the credits we underwrote began to fall off."

Preoccupied with preparing a legal defense, Milken was giving the firm only 25 percent of his prior time and effort. He recognized that Drexel, like everyone on Wall Street, was doing deals on the dangerous assumption that companies could sell assets tomorrow for more than they were worth today, and therefore could afford staggering levels of debt. But he was as much of a deal junkie as anyone else.

The Surrender

Drexel had been negotiating with the U.S. Attorney's office and the SEC for almost two years, and government lawyers were furious that the firm had not yet done the decent thing—dump Milken and plead guilty. An impatient U.S. Attorney for the Southern District of New York, Rudolph Giuliani, encouraged his subordinates to threaten Drexel with a RICO (Racketeer Influenced and Corrupt Organizations) indictment if the firm did not settle.

RICO frightened Joseph, and with good reason. Under the

statute, the government might be able to lodge a claim on Drexel's assets that would be senior to the claims of the firm's banks. Joseph believed that could lead the lenders to pull their lines of credit if Drexel were indicted.

Shortly after Thanksgiving, Joseph told the other members of the "war committee," a small group that had been set up to coordinate Drexel's resistance to the indictment, that he was thinking of settling. He also kept the twenty-two board members informed of his every move. The lone voice in opposition to settling belonged to John Kissick, forty-eight, the strapping head of West Coast corporate finance. Hugely popular within the firm, Kissick argued that admitting to guilt would be a mistake on principle because the firm did not know if it *was* guilty. Kissick had been hired by Fred Joseph in 1975 to run the West Coast corporate finance department, where he worked closely with Milken. He was torn between supporting Joseph—the man who had been his mentor—and Milken, the man who was his friend.

Two of Drexel's other stars faced a similar dilemma. Peter Ackerman, forty-three, was Milken's brilliant and aloof deputy who designed the packages of securities that the issuers offered. Leon Black, thirty-eight, was the head of mergers and acquisitions; he found the targets for Drexel's raiders. Both were busy helping Henry Kravis structure $9 billion in debt securities that Kohlberg Kravis Roberts would use to pay for the monumental RJR Nabisco buyout. Joseph had them pulled out of a meeting to discuss rumors that they might leave if Drexel sold out Milken. According to a senior officer, all Ackerman would say was "Let's see how this plays out." But neither man resigned.

Then the Giuliani team infuriated the Drexel board by demanding that the firm's employees waive attorney-client privileges in any future investigations. That meant the employees could be prosecuted later on the basis of information they had given Drexel's lawyers who were preparing the firm's defense. On December 19 the board voted overwhelmingly not to settle.

That night the corporate finance department held its Christmas party in the grand ballroom of the Waldorf-Astoria hotel. Board Chairman Robert Linton appeared onstage to sing, "Rudy the Red-Nosed Reindeer," with lyrics that made it clear Rudy was no reindeer and Drexel was remaining defiant. The crowd of about eight hundred people went wild, screaming and banging the tables. One skeptical senior investment banker recalls going over to Joseph, sticking his finger in Fred's stomach, and saying, "I hope it's not helium in there like the Macy's Thanksgiving Day balloons."

Joseph's reply came two days later. He met with the board in the morning and announced that a settlement had been worked out. Giuliani backed off on the issue of attorney-client privilege, and Drexel agreed to plead guilty to six felony counts that included dealings with Ivan Boesky. The firm would also pay $650 million in penalties and cooperate fully with the government investigations of its employees and customers.

What apparently tipped Joseph toward settling was hearing a taped conversation of accusations against Milken made by a Drexel trader. This was the first time Joseph realized the government had more against Milken than just Boesky's allegations. He was also shown some spread sheets on transactions that, combined with the tape, would lead knowledgeable people to the conclusion that Milken bent the rules too far. Joseph informed the board that Giuliani required an answer by four that afternoon, or he would hold a press conference announcing a RICO indictment.

After two years and hundreds of millions of dollars spent warring with the government, the decision came down to a board vote, and it wasn't even close—sixteen to six in favor of settling. Kissick voted no, as did Joseph in a misguided symbolic protest that infuriated employees, who thought he was being hypocritical.

The Bonuses

Especially demoralized were the employees on the West Coast, who thought they saw a sellout. Unsubstantiated rumors spread quickly in Beverly Hills that Joseph cut the deal in exchange for personal immunity from prosecution. Aware of the plunge in morale, Joseph moved quickly to hold his top producers in the high-yield department and corporate finance.

The firm seemed to have money to burn—$1.4 billion in capital, $1 billion more than required by regulations—and Joseph started spreading it around. He guaranteed key employees, although not in writing, that their 1989 compensation would equal at least 75 percent of 1988's, which had been huge. But unlike the previous arrangement Drexel had had with the high-yield group when Milken was running it, the new package did not tie compensation to the profitability of the firm.

Joseph, according to a senior manager of the firm, had long thought that Bear Stearns & Co. had made a big mistake to let Henry Kravis get away rather than meet his demands for more money. Joseph was determined to keep Ackerman, Black, and Kissick, even at the risk of paying them so much that he became, in effect, their subordinate. In April 1989 he agreed to give Ackerman at least $100 million as a reward for his performance in 1988 and for helping sell the RJR Nabisco bonds in 1989. In addition, Ackerman and Black were told that the more deals they brought in, the higher their bonuses.

When rumors got out about the special arrangements Ackerman, Black, and a few others had negotiated, morale took another nose dive. A former member of the Drexel board jeers, "The key to success was being a pig." To allow his other investment bankers to vent their anger and envy, Joseph brought in a psychologist named Ned Kennan, who is used by many companies, including KKR. What did employees tell Kennan? According to a former top investment banker, "That everybody hated Peter and Leon."

Milken's departure in 1989 forced Joseph to restructure the firm around Ackerman, Black, and Kissick: Black became one of the new heads of corporate finance, Kissick was given Milken's old job as head of the high-yield department, and Ackerman was named head of a new capital markets group.

The settlement also brought John Shad, sixty-six, out of retirement. The SEC insisted that Joseph find a Mr. Clean to install as chairman of the board of the holding company. Howard Baker, former White House chief of staff and Senate majority leader, had turned Drexel down because Joseph would not yield the CEO's title. But Shad, who had been Joseph's former boss in the early 1970s when they were both at E.F. Hutton, consulted with his old friends Nicholas Brady, now Secretary of the Treasury, and Alan Greenspan, chairman of the Federal Reserve, and took the job. Shad's $3.1 million salary went into a trust set up for the Harvard business school, to which he had pledged $20 million for the study of leadership and ethics.

The Bad Deals

Black, Ackerman, and their colleagues were determined to prove that Drexel could still do deals better than any other firm. In the first half of 1989, its market share actually *increased* to 70 percent, vs. 40 percent for the first half of 1988. But much of that came from the two big bond offerings that Drexel managed for the RJR Nabisco buyout. And now doing deals was putting the investment bankers themselves increasingly at risk. Like everyone else on Wall Street, Drexel had to compete by putting up its own money as a bridge loan. In the past Milken's network of ready buyers made this practice unnecessary.

Kissick tried hard to stop questionable deals but lacked the needed clout. As an investment banker, he knew little about selling and trading junk bonds and was still broken up over the firm's shabby treatment of Milken.

Among Drexel's worst-selling underwritings of 1989 were those that Leon Black did to help William Farley, the T-shirt titan, take over textile maker West Point-Pepperell. Farley needed over $1 billion to swing the acquisition, and Kissick questioned whether such a deal could be sold. But Black did not want to see Drexel welsh on its promise to raise the money for Farley, so he and Ackerman bulled it through. Unfortunately for the firm, Kissick's concerns were verified by the market when Drexel failed to sell $250 million of the paper and had to inventory the stuff.

Ackerman also had his fair share of fiascos. Drexel raised about $140 million to refinance the purchase of one of his clients, Edgcomb Metals, a Tulsa steel wholesaler, by the Blackstone Group, a Wall Street buyout boutique. Six weeks after the deal closed, the company's business deteriorated and over half the bonds were still in Drexel's inventory.

A wrinkle in the refinancing suggest that the motivation

behind it was not simply helping a client. Ackerman profited personally. He owned part of Edgcomb through a private partnership, and according to an informed Drexel executive received $6 million to $7 million when the company was sold. A Drexel spokesman disputes this figure as being "way off." But a senior West Coast manager says Drexel sometimes did deals in order to "cash out" its officers' positions.

Unsold private placements and bridge loans Drexel made to clients began piling up in the holding company's inventory. Like many brokerage firms, Drexel was set up as a holding company with a broker-dealer subsidiary; while the broker-dealer was regulated by the SEC, the holding company was not unless it held publicly traded securities. The SEC requires that broker-dealers mark their inventories to market; and as the public junk market slid, the broker-dealer inventory showed losses. But Drexel did not have to mark to market the private debt and bridge loans that were in the holding company's hands, and could maintain the fiction that they were worth their paper values.

By the third quarter of 1989, Drexel's holding company was stuck with an estimated $1 billion of private junk bonds and bridge loans. These represented capital commitments the firm had made to customers, and Drexel had to borrow the money to carry them and to remain in business. Says an ex-Drexel officer: "Our bridges had turned into piers."

The Customers

Meanwhile junk-bond offerings that Drexel had already sold were coming apart. Some, like the bonds of Integrated Resources, the issuer most closely associated with Drexel, were old deals. Integrated was a financial services company that sold real estate tax shelters until the 1986 Tax Reform Act eliminated most write-offs for limited partnerships and cut the heart out of its business. By June 1989 it was unable to roll over its commercial paper, but Drexel did not step up to become the buyer of last resort as the market expected. Says a former Drexel salesman: "When we let Integrated go down, the buyers lost all confidence."

But most of the deals that singed customers were of more recent vintage. One that resulted in third-degree burns was

Memorex, the maker of magnetic computer tape, for which Ackerman raised $555 million last July. Two months after the offering, the company reported a 66 percent decline in operating income, and the bonds plunged from par to 50 cents on the dollar. It turned out that foreign investors had the right to sell their Memorex bonds back to Drexel at par. When some did so, the firm booked an estimated $30 million loss. Drexel did not step in to support the market for its other customers, however.

The impact of Drexel's refusal to support Integrated and Memorex cannot be overemphasized. The firm had finally killed its famed network of buyers.

The Market

That summer Congress passed the savings and loan bailout bill, which required thrifts that owned junk bonds to sell them by 1994. The S&Ls promptly stampeded out of junk, and the secondary market began to slide.

Issuers were beginning to default on a weekly basis. Many of the exploding deals were not Drexel's, but the firm suffered the consequences more than anyone else because it depended so heavily on the business. Fees from new underwritings dropped, and trading in the secondary market became markedly less profitable. In August and September the firm began losing money. In October the losses hit $86 million.

By late summer Ackerman, who has a Ph.D. in political science from the Fletcher School of Law and Diplomacy near Boston, was telling Joseph that he wanted to move to London to write a follow-up to his doctoral dissertation on the strategy of nonviolent resistance. To hang on to Ackerman, Joseph created a position for him in London developing overseas business for the firm. This sojourn by one of the biggest producers puzzled many at the firm, but not a friend of Ackerman's, who says, "Peter wanted to get as far away as he could."

As Drexel's situation deteriorated, Joseph became more withdrawn. According to a longtime Drexel executive, "Fred sort of blew his cork and became a different human being the last year." Meanwhile Chairman John Shad and an entourage spent a good part of the fall in the Far East trying to sell junk bonds. Shad says he talked only about general market conditions in high-yield bonds and leveraged buyouts. But Drexel's former Hong Kong managing director Marc Faber says: "I took him to see Jardine Matheson, a conservative, blue-chip company. Shad asked the treasurer, 'Do you have any high-yield bonds in your portfolio?' The treasurer said, 'Of course not.' These were investors in quality. Shad was crazy to try to sell junk to these people."

More ominously, Drexel's lenders were losing their nerve. Hit with bad loans to real estate developers, many began to back away from Drexel. That was a nightmare for Joseph and Richard Wright, the chief financial officer, because without bank loans, Drexel didn't have enough capital to finance its inventory and run its business. The banks were offered the inventory of private placements and bridge loans as collateral for the lines but said it wasn't good enough. Wright's staff began to warn him that the high-yield position had to be reduced and that Drexel was on borrowed time.

Wright did not pass the dire message along to the board. Why not? Says one of his former subordinates: "It was difficult to tell whether he didn't believe the warning or whether he felt his timing was wrong."

Cash Crunch

In November, Standard & Poor's lowered its rating on the holding company's commercial paper from A2 to A3. Overnight Drexel was shut out of the commercial paper market, the source of $700 million of financing. Within three weeks, as holders refused to buy Drexel's paper when it came due, it was reduced to only $300 million of borrowings.

Desperate, Wright flew to Paris to ask Groupe Bruxelles Lambert, the French and Belgian investors who were Drexel's largest shareholders, for more money. Their reply: *Non, merci.* They wanted to see a return to profitability first. Wright took ill in Paris and was hospitalized, reportedly with an ulcer.

As the new year approached, Joseph and Shad, the head of the compensation committee, made final decisions on the bonus pool. While knowing that the firm might lose money for the year, they set the payout at a healthy $270 million, vs.

$506 million in 1988, but decided that 24 percent of that pool would be given in Drexel stock.

When the bonuses were announced in December, Leon Black was perturbed at how small his was, a mere $12 million. According to several Drexel officers, Black went home and sulked for a couple of days before Joseph relented and gave him $3 million more. Joseph, as if to compensate the firm for the cash drain, took his $2.5 million bonus entirely in Drexel stock.

Meanwhile, Drexel's financial plight was worsening. Throughout the year the firm had borrowed $650 million from its commodities trading unit. The commodities group usually borrowed gold from foreign central banks, then sold the gold and lent the cash to the holding company. But in December, when Drexel was unable to roll over more commercial paper, it could no longer pay back its commodities unit on demand.

The Crisis

The new year began badly. After months of erosion, the junk-bond market collapsed as jittery holders began dumping en masse. In January, Drexel lost $60 million.

As more and more banks refused to extend the lines of credit backing up Drexel's commercial paper, the money from the firm's commodities trading unit no longer sufficed to finance the holding company's inventory. Wright, with the approval of Fred Joseph, began to raid the broker-dealer, which still had capital in excess of the regulatory minimum, and Drexel's government-securities dealer. In late January he drained these two units of about $400 million, despite warnings from his staff that the firm would run out of capital within thirty days. He told a member of his group, "Well, maybe the salesmen can sell more commercial paper."

Neither Wright nor Joseph informed the board of directors about Drexel's precarious state. Nor did they report to the New York Stock Exchange or the SEC—which both require that brokers have a certain amount of capital to meet their obligations—that they were taking money out of the broker-dealer. But on February 2, the New York Fed got wind of the transfers and passed the word to the SEC and the exchange regulators, who were aghast. Drexel firmly believed that its longtime nemesis, Salomon Brothers, tipped off the Fed, but Salomon denies the charge.

From this point on, the regulators called the shots. On Thursday, February 8, the stock exchange officials, after consultations with SEC Chairman Richard Breeden, telephoned Wright and told him that he could not take more money from the broker-dealer without SEC approval. Wright relayed the bad news to Joseph, who was at his farm in rural New Jersey.

A meeting of the department heads who ran the firm was hastily convened, and Joseph was hooked in by phone. Wright explained that $400 million in unsecured debt was coming due within the next two weeks, with another $330 million scheduled to mature in March. Then the senior officers heard the head of the commodities trading unit explain his Rube Goldberg borrowing arrangement with the foreign central banks. And by the way, he told his dumbfounded peers, he needed his $650 million back, pronto, to repay the loans. According to a department head, recriminations began to fly about who knew what—and when—about the firm's financial condition.

On Friday, February 9, Wright was feeling the pressure. According to former Drexel officers, in the morning he and his treasurer were urging Drexel's commercial paper salesmen to sell more paper, despite widespread fears that the firm was on the edge of bankruptcy. Incredibly enough, the salesmen were able to flog millions of dollars' worth only two days before Drexel went belly-up.

In the afternoon the department heads reconvened to consider the options. About a year too late, Joseph proposed a draconian plan to save the firm: Cut costs, sell inventories of stocks and high-grade bonds, pull out of the commodities and mortgage-backed securities business, and sell off the junk holdings. Everyone was working around the clock that weekend. But when Joseph telephoned Peter Ackerman to tell him of the liquidity crisis, Ackerman resigned from the board on the spot.

Saturday was spent trying to sell operations to free up capital. But says a board member: "You don't get out of businesses in a day or a week. They were either blind and dumb or in some dream world." By Saturday night a frantic search was on for a merger partner. Desperate senior officers began calling their Wall Street competitors, saying in effect, "How about sending in a team to take a look tomorrow?" A few browsed, including Smith Barney and Nomura, but no one bought.

The End

On Monday morning rumors of Drexel's imminent bankruptcy were sweeping the world's bourses. Say a former Drexel floor broker: "When I walked out onto the floor of the [New York Stock] exchange, I could sense that something was the matter. Stories were flying that we were already out of business."

They were—almost. Drexel's only hope of salvation was its banks, which had been hounding various members of the firm for days trying to find out whether rumors of bankruptcy were true. Joseph spent the day readying a $1.1 billion bundle of securities that the banks might accept as collateral for a $300 million to $400 million loan. These securities were the same old bridge loans and private placements that Drexel hadn't been able to sell before, plus the right to income from a portfolio of leases. After giving the securities a haircut for their illiquidity, Joseph and the bankruptcy experts he had called in over the weekend put the package's worth at $800 million.

At dusk on Monday, February 12, a bevy of bankers in pinstripes, armed with calculators, marched into a seventh-floor conference room at Drexel Burnham's headquarters. Joseph knew he was not adequately prepared for the meeting and that the bankers would have serious questions about the quality of the merchandise he was offering as collateral. But he thought there was a better than even chance they would lend Drexel the money anyway. After all, he was sure that the regulators were urging the banks to help out. In fact, he figured the federal government, with a wink and a nod, had already lobbied the lenders to make the loan rather than let Drexel fail. Isn't that the way these things are done?

For their part, the bankers were angry that Drexel hadn't come clean earlier. Joseph announced to the not altogether surprised group that Drexel had a liquidity problem and needed to borrow $300 million to $400 million. According to a banker at the meeting, he said the foreign central banks that had been funding Drexel were unwilling to continue that arrangement, but that certainly Drexel's loyal commercial lenders had more courage. Then the bankers received a list of the collateral and recognized it as the same junk they had disdained earlier. They were being asked to take a credit they had already passed on.

Fred Joseph then sealed Drexel's fate. He said in response to a banker's query that the firm had missed a scheduled repayment earlier in the day to holders of some commercial paper. Says a banker who was in the room: "So the situation was already worse than we had thought before the meeting. Drexel was in danger of cross-defaulting on all its loans."

The bankers went through the motions of caucusing. After a few minutes they told Joseph that they could not make a decision that night and that they were not inclined to make the loan anyway. Joseph implored them to call their headquarters and seek approval. The bankers dutifully telephoned. The answer? Forget it.

They huddled again. Sentiment had hardened, but Joseph was not going to give up. He pleaded for the home phone numbers of the banks' top officers so that he could make personal appeals. Joseph's calls took them away from their dinner tables and televisions. But to no effect. There had been no regulatory winks and nods. By 12:30 A.M., Joseph let his exhausted troops drift home.

He, however, had one more humiliation to undergo. At 1:30 A.M. he telephoned the SEC's Richard Breeden and Gerald Corrigan of the New York Federal Reserve, who were at their homes, and informed them—as if they did not already know—that the banks had turned Drexel down. Breeden and Corrigan said that they were speaking for their respective bosses. Treasury Secretary Nicholas Brady and Fed Chairman Alan Greenspan. They suggested that Drexel file for Chapter 11 the next day or face government liquidation. It was only then that Joseph realized his firm was history. As he said to a colleague, "God has spoken."

The Reckoning

Susan C. Faludi

May 16, 1990, the *Wall Street Journal*

Susan Faludi's piece on the aftermath of the LBO of Safeway was the first hard look at the human costs of a "successful" deal. She chronicles how the senior management got rich and how the people who worked the third shift got the shaft. She won a Pulitzer Prize for her article.

O N THE EVE OF THE 1986 leveraged buyout of Safeway Stores Inc., the board of directors sat down to a last supper. Peter Magowan, the boyish-looking chairman and chief executive of the world's largest supermarket chain, rose to offer a toast to the deal that had fended off a hostile takeover by the corporate raiders Herbert and Robert Haft.

"Through your efforts, a true disaster was averted," the forty-four-year-old Mr. Magowan told the other directors. By selling the publicly held company to a group headed by buyout specialists Kohlberg Kravis Roberts & Co. and members of Safeway management, "you have saved literally thousands of jobs in our work force," Mr. Magowan said. "All of us—employees, customers, shareholders—have a great deal to be thankful for."

Nearly four years later Mr. Magowan and the KKR group can indeed count their blessings. While they borrowed heavily to buy Safeway from the shareholders, last month they sold 10 percent of the company (but none of their own shares) back to the public—at a price that values their own collective stake at more than $800 million, more than four times their cash investment.

Employees, on the other hand, have considerably less reason to celebrate. Mr. Magowan's toast notwithstanding,

285

63,000 managers and workers were cut loose from Safeway, through store sales or layoffs. While the majority were re-employed by their new store owners, this was largely at lower wages, and many thousands of Safeway people wound up either unemployed or forced into the part-time work force. A survey of former Safeway employees in Dallas found that nearly 60 percent still hadn't found full-time employment more than a year after the layoff.

James White, a Safeway trucker for nearly thirty years in Dallas, was among the 60 percent. In 1988, he marked the one-year anniversary of his last shift at Safeway this way: First he told his wife he loved her, then he locked the bathroom door, loaded his .22-caliber hunting rifle and blew his brains out.

"Safeway was James's whole life," says his widow, Helen. "He'd near stand up and salute whenever one of those trucks went by." When Safeway dismissed him, she says, "it was like he turned into a piece of stone."

Few financial maneuvers have drawn more controversy than the leveraged buyout, or LBO, a relatively old money-making tactic that was dusted off and put to extensive use in the 1980s, thanks largely to the rise of junk-bond financing.

In a leveraged buyout, a small group of investors that generally includes senior management borrows heavily to buy a company from public shareholders and takes it private. The debt is to be rapidly repaid from the company's own cash flow or from sales of its assets.

The returns on some such highly leveraged investments have been astronomical, enriching such financiers as Henry Kravis, Ronald Perelman and Nelson Peltz to a degree unheard of since the days of the Robber Barons. Proponents of LBOs argue that they are good for business and good for America, triggering long-overdue crash weight-loss programs for flabby corporations. By placing ownership in the hands of a small group of investors and managers with a powerful debt-driven incentive to improve productivity, the argument goes, companies can't help but shape up.

The Safeway LBO is often cited as one of the most successful in this regard. It brought shareholders a substantial premium at the outset, and since then the company has raised productivity and operating profits and produced riches for the new investors and top management. "We could not have done what we did do without going through the incredible trauma and pressure of the LBO," Mr. Magowan said in late 1988.

But while much has been written about the putative benefits of LBOs, little has been said about the hundreds of thousands of people directly affected by the past decade's buyout binge: employees of the bought-out corporations. In the case of Safeway, a two-month investigation of the buyout reveals enormous human costs and unintended side effects. The company dropped tens of thousands of employees from its payroll, suppliers and other dependent industries laid off hundreds more, and communities lost the civic contributions of a firm whose first store had been opened by a clergyman who wanted to help his parishioners save money.

When Safeway itself selected a group of its employees to speak to this newspaper on behalf of the company, not one of those interviewed praised the buyout. "I think LBOs are very ugly," said Carl Adkins, an inventory control clerk who described himself as happy with his job. "I think they are harmful to individual working people. I think they honestly stink."

Moreover, the evidence doesn't entirely support the argument that the LBO made Safeway a healthier institution. The supermarket chain cut plenty of muscle with the fat, both from its holdings and from its labor force, and deferred capital improvements in favor of the all-consuming debt. Many employees find the post-LBO working environment more difficult—as a company legendary for job security and fairness resorts to hardball labor policies and high-pressure quota systems.

Just before the Safeway deal was struck in 1986, Mr. Magowan's mother grew worried about the employees. The supermarket dowager wanted to be sure the LBO wouldn't damage Safeway's longstanding reputation as a benevolent employer.

Will anyone get hurt? Mrs. Magowan pressed her son at the time, according to company staff members. Will anyone lose his job?

No, Mom, Mr. Magowan promised, according to the staffers' account. No one will get hurt.

"Yes, I was greatly concerned about the people," Mrs. Magowan recalls today, in her mansion overlooking the San Francisco Bay. She declines to comment further.

Mr. Magowan's recollection: "Well, I don't ever remember such a conversation ever occurred. . . . I might have said things like, 'We're going to do the best we can for our employees and I'm hopeful that we are going to be able to keep the vast majority with the new owners.' "

In any event, before the summer was out, Mrs. Magowan's son had begun firing Safeway employees. Not long after, Safeway replaced its longtime motto, "Safeway Offers Security." The new corporate statement, displayed on a plaque in the lobby at corporate headquarters, reads in part: "Targeted Returns on Current Investment."

Before the LBO, Safeway was hardly a prime example of the sluggish, out-of-shape sort of company that LBO proponents like to target. Founded in 1926, it had grown under Magowan family leadership to encompass more than two thousand stores in twenty-nine states and in England, Australia, Canada and Mexico. Mr. Magowan's father, Robert, had largely built Safeway, and his mother, Doris Merrill Magowan, is the daughter of a founder of Merrill Lynch & Co., which helped finance Safeway's growth.

Many companies, including Safeway, had allowed their payrolls to become bloated in certain underperforming divisions, and layoffs were common throughout large American companies during the last decade.

But Safeway was already doing—albeit at a slower pace— many of the things LBO experts advocate. It was remodeling its stores and creating the upscale "superstores" that have now proved such a big success. It was experimenting with employee productivity teams, phasing out money-losing divisions, and thinning its work force with a program that included some layoffs but generally relied on less painful methods like attrition.

All these changes produced earnings that more than doubled in the first four years of the 1980s, to a record $231 million in 1985. The stock price tripled in three years, and dividends climbed four years in a row.

But all that wasn't enough for takeover-crazed Wall Street, where virtually no company was invulnerable to cash-rich corporate raiders. When the deep-pocketed Hafts began buying Safeway shares in the open market and then offered to buy the company for as much as $64 a share, management felt it had to take defensive action. Selling to the Hafts might have cost Chairman Magowan his job and, he felt, ultimately might have brought a breakup of the company.

Safeway considered and rejected a plan to fend off the Hafts through a so-called recapitalization. This was a move that its supermarket-industry competitor, Kroger Co. would use two years later to keep the same raiders at bay while allowing shareholders to realize a big one-time gain.

The decision to sell to KKR instead brought immediate benefits to some. Shareholders got $67.50 a share—82 percent more than the stock was trading at three months before—plus warrants that give them a 5.6 percent stake in the ongoing company. Employees owned roughly 10 percent of Safeway shares at the time of the buyout.

Mr. Magowan and other directors and top executives received $28 million for their shares, $5.7 million of which went to Mr. Magowan. He and about sixty other top executives also got options to buy a total of 10 percent of the new Safeway at only $2 a share; those options are now valued at more than $100 million, or $12.125 a share.

The Hafts made $100 million by selling the Safeway shares they had accumulated to KKR, and as a consolation prize, they were also given options to buy a 20 percent stake in the new Safeway. The Hafts sold that option back to KKR two-and-a-half months later for an additional $59 million.

The three investment banks that worked on the deal made a total of $65 million. Law and accounting firms shared another $25 million.

And then there are Henry Kravis, George Roberts, about a dozen other KKR employees and the seventy investors KKR brought into the buyout. KKR itself charged Safeway $60 million in fees just to put the deal together. The five KKR partners then put up a small fraction of the equity funding— 1.1 percent, or roughly $2 million—and received a 20 percent share of the eventual profits from any sale of Safeway.

KKR's investor group, half of which consists of state pension funds and which also includes banks, insurance companies and even Harvard University, got most of the rest.

Mr. Roberts rebuts the notion that too few people really benefit in an LBO. He says that some of "our seventy limited partners represent retired teachers, sanitation workers and firemen, and 80 percent of our profits go to them."

But at the largest of those investors, Oregon's public-employee pension fund, LBO investments make up only a tiny portion of investments and thus haven't had "a significant impact" on retirees' benefits to date, according to Bob Andrews, fund manager.

The immediate gains for some triggered immediate costs for others. The first employees to be fired shortly after the buyout's completion were more than three hundred staffers from Oakland corporate headquarters and a nearby division in Walnut Creek, Calif. The following spring, the entire Dallas-area division was shut down, and nearly nine thousand more employees were dismissed—employees with an average length of service of seventeen years.

"This is going to kill people," transportation manager Richard Quigley says he told his boss when he learned that layoffs would take place.

On the Friday afternoon before the dismissals went into effect, Patricia Vasquez, a fourteen-year systems analyst, heard that her name was on the list. That evening, Mrs. Vasquez, a Safeway devotee famous for her refusal to take lunch hours, packed her service citations in a cardboard box and left looking pale and drawn. The next morning her two young children found their single mother on the bathroom floor, dead of a heart attack.

That Monday, Mr. Quigley came home with the news that he, himself, would be fired. His worried wife's blood pressure began to rise. A diabetic who had been in good health for years, she was hospitalized by Labor Day weekend—and dead by September 5. Rightly or wrongly, Mr. Quigley blames his wife's death on his Safeway layoff: "She was very traumatized by it."

Told of these details and several suicides that family members and friends attribute to the Safeway layoffs, Mr. Magowan says: "I never heard of this before. If it's true, I'm obviously sorry about such a tragic thing, but any attempt to associate this directly with the LBO shows a disposition to want to believe the worst of LBOs."

For many at Safeway, firing day was only the first in a long series of financial and emotional body blows.

"The dominoes began to tumble and they crashed for a long time to come," says Ron Morrison, a former corporate systems manager. When Mr. Morrison lost his fourteen-year-job, his fiance announced she couldn't marry an unemployed man.

He found work as a transportation analyst at Del Monte, but the KKR bought that company, too—and he was laid off again, just before Thanksgiving. By the time 1990 rolled around, Mr. Morrison had not only gone through two KKR-led LBOs, he had lost his second home and was unemployed again.

"Right now I pretty much live in a cocoon," Mr. Morrison says. "You begin to pull in your tentacles because you can't afford to have any more cut off."

While at Safeway, Mr. Morrison says, he helped conduct a transportation study that trimmed millions from the company transit budget. And he wasn't the only fired employee at headquarters whose work had brought the company big savings. Refrigeration engineer Mikhail Vaynberg, a Soviet emigre, says he invented a new cooling system for the stores that cut energy costs 35 percent, saved $1.6 million a year, and was copied by many suppliers. (A Safeway spokesman says the company doesn't contest these cost-saving claims.)

After he was fired, Mr. Vaynberg couldn't find work in his field and, like many other employees fired at headquarters, says he couldn't get a current letter of recommendation from Safeway; he says his boss told him he wasn't allowed to supply a written reference because "you might use it to sue the company." (A Safeway spokesman says it is company policy not to grant reference letters for "good, sound legal reasons," but maintains that managers were allowed to make exceptions for employees laid off in the 1986 firings at headquarters.)

Mr. Vaynberg says his greatest blow came a few weeks after the layoff, when his only son dropped out of engineering school weeks shy of graduation: "The country doesn't want engineers: Look what happened to you," he told his father. Now Mr. Vaynberg, still unemployed, spends his days in a painfully clean living room, prowls the halls at night and avoids old friends and neighbors. "I am ashamed," he says, staring at his big empty hands. "I am like an old thrown-out mop."

Safeway fired its corporate employees with no notice, cut off their medical insurance in as little as two weeks and provided severance pay of one week's salary for every year of service, to a maximum of just eight weeks. And to get the pay, many employees say there were told to sign a letter waiving their right to contest the severance package later. (A company spokesman says the letter wasn't a waiver but simply an "acknowledgment" that they understood the terms.)

Mr. Magowan concedes that many of the people fired at headquarters in the summer of 1986 were "very good" employees. The cuts were made in a hurry, as he said later in a court deposition, so as "to put this whole unpleasant matter behind us as soon as possible." For such haste, Safeway would wind up paying $8.2 million to settle a wrongful termination class-action suit and $750,000 to settle a separate suit for age discrimination.

One executive who left headquarters voluntarily was accorded much better treatment. Safeway president James Rowland was granted a $1 million bonus when he retired a few months after the buyout.

Mr. Rowland advised Mr. Magowan in a memo to approve the bonus privately and divide the amount into smaller portions with labels like "paid consultant." The reason, as Mr. Rowland wrote: "Peter, I do not want to put you in an embarrassing situation."

(Mr. Rowland, reached at his Arkansas home, says he never got a "million-dollar bonus. I got my regular bonus. I just don't recall what it was. I'm not going to go back and rehash all that." He then hangs up. Mr. Magowan says Mr. Rowland wasn't paid a lump sum of $1 million. He was paid his previous year's bonus, which he had earned, plus an advance on consulting work he would do for Safeway, Mr. Magowan says. "It wouldn't have been some side deal under the table between Jim Rowland and me that nobody knew about. That's not my style.")

"I wouldn't be surprised if eleven thousand jobs were created out of" the roughly nine thousand jobs lost, Mr. Magowan announced to the press after he closed the Dallas division. He says he assumed that other grocery chains would expand to fill the Safeway vacuum. "What I'm talking about here is a theory of mine," he says later. "I will get right up front and say I don't have facts to support it." Mr. Magowan says he has not been back to Dallas since the closure.

When the Dallas division shut down, the state unemployment office had to open on the weekend—for the first time ever—just to accommodate the Safeway crowds. The Dallas employees had a thin financial pallet to cushion the blow. Their severance pay was half a week's pay for each year of service, up to a maximum of eight weeks.

And their severance checks didn't start arriving until July 1987, three months after the shutdown. Russell Webb, a twelve-year produce clerk and single father with three children didn't get his severance check for eight months. Vacation pay arrived even more slowly: First the union had to go to arbitration to get it; then, the company didn't start mailing the checks until February 1989. Safeway says the severance and other checks arrived late because they weren't part of the union contract and thus "had to be negotiated."

In addition to Mr. White's suicide, at least two others tried to kill themselves. One was Bill Mayfield Jr., a mechanic in the Safeway dairy since it opened in 1973, who slashed his wrists, then shot himself in the stomach; the bullet just missed his vital organs and he survived.

"I would say [the layoff] devastated about 80 percent of the people in the division," says Gary Jones, president of Safeway's credit union in Dallas, which eventually had to write off $4 million in loans. "Overnight we turned from a lending institution into a collection agency." At one point, more than 250 repossessed cars were sitting in his parking lot.

KKR and Safeway blame organized labor for the fall of the

Dallas division. Once the leading grocer in the area, Safeway had seen its market share fall by nearly half in the eighties. KKR and Safeway officials say the company was paying too much in wages, some 30 percent more than rivals, thus preventing it from cutting prices, remodeling stores and the like.

But rival Kroger was also a union shop, and it found a way to prosper and expand in Dallas by renovating stores and negotiating lower wages with the union. Its market share was on the rise. The Kroger case suggests that the Safeway layoffs might have been necessitated as much by mismanagement as by labor costs. Some company officials concede that Safeway had other problems besides wages in Dallas: Its stores were too small, too old and poorly designed.

While grocery competitors in Dallas eventually bought more than half the 141 Safeway stores, they were less eager to pick up the unionized workers. According to a state-funded survey of the displaced workers, stores under new management typically recalled no more than a half dozen of the forty to sixty former Safeway employees who staffed each outlet.

And wages fell sharply, no matter where the workers landed: In 1988, according to the survey, ex-Safeway employees reported that their average pay had dropped to $6.50 from $12.09 an hour.

Cindy Hale, an eleven-year Safeway employee, saw her wages fall to $4 an hour when she took an identical grocery clerk's job with AppleTree Markets, at an old Safeway store. Her new employer would only hire part-time, so Ms. Hale, a single mother, lost her medical benefits. She eventually lost her house, too, and had to send her son to live with her parents.

"But it really wasn't as bad for me as the others," says Ms. Hale.

For Dallas employees, working for Safeway had often been a total family experience, and many households lost more than one income after the buyout. The Seabolts lost three: Husband, wife and daughter all got their pink slips on the same day. Ron Seabolt, who worked in the company's distribution center for seventeen years, searched for months before taking a job as a janitor. Now he works at the post office.

Kay Seabolt, a human resources supervisor at Safeway and

a seventeen-year company veteran, counseled ex-employees for a year under a state job-placement retraining program. The program's counselors sometimes fished into their own pockets to buy groceries for those who streamed through the counseling center, an abandoned Safeway office. When Safeway sold it, the new owners evicted them.

Seared into Mrs. Seabolt's memory is the day one tattered man arrived at the office. A long-timer in the Safeway bread plant, the middle-aged baker made his way to her desk with a slow, wincing limp. He apologized for his appearance, explaining that he had just walked six miles from the temporary labor pools: His car had been repossessed. He was living in a homeless shelter. "I gave him a few job leads," she recalls, "but he was pretty shabby and I didn't hold out much hope." Before he left, she slipped him some money for bus fare, she says. "I never saw him again."

When the layoff rumors first began circulating, Clara Sanchez took to praying in the parking lot of Store No. 677. Her silent pleas went unanswered. On April 24, 1987, she and her husband, Jesse, lost their jobs. She had been a checker for twelve years; he had been an order filler in the warehouse for eighteen years.

Clara could find no work, and is still unemployed; Jesse searched for eight months before the city hired him to cut grass for $3.55 an hour. Then he washed cars for $4.50 an hour. Two months later, he was laid off. Finally, with $14,000 in unpaid bills, the Sanchezes filed for bankruptcy.

The church sent canned goods, and Mr. and Mrs. Sanchez skipped supper some evenings so their children could eat better. After a while, Mr. Sanchez was too depressed to eat anyway. "I wasn't a man; I wasn't worth anything as far as I was concerned," he says. "Why live if I can't support my kids?" One Friday night, Mr. Sanchez told his wife he was going to watch a wrestling match, but went to a friend's house instead with a business proposition: "I told him I would pay him $100 to take my life. I didn't own a gun or I would've done it myself." The friend put his gun out of reach and sent Mr. Sanchez home.

When Safeway pulled out of Dallas, the shock waves didn't stop at the supermarket doors. The shutdown led to secondary layoffs at almost all the big food and beverage vendors in town, and some construction businesses suffered. For Harry W. Parks Co., a general contractor, Safeway represented 85 percent of annual revenues; Mr. Parks had dropped most of his other clients to assist Safeway in its big remodeling program in the early eighties. After the pullout, his company nearly folded, all but three employees were laid off, and Mr. Parks had a heart attack and died.

"Safeway was his whole world," said his son, Harry Jr. "That's all he cared about for thirty years. When they pulled out, it was like his whole family died."

The North Texas Food Bank suffered, too. It lost a founding member and its leading contributor; Safeway used to donate six hundred thousand pounds of food a year.

"The bottom line," food-bank director Lori Palmer says, "is fewer people ate."

The layoffs in Oakland, Dallas and elsewhere were just one part of KKR's broad-based plan to cut costs, boost profitability and meet the stiff interest and principal deadlines set by the company's lenders and debt-holders. About a thousand of the company's stores were sold, as were forty-five plants and other facilities.

Safeway put whole divisions in Kansas, Oklahoma, Arkansas and Utah among others on the auction block. They were sold to a few grocery chains, many other LBO investors and, in some cases, real-estate investors.

The real-estate investors didn't rehire any Safeway workers: They converted the properties to video shops, thrift stores, and in one case a bingo parlor. Some were boarded up.

While grocery chains bought some Safeway stores just to shut them down and reduce competition, other chains brought whole Safeway divisions and kept most of the workers; the British and Oklahoma divisions are examples of this. In other cases, new owners retained only selected workers. In virtually all cases, though, new ownership meant pay cuts.

In what seemed at first the best deal for employees, the grocery chain Borman's Inc. bought the entire Safeway Utah division and hired virtually all the workers. But nine months later, those three thousand employees lost their jobs when

Borman sold the division, piece by piece, to local competitors and investors. Only a few of the stores in the Salt Lake City area still operate as supermarkets.

Don Schanche, a Safeway meatcutter in Salt Lake City for twenty-five years, spiraled downward from his $12.33 hourly pay at Safeway to a reduced wage scale at Borman's "Farmer Jack" outlet, to an unsuccessful appeal for any minimum-wage employment at the same store, which had been bought by his old manager. Now Mr. Schanche drives by a "for lease" sign in front of the store, which is empty, having gone belly-up. Mr. Schanche is making a living as a "job coach" in a state-funded displaced-workers program—where he is currently counseling other ex-grocery store employees following an LBO involving their employer, Alpha-Beta.

Mr. Magowan, as Safeway's CEO but no longer the man with final decision-making authority, was at first opposed to the extent of the divestiture program, people familiar with the situation say. He liked being the head of the world's largest supermarket chain. But KKR officials gave him little choice if he wanted to stay on board, these people say.

Mr. Magowan himself says that "no one twisted my arm" over the restructuring. Still, he says, he "regrets" selling promising divisions, mentioning in particular Los Angeles, El Paso, Tulsa, and Little Rock.

Still others point with regret to the loss of the company's 132-store British division—a top-performer known in-house as the "jewel" of the Safeway collection—and the sale of Safeway's successful discount chain of liquor stores, Liquor Barn, which under its new owners (Majestic Wine Warehouses Ltd.) filed for Chapter 11 bankruptcy protection in 1988.

Despite such regrets, however, Mr. Magowan is now a self-professed believer in the LBO concept. For one thing, his own performance has been rewarded under KKR, which has increased his annual compensation by about 40 percent to $1.2 million including bonus. His bonus potential has climbed to 110 percent of base pay from 40 percent before the buy-out, and he has earned the highest possible bonus every year.

Many things have gone well for the buyout group. The sale of the British division alone brought $929 million, part of the

$2.4 billion that KKR got from asset sales—or 40 percent more than KKR officials say they had projected.

Thanks to sales of some money-losing operations, Safeway's basic business could earn more without raising prices. The company's stores are now No. 1 or 2 in most of its markets. By 1989, operating profit per employee was up 62 percent from 1985, and operating margins had increased by nearly half. The company is producing nearly twice as much annual cash flow as it needs to cover yearly interest payments. As a result, Safeway has been able to pay bank lenders ahead of schedule and negotiate lower interest rates.

Finally, KKR and Safeway officials also credit a new combination of incentives and quotas that they say make workers more entrepreneurial and at the same time more accountable.

Mr. Magowan says that employees are thriving in this post-LBO culture: "I am convinced that today's typical Safeway employee feels better about the company than he or she has at any point since the buyout." Store managers, he says, "genuinely enjoy this extra responsibility of meeting new quotas."

Not every part of the new Safeway picture is as rosy as Mr. Magowan portrays it, however.

The public offering completed recently didn't quite go as planned. The offering's underwriters knocked the price down to $11.25 from the $20 a share envisioned last summer. Mr. Magowan himself concedes, "I think if we had known right at the start that this was the price that we would've gotten, we probably wouldn't have come out with our offering." He blames the much-publicized problems of other leveraged companies for unjustly tainting Safeway's offering and driving away stock shoppers.

But some potential investors say that it was Safeway's own financial condition that turned them off.

The company labors under an interest bill of about $400 million a year, a negative net worth of $389 million, and a remaining $3.1 billion in debt. The company's net income was only $2.5 million last year (after accounting for nonrecurring expenses), down from $31 million the year before. Safeway lost a whopping $488 million in 1987, the first year of the LBO.

A large amount of capital improvement has been post-poned, with such annual spending falling from an average $600 million to $700 million in the three years before the buy-out to an average of $300 million in the years since. The company estimates it must spend $3.2 billion on store remodeling and openings over the next five years. And Safeway now has few assets left that it can justify jettisoning.

When Mr. Magowan in 1988 sat down with a group of specially selected employees to tell them the story of "our growing success," the workers had a different story to tell him, as chronicled by the company's own magazine, *Safeway Today*.

"The morale in Richmond [Calif.] right now is down to rock bottom," Vince Macias, a twenty-five year trucker, told the boss. He added that drivers were forced to pull as much as sixteen-hour shifts and were so overworked they were "dangerous" on the highways.

"The morale is so bad in some of our stores," Christie Mills, a San Jose employee, told him, that it's driving away customers.

"There aren't many of us, and hours are cut back so much," said Cheryl Deniz, a bakery clerk. "I don't let the customer see it, but inside I'm miserable. . . . I want to be happy when I wait on them. . . . I try my best, but sometimes I'm so overloaded. It's unfair to the customer, and it's unfair to the employee. . . . And some of you feel the same way."

Mr. Magowan looked around the room. "I see everybody nodding their heads to what you are saying," he told her. Then he added: "I've heard this before."

(A Safeway spokesman says the company immediately followed up on the workers' complaints and that Mr. Magowan personally wrote letters to those employees who voiced concerns.)

Certainly many employees have emerged unscathed from the LPO and feel comfortable working under the new regime. A good number of them even applaud the company for its rapid surfacing from the debt depths.

But among a group of workers that Safeway supplies to this newspaper as a sampler of "happy employees," no one interviewed is praising the LBO

"We've recovered well," says Jim Ratto, a Safeway liquor merchandiser. "But personally, I think Safeway would have been better off if we had never gone through the leveraged buyout. It definitely added some problems, and the company would have been farther ahead now if it had never happened."

"Safeway's made a beautiful comeback, we're getting on our feet again, and I have no complaints," says George Voronin, an affable wine steward who says, "I always try to look on the positive side." But even Mr. Voronin adds, "When someone comes in and takes all your funds and sells your stores, isn't that what we in the United States call dishonest?"

The new esprit de corps trumpeted in the executive suite is less apparent in the grocery aisles, where store employees say the KKR-inspired quotas—based on complex return-on-market-value formulas—create anxiety as well as productivity. And the pressure mounts as one goes down the chain from manager to checker.

While Safeway executives call the quota program an "incentive" plan, some store managers refer to it as "the punishment system." That's because store managers say if they don't make the week's quota, they can be penalized. In some divisions they report that they must work a seven-day week as penance. Working a month without a day off isn't unusual, managers in the Washington and California divisions say. In some stores managers who miss quota say they have to pull 6 A.M. to 6 P.M. shifts.

Mr. Magowan says corporate headquarters sets no such penalties. "I have never heard of any such program," he says. "I simply do not believe for one second that this is any widespread activity." A company spokesman says that at least 50 percent of store managers are meeting their quota.

Even among the list of satisfied employees that Safeway provides, many aren't profiting from the incentive plan. Either they are too low on the totem pole to get a bonus (with a few exceptions, only department heads and higher qualify), or their departments aren't generating enough sales volume to meet the demanding quotas. Mr. Voronin, whose wine department has been on the incentive plan for two years, has yet to get a bonus. Mary Wise is head of the floral department, but the company hasn't yet cut her into the plan. She says she doesn't mind: "I leave feeling good, knowing I did the job right, and for me, that's my bonus." She adds, "But I'm one of those people you look at and say, 'Oh, why is she always so happy?' "

In Seattle, only one of more than a dozen store managers in one district expects to meet quota this year, managers say. Last year, none made more than 20 percent of their bonus potential, the store heads say. A Safeway spokesman says most managers in that region are making their quota.

On Safeway's home turf in the San Francisco area, managers are "stepping down" and becoming checkers. Some have been forced to turn in their manager badges when they didn't meet quota; others say they are voluntarily taking lower status and pay—out of exhaustion.

"A number of store managers have stepped down, this year particularly," a company spokesman acknowledges. "In recent years, the job has gotten tougher."

In the wake of the LBO, the company was able to squeeze labor concessions from the unions, using the Dallas shutdown as an object lesson of what can happen when labor costs are deemed too high. With the debt hovering overhead, you could "get the labor concessions you deserve," Mr. Magowan says.

"It was like coming to the table with a gun at our heads," recalls Ed Hardy, a United Food and Commercial Workers negotiator. While the company's average hourly wage rate has risen slightly in the last three years—the exact amount is confidential, Safeway says—the small increase trails the inflation rate.

The strategy of catering to the upscale of many stores has also enabled KKR to cut service workers' wages even further. To staff trendy specialty departments, Safeway has hired "general merchandise clerks," a classification that pays as little as half the wages of food clerks.

This disparity troubles even the upbeat floral manager Mary Wise. "Gosh, you can barely live on what they are paying them," she says. She broached the subject with Mr. Magowan at the 1988 meeting. These specialty clerks are performing a job that requires training and skill, she said, and "Safeway should pay them accordingly."

Mr. Magowan's response, as quoted in the company's magazine: "The problem, Mary, is this. The reason we got the lower GMC [general merchandising clerk] rate was to allow our labor costs to be competitive." But he reassured her that the company was taking steps to make up for the low pay. "What I've suggested from time to time is saying, 'Do you like weekends off? Do you like to work eight to five?' . . . We'll give you the lower rate but a better schedule.' That might make them very happy."

In one division, Safeway has extended the incentive program beyond the department manager level in an experiment aimed at letting all workers benefit in the enhanced productivity they are generating. Employees in the Denver division took a 14 percent cut, but were assured that, on average, the new profit-sharing plan would more than make up the difference. The company acknowledges this hasn't happened in nearly half the cases; the union estimates that even fewer increased their earnings.

Store employees in Denver also complained about the way the incentive system was linked—as it is throughout the company—to grievances and work-related medical claims. "Managers have been saying to people, don't file workman's comp because it will hurt the bonus," says Charles Mercer, president of the Denver local of the United Food and Commercial Workers. Mr. Magowan concedes that the Denver bonus plan is "not very popular."

Mr. Magowan's assertion that Safeway's culture is more collegial now also doesn't always square with the view from the retail floor. In stores around the country, employees report that management is pushing out older, skilled and well-paid employees, turning to cheap part-time help (who don't get medical insurance and other benefits) and piling extra work on the remaining staff. Union officials estimate that the average age of the stores' work force has dropped ten years since the buy-out; a company spokesman disputes this, but says Safeway doesn't track age.

"Safeway used to be one of the best places to work of the retail grocers," says Rowena Schoos, a middle-aged Safeway meatcutter in Oregon for five years. "But after the buyout, they started cutting hours to the nitty-gritty, the store managers went into mass panic, and Safeway just turned into a burnout company."

Ms. Schoos recently left herself, after she was cut back to sixteen hours a week and lost her medical benefits. Like many of the older and well-paid meatcutters, she says, she was relegated to the "extra board," a tour of duty that can require driving more than a hundred miles a day to different stores to fill in where needed.

For the older butchers, many of whom suffer physical injuries from the years of toting and carving, the assignment is the final shove out the door. Ms. Schoos, for example, has two herniated discs, which she attributes to years of lugging hundred-pound carcasses.

A Safeway spokesman responds, "That's just another case of an isolated situation. She was just not performing the job adequately," and thus her hours were cut.

The company also says that meatcutters' numbers have been reduced primarily because a gradual shift to pre-packaged goods in meat processing has lessened the need. Employees in the meat department argue that even with the changes, much of the work still requires a butcher's expertise and that the cutbacks have been too severe.

While on the extra-board circuit, Ms. Schoos had the opportunity to observe the LBO-fallout at many stores. "It was the same thing everywhere I went," she recalls. "The managers were desperate to meet quota and the older people always got it the worst. They'd bust them back to lower positions. One produce manager was told he had a 'choice'—go back to being a checker or get fired. One lady asked for a break, and the manager cut her from forty to eight hours."

In response, Mr. Magowan produces a recent employee survey conducted in the Portland, Ore., division that finds that more than 80 percent of employees feel Safeway offers advancement opportunity and other advantages. "These would be good scores to decertify the union should we ever wish to do so," Mr. Magowan says, adding, "which we have no intention of doing, whatsoever."

Closer to headquarters, at the Market Street store in San Francisco, employees report a grind of tension and overwork. Some say they are shouldering as many as nine different jobs.

In the meat department, the butchers' numbers have been cut back sharply and inexperienced clerks take up the slack. "Everyone is burned out," says another employee, who points to a counter where overripe meat is on display, the result of a hasty stocking effort. "It's a whole new ball game and everyone's discontented."

In the Market Street store, employees complain that clipboard-toting managers patrol the floors, closely monitoring performance and filing a blizzard of disciplinary reports. A company spokesman disputes these accounts: "There is no ROMV [Return on Market Value] police."

Last month, at the Market Street store, food clerk Steve Dolinka lost his job after twenty-five years of service. His malfeasance: He says he forgot to pay for the cup of soup and toast he ate at the deli on his lunch hour. Mr. Dolinka apologized, shelled out the few dollars that his food cost, and explained why he was so distracted—his mind was on a murder trial that had ended a few weeks earlier. A gas-station robber was before the court charged with slitting the throat of Mr. Dolinka's fifteen-year-old son in 1982 in an assault that the investigating detective called "the most brutal in my experience."

"My wife says I've been forgetting things a lot lately," Mr. Dolinka says.

"In our business, employee theft is a serious problem," a company spokesman says of Mr. Dolinka's expulsion. "And every employee is treated the same way."

Mr. Dolinka says he doesn't blame his manager for the firing. "The way it works here, I don't think any of the managers have the freedom to make these decisions. It's all coming down from company policy, and they have got to follow it like their bible."

To all such reports from the store front, Mr. Magowan says he's skeptical: "Our productivity is up," he points out. Employees are donating more to Easter Seals, and workers compensation claims are down, he says. And when the earthquake hit, "our employees stayed up all night cleaning up their stores."

"Are these acts of a disgruntled work force?" he asks. "I don't think so."

George Roberts, one of KKR's two principal partners, notes that workers at many corporations are being asked to do more, whether an LBO is involved or not. Employees "are now being held accountable," Mr. Roberts says. "They have to produce up to plan, if they are going to be competitive with the rest of the world. It's high time we did that."

The Biggest Looniest Deal Ever

Carol J. Loomis

June 18, 1990, *Fortune*

Carol Loomis is the best writer in the recent history of Fortune *magazine. And "The Biggest Looniest Deal Ever," her masterful yarn about the rise and fall of madman Robert Campeau, is vintage Loomis—the big story, deeply reported, and well told. She answers one of the decade's great questions: How could supposedly careful and conservative investment banks and commercial banks lend billions to a nut like Campeau?*

IN THE DOOM-LADEN DAYS when Robert Campeau was obsessively chasing Federated Department Stores, a moment flashed when he might have been derailed. It came at 8 A.M. on February 16, 1988, in New York City, as the directors of May Department Stores, then the third-largest U.S. chain to Federated's first, gathered for a suddenly called special meeting. The directors knew their mission: They were to bless a giant deal in which May, well capitalized and tightly managed, would make a white-knight bid for Federated. Across town Federated's representatives, themselves poised to enter a board meeting, were eagerly anticipating May's call—and an offer they expected to be $67 a share.

But May's fifty-four-year-old chief executive, David Farrell, normally punctual to the second, was late this morning. "When he finally came in," says one of the waiting May directors, "his face was long. I knew then we weren't going to be approving any deal." Soberly, Farrell explained that he and his executive team had concluded that the challenge of taking over Federated—huge, sprawling, and run by managers who would not necessarily cotton to May's exacting ways—seemed too great to risk. An apologetic telephone call went to a stunned Federated, and the episode was closed. No word of it leaked out.

Six weeks later, on April Fool's Day, Campeau—a Canadian entrepreneur successful in real estate but inexperienced in retailing—captured Federated. Then sixty-four, Campeau had a widely publicized history of emotional breakdowns, volatile behavior, and aggressive business practices. In this fit of boldness, sashaying in where May had feared to tread, he paid $73.50 a share, for a total of $6.5 billion, almost all borrowed.

The price, the debt, and the man. Together they created a financial megabomb that was barely built before it was detonated by a business that *had* to deliver and didn't. Less than two years down the road, on January 15, 1990, a reeling, shellshocked Federated went into Chapter 11. Its brother in bankruptcy was Allied Stores, which Campeau had nabbed earlier for $3.6 billion, also in a hostile assault, on another appropriate day, Halloween 1986.

In ways that even witches could not have foretold, these collapses will be long and despairingly remembered. Behind them, for one thing, is an incredible list of financiers who thought it was a neat idea to give Campeau all those billions and who now are feeling the consequences: Citibank and a string of other U.S. banks; Sumitomo and ten other Japanese banks; three investment banks, First Boston, Paine Webber, and Dillon Read; a giant mortgage lender, Prudential Insurance; innumerable junk-bond buyers, among them such big-time players as Equitable Life Assurance and Fidelity Investments, the world's largest mutual fund company; and two of North America's most sophisticated real estate operators, the Reichmann family's Olympia & York and Edward J. DeBartolo Co.

In their wake are the other direct, and largely innocent, victims: perhaps 300,000 vendors and suppliers, many of them paid shortly before the bankruptcy with rubber checks; 101,000 employees wondering what happens next; 250 retired executives who are not receiving deferred compensation and supplemental retirement benefits they are owed; and even a booster club from Miamisburg, Ohio, whose members had counted inventories at a Federated store to raise money for the high school band and were stiffed for $3,514.40.

Other ripple effects look more like tidal waves. Trying to generate sales that would keep them alive, the Campeau stores took the cleaver to prices and drove their competitors to do likewise. The 1989 holiday season grew ugly for many retailers, especially the highly leveraged, forced to watch their cash flows shrink. One of those was R.H. Macy, which suffered a $39 million loss in its Christmas quarter, against $78 million in profits a year earlier, and whose creditors are nervous. Says a bemused retailing consultant: "One man, one company. They simply managed to throw a whole industry into turmoil."

Make that several industries. The early signs of profound trouble in the Campeau empire, which surfaced last September, jolted the junk-bond market out of dreamland and sent it into a nightmarish slide that rattled Wall Street and helped push Drexel Burnham Lambert into bankruptcy. Federated and Allied junk bonds headed south, no surprise. But so did the junk bonds of nearly all other issuers, as well as the shares of all companies the market perceived to have too much debt.

Thus did an age of excess unravel, with Robert Campeau as the catalyst and also the symbol of excess carried to its dumbest, most egregious limits. When the financial history of the 1980s is written, when the tales of leverage are limned, the $25 billion RJR Nabisco buyout will no doubt be viewed as the epochal transaction. But the Campeau drama has no rival for absurdity as it proceeded and for shattering effects as it ended.

The overarching wonder of this affair is that so many supposedly shrewd lenders forked over so much money to a man whose instability would probably keep him from being hired as a Bloomingdale's salesclerk. Among the credulous was William Mayer, head of merchant banking at first Boston, who recently took a weak stab at explaining just why the firm entrusted hundreds of millions to Campeau: "In the market of the time, it seemed perfectly plausible."

In the willing suspension of disbelief that occurred then, the prices that Campeau paid were, of course, called justifiable. But some mathematics show just how stretched his two deals were. In buying first Allied and then Federated, and after setting up initial assumptions that he would sell twenty-five divisions and pay down more than $5 billion in debt, Campeau was to be left with eleven divisions and the servicing of about $7.9 billion in new and old debt. Most of the debt was to be carried directly by Federated and Allied, the rest by other Campeau companies that borrowed to finance the purchases. Assume, conservatively, that the blended interest rate on that $7.9 billion was 11 percent. That would be annual interest of $869 million.

Yet in their best years ever, which in the cyclical department store business seldom appear consecutively, the 11 chains Campeau planned to keep had made pretax, pre-interest profits totaling only $680 million. So even on this conservative 11 percent assumption and even ignoring the ups and downs of this business and the general hazards of an LBO, Campeau was looking at a prospective annual gap between interest and the operating earnings available to pay it of nearly $190 million. In truth, Campeau's blended rate of interest turned out to be higher, in part because he paid rates of 16 percent and 17¾ percent on two Federated junk-bond issues that accounted for around $700 million of the company's debt.

But don't leveraged companies think of cash flow rather than earnings? They do, constructing a cash flow figure called EBITDA—earnings before interest, taxes, depreciation, and amortization. But this amount is not entirely available to service debt, since it must also cover capital expenditures. These are significant in the department store business: Even if expansion halts, the refurbishing and freshening of existing stores is an absolute necessity and a steady drain on cash flow. As a result, "free cash flow"—the amount legitimately available to pay interest—typically does not differ much from operating earnings.

Campeau, nonetheless, had definite ideas for handling his debt. Most important, he planned to secure annual savings of perhaps $300 million by cutting the payroll and streamlining operations. The payroll indeed fell, and in time the Allied and the Federated corporate bureaucracies were reduced to one. But what counted was profits, and in the bitterly competitive retail industry, they did not begin to meet the expectations that Campeau, ever the optimist, had built into his projections. Even a small shortfall would have been a killer: There was no room for error in these deals.

There were lenders who thought from the start that the transactions were uneconomic. One was Bankers Trust, a big player in the leveraged-buyout business, which declined to finance both takeovers. The bank is unwilling today to spell out its reasons. But a clue to its thinking may be culled from some comments CEO Charles Sanford made to security analysts in January. "Optimistic growth assumptions," he said, can plunge a buyer into trouble: "If you look back at transactions gone bad, more often than not the problem was paying too much."

Most of the lenders who saw things differently are not seeking publicity today. If victory has a thousand fathers and defeat is an orphan, this baby, in the sense of there being *anyone* willing to claim parentage, is an outright virgin birth. Partly because the bankruptcy is a sump sure to breed lawsuits, few people will speak freely on the record. Off the record, the principals tend to shift the blame away from themselves and on to some nearby convenient back.

Campeau himself is not speaking to the press, and neither are Federated's top executives. Bruce Wasserstein, the investment banker, is an especially interesting nontalker, since it was his fame and financial resources that originally converted Campeau from a Canadian mystery man to an American presence. For this article Wasserstein agreed to an interview, provided no shred of it would be quoted or attributed to him. *Fortune* said no to the terms and the interview.

To understand all that happened in this wrong-headed affair, it is necessary to understand Bob Campeau's status when it began four years ago. Though he was largely unknown in the U.S., he had put his stamp on Canada. A French Canadian, he was born to a poor, devout Catholic family in an Ontario mining town, dropped out of school at fourteen, and later fell almost by accident into homebuilding. Physically slight but smart and superenergetic, he went on to earn a nationwide reputation for creative, well-constructed real estate developments. "A Campeau-built house" is to this day a term that connotes quality in Canada. Toronto's impressive downtown skyline boasts several buildings put up by Campeau Corp., including the dramatic tower, Scotia Plaza, in which the company makes its headquarters.

The boss had meanwhile exhibited his unconventionality and high-strung temperament. He suffered two mental breakdowns, the first in 1970—after which he added to the board of Campeau Corp. the head of the psychiatric clinic where he had been treated—and the second in 1985. Campeau also developed a reputation for cheating at golf. In 1980 he audaciously tried to take over a bastion of English Canada's banking establishment, Royal Trustco. Repulsed in that assault, he emerged with a conviction that he could never crack what he saw as a closed society.

The double life he had once led did not improve his chances. For public consumption, he was married and the father of a girl and two adopted boys. Back street, he had a mistress, Ilse Luebbert, by whom he fathered a daughter, Giselle, and a son, Robert Jr. In 1969 he was divorced from his wife and shortly after married Ilse, who then bore him another son, Jan Paul. German by birth, Ilse, fifty, is regally tall and, says an American acquaintance, "attractive—if you're into Valkyries." She served on the Campeau board until last fall and remains her husband's closest business confidante.

By 1986 the shared confidences included Campeau's determination to move into U.S. retailing. He viewed the American culture as free and open, and he was drawn to retailing by a vision of linking it to real estate. His target of choice was Allied, then the sixth-largest department store chain. As the Canadian saw it, Allied's lead chains—Ann Taylor, Bon Marché, Brooks Brothers, Jordan Marsh, Maas Brothers, and Stern's—would provide anchor and specialty stores for the shopping centers he planned to develop.

Campeau Corp.'s profits were then under $10 million a year (in U.S. dollars), and its common stock had a market value of about $200 million. Allied was thirty times as big in profits and ten times as large in market value. Bob Campeau had little spare cash, but he was a real estate man accustomed to borrowing however much creditors would lend. In 1986 the U.S. leveraged-buyout market was in a state of heat, and he correctly assumed he could get whatever it took to buy Allied.

In the Campeau saga, the taking of Allied and its early history under the Canadian are seldom given the attention they deserve. Allied was the evidence that lenders had to look at as they surveyed Campeau's plans for buying Federated, and in the kindest reading possible, the evidence was mixed. Certain financial accomplishments were visible: Campeau had moved fast on divestitures, for example, and was ahead of schedule in paying down debt. But his erratic, undependable, overreaching nature was also on display.

An early punching bag was Paine Webber, the first investment banker that Campeau turned to when he began his American campaign. Paine Webber advised Campeau for several months in the spring and summer of 1986, as he pursued a friendly merger with Allied. But when hostilities began to look inevitable, Campeau concluded he needed a more high-powered banker and engaged First Boston. Paine Webber was sent to the sidelines.

In Paine Webber's pocket, however, was a contract, signed in September, providing without qualification that the firm would be paid $5.75 million if and when Campeau acquired Allied. So when that acquisition was done, Paine Webber rendered its bill for the $4.6 million still owed it—and Campeau refused to pay, claiming that Paine Webber had contributed nothing to his victory. Paine Webber eventually sued, collected, and went its way, supposedly wiser.

First Boston had by then forged an enduring relationship with Campeau. The firm was brought into the picture in September 1986 by Allen Finkelson, a Cravath Swaine & Moore partner who was Campeau's lawyer and whose help Campeau enlisted when he was looking for new investment-banking firepower. Finkelson put Campeau together with merger and acquisition experts from three firms, who came in relays to meet him at his Waldorf Towers suite in Manhattan. A banker involved has a snapshot memory of how Campeau perched on the couch as they talked—"his feet tucked up, a shirt button popping open across his stomach."

One firm in this beauty contest, Shearson Lehman, bowed out because it had a client conflict. The meeting between Campeau and another, Morgan Stanley, went poorly. Says Eric Gleacher, then head of mergers and acquisitions at the firm: "When we got down on the street, I said to the guys with me, 'I don't know about you, but I didn't understand a word he was saying.' Turns out, they didn't either." Gleacher called up Finkelson and said, "Count us out."

But First Boston's Bruce Wasserstein and Campeau clicked. Wasserstein was then a thirty-eight-year-old M&A rocket, celebrated both for his creative thinking and for his determination to make First Boston a player in every deal going. He had a "dare to be great" speech aimed at stroking his clients' egos, and in that first meeting he laid it very effectively on Campeau, a willing subject if ever there was one.

In the next few weeks the two men turned their guns on Allied, which tried frantically to escape by making a deal with Edward J. DeBartolo, a shopping center developer who had his own vision of melding real estate and retailing. Campeau's counteroffensive was a tender offer at $66 a share, a bid more than $20 above the price two months before. But on October 24, he suddenly abandoned the offer and instead bought huge blocks of Allied's stock in the open market at $67, raising his stake to a controlling 53 percent in thirty minutes. Allied sued to undo this "street sweep," claiming it subverted the tender-offer rules, and was supported by the SEC. The court, however, let the sweep stand. Soon after, the commission forbade such tactics.

The Allied sweep was a Wasserstein brainstorm, and he was the man without whom this deal could not have been done. His prestige lent Campeau credibility in the financial markets, and his clout at First Boston produced hard cash. Initially First Boston promised Campeau all the money he needed to acquire more than 50 percent control, a giant $1.8 billion. But when Citibank stepped up with an offer of bank financing, First Boston was able to reduce its contribution—a bridge loan—to $865 million.

Despite the knockout punch of the street sweep, and a

merger agreement signed on Halloween, the Allied deal promptly turned into a cliffhanger. The master plan called for a Campeau company to merge with Allied and simultaneously buy the stock still outstanding. For tax reasons, that transaction had to be completed by the end of 1986. By the same date Bob Campeau had to come up with something he didn't have: $300 million in equity capital to add to the more than $3 billion in debt First Boston and a Citibank syndicate were making available for the merger. A partial solution was provided by Citibank itself, which lent Campeau Corp. $150 million that it could contribute to Allied as "equity." A possible lender of the other $150 million was, of all people, DeBartolo.

But while Santa Claus came and went and while squads of negotiators filed in and out of a Manhattan conference room, Campeau kept haggling with DeBartolo about terms on an amount that constituted less than 5 percent of the value of the deal. Recalls an exasperated witness: "That was when I knew for sure that Campeau was Looney Tunes." An Allied stockholders' meeting to approve the merger was postponed from December 29th to the 30th, and then to the 31st. Only hours before the throngs gathered in Times Square to ring out the year, a wrung-out set of negotiators concluded a transaction in which Campeau Corp. borrowed the money Campeau still needed from DeBartolo. As he left the scene, a Campeau adviser recalled a half-jesting question posed earlier by Citibank's lead negotiator, Carolyn Buck Luce: "What have we created?"

So it was that Bruce Wasserstein, First Boston, and Citibank—with a last-minute boost from Edward DeBartolo—godfathered Campeau's entry into U.S. retailing. When Campeau hosted a victory party at the Metropolitan Museum of Art some weeks later, he toasted Wasserstein and lawyer Allen Finkelson, and lectured—"unintelligibly," says a guest—about currency rates. Pierre Trudeau, Canada's former Prime Minister and Campeau's fellow French Canadian, was there, as was the cardinal of Toronto. A raft of American politicians and business leaders were also invited, but few showed. Instead the tables were occupied by advisers, lenders, and others who had pocketed the deal's $210 million in fees.

Now that the prize was won, it had to be made to work—ah, yes, *that* challenge. Campeau announced that he would sell sixteen of Allied's twenty-four divisions, though certainly not such gems as Brooks Brothers and Ann Taylor. He visited Allied's chains to discuss plans for cutting costs, and he prepared to restructure his debt, to stretch some due dates out ten years or more.

One financing step took place in March 1987: a $1.15 billion junk bond and preferred stock offering whose proceeds were to be applied to paying off First Boston's bridge loan. The Toronto *Globe and Mail's* magazine, *Report on Business*, chose this sensitive moment to publish an article about Campeau that dwelt lingeringly on his mental illnesses and marital history. But the market, bubbly at the time, ignored these disclosures.

Equally unwisely, the buyers paid little attention to the fact that Allied was permitted under the bond indentures to sell one business and, instead of paying down debt with the proceeds, buy another. That clause would come back to haunt the Allied bondholders. Finally, the preferred stock part of the offering permitted Allied to pay dividends "in kind"—that is, in more shares—instead of in cash. Campeau was among the first big users of these payment in kind, or PIK, securities, which later became a financing mania.

Hard as it is to believe today, Allied's offering was a solid success. And so, largely, were the efforts to sell divisions. Many people attest to Campeau's tenacity and to his charm—and both were valuable as he unloaded the divisions. Says a man who used to work for Campeau: "He is simply the best salesman I have ever met."

But according to a story that investment banker Felix Rohatyn of Lazard Frères has told friends, Campeau was erratic even in this endeavor. In 1987, Rohatyn and a client, the Limited's Leslie Wexner, met in Manhattan late at night with Campeau to discuss one of the divisions up for sale. After a while, Campeau grew agitated and began to circle the room nervously. "You think I did right in buying Allied?" he asked the visitors. "I hope I didn't overpay. I think I didn't overpay." Dismayed and concerned about this behavior, Rohatyn and Wexner left hurriedly. The retailer did not buy a Campeau division.

By year-end 1987, Campeau had nevertheless shed about $1 billion of properties and paid down that much debt ahead of schedule. Concurrently he received a commitment from Prudential for up to $460 million in mortgages on properties he had retained, and he changed bankers, replacing Citibank with Security Pacific Bank, which had come calling with very attractive terms on a $1.45 billion loan commitment. Uncharacteristically filled with caution, Citi would not match those terms because it was unsure that Allied's retail operations were chugging along as they should.

That was indeed the burning question: Were they? Campeau had by that time been through two Allied bosses and just hired a third. The first was Thomas Macioce, Allied's CEO during the takeover fight, whom Campeau not only left in his post but also made chairman of Campeau Corp. Macioce lasted three weeks. Today owed $5 million in deferred compensation by Allied, he has filed papers in the bankruptcy court that claim Campeau "undermined" him, refusing to let him exercise his executive powers.

Next Howard Hassler, Allied's chief financial officer, moved up to be president and chief operating officer. He resigned eight months later over disagreements with the boss, at which point Campeau announced that he would run Allied himself. Even then, however, he was wooing an experienced retailer, Robert Morosky, who a few months before had abruptly left the Limited, where he was second in command to Wexner.

During the negotiations Morosky, then forty-six, took his wife to Toronto, where they spent a pleasant day with the Campeaus. The couples, Morosky says, shared an interest in the Catholic church and family. In his due diligence, Morosky somehow failed to uncover Campeau's unchurchly family life, nor did he learn that executive turnover at Campeau Corp. had been high. Had he known those things, Morosky says now, he might have thought twice before joining up. Instead, he took over as Allied's president in November with a contract that promised he would be CEO in six months.

In November, Allied also released financial results for the first nine months of 1987, which became the tea leaves of record available to lenders as they later weighed the Federal deal. Absolutely nothing about the figures was reassuring. Operating earnings for the nine months were $44 million, and the smallness of the capital spending budget, held down in part because Campeau was busy shedding divisions, pushed free cash flow to just over $100 million. But interest paid was a thunderous $244 million.

So what do you do when you have a limping retailer in tow? If you're Campeau, you buy a spry one and cripple it as well. In the late summer of 1987, he began making plans to go after Federated, owner of an avenue of names: Abraham & Straus, Bloomingdale's, Bullock's, Burdines, Filene's, Foley's, I. Magnin, Lazarus, Rich's, and—an apple among peers—Ralphs Grocery, a California supermarket chain. In honor of Federated's hometown of Cincinnati, and its most famous ballplaying gambler, this quest was code-named Project Rose.

Once the class of its industry, Federated had fallen in prestige and profit margins during the 1980s. Though he was no admirer of the company's top management, Campeau thought Federated was a better-run operation than Allied. He also envisioned one vastly slimmed corporate staff and other efficiencies to be gained by combining the two companies.

Morosky knew from the start that Campeau wanted to acquire other chains, but he was startled to hear shortly after he was hired that the target was Federated, which was three times Allied's size. Says he: "You really couldn't say that we had Allied in shape yet, and here we were proposing to take on a job that would be Herculean and loaded with financing problems. I told Bob that it would be like acquiring the U.S. Navy. But in the end, I voted yes just like everybody else."

On January 25, 1988, Campeau hit the market with a $47-per-share bid for a company whose stock had been selling at $33 four weeks before. He was eventually driven up to the final price of $73.50 as his attack set off a media circus and propelled Federated into an intense search for an escape. Meanwhile, he shocked one of the unsuspecting lenders, Prudential, with which he had just done business. Says Garnett Keith, vice chairman of Prudential: "We were appalled that anyone who had hocked himself to the gills could turn around and add another layer on top of that."

Campeau's initial bid for Federated was followed by the prolonged takeover battle called "store wars," in which May aborted its takeoff but Macy's ultimately screamed into full flight. In the weeks of war, Campeau was . . . Campeau. He scheduled meetings for 3 A.M. Using a Gulfstream III that belonged to Allied, he disappeared on trips, taking Citibank's Lawrence Small, who had helped bring Campeau's business to the bank, to the Calgary Olympics, and Ilse back home to Germany. He was en route to Germany, in fact, when the Federated board suddenly agreed, after weeks of refusal, to a face-to-face meeting with its northern nemesis. He did not speed back. Instead a team headed by Wasserstein appeared before the Federated board. To the end, the directors never did meet Campeau.

His absences signaled no waning of desire. On the contrary, he had become fixated on Federated. Davis Weinstock, a New York City public relations consultant then working with Campeau, recalls his client's mood: "I knew as the deal went on that he was either going to win or die. He was not going to be reasonable. He was flying."

He was also not to be hauled back to earth by his investment bankers. Their ingrained propensity to indulge the folly of clients—deals create fees and reputations, bigger deals create bigger fees and bigger reputations—was intensified by special circumstances at First Boston, which was riven by internal rivalry. Wasserstein and his co-head of investment banking, Joseph Perella, had been waging a turf battle with CEO Peter Buchanan and the other traders who dominated the firm. Beat back, the two rebels abruptly left First Boston to form Wasserstein Perella & Co., taking a clutch of First Boston people with them. The date was February 2, one week after Campeau made his bid.

Campeau quickly said he would work with both Wasserstein and First Boston. From the former he wanted advice; from the latter, a bridge loan and the firm's capacity to market and trade junk bonds. For its part, First Boston was left with a decimated mergers department and an ego-driven determination to prove it could nonetheless pull off this deal.

With everyone rabid to do a takeover, the bids for Federated passed the bounds of rationality. That could not have been proved, however, by the investment bankers' computers, which kept turning out deal analyses—"iterations" is the buzzword—that validated whatever price Campeau and his opponent, Macy's CEO Edward Finkelstein, had decided they needed to pay. Even today some members of Campeau's group argue that the price for Federated could not then have been 6too high if Finkelstein, a master retailer, was willing to pay as much. The argument is frail because there is no evidence that Finkelstein could have coped with Federated had he bought it. Macy's itself has hardly turned out to be an LBO luminosity.

In any case, the battle between Campeau and Macy's was intricate and also frustrating for Federated's directors, who were by then both playing auctioneer and yearning for calm. One of the board's attorneys, James C. Freund of Skadden Arps Slate Meagher & Flom, says the directors had a favorite, not named Campeau. They would have preferred to see Finkelstein, an experienced, respected merchant—and a man, yes, whom they had actually met in the flesh!—buy the company. But they also had a legal responsibility to get the highest price for shareholders, and Campeau offered that price. On March 31, 1988, the board prepared to declare Campeau the winner, only to watch Macy's lob in still one more, higher bid.

At that point somebody desperate for peace—reports say it was Joseph Flom, the lead Skadden Arps lawyer advising the Federated directors—whispered "compromise," and suddenly Campeau and Finkelstein were in a long meeting that stretched beyond midnight. From the tryst came this all-time April Fool's joke, better known then as a "win-win" pact. Macy's would drop out of the bidding in return for the opportunity to buy I. Magnin and Bullock's, two divisions it coveted, for $1.1 billion. Macy's would also be granted $60 million to cover expenses and fees. Campeau was to get the rest of Federated. Suits us, said the Federated board when daylight came, and that was it.

The final merger agreement included hogtie provisions, however, that suggest the board had definite qualms about the new owner. Campeau was required, for example, to retain Federated's employee benefit plans, and he was forbidden to withdraw equity capital from the company for a year. And to give these promises bite, three Federated directors were to go on Campeau Corp.'s board as watchdogs.

The requirement about equity capital grew from the deal's financing, which was a Campeau special: enormously complex, tortuous to arrange, and rewarding to the advisers and bankers, who took home more than $350 million in fees. Among the components was a $2 billion bridge loan from investment banks First Boston, Dillon Read, and—ready?—Paine Webber.

Once burned but plainly not twice shy, Paine Webber ponied up $500 million for this transaction. In explaining this bizarre behavior, Paine Webber cites the need to be competitive. The firm was not a contender in bridge loan financing, and it wanted to put itself on the map. Paine Webber says that it has since made money on bridge loans. But hardly on this one: Though much of the bridge loan was paid down, Paine Webber is today an unsecured Federated creditor owed $96 million.

The $6.5 billion deal also included a large bank loan commitment from a Citibank and Sumitomo syndicate and $1.4 billion in equity, a bounteous sum by LBO standards. But under the microscope, this equity specimen could be seen as mostly Campeau debt. One of the contributors to the $1.4 billion pot was the wealthy Reichmann family of Toronto, owner of the immensely successful real estate company Olympia & York. The Reichmanns admired Campeau's real estate skills and even owned some Campeau Corp. stock and convertible debentures. When Bob Campeau showed up hat in hand, they refused to become equity investors in the Federated deal but did buy $260 million more of Campeau Corp.'s convertible debentures, from which $227 million was passed along to Federated. There is no evidence that the Reichmanns, brilliant though their reputation is, dug deeply into the economics of this transaction. In other words, they seem to have goofed.

Ed DeBartolo, having been repaid the money he had lent for the Allied deal, decided on another fling, a risk equivalent to trying bungee jumping twice. He lent a Campeau Corp. subsidiary $480 million and received 7.5 percent of Federated's stock—Campeau held the rest—along with 50 percent of a partnership that had ambitious plans for developing five to ten shopping centers and malls a year. Another chunk of the $1.4 billion in equity came from a $500 million, steep-interest loan that Bank of Montreal and Banque Paribas made to that same subsidiary and that had to be repaid in one dangerous year.

Campeau wrenched the remaining millions of equity capital that he needed from a party that certainly couldn't spare it: Allied. Though he had vowed to keep Allied's Brooks Brothers clothing stores, he now sold them to Marks & Spencer for a splendid $750 million. Most of that went to pay down bank debt. But with $193 million left over, Allied took advantage of the loose covenants in its junk-bond indentures and bought 13.8 percent of Federated's stock. Though the fine price Campeau received for Brooks Brothers muted criticism of this brassy maneuver, the implications for Allied's bondholders were huge. Campeau had in effect exchanged a stake in Brooks Brothers, an income-producing property, for a stake in Federated, a debt-loaded entity whose ability to pay dividends to Allied was nil.

With that final off-the-wall piece of the capitalization in place, Federated was launched as a leveraged buyout on July 29, 1988. Not quite eighteen months later it slid haplessly into Chapter 11. It is fair to say that almost nothing good happened to the company in the interim. That was not apparent, however, from Campeau's public statements, which brimmed with hope and cheer and swell thoughts. Perhaps the most pretentious of these appeared in an expensive, self-congratulatory book that Campeau Corp. published about itself in early 1989. It included a corporate credo that began: "Because we can be no more than what we aspire to be, we will always aspire to be more than the best of what we are."

The "we" who aspired, alas, kept expiring. Days after he had clutched the billions needed for Federated's stock, Campeau confronted Robert Morosky, the man who was supposedly going to run the entire Federated-Allied retailing empire, and told him he would not be made CEO after all, regardless of what it said in Morosky's contract. It seems that

Campeau had sourced on Morosky, in part, no doubt, because the Federated organization had immediately judged him to be an arrogant no-goodnik. Not willing to be anything other than CEO, Morosky quit.

Campeau thereupon began stalking the Federated officers who had just taken their golden parachutes and split. His first choice, Allen I. Questrom, fifty, who had been a Federated vice chairman, rejected the CEO's job because he thought Campeau's retailers too leveraged. The next offer went to John Burden III, fifty-three, another former vice chairman, and he accepted with the stipulation that he would serve only eighteen months. Burden was a merchant by training and needed an operating executive and numbers man as president. That job went to James Zimmerman, forty-six, who had been expertly running the Rich's division. The weird upshot: Campeau, who had thought he needed an outsider to shape Federated up, ended up with two insiders in charge.

While the financial world was still digesting these bewildering events, Campeau suddenly announced that allied would sell Ann Taylor, another of those beauties he had sworn faithfully to love, honor, and cherish. The reason was that $500 million loan from Bank of Montreal and Paribas, coming due all too soon. In a Tinker-to-Evers-to-Chance Transaction, Allied cavalierly used the Ann Taylor proceeds to raise its stake in Federated to 50 percent, buying the shares from a Campeau subsidiary, which promptly relayed cash to the two banks to erase that $500 million loan.

You didn't have to be an Allied bondholder to despise what was going on; catcalls were coming from everywhere. In the early fall of 1988, First Boston was rebuffed when it tried to offer $1.15 billion of Federated junk bonds at rates averaging 14 percent. Only after the firm cut the offering to $723 million and reset the coupons to a dizzying 16 percent and 17¾ percent was it able to sell the bonds. The cutback was a blow to First Boston, since the proceeds were slated to repay the $1.1 billion still outstanding on the bridge loan that it, Paine Webber, and Dillon Read had made. Instead, the three bridge lenders were left holding about $400 million of their loan. Call it justice.

The mauling he got in the junk market infuriated Campeau, and he drastically revised his financial strategy. On Federated's books was an $800 million mortgage bridge loan, due in early 1990, that Campeau had been planning to refinance with longer-term money. Citibank, ever accommodating, appeared ready to deliver the dollars. But in late 1988 Campeau resolved instead to raise $2 billion or $3 billion or $4 billion—whatever a willing world would give him—and use the money not only to refinance the $800 million but also to eliminate the vile junk debt. He embarked on an extended, manic search for the money. A half-year later, at the Campeau Corp. annual meeting in July 1989, he was still saying that new mortgage financing was almost in hand.

Today most of the other principals in the Campeau catastrophe excoriate Campeau for not having accepted the Citibank financing at an early date. They argue that this debt could have saved Federated from Chapter 11, but it is hard to see how. The refinancing would not have cut interest costs appreciably; it might even have raised them. And interest, have no doubt, was the scourge of this company.

An inseparable problem from the interest costs was operating profits that just didn't measure up. For a while during 1988, the profit picture at Federated and Allied was blurred by charges related to large layoffs and the consolidation of certain functions, such as data processing, that each company had handled separately. But by 1989 it was possible to see clearly that these two companies were doing terribly. For example, compare Federated's expectations for 1989 with its actual performance: In the fall of 1988 the company was projecting profits before interest, taxes, depreciation, and amortization of $740 million. The reality was a horrifying half of that, $372 million. Meanwhile, the claims on this money—modest capital expenditures of $111 million and immodest interest of $516 million—ran to $627 million.

Without question, the widespread publicity about Campeau's troubles that began in September 1989 hurt store traffic, particularly in the high-profile operations like Bloomingdale's. But that excuse is a thin one, because both Federated and Allied had reported weak profits much earlier in the year. Take Allied, which in the first few months of 1989 needed to refinance Security Pacific's loan. It turned to Citibank, which didn't want the business. But on April 7 a Citi syndicate finally made the loan, collecting especially large fees—more than $40 million for a $1.1 billion commitment. Citi also put a close watch on Allied. For example, the company was supposed to show earnings before taxes and interest of at least $35 million for the quarter that was to end on July 31. But Allied couldn't even do that. Pretax, pre-interest earnings were only $24 million.

The engine of trouble does not appear to have been sales, for which projections were being met. Instead, the problem was markdowns and promotions, tactics that made the sales largely profitless. Still more fundamentally, inventories seem to have been out of control. Federated's, for instance, leaped 26 percent between July 1988 and July 1989, a jump that both strained working capital and forced the stores to shove goods out the door just about any way they could.

The inventory problem is partly traceable to one of John Burden's merchandising strategies. He wanted the stores to be deep in "basics"—that is, white shirts, men's underwear, women's panty hose—and his buyers appear to have carried that notion to a perilous extreme. But a former Federated executive says the problem rose more precisely from the fact that nobody was minding the store: "We just didn't execute well. Nobody seemed to be paying attention."

The somebodies who could have done so certainly included Burden and Zimmerman, who must instead have been out to lunch. A Canadian cadre was also assigned to this case. One of its members, Ronald Tysoe, thirty-seven, took up residence in Cincinnati, where he served as a real estate expert and as Campeau's man on the spot. In Toronto the troops included Campeau Corp.'s president, James T. Roddy, forty-seven, and Carolyn Buck Luce, thirty-seven, who had improbably moved from Citibank to First Boston to Campeau. Her main job, both pinchingly difficult and imperfectly carried out, was to arrange financing for this intricate, wobbly structure that Bob Campeau had cobbled together.

Roddy, serious, ruddy-faced, and sometimes abrasive, had once been an executive of Peoples Jewellers, a Canadian retailer. This background made him think he had some expertise to bring to Federated and Allied. But Burden and Zimmerman did not want orders from Canada, and Bob Campeau did not insist that they accept them. Finally, last spring, both Roddy and Buck Luce resigned. As it always is and must be, the ultimate responsibility for the crumbling of the retail operations rested with the boss—initials, R.C.

Reviewing the deterioration in the business and the impossible burden of debt, one principal in this affair says that Chapter 11 filings could logically have occurred as early as the spring of 1989. But Campeau was then still aspiring to be more than he could be and not even entertaining ideas of default.

Personally, he was also being his usual outrageous self. In May 1989 he was honored by the New York United Jewish Appeal at a fund-raising cocktail party held at Bloomingdale's. Rising to speak and graciously pledging $50,000, he suddenly veered into a lecture about the unfortunate tendency of Jews to be oversensitive and even paranoid. "I like Jews," one listener distinctly recalls him saying. Campeau observed that he had frequently dealt with Jews in Canada and found them "honorable." He drew comparisons between Hitler and Napoleon, identifying both as "murderers" who differed in that Hitler's target was Jews. His audience, made up mainly of apparel manufacturers, cringed.

Just about that time, the Reichmann family, devout Orthodox Jews whom Campeau certainly included among the Jews he liked, was beginning to take a belated but intense interest in the man's empire. The Reichmann brothers—Albert, sixty-one, Paul, fifty-nine, and Ralph, fifty-six—had been unhappily startled in April to receive an emergency loan request from Allied for $75 million. They sent the money, but by June they also had consultants from McKinsey & Co. burrowing into the economics of the retailing operations. McKinsey produced findings that this family of real estate experts easily understood: The businesses did not have—and weren't likely to have—enough free cash flow to service their debt. By late summer, Campeau himself had reluctantly accepted that fact and had entered into grave talks with the Reichmanns.

From that point on, though there were rumors of a grandiose Reichmann rescue, a restructuring of Federated and Allied was inevitable. The only question was whether it would be done inside Chapter 11, a process that Bob Campeau doubted the stores could survive, or outside it. The outside route required that the holders of Federated and Allied junk bonds—debt so junior that it was essentially equity—be persuaded to exchange their securities for new pieces of paper carrying terms that would ease the companies' interest burden. Willing to try that plan, the Reichmanns exacted an agreement from Campeau that Bloomingdale's would be put on the block, promised the stores $250 million in working capital, and said the family would possibly commit more money if a junk-bond deal could be devised.

The plan never had a prayer. The reports of trouble that oozed out in September exacerbated the retailing problems to the point that bankruptcy was inevitable. In this climate nobody even cared to consider paying up for Bloomingdale's. Operationally, Campeau's last sources of credit—vendors and the factoring companies that finance them—began to slide away and refuse to ship merchandise. The suppliers that stoutly accepted credit risk to the end, including the largest factoring company, CIT, are in the crowd stuck with bounced checks.

Many of the stores suffered miserably in this chaotic period. Says a former Federated executive: "I walked into Bloomingdale's before Christmas, and I almost cried. It was dirty; it was schlocky; there were round tables in the aisles. It was criminal."

By that time planning for the Chapter 11 filings was in full, if covert, swing. The management structure was also undergoing drastic change. In January, days before the filing, Campeau Corp.'s board, by then strongly influenced by the Reichmanns, stripped Bob Campeau of authority over retailing and put the operation on its own. Then the board put Federated, Allied, and sixty-five subsidiaries into Chapter 11.

As boss of what is now called Federated Stores Inc., the directors installed G. William Miller, sixty-five, who was once the head of Textron, then chairman of the Federal Reserve Board, Secretary of the Treasury, and still later a Federated director who went on the Campeau board as one of three, ahem, watchdogs. In his new job Miller proceeded to form a management team. Burden resigned. Zimmerman stayed on, and so did Tysoe.

To head retailing, Miller got the fellow Campeau couldn't, Allen Questrom, who was persuaded to leave the job of CEO at Neiman Marcus and take on this monumental challenge. Questrom did not sign on unprotected: Under his employment contract, a $10 million trust fund has been established to guarantee that he gets paid. Not similarly swaddled, vendors have been asked to resume business as usual, and most have complied. Few truly see an alternative, since they cannot afford to lose customers this big.

In the Cincinnati court handling this case, the long rolls of creditors include some names that were accomplices before the fact: First Boston is owed $425 million, which is unsecured. Citibank, which sold off many of its Federated loans to smaller banks, is a secured creditor due $288 million. The bank is also still trying to make money off this crowd: It has signed up to finance Federated as it plows through bankruptcy.

Ed DeBartolo is due his full $480 million loan but is considered to be relatively well secured, in part by shares of Ralphs Grocery. The Reichmanns' Olympia & York is owed $525 million by Campeau Corp., which is not in bankruptcy—though neither is it paying interest on most of that debt. Olympia & York also has a 38 percent fully diluted common stock position in Campeau Corp., for whatever that means. Last August the stock was at an irrational $16 per share; now it bumps along around $1.

Bob Campeau has lost control of his company. That stark fact must trouble him the most, because he has for many years fanatically protected his equity. Furthermore, most of his Campeau stock, in which he has a 43 percent fully diluted position, is collateral for loans. The biggest of these is $150 million he owes to National Bank of Canada. Campeau has recently announced plans to buy back the stock that bank holds for $80 million, half of that to be paid promptly, the rest when the bankruptcy court approves a plan for getting Federated and Allied out of Chapter 11. But no one knows where that money will come from, since Campeau is not assumed to be flush with cash. Says a longtime associate: "This is a man who had all of his eggs in one basket, Campeau Corp. I know one thing: He's scrambling."

And the prospects for Federated and Allied? Convoluted. They include a possible entanglement in something called a "fraudulent conveyance" suit, an action based on the premise that a seller cannot make a deal through which a company becomes so burdened by debt that it is unable to pay existing claims, such as outstanding bonds or rents, or those that will arise as it plies its trade, such as the bills due vendors. Says Lewis S. Rosenbloom, a bankruptcy specialist with the Chicago law firm of Winston & Strawn: "Creditors have a right to expect that a company that has historically been profitable and never had its viability threatened will continue after it is sold to be able to satisfy its obligations in the ordinary course of business."

In the Federated and Allied situations, no fraudulent conveyance action has yet been brought, but reports persist that one or more are coming. All manner of folk could be sued by creditors, among them Campeau for piling on the debt, various lenders for letting him do it, and the former Federated directors for playing along. Indeed, a spokeswoman for Federated Stores Inc. mentioned the possibility of fraudulent conveyance suits as a reason current management—including former Federated director Miller—could not be interviewed.

Litigation, therefore, could interfere with Bill Miller's goal to get the bankruptcies over quickly. So could the deep complexity of the Chapter 11 filing and various operational imponderables. The question of how much debt the two retailing businesses can stand is unanswerable at present because their health is undeterminable. Says one investment banker close to the facts: "At this point, nobody really knows what the normalized cash flow of these companies is. When we do, we can reach some conclusions about the debt."

An experienced retailing consultant adds his opinion that the Federated and Allied chains have the strength to survive this trauma—"if only their creditors will let them." His reading makes sense. But wouldn't it have been grand if the creditors had headed off this trauma altogether, by refusing to let

Bob Campeau have money when he first went south to get it? Restraint of that kind might have prevented the preposterous deals that made the Eighties the Eighties—and whose repair will make the Nineties the Nineties.

Michael Milken Free at Last!

Tad Friend

May 1991, *Esquire*

Esquire's "Michael Milken Free at Last!" takes the reader behind the scenes of Milken's last days as a free white man. Tad Friend recounts how the so-called genius of junk bonds allowed himself to get eaten alive by the horde of PR flacks, lawyers, and journalists who surrounded him. I especially like Friend's treatment of the press's antics. When was the last time you heard of a **New York Times** *reporter calling another journalist "a psychotic bitch"?*

Manhattan, November 21, 1990: The Sentencing

MICHAEL MILKEN WALKED INTO COURTROOM 318 at exactly 10:00 A.M., and two dozen journalists scrawled "MM looks nervous." That rare banker who had achieved tabloid fame (JUNK BOND KING BEGS FOR MERCY!), Milken had long been written about as a reclusive guru, a vastly rich and vulpine manipulator—but up close he proved merely nervous. And rather humdrum. When he had walked up the courthouse steps in his dull gray suit, the onlookers seemed amazed that this wan figure was the famous Milken. "Hey, junk bond man!" they'd shouted at him, giddily. "Yo, Michael baby!" He didn't look up.

In court now, Milken sought his wife Lori, in the front row, his eyebrows soaring in dismay. Finding her, her white, alarmed face, he made an effort to smile toward her without catching the eye of anyone else in the huge gallery of reporters, lawyers, and epiphany chasers.

Richard Sandler, Milken's childhood friend, personal

lawyer, and self-appointed image guardian, sat beside him at the defense table with a look of dry terror. Stephen Kaufman, the lawyer brought in to ease the contentious final round of plea discussions with the government—discussions that led to Milken's pleading guilty to six counts of false filing, securities fraud, and conspiracy, and his paying $600 million in April 1990—stood with his arms folded, his Mount Rushmore face grave. Arthur Liman, Milken's $450-an-hour lead attorney, formerly the Senate's counsel in the Iran-contra affair and probably the best-known white-collar defense lawyer in the country, stood alone, mulling over his forthcoming plea for clemency. He brooded with his hands clasped behind his back, like a ship's captain in a storm.

When the lawyers began chatting idly, Milken leaned toward Liman and Martin Flumenbaum, another lawyer in Liman's firm, as if they were the most fascinating conversationalists in the world, which they are not. Milken and his attorneys had grown intimate during the four-year investigation; when one of his lawyers had told him a joke about a white-collar criminal quartered with a surly felon (the punch line is, "All right, husband, come up here and suck your wife's cock"), Milken, facing the likelihood of his own imprisonment, managed a game smile.

At the government's table, the federal prosecutors sat poised but expressionless, the very figures of bland moral authority.

In the press box, the rivalrous Kurt Eichenwald of the *New York Times* and Laurie Cohen of the *Wall Street Journal*, who had done so much to shape the public perception of Milken, peered at him like jewelers considering an uncut diamond of enormous wealth.

Then Judge Kimba Wood strode in and everyone stood in sudden silence as she assumed the bench.

The Holy War

Michael Milken, at age forty-four still the most private of men, was about to receive the most publicly awaited verdict in the Wall Street corruption cases. Though he'd pleaded guilty only to minor infractions, Milken was a major figure: As the head of Drexel Burnham Lambert's arrogantly profitable high-yield-bond department, he became famous. When he began raising huge sums of money for hostile—not to say bellicose—takeovers ($1.1 billion for Ron Perelman's acquisition of Revlon, $2.5 billion for Kohlberg Kravis's purchase of Beatrice), he became infamous.

Milken became shorthand for Drexel, and Drexel shorthand for the noxious 1980s. As Phil Donahue said when he did a show with two hundred former Drexel employees: "I mean, you are mostly white, mostly northeastern, Yale-Harvard types. You are mostly Republican. You were raised in Connecticut. You never ride the subway. So who gives a damn about you guys?"

All prominent criminal cases are instinct with the rhetoric of a crusade, but this one became a Holy War, pitting Milken's supporters against the government, against Drexel, against "unfriendly" journalists, against the tidal wash of public opinion. No one was neutral about Michael Milken: He had an elusive, Zelig-like quality that entranced journalists and made him a vessel for the public's hopes and fears. The government pursued him as if he were Al Capone; his lawyers sheltered him as if he were Mother Teresa.

And by largely denying the press access, Milken himself all but disappeared under the weirdly futile barrage of charges and countercharges; it was as if the world's largest armies had crowded into Monaco and begun bopping one another with rolled-up newspapers. Former Drexel managing director Chris Anderson wrote Judge Wood, "We all created him, because Michael the product was so easy to sell. We created an image of mystery, of mastery. Someone larger than life and all-powerful . . . Michael was my product . . . he was [Drexel CEO] Fred Joseph's product . . . and mostly, he was [chief prosecutor] Rudolph Giuliani's product." In his own rambling and emotional eleven-page letter to Judge Wood two weeks before sentencing, Milken wrote, "Much of my life during the past four years has been like a Ping-Pong ball, with every cause on either side of the issues using me as a symbol for their own uses," and pleaded, "let me return to a life of anonymity."

Your view of Milken—and of how he should be sentenced—depended on whether you were one of the few he'd made rich or the many who believed he had subtly impoverished the whole country. Hundreds of Milken's clients and fellow employees wrote supplicatory letters to Judge Wood declaring Milken an angel, the man who funded the American Dream. Steve Wynn, owner of the Golden Nugget Casino and a favored Milken client, once said of his benefactor, "I love him. He is my favorite living human."

But many agreed with columnists like Michael Thomas and Ben Stein that the whole junk-bond market was a fraudulent Ponzi scheme (in which you sell to Peter to pay Paul) that fed America's growing national debt. One California man had written Judge Wood, "My family and I . . . wish to express our desire to see [Milken] hung by his balls until death."

The ordnance numbers alone explained why Milken's story would be the inspiration for, or play an important role in, at least eight books: Milken made well over $2 billion in the 1980s; $550 million from Drexel in 1985 alone. The government subpoenaed over 1.5 million documents from Drexel, which spent over $40 million compiling them. The Securities & Exchange Commission spent at least $4 million and fifty thousand man-hours pursuing the investigation; Milken's chief counsel, Liman's firm of Paul, Weiss, Rifkind, Wharton & Garrison, billed $13 million in the first three years alone, and three other law firms worked on Milken's behalf. Over 150 lawyers were eventually involved in one capacity or another. "This case is like a Chinese menu," says Milken's lawyer Stephen Kaufman. "You don't know what to look at first."

The case gorged itself on animus and deceit. A fairly typical head-butting, chosen almost at random from a lengthy card of fifteen-round bouts, was that between the *Wall Street Journal*'s Laurie Cohen and Michael Armstrong, the lawyer for Milken's brother, Lowell, who had worked with Milken in Beverly Hills and who had also been indicted. Cohen says, "During the first round of plea negotiations between Milken and the government, in January 1989, I was getting out-and-out-lie denials from Michael Armstrong that negotiations were occurring. Armstrong later told me there were situations when it was okay to lie if it would be better for your client."

Armstrong replies, "I don't think I lied to her, but I didn't go out of my way to put her straight. I did later tell her there are circumstances when you have to lie for your client." Not content to leave it there, Armstrong adds, "Laurie Cohen, in my view, was totally in the government's pocket. She had a direct pipeline into the government, and she shamelessly slanted her stories. I think she got conned."

To resolve the Holy War before sentencing, Judge Wood had earlier ordered a rarely held Fatico hearing to examine the pattern of Milken's alleged criminal behavior, a decision the defense hated. "Fatico hearings are for people whose names end in vowels," as one Milken attorney put it, referring to mafiosi. "We began to think that [Wood] wanted more exposure on the case, that she was ambitious." The defense did surprisingly well in the Fatico hearing—Judge Wood found that the government didn't prove any of the three alleged crimes it presented, though it did prove obstruction of justice—and with a probation report favorable to Milken, it felt reason to be hopeful.

The consensus among white-collar defense lawyers, many of whom had crowded the courtroom to see this signal moment in their profession, was that Milken would get three or four years. (The other big Wall Street crooks, Ivan Boesky, Dennis Levine, and Martin Siegel, had gotten, respectively, three years, two years, and two months.)

But the defense—and the government—still saw Wood as a wild card: Pretty and warm outside the courtroom, she emanated chilly rectitude within it. One of the first female partners at a large Manhattan law firm, she had only been appointed a federal judge in 1988 and so had little experience on the bench. The defense team had carefully combed her few opinions for clues about her disposition (and had even looked into the divorce that ended her first marriage, and her happy second marriage to a *Time* columnist). They were worried by her inexperience—one attorney privately called her "amateur hour" after she made a big procedural mistake during the Fatico hearing—but believed her careful and intelligent. They had concluded with a sort of collective shrug that the book on her was fairness. Which meant they had no idea what she'd do.

The Sentencing

Judge Wood, looking customarily austere in her black robe, briskly asked Arthur Liman if he wished to say anything. Liman unlimbered himself and walked to the rostrum, where he canted his knowing, raddled face toward Wood. Though he can muster thunderheads of moral authority, Liman chose to ease into his remarks, blending the statesmanlike and the folksy in the throaty mumble that has earned him the nickname Martha (as in, "Hello, I'm Martha Liman"). "What is Michael Milken really like, not the myth?" he asked, and the ranks of journalists made small peevish sounds among themselves, expecting to hear brazen myth.

Liman touched lightly on Milken's affinity for children, his concern for the sick and the handicapped, his family values, then read a letter from a friend of Milken's about how sweet Milken had been when her daughter, Stacy, suffered brain damage. "Michael not only helped me emotionally, he was involved with Stacy's care and rehabilitation. . . . He was always including her in social and family functions, helping her to relearn her social skills. He was never afraid of appearing foolish if it helped make someone happy." Milken, who had been heaving great sighs, put his left hand to his eyes and began sobbing. The courtroom artists flipped a page and began new sketches.

Jigsaw Man

What Michael Milken is really like was an obsessing puzzle. The best Milken stories—that he kept a chart of his net worth over his bed; that in the early 1970s when he rode the bus to work before dawn he wore a miner's head lamp to read spreadsheets—were myths, and none of the easy formulas quite fit.

Milken was in large part the all-American boy. Born on the Fourth of July, he helped his accountant father prepare tax returns at age ten, became his high school's prom king, and married his childhood sweetheart. He avoids all artificial stimulants and has a collection of Marvel Comics (though his spokesman denies it). Milken became astoundingly wealthy and bought Clark Gable's old house in Encino, California, but he gave his three children only ten dollars a week in allowance and made them read Shel Silverstein's *The Giving Tree*. As his lawyer Richard Sandler says, "Think of Michael's family as *Ozzie and Harriet* to the extreme."

But Milken also had a bit of Elvis in him: His nickname at Drexel was The King, he wore a toupee, he traveled with a bodyguard, he sought to purchase rights to all pictures of himself, and he associated with an excessive number of has-been TV stars. (He appeared with Barbara *I Dream of Jeannie* Eden and Jamie *M*A*S*H* Farr at one fundraiser, and with Dennis *McCloud* Weaver at another; and Henry *Happy Days* Winkler and Monty *Let's Make a Deal* Hall wrote on his behalf to Judge Woods.)

Yet it was as a businessman, of course, that Milken became legend. His salesmanship of the notion that a portfolio of high-yield, or "junk," bonds (bonds issued by small or struggling companies) would earn a higher return than bonds issued by rated companies earned him a devoted clientele of investors and mutual-fund managers and businessmen whose companies prospered because Milken could single-handedly make a market for their bonds. He raised over $100 billion in junk bonds, and by 1986, when junk was at its peak, Drexel made 46 percent of the market.

Milken's focus on work and work alone was extraordinary (one reporter discovered that he couldn't remember the name of his best man or how to spell his wife's middle name). He could decipher a company's spreadsheets as quickly and fluently as a radiologist reading an X-ray, and indeed Milken spoke of himself as a doctor to ailing companies—a lofty metaphor that disguised the grindingly mundane sixteen- to twenty-hour workdays that began at 4:30 A.M. Milken was involved in five hundred phone conversations a day and once testified, alarmingly, that he ate lunch at his X-shaped desk in "from one to five minutes."

It worked. By the end of 1986 Drexel was the Street's most profitable investment bank, with after-tax earnings of $545.5 million. And though his high-yield department numbered over two hundred people, and Drexel as a whole almost ten thousand, for all intents and purposes Michael Milken *was* Drexel. Milken's 1987 compensation of $310 million was 82 percent of the company's operating profit.

The money was insane. Milken's 517 employee partnerships, set up to hold stocks and to trade bonds back and forth between Drexel and the firm's clients, taking a hefty and possibly improper profit each time, made over $2 billion for Milken and his friends in the 1980s, over $1 billion for Milken alone

But also among Milken's multiple personalities was a mystic, a faith healer. He gave his junk-bond pitch with wide-eyed, zoned-out religious fervor, believing he could save small companies that couldn't raise money anywhere else, and he gave $360 million and considerable time and thought to 270 charities. Like many evangelists, he lacked introspection, and was happiest solving the problems of others, whether crippled children or crippled companies. At times he said the United States had made a mistake by lending to Argentina and not to Oakland; at other times he proposed elaborate schemes for refinancing Third World debt. He didn't see the contradiction, because he was less a deep social thinker than a Mr. Fix-it with an M.B.A., a visionary perpetually seeking a vision.

The Sentencing

Arthur Liman read on, his clarion sentiments falling upon a courtroom quiet save for Milken's intermittent sobs. Liman avoided the great conundrum—why, when you earn $530 million a year honestly, must you try to earn another $20 million through chicanery?—and repeatedly portrayed Milken as a man with a social conscience, to distinguish him from Dennis Levine (whom Liman had represented but whose "personal values" he now blithely disparaged to aid his current client) and Ivan Boesky, the ferret-faced arbitrageur famed for his purchase of inside information with suitcases of cash and for his bald motto, Greed is good.

Ivan the Credible

Ivan Boesky, of course, had used the symbol of Mike Milken as shrewdly as anyone in the whole case; when the government announced that Boesky had pleaded guilty on November 14, 1986, subpoenas were on their way to Milken's office in Beverly Hills. Eager to cooperate and reduce his sentence (he paid a fine of $100 million and was later sentenced to three years), Boesky had told the government that Milken was the real insider-trading kingpin. Milken and Drexel strongly denied wrongdoing and hired the most expensive lawyers in the country.

Lowell Milken's lawyer, Michael Armstrong, would later put the defense's theory to Assistant U.S. Attorney John

Carroll—that Boesky was really the kingpin, that he had conned them into thinking he had a lot of information about Milken to get a light sentence, and that the government was going after Milken to justify its lenient treatment of Boesky. Armstrong says Carroll sheepishly replied, "Well, have you ever known anyone to lie about everything?"

Certainly Milken and Drexel were surprised by the government's unwillingness to resolve matters with a consent decree and a modest fine—the traditional disposition of white-collar unseemliness. "There was a venom in this investigation that I've never seen before," says Drexel lawyer Peter Fleming. "The SEC basically told us, 'Go fuck yourself.' the *Wall Street Journal* [which ran numerous stories outlining the government's investigation] was our best source of information."

Milken's lawyers came to focus their anger on Bruce Baird, then chief of securities fraud for New York's Southern District, and a self-described "bad cop" who has said he feels more sympathy for mobsters than insider traders. In the related Princeton/Newport case, defense attorney Jack Arseneault said Baird had told him that he was just using them to go after Drexel: "We have bigger fish to fry, and we will roll over you to get where we want to go." (Baird calls this quote "a fantasy.")

Gary Lynch, then the SEC's enforcement director, suggests that rather than seeking resolution, Drexel was fishing for the government's evidence. Lynch adds that the government was unconciliatory because it had a "very real concern here with destruction of documents." At Milken's sentencing hearing, one trader testified that after being subpoenaed, a nervous Milken turned on a faucet in a bathroom meeting and said to him, "Whatever you need to do, do it"; another testified that when he was gathering records for the government, Milken told him, "If you don't have them, you can't provide them."

Drexel

Early one evening in November 1988, Drexel CEO Fred Joseph was preparing to go to a black-tie dinner in midtown Manhattan. According to a senior Drexel official, as Joseph left the office, the lawyer he most trusted, Tom Curnin, came up to him and said, "I've got to talk to you." They got into a company car, and as their driver skated the fifty blocks through the dark and rainy streets, Curnin told Joseph that the government had convinced two of Milken's traders to testify against him in return for immunity, and he sketched the damage their testimony would do. Curnin also said the government had strong evidence that Milken had engaged in illegal trades with a firm called Solomon Asset Management. "Fred," Curnin said, "Mike did the stuff he said he didn't do."

Fred Joseph and Michael Milken were the two best salesmen at Drexel, and Joseph, a shrewdly gregarious bantam who had fought on the Harvard boxing team, had acted as Milken's public face, explaining Milken's dodgier-looking maneuvers, handling the press's interest in Drexel's exploding profits. For two years Fred and Mike had fought the investigation side by side; friends of both described their relations as a marriage.

But Joseph's conversation with Curnin crystallized his growing doubts. "Fred came to believe that he made one really bad mistake," says a senior Drexel executive. "He trusted the wrong guy. He decided Michael conned him, set him up."

Drexel began serious negotiations. The government insisted that the firm fire Milken and withhold his 1988 compensation. There was furious discussion among Drexel's lawyers and executives about the propriety of firing their economic mainstay—"We've heard nothing for two years but what a great guy he is," as one participant put it, "and now you're going to cut his nuts off"—but Drexel finally agreed that Milken had to go.

The government was equally resolute about the fine: U.S. Attorney Rudolph Giuliani began by demanding $750 million. The government had planned to seek a lower amount, having estimated Drexel's cash reserves at $400 million to $500 million, but a *Wall Street Journal* story by Laurie Cohen put Drexel's reserves at $700 million, so it raised its price (a prosecutor later said privately that Cohen's story had made the government at least $200 million). Drexel reluctantly said it actually had $500 million in reserve, but the government's price stayed high, and the haggling became acrimonious.

According to someone in the room, at one point Bruce Baird said to Joseph, "This is outrageous! You're talking about money and I'm talking about justice!" Joseph replied, "I'm talking about the jobs of people I'm going to have to fire—and you get the same headlines for $200 million."

Milken began phoning Joseph and other Drexel officials to urge them not to settle, suggesting that the bank was really caving in, not to the evidence but to Giuliani's threat to indict Drexel under the controversial Racketeer Influenced and Corrupt Organizations (RICO) Act, originally intended as a weapon against the mob. A RICO indictment would have allowed the government to freeze Drexel's assets, in which case Drexel estimated it would have had to file for bankruptcy within days.

In the course of his rambling, pleading phone calls, Milken repeated a parable about persecution: The government lawyers were the Nazis, and Drexel officials were the good Germans who hadn't stood up for the Jews. Though Milken is famous for never maligning people, he clearly felt Joseph had made him a symbol of the "bad" Drexel to save the "good" Drexel—had made a pragmatic decision to sell him out.

Once the break came, it came fast and ugly. One Milken adviser says bitterly, "Fred Joseph wasn't misled by Michael. He knew what was going on every step of the way, and now he's trying to distance himself. Fred basically convicted Michael—he stabbed him in the back."

Drexel officials say that after the SEC filed its charges against Milken and Drexel in September, Milken's friends and his public relations firm tried to discredit Drexel by directing journalists to employees loyal to Milken who would bad-mouth the firm, and by spreading the canard that Joseph had made a secret deal with the government to plead the company guilty in return for personal immunity. His PR firm denies any such campaign.

On December 21 the government told Drexel that unless it settled it would be indicted at 4:00 P.M. The Drexel board met and, after much debate, concluded that the government's case was only getting stronger, that they couldn't survive a RICO hit, and that they were defending the wrong man. It finally voted sixteen to six to plead guilty to six felony counts and to pay $650 million.

In April 1989 Drexel cut four thousand jobs. In February 1990 it went bankrupt. Drexel managers now wish they'd taken the RICO hit and gone into bankruptcy after the 1988 indictment, rather than sinking into the shabby penury that finds them with Chinese take-out menus in their "reception area" (two chairs). As one executive puts it, "If you're on a sinking ship surrounded by flesh-eating sharks and you have an insufficiently provisioned lifeboat, you take the lifeboat. Two weeks later when you're sunburned and dehydrated and you're sinking anyway, you're going to wish you'd jumped in with the sharks. We would have lost anyway—Michael would have pleaded and hung us out to dry—but we would have felt better about it. It would have been the right thing to do."

The Plea

After Drexel settled, the government gave Milken a "drop dead" date in March 1989, by which time he had to plead guilty to two counts and pay a fine of about $250 million or be indicted. A week after the deadline Arthur Liman called acting U.S. Attorney Benito Romano and said, "We'll take your last offer of two counts." (The call was an unexpected and almost clandestine capitulation that other Milken advisers strongly denied or were unaware of until very recently.) But the government's case had gotten stronger since the last discussions and the indictment was about to come down. Without even looking at the other prosecutors in the room, Romano said calmly, "The time has passed."

On March 29, Milken was indicted under RICO on ninety-eight counts of securities fraud, largely on allegations having to do with Ivan Boesky and Princeton/Newport. His brother, Lowell, and trader Bruce Newberg were also indicted. Bruce Baird put Milken's arraignment photo up on his bulletin board, using it as a mental dart board.

But by the time the next round of discussions began, in late 1989, Baird had left the government for private practice and Milken was facing the threat of a superseding indictment. The superseder would have doubled the number of illegal relationships Milken was accused of from two to four. The number of counts would also have increased, and one Milken adviser says, the realization began to sink in that there was "a very high risk of being convicted of more than five or six counts if you're indicted on over a hundred."

Two factors finally convinced Milken to settle; both involved his relatives. The first was that FBI agents visited Milken's grandfather, Louis Zax, who is ninety-two and has two hearing aids, to question him about stock transactions. Zax was badly shaken by the encounter, and after Milken heard the news he turned to a friend and said, "This is never going to stop, is it?" (One reporter who had obviously been following Milken had earlier called up a woman named Jonie Noah and said, "We saw you hugging Michael Milken and if you tell us about your relationship with him, we'll protect you." "I'm his sister," she said. The reporter rang off quietly.)

The second factor was Lowell. Michael Armstrong says, "Lowell was in that indictment to put pressure on Michael, and when I said this to the prosecutors they smiled and looked away—they didn't argue." The government had told Liman and Kaufman that they wouldn't link the dropping of Lowell's indictment to Michael's plea bargain (on the theory that if Lowell was guilty enough to indict, he should have been guilty enough to prosecute). Then the prosecutors realized that Michael wouldn't plead and leave Lowell to fight alone, and they reversed themselves. Milken's lawyers accuse Attorney General Richard Thornburgh himself of decreeing Lowell a bargaining chip. "It smacks of hostage taking, of *Sophie's Choice,*" one says angrily.

His lawyers told Milken that if he accepted the six-count plea, he was facing three to five years, possibly much less. All Milken's family members urged him not to settle, and Lowell was especially vehement, vowing to fight on with his brother. But Milken's friends suggest that once he sold himself on the idea that he was saving Lowell, on the idea of being a martyr, he felt he could accept the plea. Still, the decision wasn't made easily. A friend who was with Milken when he decided to settle says, "It was like watching a person have stomach surgery without anesthesia."

When Milken finally agreed to a plea late on April 20,

1990, an hour before the government's threatened superseding indictment, he destroyed himself in the court of public opinion and left many of his supporters feeling betrayed. But his true disciples—and his PR firm—kept the faith.

All the King's Lawyers and All the King's Men

Milken had always valued privacy and had mistrusted journalists; as one adviser puts it, he "made a conscious effort to be rude to the press." But he slowly came to realize that his decision to take the high-yield unit from New York to Beverly Hills in 1978 and to avoid publicity until it was thrust upon him by Ivan Boesky was a huge mistake. David Vise, who covered the story for the *Washington Post*, says, "Michael was really hurt by the decision not to talk to the press until it was too late—it fueled the basic journalistic instinct that if people refuse to talk they must have something pretty significant to hide. The game was over, and the rest was damage control."

The government sought to increase that damage. In fact, certain government officials appeared to have quite shrewdly—if illegally—fed the press details of the investigation. From the day Boesky pleaded through 1988, Milken's worsening image was molded by the detailed stories about the government's investigation that James Stewart and Daniel Hertzberg wrote for the *Wall Street Journal*. "It is the *Journal* more than any other publication," says another reporter who covered the story, "that built the story line of this trial into 'Is the government going to catch the bad guys?' " (Stewart and other reporters suggest that many of their sources were not in the government, and that the defense knew it.)

The government was especially canny when it highlighted Milken's 1985 salary on the indictment's second page. That one huge number became Milken's tar baby. As one reporter notes, "Americans don't have sympathy for anyone who earns $550 million a year."

In April 1988, far too late, Milken and his lawyers hired a top-notch public relations firm: Robinson, Lake, Lerer & Montgomery. Robinson, Lake was helpful with reporters' queries, and many journalists came to like and trust Ken Lerer, who handled Milken's account, even though, at $275 an hour, he usually got more out of their conversations than they did. Lerer is personable and self-effacing, with trustworthy spaniel eyes, the sort of person even his detractors say would be your friend if he weren't being paid to be your friend. Lerer, who dealt with over five hundred requests for Milken interviews in two and a half years, felt boxed in by Milken's strategic decision not to talk about the case and by his previous silence. "If you told the press Michael was giving a speech, they wrote that he was trying to improve his image," Lerer says, "and if you didn't tell them he was speaking, they wrote that he was a crazy recluse."

Lerer downplays his firm's role in the case, saying Robinson, Lake mostly answered reporters' questions, but clearly the firm was doing *something* that ran up monthly bills that were regularly over $100,000. Thematically, Robinson, Lake sought to portray the innocent, persecuted Michael Milken who had become a crusade for his friends and his lawyers. Many reporters questioned this Peter Pan image: Should, for instance, the sixfold increase in Milken's charitable gifts after the investigation began, from $31 million in 1986 to $205 million in 1987, be seen as the increasing generosity of a philanthropist who had established his foundations in 1982— or as image polishing?

Connie Bruck, who wrote an unflattering book about Milken called *The Predators' Ball*, says of the PR effort: "They were clever. They needed to humanize him because he was seen as this robotic figure, so they went with the kids theme and the philanthropy, which he does believe in. They re-created him along the lines that had been there, which is why they could get so emotional about him, because it was Michael—only, it hadn't been Michael before."

"Robinson, Lake also focused reporters on questions of process," says *Newsday*'s John Riley, "questions about the use of RICO, the use of leaks, about the credibility of Ivan Boesky, about Rudy Giuliani's personal ambitions." (Giuliani later used his crime-busting reputation as a springboard for his unsuccessful mayoral race in New York.) Robinson, Lake seemed to be following the old legal saw: If you have the facts, argue the facts; if you have the law, argue the law; if you have neither, attack the other guys. All the other guys.

As a result, the firm was often at the center of controversy. Robinson, Lake's first big decision concerned how to handle *The Predators' Ball*, published in June 1988. Bruck, a disarmingly solicitous reporter, painted a damaging portrait of Drexel as the Cosa Nostra of the business world and of Milken as a sort of corrupt idiot savant. Drexel, after wavering, as it did when faced with nearly any decision during this period, decided to ignore the book.

But Ken Lerer and his partner Linda Robinson came to Drexel and, one Drexel official recalls, said that "they had had a meeting with the *Journal* about the book without consulting us and were calling reviewers to point out the errors." Several reviewers wrote about the clumsy attempt to influence them, and the *Journal*'s front-page story increased rather than dampened the controversy. "Going to war over the book made it a best seller," a senior Drexel executive says. (The book was briefly a *New York Times* best seller.)

In early 1990, Lerer, exasperated by a series of virulently anti-Milken columns Ben Stein had written for *Barron's*, leaked to the *New York Post* and other newspapers an obsequious letter that Stein had written Milken in November 1988 asking for a job as "an in-house analyst of the fairness of the deals you put together." Lerer's well-taken point was that Stein had a clear conflict of interest, but some journalists who received Lerer's press kit on Stein, complete with a description of a controversial article Stein had written about Joan Rivers, thought Lerer had gone too far.

Stein, while regretting having written Milken, says, "I'm unaware of any comparable thing to attacking a journalist in this way—even when I was working for Nixon, we never thought of it." Stein also says that at the time, Lerer denied leaking his letter. Lerer, somewhat amazingly, doesn't deny his denial.

According to several reporters, the firm also encouraged them to pursue stories that would discredit witnesses cooperating against Milken (such unsubstantiated rumors as one trader's alleged insider trading with Hollywood producer Jon Peters and another's alleged cocaine problem). Several Drexel employees and businessmen who wrote to the court on Milken's behalf say that the firm offered to edit their letters. According to a former Robinson, Lake employee, the firm also ghostwrote Milken-is-a-good-guy op-ed pieces by businessman Reginald Lewis and *Spin* magazine chairman Stephen Swid, among others. Two Robinson, Lake employees also say the firm keeps files on journalists containing stories they have written and a rating of perceived "friendliness." (Lerer strongly denies these charges.)

Ironically, the one event that came to symbolize Milken's PR campaign wasn't Robinson, Lake's doing: The week after the SEC filed charges against Drexel and Milken, in September 1988, Milken took seventeen hundred underprivileged children to a Mets game at Shea Stadium. The press was not informed, but New York's chancellor of education happened to mention Milken's plans at a Drexel breakfast meeting where reporters were present. The resulting pictures and publicity haunt Milken to this day. As one Milken lawyer says— while trying to shift the blame to Drexel's corporate public relations team—"It was seen as an attempt by Milken to make himself into a hot-dog vendor, a common person. It was a disaster."

Robinson, Lake's strategy with newspapers was to begin allowing cautious access to Milken so that reporters could get to know the man they were assailing. The firm arranged off-the-record meetings with reporters and editors at the *New York Times*, the *Los Angeles Times*, and the *Washington Post*, and eight on-the-record profiles, with the caveats that Milken wouldn't talk about the case and his lawyers would vet all quotes. Reporters found the mystery man sweet-tempered and appealing—when he wasn't eerily mechanical and Stepford-like. Yet if they emerged liking Milken they felt uneasy. "Journalists are most often on the side of prosecutors, trashing the high and the mighty," says *Business Week*'s Chris Welles. "You always look better when you're saying, 'Go get those bastards.' It probably hurt me that I was taking a more dovish line—people wonder, 'Have you sold out to this guy?'"

At one time or another, almost every reporter on the case was considered an apologist for the government or the defense. Kurt Eichenwald, the *New York Times*'s tightly wound Wall Street-beat reporter for the last two years, was often accused of bedding down with the defense. Eichenwald and Connie Bruck had a brief conversation in the hallway during a break in Milken's Fatico hearing that flared into a debate about how to cover the story. Bruck said the testimony of a Milken trader was damaging to Milken, and Eichenwald said that what the trader had described was not proof of Milken's obstructing justice.

"I can't believe you'd be so naive as to think there would be a manipulation and Milken wouldn't be behind it," Bruck said.

"I guess that's the difference between coming in with your mind made up and coming in to listen to the evidence," Eichenwald said.

Bruck walked away, then slammed Eichenwald in the *New York Post*, declaring that Arthur Liman could have written his stories.

Eichenwald says, "If you try to stay in the middle, it's very difficult—you get criticized from both sides. The only person who really knows my opinion is my wife." In fact, though Eichenwald's stories were relatively sympathetic to Milken, they were within the range of objective reporting. His problem, really, was that the *New York Times* was beaten by the *Wall Street Journal* or the *Washington Post* on almost every development since the case began. Because the government triggered all the developments, Eichenwald was, by default, seen as close to the defense.

Eichenwald's relations with the *Journal*'s Laurie Cohen were deeply fractured by their different sources and their temperaments. Eichenwald is hermeneutic and self-examining, fond of posing rhetorical questions and then saying they're unanswerable as posed, while Cohen has the instincts of a Doberman. During a previous trial, Cohen had the *Journal*'s lawyer call the judge to evict Eichenwald from her chambers, where he had gone as a pool reporter. Eichenwald, understandably furious, came over to Cohen and, she says, called her "a psychotic bitch." (Eichenwald says he asked, "Are you psychotic?")

Cohen and Robinson, Lake were even more frankly confrontational. Cohen says, "Basically, every time I wrote a story they complained. It was unceasing. They kept making it seem like Kurt Eichenwald was the smart reporter and I was the dumb one. But I feel most of my reporting was borne out by the results."

Lerer says that Cohen was used by the government to pressure Milken, and points in particular to the eighteen stories Cohen wrote about the government's investigation that said a superseding indictment would be filed soon. In February 1990 Lerer wrote to the *Journal*'s managing editor, Norman Pearlstine, with statistics on the number of times the *Journal* had run stories using "blind" sources about the superseding indictment. Lerer admonished Pearlstine for "continuing to provide a forum for those who want to hurt Michael Milken." Pearlstine's deputy managing editor, Paul Steiger, wrote back, "You are wasting your client's money and our time."

The Sentencing

Liman concluded his speech with a "prayer to the court" for a sentence of community service and sat down. Milken clasped Liman's arm thankfully. Both knew that Judge Wood had already made her decision and that Liman's hour-long speech was pointless in that regard; this last artillery round was lobbed toward press notebooks.

Judge Wood, who had been nodding throughout Liman's remarks, said, "Thank you, Mr. Liman, for a very fine presentation," and asked Milken if he had any comments. Milken stood and, in a choked voice, said, "What I did violated not just the law but all of my own principles and values. I deeply regret it and will for the rest of my life. I am truly sorry."

Judge Wood, looking down compassionately, said, "Thank you, Mr. Milken. Your letter was a very moving one, as was the letter from your wife, Lori, and I thank you for writing to the court." One defense lawyer in the courtroom, speaking in the standard litigator's lexicon of sexual threat, says he was enormously heartened: "If you're going to fuck somebody, you don't look them in the eye and thank them by name for their letter."

Assistant U.S. Attorney Jess Fardella then briefly and unemotionally addressed the court, admitting Milken's virtues but asking for "substantial incarceration."

Fardella sat down and Judge Wood, after taking a breath, began to speak in her pearly, authoritative tones. Milken was hunkered down in his chair, but his lawyers leaned forward as if Wood were whispering, alert to every nuance—which meant that their hopes veered wildly. They rose when Wood said she wouldn't sentence Milken as "a verdict on a decade of greed"; sank when she said, "You may have committed only subtle crimes not because you were not disposed to any criminal behavior but because you were willing to commit only crimes that were unlikely to be detected"; but rose again when she said, "I have given considerable thought to whether a sentence of lengthy community service would be an adequate penalty here."

Drexel lawyer Peter Fleming, a spectator, says, "I was thinking two years, six years, two years, depending on where she was in her remarks."

Her voice still calm, Judge Wood said she was going to impose a sentence with both a prison term and community service to deter others from following Milken's path. She continued, almost casually, "Because changes are likely to take place in community programs between today and the day you are released from prison, it would be inappropriate to select a particular program for you today." The defense shot each other unhappy glances. This was going to be a severe rebuke.

Judge Wood paused, then said, "Mr. Milken, please rise."

Though Liman usually stands with his clients to hear the sentence, he made an intuitive decision that Milken, who had been seen as overprotected for four years, would want to stand alone. But he had to give Milken an arm up and steady him with a hand to the back as he faced the bench, shaking.

Judge Wood, glancing at her notes, said, "I sentence you to a total of ten years in prison"—there were gasps in the audience—"and I also sentence you to three years of . . . full-time community service."

Milken sat down, and in the clamor turned to his lawyers and asked what had happened—in shock, he didn't know what he'd gotten. "I thought she had misspoken," says Michael Armstrong, who was sitting behind the defense table. "My mind groped for any explanations."

A huge cordon of gawkers formed on the courthouse steps, six boom mikes and four TV crews hovered around the crowd, all waiting for Milken to emerge. Journalists, shivering in their overcoats and shaking their heads in astonishment, bounced leads off one another: The most popular seemed to be, "The eighties are over." Half an hour later Ken Lerer came out and, almost offhandedly, murmured to a few reporters that there would be no statement. Milken, vanishing as usual, had gone out the back.

The Aftermath

Curiously, Judge Wood's findings comforted both sides: Kurt Eichenwald felt she had justified his approach; so did Laurie Cohen. "The government can say he got ten years," one Milken adviser points out, "and the defense can say he was basically acquitted of the Fatico charges. It's an incredible ending. You still can't find any common ground." (In February, Wood ruled that the total loss to investors from Milken's crimes was only $318,000, and recommended that Milken serve thirty-six to forty months before being paroled. The *Times* viewed it as a vindication of Eichenwald's analysis of the intent of Wood's sentence and ran a story on its front page; the *Journal* played it small on page B4.)

Following the sentencing, the judge's picture appeared in the *New York Times*, and friends flocked to tell her how pretty she looked, then cast around for a graceful way to say, "What a great sentence." She turned down more than fifteen interview requests in the first week alone. "It might never be appropriate to comment on a case like this," Wood says. Her name was frequently mentioned for a vacancy on the Second Circuit Court of Appeals, and her cockiest supporters speculated that she would eventually replace Justice Sandra Day O'Connor on the Supreme Court.

The sentence left the government's lawyers pleasantly shocked. "I never in my wildest dreams thought we'd be as successful as we were," says Bruce Baird. "The case caught the imagination of the times and had a maximum deterrent value." Though they believed Judge Wood had given the stiff sentence to encourage Milken to cooperate (if he did, Wood said, she would consider reducing his prison time), the prosecutor's office quickly spawned a joke about Saddam Hussein looking into a mirror and saying, "Mirror, mirror, on the wall, who's the meanest of them all?" The mirror answers, "Qaddafi," and Hussein runs out and tells his advisers to slaughter a million lambs. Hussein asks again, and the mirror answers, "Arafat," so Hussein runs out and tells his advisers to slaughter a million Kurds. He questions the mirror a third time, then runs out and asks his advisers, "Who Kimba Wood?"

On March 3, Milken entered the minimum security camp in Pleasanton, California, where he shares 360 square feet with three other men, earns up to 40 cents a day, and is forbidden to wear his toupee. Though Milken still had an estimated $1.5 billion fortune, much of it was expected to leak away as he settled the more than fifty civil suits against him. The $400 million Milken paid the government to reimburse civil-suit plaintiffs was invested in treasury notes, earning $7\frac{1}{4}$ percent—surely the last investment vehicle Milken would have chosen. In the final irony, Drexel was planning to sue Milken, and Milken, who is still owed his 1988 compensation (roughly $100 million), may well sue back. The lucrative marriage of Milken and Joseph was headed for a lucrative divorce—lucrative for the lawyers, at least.

The mood among Milken's lawyers, who were widely criticized for not having strong-armed Milken into pleading earlier and on more favorable terms, was by turns funereal and outraged. "Unless we're the biggest bunch of boobs that ever came down the pike," Stephen Kaufman says with restrained anger, "we wouldn't have pleaded a man to get a ten-year sentence." He adds musingly, "Lowell [a hostage]—a wasted bullet . . . Michael's good deeds—nothing. . . . It's a tremendous disappointment. What the hell do you offer as a lawyer? You offer judgment."

Shortly before he went to jail, Milken had another in a series of meetings with prosecutors. Instead of naming criminals in the S&L industry, Milken launched into a wandering philippic about why the debt his name had been synonymous with was good for America. Afterward, back at Arthur Liman's law firm, Milken trailed aimlessly after his attorneys. His trench coat was unbuttoned; he had put on weight. His head was down and he scuffed his feet dejectedly through the carpet. He looked less like the top of the pyramid, the most notorious and powerful businessman in the country, the symbol of a decade, than like a small boy kept after school. "Everyone else gets to move on to the rest of their lives except him," says a close friend. "He gets to go to jail and think about what it all means."

Sullied Solly

Michael Siconolfi
and Laurie P. Cohen

August 19, 1991, the *Wall Street Journal*

The Treasury auction scandal at Salomon Brothers was the capper to the Gaga Years and the incident that toppled John Gutfreund, the biggest swinging dick, to use Salomon lingo. Hardly anyone shed a tear for him, not even at Salomon.

JOHN H. GUTFREUND's thirty-eight-year career at Salomon Brothers Inc. ended with two calls from the Federal Reserve Bank of New York.

On Thursday afternoon, Mr. Gutfreund, a legendary Wall Street survivor, was still insisting he would ride out his firm's unfolding treasury-bidding scandal. In meetings that day with top Salomon executives, Mr. Gutfreund's message was clear: He planned to tough it out. Nestled in his elegant forty-third-floor office overlooking the Hudson River, he told Salomon executives: "A lot of people are upset, the stock's down big, but we'll work our way out of this."

But then came the calls from powerful New York Fed President E. Gerald Corrigan, one on Thursday night and one early Friday morning. Mr. Corrigan was furious about Salomon's admissions that it repeatedly violated rules at the Treasury's multibillion-dollar note auctions. He demanded that Mr. Gutfreund take immediate action.

He got it. Less than six hours after the second call, Mr. Gutfreund offered to resign as Salomon's chairman and chief executive and Thomas W. Strauss offered to resign as president. Yesterday, amid new sanctions levied by the Treasury Department, the Salomon Inc. board accepted their resignations along with that of Vice Chairman John W. Meriwether in an attempt to stanch the worst scandal in the big investment bank's eighty-one-year history. Billionaire investor Warren Buffett, looking to protect his 16 percent Salomon stake, took the reins as interim chairman and chief executive. In his first move yesterday, Mr. Buffett named Deryck C. Maughan, an eight-year Salomon veteran recently based in Tokyo, as chief operating officer.

For the sixty-one-year-old Mr. Gutfreund, the week's events cap one of the swiftest falls for a leading Wall Street chief executive. Just a few weeks ago, Salomon was reveling in record six-months earnings, driven largely by profits from bond trading. But Wall Street executives say it was Mr. Gutfreund's hubris that led to his downfall and to the scandal that has crippled the firm he epitomized, which he once boasted was "the greatest trading organization the world has ever known." The swagger that made Salomon one of the most feared trading powers on Wall Street may evaporate with Mr. Gutfreund's departure.

At Mr. Buffett's first meeting with Salomon employees, he suggested the investment bank should take fewer risks. In a pep talk to about one hundred Salomon managing directors in the firm's thirty-ninth-floor conference room Friday evening, Mr. Buffett said any action by Salomon even approaching impropriety won't be tolerated. "Anything not only on the line, but near the line, will be called out," a senior managing director said Mr. Buffett told them.

For Salomon, the tough times are only beginning. The embattled investment bank is struggling to reassure nervous creditors. Securities firms such as Salomon borrow heavily to fund their trading and other activities, so a funding crisis is potentially devastating. More than $1.1 billion of Salomon's commercial paper, or short-term IOUs, is coming due in the next few weeks.

Salomon can turn to a $2 billion backup line of credit from banks led by Citibank and Bank of America. But major credit-rating agencies said late last week they may downgrade Salomon's $7 billion in long-term debt and $7.7 billion in commercial paper, an action that would increase Salomon's borrowing costs.

Yesterday morning, just as the Salomon Inc. board meeting began, the Treasury Department barred Salomon from bidding at further Treasury auctions until "appropriate steps are taken to address irregularities, and pending the results of ongoing investigations." A few hours later, after Mr. Buffett was formally voted chairman—and after several phone conversations between him and Treasury Secretary Nicholas Brady—the Treasury reduced the scope of Salomon's suspension and said the firm could continue to bid at auctions, but only for its own account. This damages Salomon's power as a bond firm by prohibiting it from buying Treasury securities at auctions on behalf of clients.

Says a Salomon Brothers executive: "We're not out of the woods at all."

Salomon faces other major hurdles. Government regulators promise a top-to-bottom investigation of all of Salomon's trading activities. Defections are sure to rock the firm, as bonuses are threatened. Salomon will have to set aside reserves for possible substantial government fines and for potential civil liability from burgeoning investor lawsuits. That could wipe out some or all the firm's record six-month earnings this year of $451 million.

Mr. Gutfreund, a one-time bond trader, kept his tough-guy image to the end. Late Friday, after formally offering to resign, Mr. Gutfreund, dressed nattily in his trademark dark suit and white shirt, told top executives at a closed-door meeting: "I'm not apologizing for anything to anybody. Apologies don't mean [expletive]. What happened, happened."

The same arrogance that enabled Mr. Gutfreund to build Salomon into the dominant force in the $2.3 trillion Treasury securities market also led to his becoming ensnared in a government trap that became his undoing. The seeds of his demise were sown shortly after the Treasury's May 1991 auction of $12.26 billion of two-year notes. Within days of the auction, institutions caught in a "squeeze" complained to both the Securities and Exchange Commission and the Treasury that they believed Salomon had cornered the market in the notes, grabbing much more than the 35 percent limit to which it was entitled at the auction.

In the wake of those complaints, government officials carefully laid out a plan of attack for uncovering potential wrongdoing by Salomon.

In a series of conference calls the week after the auction,

officials of the SEC, the Justice Department, the Treasury and the Federal Reserve agreed that rather than informing Salomon of their concerns, they would quietly monitor trading in the new two-year Treasury notes. These officials agreed that Salomon shouldn't, under any circumstances, be told that it was under investigation.

For the next three weeks, officials of the SEC, working with Treasury and the Justice Department, pieced together how they believed Salomon might have cornered the market. Because the agencies didn't want to let on that they were investigating Salomon, they waited until the securities bought at auction went through a New York-based clearing firm. With records subpoenaed from that firm, they could retrace the commitments Salomon had made to clients before the auction occurred and the delivery of those securities in the after-market.

By mid-June, suspicious regulators sent subpoenas for documents to about five Salomon clients. They quickly noticed a discrepancy in at least one case. One large New York firm that is a Salomon client appeared to have sold back to Salomon some $500 million of notes soon after the auction. That meant that Salomon itself had bought far more than the 35 percent of the two-year note issue to which it was entitled.

Salomon was only notified that it was under formal investigation by the SEC and Justice Department during the last week of June, when it received subpoenas for documents and trading records.

Martin Lipton, a founding partner of the elite New York law firm of Wachtell, Lipton, Rosen & Katz, was immediately contacted by Mr. Gutfreund and told about the subpoenas. Mr. Lipton, working with Wachtell partner Lawrence Pedowitz, a former top prosecutor in the U.S. attorney's office in New York, quickly determined that if the SEC and Justice Department were focusing on the May auction, the Wachtell lawyers should undertake to learn everything the government was looking at, too.

After the July 4 holiday, the Wachtell attorneys began interviewing each of the traders and clerks on Salomon's government-bond desk in its cavernous trading floor in the World Trade Center here.

Paul Mozer and Thomas Murphy, the desk's two top traders, who were both managing directors, hired their own lawyers.

Salomon hasn't released details of the internal investigation. But according to individuals familiar with the report, Wachtell concluded that Messrs. Mozer and Murphy had, on at least five occasions, violated bidding rules at Treasury auctions. The most recent violation, the lawyers concluded, occurred in the May auction. Lawyers for Messrs. Mozer and Murphy declined comment.

Salomon has disclosed that it violated government bidding rules in at least four Treasury-note auctions in the past eight months. The firm admitted that it had submitted bids in the names of customers who hadn't authorized it to do so, and repeatedly violated Treasury rules that bar anyone from buying more than 35 percent of a Treasury issue at an auction. Yesterday, Salomon fired Mr. Mozer, whom the firm paid $10 million last year, and Mr. Murphy.

Its most damaging admission, though, was that Messrs. Gutfreund, Strauss, and Meriwether were told in April that Salomon had made an illegal bid in a Treasury-note auction sale, but didn't report the wrongdoing to the government until last week.

Salomon conceded last week that just before a Treasury auction in February, one of the fired managing directors—believed to be Mr. Mozer—persuaded a customer to play a "practical joke" on a Salomon employee. As a result, Salomon submitted a phony $1 billion unauthorized bid in the name of a customer, purchased the securities, but never told the Treasury about the incident.

Mr. Mozer apparently realized the end was near in late April. At a news conference yesterday, Mr. Buffett said that Mr. Mozer at that time received a copy of a letter from a regulator seeking information from a Salomon client about a discrepancy in bids in connection with a February auction. Although the government didn't have any knowledge of wrongdoing at that time, Mr. Mozer was apparently concerned enough to report another unauthorized bid to Mr. Meriwether, who in turn discussed the problem with Messrs. Gutfreund and Strauss.

Government regulators were shocked and angered by the wrongdoing admitted by Salomon, which has tarnished the integrity of the $2.3 trillion Treasury market. One government official fumes about the "level of arrogance." He says it is shocking that Salomon "could do it at the February auction, learn about it in April, not tell us, and do it again in May."

But on top of that, Salomon's strategy of beating the government to the punch by publicly disclosing wrongdoing before the government could complete its investigation further angered regulators.

Mr. Lipton phoned the SEC, the Justice Department, the Treasury and the Fed on the morning of August 9, told officials at those agencies of the general conclusions of the Salomon internal report and agreed to meet the following Wednesday.

But the same day, Salomon released a statement to the media saying it was under investigation in connection with its submission of bids in certain Treasury auctions.

On Wednesday, Salomon supplied additional details to the government based on the conclusions of its internal report. The actual report itself wasn't shared. Government officials were furious. The amount of wrongdoing that the internal report found went well beyond what Wachtell had previously disclosed. Indeed, the SEC, the Fed and Justice hadn't any idea of the February "practical joke" or of the failure of Messrs. Gutfreund, Strauss, and Meriwether to do anything about it.

According to attorneys with knowledge of the investigation, Wachtell was worried that damaging and misleading information might be conveyed to the press by government lawyers. Wachtell was concerned that if information was going to get out, it should reach the public with Salomon's own spin. Wachtell also hoped that the appearance of full disclosure to the public would help it avoid a long, drawn-out investigation and constant publicity, as occurred during the Drexel investigation that began in 1986 and ended only last year.

Messrs. Mozer and Murphy are understood to differ sharply with the official Salomon version of events, claiming that in certain instances, customers had authorized the use of their names for purposes of bidding. The two apparently also reject the idea that Salomon led a market squeeze in May. They will likely tell their stories to government officials before too long.

Mr. Gutfreund's downfall is particularly ironic since he often boasted that his firm was untouched by Wall Street's insider-trading scandal. He was one of the most vocal critics of Drexel Burnham Lambert Inc. and Michael Milken, its fallen junk-bond king.

Only a month ago, fresh from record six-month earnings, Salomon scored a significant coup but alienated rival Merrill Lynch & Co. by snatching the lead role in Time Warner's stock offering from Merrill Lynch after a secret meeting between Mr. Gutfreund and Time Warner Chairman Steven J. Ross.

Nor had Mr. Gutfreund made many new friends in recent years. Gossip columnists regularly poked fun at Mr. Gutfruend and his second wife, Susan, a former flight attendant, for their extravagant society parties. Salomon and Mr. Gutfreund also were hurt by the firm's depiction in the best-selling book *Liar's Poker*, which chronicled the bawdy antics of some Salomon traders. At Salomon's 1990 annual meeting, Mr. Gutfreund admitted that the book had made the firm "a laughing-stock" and caused tension with clients. But, he added, "We have overcome that by doing our job well."

The biggest blow to the firm may not be the loss of Mr. Gutfreund or even the easygoing Mr. Strauss. Rather, Salomon executives are worried about defections stemming from the resignation of the forty-four-year-old Mr. Meriwether, who ran the firm's highly profitable bond-arbitrage group.

These high-tech traders employ rigorous mathematical methods to make huge bets on tiny price discrepancies between securities. Mr. Meriwether's close-knit group was thrust into the spotlight earlier this year when it was disclosed that Lawrence Hilibrand, a thirty-one-year-old managing director in the group, made $23 million in salary and bonus last year. (Mr. Meriwether made about $10 million last year, people familiar with the firm say.)

The debate over Mr. Meriwether's fate boiled over Friday, when the Salomon Brothers board met. At the board's behest, Messrs. Gutfreund, Strauss, and Meriwether left the room, and the board began discussing their futures. "Is John out?" one board member asked. "Absolutely," was the reply. "Is Tommy out?" "Absolutely." But they disagreed about Mr. Meriwether.

While a majority of the board members wanted Mr. Meriwether to resign, others argued that he should be given a chance to defend himself and stay on in a limited capacity, given the money he earned for the firm.

Yesterday, Mr. Meriwether's opponents won out and Mr. Meriwether tendered his resignation. But he insisted he shouldn't be held responsible, even though he directly oversaw the activities of Messrs. Mozer and Murphy. "When I learned of their improper conduct, I immediately reported what I knew to the appropriate senior officers of the firm and to our inside counsel, and I concurred in the decision that they would promptly notify the regulatory authorities," Mr. Meriwether said in a statement.

Privately, Salomon insiders say Mr. Meriwether was fuming. On Friday, he told associates he objected to "being joined at the hip" with Messrs. Gutfreund and Strauss. In his statement, Mr. Meriwether said: "I am confident that the internal and governmental reviews of the situation will confirm that I acted properly at all times, but I believe that my resignation today is in the best interests of the firm."

At a crowded news conference yesterday afternoon, Mr. Buffett made clear that he wouldn't be running Salomon for long. "I do not want this job to last any longer than necessary," he said.

"The most important job we have is to come clean in an aggressive way" to regulators, Mr. Buffett said. He added: "My job is to clean up the sins of the past and capitalize on the enormous attributes that this firm has."

Mr. Buffett conceded that Salomon's freewheeling, aggressive style probably contributed to its current difficulties. He said that style would be toned down. "There were aspects of the culture that could have contributed to that," Mr. Buffett said. "[It is] what some might call macho, some might call cavalier."

He said the "behavior and goals" of the top officials will change. "Do I think everyone will get the message? No," Mr.

Buffett said. But he said those people will " be out" of the firm
quickly. "I intend to set an example that people will take
quite seriously."

Right now, Salomon's biggest hurdle is to convince customers and creditors that it is worthy of keeping their trust
and that it is a creditworthy institution. It must also persuade
the Federal Reserve Bank of New York that it deserves to
maintain its designation as one of the forty primary dealers
allowed to trade directly with the Fed.

Losing its primary dealership would be a major blow.
That's because many institutional investors will only do business with a primary dealer when buying and selling U.S.
government and other securities. The New York Fed is considering penalties ranging from temporarily suspending its
trading relationship with Salomon to revoking Salomon's primary dealership and forcing it to reapply. With the central
bank's credibility on the line, some on Wall Street believe the
Fed will be forced to make an example of the firm.

The Treasury's suspension of Salomon from bidding for
customers at auctions may give rivals a rare opportunity to
make inroads into Salomon's long-standing relationships
with some of the world's biggest investors.

Salomon's Treasury bond desk is crucial to many of its
other businesses. For instance, Treasury securities are the key
to many of the sophisticated financial transactions—such as
swaps, futures and options—in which Salomon is considered a
leader.

Like other securities firms, Salomon funds its huge trading
positions with a combination of equity, long-term debt, commercial paper and bank borrowings. Salomon, say analysts, is
vulnerable because of its heavy reliance on commercial paper,
with $7.7 billion of such debt now outstanding worldwide.
Salomon must refinance $1.1 billion of that within the next
two weeks.

"Rolling over" that $1.1 billion, say analysts and U.S.
officials, will be the first big test of what Salomon's creditors
now think of the firm.

John G. Macfarlane III, Salomon's thirty-seven-year-old
treasurer, is confident Salomon can deal with the situation,
even if buyers balk. "Were we not to roll over any of the

outstanding commercial paper, we would have no difficulty funding all of our assets, because we have adequate alternative sources of funds," he says. In stages, he says, the firm would borrow against unencumbered securities it currently owns, which amount to $9.3 billion in market value; utilize bank lines that "have been reconfirmed with most of our major U.S. lenders" and draw down the $2 billion commercial paper backup funding that the firm has never used.

If all else failed, Salomon could begin selling off assets, 71 percent of which consist of highly liquid U.S. Treasury securities, U.S. federal agency securities, and debt issued by major foreign governments such as Japan and Germany.

The strength of Salomon's liquidity management, says Mr. Macfarlane, rests in its diversity of instruments, maturities, currencies and lenders. "We're in good shape; from a liquidity standpoint, I don't think we're vulnerable," says Mr. Macfarlane. He adds that as Salomon has presented its funding position to lenders since the crisis broke, "the response has been quite favorable."

"Salomon has strong financial management plus a good alternative liquidity system in place," says John J. Kriz, a vice president at Moody's Investors Service Inc. "In Salomon, you are looking at a company with a healthy level of capital. It's profitable, has good quality assets, has good businesses and is liquid."

A big German bank said that some European institutions had quietly lowered their trading limits with Salomon. Big U.S. banks have mostly stood by Salomon and not cut either lending or trading lines, but a spokesman for one New York bank says that top management was reviewing the situation daily. At the least, some analysts expect banks to increase the cost of the loans and credit lines they extend to Salomon when they mature.

A Liar's Obituary

Michael Lewis

August 21, 1991, the *Wall Street Journal*

Michael Lewis, author of Liar's Poker, *is John Gutfreund's worst nightmare—a well-informed wiseguy who likes nothing more than to make fun of pompous CEOs like Gutfreund. "Liar's Obituary" is Lewis at his most lethal.*

W E MAY NEVER KNOW the truth about what happened at Salomon Brothers over the past few years. I'm not even sure that it matters. The firm has admitted to breaking the rules in four separate U.S. Treasury auctions, to using the names of its customers fraudulently, and to submitting an illegal bid for $1 billion in U.S. Treasury bonds as a "practical joke."

The firm's managers at first pleaded total ignorance of the deeds, and then a few days later altered their story, confessing they had known of the violations since April. They now say that they simply forgot to inform the relevant officials. Last weekend, facing growing outrage and certain dismissal, Salomon's three most senior executives—John Gutfreund, Thomas Strauss, and John Meriwether—resigned.

They did not accept blame. They denied any serious wrongdoing. Messrs. Gutfreund and Strauss sounded less like disgraced executives than like a pair of ungrammatical martyrs. The two said in their public statements: "We cannot let our unfortunate mistake of not taking prompt action, when in April we learned of the unauthorized bid at a February Treasury auction, to harm the firm. We are taking this action to protect the firm, its nine thousand people and its clients."

I would be surprised if anyone at Salomon actually believes that Messrs. Gutfreund and Strauss had no idea that the

364 • A Wicked Hangover (1990–1991)

traders who sat a few yards from them were routinely breaking the rules. I certainly don't. While at Salomon in the mid-
eighties, I watched several U.S. Treasury auctions, and never
were either Mr. Strauss or Mr. Gutfreund far from the action.
They usually helped to prepare the bids. What is more, the top
management of Salomon receives daily reports on the firm's
bond holdings.

Even if the gentlemen somehow succeeded in turning a
blind eye to all five of the auctions in which Salomon has
admitted wrongdoing, they could hardly have failed to notice
the larger-than-legal holdings on the Salomon balance sheets.
And if they knew, as they have admitted, of a single violation
in April, how did they permit the occurrence of another, larger
violation in May?

American financial scandals are seldom what they pretend
to be. The securities laws have always been used to punish
financiers for perfectly legal activity. This was true of the
legendary U.S. Senate investigation of 1934, when J. P. Morgan Jr. was dragged before the Senate to discuss his role in this
nation's financial collapse, only to be ridiculed for having
paid no income tax in the previous three years. His real crime
was undisguised piggishness. This was also true in Michael
Milken's conviction for breaking six laws few people even
knew existed. His real "crimes" were creating junk bonds and
leveraged buyouts and loitering in the vicinity of the savings
and loan crisis.

I think it's fair to assume that most of the people who are
angry at Salomon Brothers neither know nor care about the
laws it has broken. The firm's real crime was its curious
attitude toward the truth.

This is worth trying to explain. Why did Mr. Gutfreund
tell such stupid stories? The first answer is that he thought,
not unjustifiably, that they would be believed.

The chairman of Salomon Brothers has always had a gift
for disinformation. Not long ago I was treated to a trivial but
amusing dose of this, after I published my book, *Liar's Poker*,
about my three years with the firm. In it I described the ritual
Salomon trading floor game (of betting on the serial numbers
on hidden banknotes) that gave the book its title. The description included a story of a million-dollar hand, in which John

Meriwether bluffed John Gutfreund. I had been told the story by (among others) Mr. Meriwether himself. I had no reason to doubt him. I had watched with my own eyes as John Gutfreund gambled away enormous sums of money at liar's poker, and viewed the million-dollar hand as no more than an extension of his daily routine.

Salomon Brothers' response to the publication of this story boggled my mind almost as much as it inflated my royalties. Acting under instructions from Mr. Gutfreund, the Salomon Brothers public relations man told reporters that the game occurred, but that it had been a practical joke. He was widely disbelieved. A few weeks later the Salomon spokesman mysteriously changed his story: The game had happened, and was presumably serious, but it had not involved Mr. Gutfreund. It had involved another managing director, who had recently died, and so was unavailable for comment. The Salomon spokesman was again ridiculed. Months later I opened a newspaper to find Mr. Gutfreund himself claiming that the story was pure fiction.

The point of all this is not that you should believe my story, agreeable to me as that would be, but that you couldn't logically believe all of theirs.

People who haven't worked on Wall Street have trouble understanding that the market often values lies more highly than the truth. I offer this less as criticism than as simple observation; to see how such intelligent people could get caught in such silly lies you have to understand the peculiar rules of their daily game. Traders spend a large part of their day pretending to their rivals to be selling when they want to buy, and buying when they want to sell. Salesmen spend an even larger part of their day overpraising mediocre investments to their clients. This is less venal than it sounds. Everyone who deals with financial intermediaries knows better than to believe everything he hears. Anyone who doesn't is regarded as a fool.

The history of Salomon Brothers is littered with the bodies of people stupid enough to believe what they were told by their superiors. One small example: Young people who entered the firm in the mid-1980s were told by Mr. Gutfreund to trust the firm to decide where in the firm they should be employed; that no one would *ever* suffer for working in a dying market. As a result, hundreds of perfectly capable but trusting people ended up selling municipal bonds and money-market instruments. One day in October 1987 they arrived at Salomon Brothers to learn that Mr. Gutfreund had fired their entire departments. Like any good bond trader, Mr. Gutfreund was able to put a price on anything, including his word. When the cost of keeping it became too high, he sold.

Only I don't believe that he was always as cynical as that. Throughout his career Mr. Gutfreund had a natural ability to confuse his self-interest with high principle. He was less cynical than carefully self-deluded. In 1987, for example, he used several hundred million dollars of shareholders' funds to pay Warren Buffett to save himself from the wrath of Ronald Perelman, the corporate raider who wanted to take over Salomon; Mr. Gutfreund did this, he claimed, only because Mr. Perelman was not the sort of person who should run an investment bank. I think he really believed it.

The same year he loudly declined to accept a bonus, while awarding himself stock options worth even more than the forgone bonus. Still, he was able to convince himself and others that he was making a genuine sacrifice. If you read the press cuttings, you'll find that in most cases John Gutfreund was taken at his word. The current scandal may well have occurred because the chairman thought he would be believed once again. But for the first time in his brilliant career, he fooled only himself.

Fall of the House of Roehm

Cathy Horyn

September 10, 1991, the *Washington Post*

When Henry Kravis's trophy wife Carolyne Roehm closed the shutters on her fashion business, the eighties came to an unofficial end. Her hubby Henry seems to have decided that it was cheaper to let her buy all the clothes she wanted rather than make all the clothes she wanted. In "Fall of the House of Roehm," Washington Post fashion writer Cathy Horyn chips away at "the veneer of her success story—from ambitious Carolyne Jane Smith back in Kirksville, Missouri, through a brief marriage to Axel Roehm, to Mrs. Henry R. Kravis of Park Avenue."

IT WAS A GOOD RUN while it lasted—the extravagant ensembles for a thinning society, the familiar crush of pals in the front row, the gorgeous life played out in the press—but yesterday it came to end. Carolyne Roehm, whose clothes were seldom as intriguing as her lifestyle, announced she is closing her Seventh Avenue fashion house.

The news was broken early yesterday in the *Wall Street Journal* on a tip that Roehm's newly appointed president, Kitty D'Alessio, was seen last week discussing a severance agreement with Henry Kravis, Roehm's husband and her company's backer. By midday, the forty-year-old designer, who only a few weeks ago sounded characteristically upbeat about the future of her six-year-old company, was preparing a statement with members of her staff, including D'Alessio.

"I have come to this decision after weighing all the pros and cons of continuing my business, and in the wake of a personal family tragedy that has caused me to reevaluate my plans for the future," Roehm said in the statement, referring to the July automobile accident in which Kravis's nineteen-year-old son, Harrison, a freshman at Brown University, was killed. She went on to say that "if any sense is to be made out of tragedy, then an improvement in one's vision and one's quality of life, and the impact one can have on others, is the only benefit. I shall spend the next year trying to find that vision, spending more time with my husband and my family."

D'Alessio, a former president of Chanel who was hired in June to revive Roehm's troubled business with new products, said in an interview that Roehm gave the news to her staff and then left for the day. "She's just worn out," said D'Alessio, who acknowledged that rumors about the company's demise had been circulating for several weeks. Even so, Roehm put out a resort collection in early August, and she and D'Alessio had been planning to make a business trip to Europe next week. "I have nothing further to add to Carolyne's statement, but I just personally want to add that I would have loved to see our plans go through."

For Roehm, those plans came too late. Unlike her competitors in the exclusive 550 building on Seventh Avenue—notably Bill Blass, Oscar de la Renta and Donna Karan—Roehm had not established a product and licensing base by which to subsidize a high-priced dress business, in which a simple evening gown can cost upwards of $2,000. And yet, according to people familiar with her company, she poured millions into it—for the best European fabrics and embroideries, the weekly displays of flowers, the advertisements for which she herself modeled and the media attention that comes from status and glamour.

"She always spent money like it was water," says an individual whose firm worked for Roehm.

It was no secret that Kravis, a principal partner in the leveraged-buyout firm of Kohlberg Kravis Roberts & Co., had helped her start her business in 1985, after she had spent nearly a decade working as a design assistant for de la Renta. According to sources in the *Journal* article, Kravis invested more than $20 million in Carolyne Roehm Inc. Others familiar with the design house do not dispute that figure.

"She's been wanting to do this for some time," said a

colleague, referring to the decision to close. "I guess Henry's been a contributing factor in the whole thing."

While Roehm's statement said that Kravis stood ready to help her business "through this tumultuous time in the fashion industry had I not decided to suspend business operations," she has occasionally expressed misgivings about the time she spent on her business and on fashion industry benefits, notably last November's 7th on Sale project. She was widely praised for her efforts in that event, which raised more than $4.5 million for AIDS patients.

But if her husband, who helped engineer the buyout of RJR Nabisco, had indeed grown weary of supporting a fashion house in the midst of a recession, as many insiders speculate, that too would come as no surprise. There is less room now at the top of the luxury market for another designer of pretty suits.

"You could just as easily buy the same look at Bill Blass or Oscar," said one insider.

And yet the veneer of her success story—from ambitious Carolyne Jane Smith back in Kirksville, Mo., through a brief marriage to Axel Roehm, to Mrs. Henry R. Kravis of Park Avenue—impressed nouvelle society and its followers. She didn't seem to mind incorporating that life into her public relations or advertisements, though after a while the publicity seemed to overtake both Kravis and Roehm. Even their horse barn in Connecticut, with its temperature-controlled riding arena, was grist for the PR mill.

On Seventh Avenue, where Roehm is well liked, yesterday's news was met with surprise and some sadness. "I don't like hearing about any designer going out of business," said Joan Kaner, a vice president of Neiman Marcus who had only a few weeks ago seen Roehm's resort collection. "In fact, we thought it was one of her strongest. We were planning to buy it."

"I am surprised," echoed Jack Alexander, an assistant to de la Renta and a longtime friend of Roehm's. "I know how much she loved doing what she did . . . I know this is going to be tough for her."

Poverty and Wealth in America

Washington Post editorial board

September 30, 1991, the *Washington Post*

So where did the Gaga Years leave us? As this
Washington Post *editorial points out, the rich got
richer, and the poor got left behind. Welcome to
the nineties.*

POVERTY AND WEALTH in the United States are increasing
together. The poverty rate rose significantly last year, the
Census Bureau has just reported. As the White House somewhat defensively observes, much of that jump is doubtless the
effect of the recession. The larger and more ominous pattern
is one of an increasing distance between rich and poor not
merely from year to year, but from decade to decade.

The poor were left entirely out of the great boom of the
1980s. In 1989, before the recession began, the poverty rate
was higher than it had been a decade earlier. The poorest fifth
of the population were living on incomes that were actually
lower than in 1979, even counting tax cuts and social welfare
benefits. But the incomes of the top fifth were a great deal
higher, any way you count it, than a decade earlier.

One out of every five American children now lives in
poverty. More than two out of every five black children live in
poverty. It is the children who are the crucial part of this
disaster. You could make quite a bonfire of all the speeches
delivered over the past year on the urgent need to improve the
capabilities of the American labor force and maintain its competitive edge in the next century. But children who live the
first eighteen years of their lives in the squalor and duress of
poverty only rarely manage to acquire the kinds of skills that
make them valuable to employers. The disappearance of un-

skilled jobs is irreversible, but the country isn't responding to its own national interests. Just as slow economic growth is increasing poverty, the rising numbers of poor people will contribute to slow economic growth.

Here in Washington it's conventional to shrug and say that the changes overtaking the world in the past decade have made these social forces difficult to remedy. But all the other industrial countries have been living in the same world, and their poverty rates are generally far below the United States'—particularly among children.

Behind the statistical tables published by the Census lies the unhappy reality of a country in which economic and social differences are becoming wider, and the social class structure is becoming more rigid. It's a fair generalization to say that through the first two-thirds of this century, distinctions of class became progressively less important, and the opportunities to move up the ladder expanded. That stopped sometime around the early 1970s and since then, despite the booming 1980s, American society has been moving in the opposite direction. Vigorous government action could correct that unhealthy drift, as the Europeans have demonstrated. But on this crucial question, Americans have chosen so far to pursue the politics of indifference.

PERMISSIONS